Artificial Intelligent Towards Sustainable Impact Accelerator through Education, Research and Ac

This book emphasizes the importance of incorporating sustainability concepts through the lens of education, research, and advocacy. A core focus is artificial intelligence (AI) and its developing role in relation to education, research, and advocacy to advance sustainable development. By providing a comprehensive perspective, the reader learns that research and education must work together to generate innovation, advocating responsible AI development and deployment. To enable the development of change agents in their fields, the authors emphasize the importance of incorporating sustainability ideas into a variety of educational programs. On the topic of creating purposeful learning environments, AI is examined as a tool to strike a balance between flexible, student-centered approaches and curriculum standards, in consideration of the sustainability impact factor.

This book aims to align with the United Nations Sustainable Development Goal (SDG) No. 4 on quality education. It also examines how research aids in the development of sustainable practices and the discovery of novel solutions. Researchers can contribute to evidence-based decision-making by encouraging interdisciplinary collaboration and interacting with stakeholders. Furthermore, the reader learns that advocacy can be used by both individuals and groups to effect real change through awareness-raising, influencing public opinion, and advocating for legislative changes. The ethical issues, legal frameworks, and the role of advocacy in forming responsible AI practices for capacity building are discussed. Each topic is supported by case studies, best practices, and practical insights, making this book a useful reference for research and practice.

Developed by experts in their respective fields of science, technology, and engineering with experience in education, research, and advocacy, this book would serve scholars with innovative insights for their research. Practitioners may also utilize this book for their professional work to apply the latest advancements and optimal methodologies.

Samsul Ariffin Abdul Karim is an associate professor at UUM's School of Quantitative Sciences, Research Fellow at ISIDM, and Founding Director of CSAM. He has published over 223 works, including 80 book chapters, and has received UTP's education and publication awards. He is also a Certified Wolfram Technology Associate.

Chockalingam Aravind Vaithilingam is a professor at the Faculty of Innovation and Technology at Taylor's University, Malaysia. He also heads the Clean Technology Impact Lab, which is aligned with SDG 6 and SDG 7 as part of Taylor's University's future-focused education, research, and advocacy strategy.

Ari Happonen is an adjunct and associate Professor, a project manager/principal investigator, and university-industry collaborator at the LUT School of Engineering Science in Lappeenranta University of Technology, Finland. He contributes to software engineering, Createch research, ICT and sustainability, AI solutions, and hackathon- and education-related research.

Artificial Intelligent Towards Sustainable Impact Accelerator through Education, Research and Advocacy

Edited by Samsul Ariffin Abdul Karim,
Chockalingam Aravind Vaithilingam
and Ari Happonen

CRC Press
Taylor & Francis Group
Boca Raton London New York

CRC Press is an imprint of the
Taylor & Francis Group, an **informa** business

Designed cover image: Shutterstock

First edition published 2026
by CRC Press
2385 NW Executive Center Drive, Suite 320, Boca Raton FL 33431

and by CRC Press
4 Park Square, Milton Park, Abingdon, Oxon, OX14 4RN

CRC Press is an imprint of Taylor & Francis Group, LLC

ISBN: 978-1-041-06006-2 (hbk)
ISBN: 978-1-041-04890-9 (pbk)
ISBN: 978-1-003-63343-3 (ebk)

DOI: 10.1201/9781003633433

Typeset in Palatino
by Apex CoVantage, LLC

Contents

About the Editors

Samsul Ariffin Abdul Karim is an associate professor at the School of Quantitative Sciences, UUM College of Arts & Sciences, Universiti Utara Malaysia (UUM). Previously, he has worked at Universiti Teknologi PETRONAS (UTP) and Universiti Malaysia Sabah (UMS). He is a research fellow at the Institute of Strategic Industrial Decision Modelling (ISIDM), UUM; Senior Research Fellow of the Quaternion Fourier Transform Research Group (Q-FourT), Hasanuddin University, Makassar, Indonesia and the founding director of the Computational Statistics and Applied Mathematics (CSAM) research center. He received his PhD in mathematics from Universiti Sains Malaysia (USM) and is a professional technologist registered with the Malaysia Board of Technologists (MBOT) (No. PT21030227). His research interests include numerical analysis, machine learning, approximation theory, optimization, wavelets, and STEM education in science and engineering. Dr. Samsul has authored more than 223 research articles (indexed by Scopus) in journals and conference proceedings, including five edited conference volumes and 85 book chapters. He has also published 13 academic books. His scholarly achievements have been recognized through awards such as the Effective Education Delivery Award and Publication Awards at UTP Quality Day (2010–2012), as well as the Book Publication Award (2020) for his volume on *Water Quality Index Prediction Using Multiple Linear Fuzzy Regression*. He is also a **Certified Wolfram Technology Associate (Mathematica Student Level).**

Chockalingam Aravind Vaithilingam is a professor with the Faculty of Innovation and Technology at Taylor's University, Malaysia. He obtained his PhD in electrical engineering from Universiti Putra Malaysia (UPM). He holds a doctoral degree in electrical power engineering, with his PhD work earning Gold at MTE 2013. He is a frequent speaker on various international and national platforms. He is the program director for the Electrical and Electronic Engineering Program, which is the first program within the school to be ranked in the QS 2023 narrow subject. He is also a professional technologist with the Malaysian Board of Technologists, a member of the Society of Engineering Education Malaysia, a senior member of IEEE, and a member of IET UK. He also heads the Clean Technology Impact Lab aligned with SDG 6 and SDG 7 as part of the future-of-education research and advocacy strategy of Taylor's University. He has published over 150 indexed disseminations and secured projects with a total grant value of USD 287,703, of which 50.6% has been as principal investigator since 2007. He is also the developer of the multiple award-winning CODE design-thinking enterprise framework, which he used to develop teaching, learning, research, and consulting solutions.

Ari Happonen is an adjunct and associate professor, a project manager/principal investigator, and a university-industry collaborator at the LUT School of Engineering Science in Lappeenranta University of Technology, Finland. Prof. Happonen has special research interests in digitalization, ICT for sustainability, robotization, hackathons, code camps, digital transformation, experimental and innovation-boosting activities, and modern waste-reduction and sustainability-enhancing methodologies. His research focuses mainly on practical and efficient industry-related applied research collaboration activities in B2B and B2C contexts. He contributes to software engineering, Createch research, ICT and sustainability, AI solutions, and hackathon- and education-related research areas. He also actively participates in education and teaching development efforts, with 20+ years of experience. He works as an intermediary in multiple research projects between universities and innovative frontline companies.

Contributors' Bios

Dharel P. Acut
Cebu Technological University
Philippines

Hafisoh Ahmad
School of Engineering
Taylor's University
Selangor, Malaysia

Priscilla Pomaa Annor
Busara Africa
Ghana

Noratiqah Mohd Ariff
Department of Mathematical Sciences
Faculty of Science and Technology
Universiti Kebangsaan Malaysia
Bangi, Selangor, Malaysia

Afizan Azman
School of Computer Science
Faculty of Innovation & Technology
Taylor's University Lakeside Campus
Subang Jaya, Selangor, Malaysia

Mohd Aftar Abu Bakar
Department of Mathematical Sciences
Faculty of Science and Technology
Universiti Kebangsaan Malaysia
Bangi, Selangor

Kah Yoong Chan
Faculty of Engineering
Multimedia University
Selangor, Malaysia

Jia Qi Cheong
Department of Business and Management
University of Teknologi MARA (UiTM) Seri Iskandar, Malaysia; Centre for Economic Development and Policy

Chong Shyue Chuan
Tunku Abdul Rahman University of Management and Technology

Gwo Chin Chung
Faculty of Engineering
Multimedia University
Selangor, Malaysia

Manee Sangaran Diagarajan
School of Engineering
Faculty of Innovation and Technology
Taylor's University Lakeside Campus
Subang Jaya, Selangor, Malaysia

Lydia Yoke Yean Foong
Director, Curriculum and Educational Development
Centre for Future Learning
Taylor's University
Selangor, Malaysia

Manuel B. Garcia
FEU Institute of Technology, Philippines
Korea University
South Korea

Hui Hwang Goh
School of Engineering
Taylor's University
Selangor, Malaysia.

Norhidayah Hamzah
School of Computer Science
Faculty of Innovation & Technology
Taylor's University
Selangor, Malaysia

Ari Happonen
LUT University
Finland

Victoria T. Hasheela
Department of Computing, Mathematical and Statistical Science
University of Namibia
Windhoek, Namibia

Husna Sarirah Husin
School of Computer Science
Faculty of Innovation & Technology
Taylor's University
Selangor, Malaysia

Intan Izafina Idrus
School of Engineering
Taylor's University
Selangor, Malaysia

Samsul Ariffin Abdul Karim
Institute of Strategic Industrial Decision Modelling (ISIDM)
School of Quantitative Sciences, UUM College of Arts & Sciences
Universiti Utara Malaysia
Sintok, Kedah Darul Aman, Malaysia
Computational Statistics and Applied Mathematics (CSAM) Research Group
School of Quantitative Sciences
UUM College of Arts & Sciences, Universiti Utara Malaysia
Sintok, Kedah Darul Aman, Malaysia

Muhammad Khujaev
American Degree Transfer Program
School of Liberal Arts and Sciences, Faculty of Social Sciences and Leisure Management
Taylor's University
Subang Jaya, Selangor, Malaysia

Sarmela Nadarajan
Department of Mathematical Sciences
Faculty of Science and Technology
Universiti Kebangsaan Malaysia
Bangi, Selangor, Malaysia

Asokan Narayanasamy
SONA Medical College of Naturopathy and Yoga
Salem, Tamil Nadu, India

Muhammed Haziq Muhammed Nor
Department of Mathematical Sciences
Faculty of Science and Technology
Universiti Kebangsaan Malaysia
Bangi, Selangor

Kingsley Ofosu-Ampong
Heritage Christian University
Ghana

Samuel Owusu-Ansah
University of Ghana
Ghana

Wai Leong Pang
School of Engineering
Taylor's University
Selangor, Malaysia

Kalaivaani P. C. D.
Faculty of Computer Science and Engineering
Kongu Engineering College, Perundurai, Erode
Tamil Nadu, India

Divya Rose Peter
School of Education and Social Sciences Management and Science University Sdn. Bhd.
University Drive, Off Persiaran Olahraga
Shah Alam
Selangor Darul Ehsan, Malaysia

Alia Muhammad Radzi
Department of Mathematical Sciences
Faculty of Science and Technology
Universiti Kebangsaan Malaysia
Selangor, Malaysia

Gajjala Hrithvik Reddy
American Degree Transfer Program
School of Liberal Arts and Sciences, Faculty of Social Sciences and Leisure Management
Taylor's University, Subang Jaya
Selangor, Malaysia

Thimmareddy Sharat Chandra Reddy
American Degree Transfer Program
School of Liberal Arts and Sciences, Faculty of Social Sciences and Leisure Management
Taylor's University, Subang Jaya
Selangor, Malaysia

Rajalaxmi R. R.
Faculty of Computer Science and Engineering
Kongu Engineering College, Perundurai, Erode
Tamil Nadu, India

Yee Wei Sim
School of Engineering
Taylor's University
Selangor, Malaysia

Sunitha Sivakumaran
Pusat Pendidkan Khas Sinaran Taarana
Selangor, Malaysia

Murugan Thangiah
School of Liberal Arts & Sciences
Faculty of Innovation and Technology
Taylor's University
Selangor, Malaysia

Wong Hock Tsen
Faculty of Business, Economics and Accountancy
Universiti Malaysia Sabah
Kota Kinabalu, Sabah, Malaysia

Micheal Tuape
Software Engineering
LUT School of Engineering Sciences
Lappeenranta, Finland

Chockalingam Aravind Vaithilingam
School of Engineering, Faculty of Innovation and Technology
Taylor's University Lakeside Campus, Subang Jaya
Selangor, Malaysia

Sing Yun Wong
Faculty of Business, Economics and Accountancy
Universiti Malaysia Sabah
Kota Kinabalu, Sabah, Malaysia

Sook Jhee Yoon
Expert, Academic Policy and Curriculum
Centre for Future Learning, Taylor's University
Selangor, Malaysia

Sarani Zakaria
Department of Applied Physics
Faculty of Science and Technology
Universiti Kebangsaan Malaysia
Selangor, Malaysia

Preface

This book, ***Artificial Intelligent Towards Sustainable Impact Accelerator through Education, Research, and Advocacy,*** explores how education, research, and advocacy (ERA) play vital roles in driving sustainable development. It highlights the transformative power of education in equipping individuals with the knowledge, skills, and mindset needed to shape a sustainable future. Through both analytical discussions and real-world examples, the book underscores the importance of embedding sustainability principles into diverse academic programs, enabling learners to act as agents of change in their communities and professions.

Equally, it reflects on the significance of research as a driver of innovative practices and sustainable solutions. By fostering interdisciplinary collaboration and engaging multiple stakeholders, research strengthens evidence-based decision-making and supports long-term societal progress. Alongside this, the book emphasizes the role of advocacy in shaping public opinion, raising awareness, and influencing policy. Practical strategies for effective communication and illustrations of successful advocacy initiatives demonstrate how both individuals and organizations can generate meaningful impact.

A particular focus is given to the adaptation processes within higher education, where interactions across institutional, social, and policy levels are critically examined. By applying established social science concepts and theories, the book offers fresh insights into how higher education systems adapt and respond to shifting global challenges. Its findings are designed to benefit a wide readership of educators, researchers, policymakers, and practitioners who seek to deepen their understanding of change within higher education.

The overarching aim of ***Artificial Intelligent Towards Sustainable Impact Accelerator through Education, Research, and Advocacy*** is to inspire readers to recognize their own capacity to contribute to a sustainable future. The work provides actionable perspectives for those engaged in teaching, research, activism, or policymaking, offering pathways to promote social equity and environmental responsibility.

Since the adoption of the United Nations Sustainable Development Goals (SDGs) in 2015, all member states have committed to meeting the 17 global targets by 2030. This book places particular emphasis on SDG 4: Quality Education, which includes targets such as expanding access to affordable higher education and increasing the proportion of youth and adults with digital and vocational skills (Targets 4.3 and 4.4, respectively). Despite progress, challenges remain—while millions of children are now enrolled in school, an estimated 272 million remain excluded from formal education as of 2025.

Beyond SDG 4, the discussions also connect to SDG 8 (Decent Work and Economic Growth) and SDG 10 (Reduced Inequalities), where artificial intelligence offers promising tools to bridge rural–urban education divides through cost-effective, inclusive learning technologies.

This book is intended for postgraduate students, researchers in R&D, practitioners, policymakers, and scientists who seek to deepen their understanding of how education, research, and advocacy (ERA) can accelerate sustainable impact. By integrating these three pillars, the book provides valuable insights for advancing theory, shaping policy, and guiding practical applications. It is especially relevant for those committed to linking innovation with social responsibility, ensuring that knowledge and technology contribute meaningfully to sustainable development.

The editors extend their sincere gratitude to all contributing authors for their commitment and expertise in producing high-quality chapters, as well as to the reviewers whose constructive feedback has been invaluable in strengthening this volume.

The first editor was fully supported by Universiti Utara Malaysia through Geran Penjanaan Penyelidikan Universiti 2025 [SO Code: 22139] (A Machine Learning-Based Scattered Data Interpolation for Image Enhancement) and the Ministry of Higher Education (MOHE) of Malaysia through the **Fundamental Research Grant Scheme [FRGS/1/2023/ICT06/UMS/02/1] (New Scattered Data Interpolation Scheme Using Quasi-Cubic Triangular Patches for RGB Image Interpolation)**. Finally, a special thank-you to the Institute of Strategic Industrial Decision Modelling (ISIDM), the Computational Statistics and Applied Mathematics (CSAM) Research Group, and the School of Quantitative Sciences, Universiti Utara Malaysia, for their tremendous computing-facilities support. Finally, our deepest gratitude goes to the dedicated team at Taylor & Francis/CRC Press for their unwavering support and tireless efforts in bringing this book into publication.

Samsul Ariffin Abdul Karim
Universiti Utara Malaysia, Malaysia

Chockalingam Aravind Vaithilingam
Taylor's University, Malaysia

Ari Happonen
LUT University, Finland
September 14, 2025

1

Artificial Intelligence toward a Sustainable Impact Accelerator through Education, Research, and Advocacy: An Overview and Pathways for Continuous Improvement

Samsul Ariffin Abdul Karim

1.1 AI for Sustainable Impact Accelerator through Education, Research, and Advocacy

The idea of a sustainable impact accelerator reflects the need for a deliberate and structured approach to advancing sustainable development. It recognizes that progress cannot depend on a single strategy or isolated effort but instead requires the combined strength of education, research, and advocacy. These three elements act as reinforcing pillars, each contributing uniquely while amplifying the effectiveness of the others.

Among these three elements, education provides the foundation. It equips individuals, communities, and institutions with the knowledge, values, and critical thinking skills necessary to understand today's global AI challenges. Beyond the classroom, education nurtures awareness, shapes attitudes, and cultivates a sense of responsibility toward social and environmental well-being. By embedding sustainability into learning processes, societies can prepare future generations not only to adapt but also to innovate solutions to complex issues.

Research plays a complementary role by generating the evidence base required for meaningful action. It offers new insights, develops innovative technologies, and provides tools for evaluating impact. Rigorous research ensures that decisions are not made on assumptions only but are instead grounded in tested knowledge. From research, we may have varieties of impactful innovations. Moreover, interdisciplinary research strengthens connections between scientific discovery, social realities, and practical implementation, bridging the gap between theory and application.

Advocacy serves as the mechanism that transforms knowledge and evidence into momentum for change. It brings voices together, communicates findings to wider audiences, and pushes for policies that align with long-term sustainability goals. Advocacy ensures that the benefits of education and research do not

DOI: 10.1201/9781003633433-1

remain confined within institutions but reach decision-makers, communities—especially rural areas—and industries where change must occur.

When education, research, and advocacy (ERA) are viewed together, they form a powerful accelerator for sustainable impact. Education builds awareness and capability, research generates knowledge and innovation, and advocacy translates both into action and influence. This synergy creates a cycle of continuous quality improvement (CQI), where learning inspires research, research informs advocacy, and advocacy strengthens education. Figure 1.1 shows the proposed CQI based on the proposed ERA model.

The United Nations Sustainable Development Goals (SDGs), shown in Figure 1.2 (United Nations, 2019), provide a global framework for this integrated approach. They highlight areas where progress is most urgently

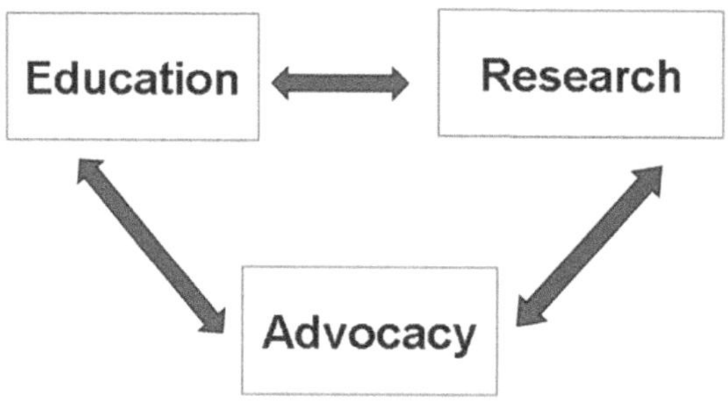

FIGURE 1.1
The proposed CQI ERA cycle.

FIGURE 1.2
UN SDGs.

needed and offer a common language for collaboration. By aligning ERA with the SDGs, societies can move beyond fragmented initiatives toward cohesive strategies that deliver long-lasting results. This finding, therefore, positions the sustainable impact accelerator as not only a conceptual model but also a practical pathway to achieving meaningful global transformation.

1.2 Summary

The subsequent paragraphs present the overall structure of the book and offer an executive summary of each chapter. It is important to note that every chapter constitutes a self-contained contribution that may be read independently without loss of coherence.

The chapter **Make a Difference Enterprise (MADE): Catalyzing AI-Driven Design Thinking in Student Learning** is a cross-border collaborative learning platform that empowers students as changemakers through AI-driven design thinking. Cocreated by Taylor's University, Malaysia, and partner institutions in India, MADE brought together 51 students and ten mentors for an immersive seven-day workshop. Interdisciplinary teams applied design thinking, AI tools, and ethical reasoning to cocreate solutions to real-world problems aligned with the SDGs. Guided by the imPACT framework—innovation, mobilization, partnership, action, cocreation, and transformation—students gained future-ready skills, with 88% reporting greater confidence in AI, 75% stronger problem-solving abilities, and 92% improved intercultural collaboration. MADE demonstrates how curriculum innovation can integrate technology, creativity, and social responsibility for lasting educational and societal impact.

The chapter **Student Engagement and Motivation toward Education 4.0** is motivating and actively engaging students beyond getting their degree, building their life and career for the next 30 years after graduation, and making them realize that lifelong self-learners are the present challenges and opportunities in higher education, along with localized educational and social issues. Students need to be motivated to involve themselves and actively engage to develop higher-order thinking skills, learn how to learn, use metacognition, and understand transdisciplinary subjects to solve societal problems. Three types of transformations—technological, strategic, and learner characteristics transformations—identified and discussed by the author, are to be embedded in the teaching-learning process to enhance student engagement and motivation toward Education 4.0.

The chapter **Determinants of Successful Integration and Adoption of AI in Education: A Structural Equation Modeling Approach** explores the factors driving AI adoption in Ghanaian higher education. This study applies the diffusion of innovation theory and UTAUT2 to examine key influences such as interoperability, pedagogical alignment, and ethical considerations. Analyzing data from 230 participants across 34 universities, the research confirms a 77.3% explanatory power for the adoption of AI, emphasizing the need for structured implementation strategies. The findings offer valuable insights for policymakers and institutional leaders to foster sustainable AI integration in resource-limited settings.

Artificial intelligence (AI) is revolutionizing educational assessment, offering new pathways for sustainable and equitable learning. The chapter **Artificial Intelligence for Equitable and Sustainable Assessment** explores how AI-driven innovations can transform traditional evaluation methods into ethical, inclusive, and impactful practices. Through a deep dive into key frameworks, principles, and a case study from a Malaysian university, this chapter provides essential insights for integrating AI into assessment design while safeguarding academic integrity and fairness. With a focus on accessibility, reliability, and future-ready learning, this chapter serves as a vital resource for educators, researchers, and policymakers looking to harness AI for meaningful, adaptive, and globally sustainable education.

The chapter **AI Ethics in Education** presents the ethical concerns in the deployment of AI in education. The integration of AI in education raises critical ethical concerns that impact multiple stakeholders, including learners, educators, policymakers, technology developers, and institutions. While AI enhances personalized learning, automates assessments, and optimizes administrative tasks, it also presents challenges related to data privacy, algorithmic bias, and the digital divide. Ethical concerns arise from the potential misuse of learner data, the lack of transparency in AI decision-making, and the risk of over-reliance on automation, which may compromise human judgment and creativity in education. Addressing these challenges requires collaboration among stakeholders to establish clear ethical frameworks, regulatory policies, and AI literacy initiatives. A human-centered approach to AI integration, emphasizing fairness, accountability, and transparency, is essential to mitigate risks while maximizing benefits. This chapter explores the ethical dimensions of AI in education and proposes strategies to uphold integrity, inclusivity, and trust in AI-driven learning environments.

The chapter **A Job-Based Course Recommender System Using Unsupervised Machine Learning for Text Clustering to Promote a Multidisciplinary Curriculum** presents a framework for a recommender system that guides university students to choose combinations of courses to acquire the skills needed for their future job interests. The study was done using clustering analysis on courses provided by a public university in Malaysia. It was found that the recommender system produced satisfactory multidisciplinary course combinations when evaluated across distinct fields.

Hence, these results could help in real applications promoting a multidisciplinary curriculum using technology.

Due to the rapid integration of AI in education, careful evaluation of its impacts is required. The chapter **The Integration of Artificial Intelligence in Education: A Systematic Review of Pedagogical, Ethical, and Systemic Dimensions** provides a systematic review that synthesizes 92 studies to map AI applications, highlighting opportunities and challenges across educational, ethical, and systemic dimensions. Key uses include intelligent tutoring systems (ITS), adaptive-learning platforms, and chatbots, offering strong potential for personalized learning and scalable support. Effectiveness depends on human-centered design, with hybrid human–AI collaboration shown to strengthen rather than replace instructor roles. Central to sustainable adoption are trust, transparency, and ethical governance. Barriers include algorithmic bias, data privacy risks, and unequal implementation, which risk deepening digital divides. Current research is limited by short-term, small-scale studies; higher education bias; and fragmented inquiry across technical, pedagogical, and ethical domains. This review proposes a future agenda prioritizing longitudinal real-world studies, participatory design, context-specific ethical frameworks, and robust theoretical models to guide responsible and equitable AI adoption in education worldwide.

The chapter **Exploring the Influence of Artificial Intelligence on Education: Perceptions and Attitudes among University Students** presents a study investigating students' perceptions of AI in higher education through survey data collected in 2025 from 1,014 students across seven universities. Findings reveal that students appreciate AI's capabilities for personalized learning, real-time feedback, research and writing assistance, and AI-powered tutoring and support. Students also expressed concerns about AI dependency, data privacy, and potential biases in AI systems.

The chapter **Social and Emotional Learning with Purpose** delves into the critical role of social and emotional learning (SEL) in education today, particularly in response to the digital age and the lasting effects of the pandemic. As students increasingly seek social and emotional skills to navigate their academic and personal lives, this chapter explores how educators can effectively integrate SEL into the curriculum. By fostering supportive and engaging environments, SEL empowers learners to build meaningful connections and develop essential life skills. Addressing both the opportunities and challenges of implementation, this chapter makes a compelling case for SEL as a cornerstone of modern education.

The chapter **AI in Education—Transforming Teaching and Learning in the Digital Age** presents how AI is transforming education by making learning more personalized, accessible, and efficient. AI-powered systems can adapt to individual learning styles, offering customized lessons, instant feedback, and interactive content. Educators benefit too, with AI automating tasks like grading and attendance, freeing up time for creative, student-centered teaching. ITS and language translation tools help bridge gaps, making quality education available to diverse and remote communities. While AI brings exciting opportunities, it also raises challenges around data privacy, fairness, and ethics. Balancing innovation with human values is key to creating a smarter, more inclusive educational future.

The chapter **Introduction: The Promise and Peril of AI in Education** presents how AI has progressively shaped education, evolving from rule-based ITS in the early 2000s to today's generative AI, such as ChatGPT and other advanced adaptive-learning platforms. Early implementations focused on personalized learning, providing automated feedback and customized lesson plans based on student performance. However, recent advancements have introduced AI-driven grading systems, virtual teaching assistants, and automated administrative tools, raising new ethical concerns alongside their benefits.

The chapter **Purpose-Led Learning Using AI for Data Analytics with SMEs in Malaysia** highlights how small and medium-sized enterprises (SMEs) are crucial drivers of economic growth in Malaysia. However, many lack the technical capacity and data-driven strategies to remain competitive. This chapter presents a purpose-led learning model that integrates AI techniques and data analytics into an experiential education framework, enabling students to cocreate data-driven solutions with real SMEs. Through the data analytics and machine learning module at Taylor's University, students engaged with SMEs' raw operational data, applied AI-based predictive analytics, and produced actionable insights to enhance business decision-making. This initiative not only built students' technical and soft skills but also fostered data literacy among SME owners. The project demonstrates how purpose-driven learning can bridge academia-industry gaps, support Malaysia's digital transformation, and align with UN SDG 8 (Decent Work and Economic Growth) and UN SDG 9 (Industry, Innovation, and Infrastructure).

The chapter **Inclusive Education through AI: Translating Speech-to-Sign Language for Deaf and Mute Learners in Online Platforms Using Generative Adversarial Network** delves into the role of generative AI, especially GAN-based translation systems, in addressing the communication barriers faced by deaf and mute students through real-time conversion from natural language to sign language. It discusses the design of such systems, the ethical challenges they pose, and the critical need for diverse datasets, revealing both the opportunities and intricacies of implementing these technologies in educational environments. The research underscores the potential of AI to enhance inclusivity, offering a perspective on creating a more equitable and accessible education for every special-needs learner.

The chapter **Empowering Innovation through a Generative Artificial Intelligence-Integrated Design Thinking Framework for Value-Driven Product Development** proposes **CODE© (Conceptualize, Organize, Deploy, Evolve)** as a design thinking framework enhanced with generative AI to guide students from ideation to market-ready solutions. Acting as a digital mentor, it strengthens critical thinking, creativity, and entrepreneurial value through integrated tools such as the Value Proposition, Communication, and Management Canvases. Since 2024, CODE© has been applied in academic projects, workshops, and engineering capstones, producing industry-relevant outcomes while fostering lifelong skills in value creation, ethical reasoning, and ambiguity management. In 2025, all users recommended the tool, with half applying it to entrepreneurial ventures, highlighting its enduring relevance in both education and practice.

The chapter **Artificial Intelligence toward Sustainable Impact Accelerator through Education, Research and Advocacy: Critical Assessments** offers a comprehensive evaluation of AI's influence across these three interconnected pillars. It highlights both the transformative potential and the inherent challenges of integrating AI into academic and institutional contexts. A key outcome of this study is the development of two practical tools—AI ethics and academic honesty declaration forms—designed for lecturers and instructors. These forms serve as guiding instruments to promote responsible AI use, safeguard academic integrity, and foster ethical awareness among students in the classroom setting. Finally, the chapter **Artificial Intelligence and the Sustainable Impact Accelerator: Advancing Education, Research, and Advocacy beyond IR4.0 and Society 5.0** serves as a concluding synthesis of the book's central contributions. It highlights how the three core pillars—education, research, and advocacy (ERA)—interact to drive meaningful change while also providing a structured framework for CQI.

1.3 Declaration on the Use of Generative AI and AI-Assisted Technologies

During the preparation of this work, the author used ChatGPT to improve readability and draft structure. All outputs generated by the tool were carefully reviewed, edited, and validated. The findings, interpretations, and conclusions presented are entirely the author's own work. The author accepts full responsibility for the originality, accuracy, and integrity of the final content.

Acknowledgment

This study was fully supported by Universiti Utara Malaysia through Geran Penjanaan Penyelidikan Universiti 2025 [SO Code: 22139] (A Machine Learning-Based Scattered Data Interpolation for Image Enhancement) and the Ministry of Higher Education (MOHE) of Malaysia through the Fundamental Research Grant Scheme **[FRGS/1/2023/ICT06/UMS/02/1]**

(New Scattered Data Interpolation Scheme Using Quasi-Cubic Triangular Patches for RGB Image Interpolation). Finally, a special thank-you to the Institute of Strategic Industrial Decision Modelling (ISIDM) and the Computational Statistics and Applied Mathematics (CSAM) Research Group, School of Quantitative Sciences, Universiti Utara Malaysia, for their tremendous computing-facilities support.

Reference

United Nations SDGs. (2019). https://sdgs.un.org/goals

2

Make a Difference Enterprise (MADE): Catalyzing AI-Driven Design Thinking in Student Learning

Manee Sangaran Diagarajan, Chockalingam Aravind Vaithilingam, and Murugan Thangiah

2.1 Introduction: Background and Context

The rapid advancement of artificial intelligence (AI) is transforming multiple industries, including education, where it is increasingly adopted to enhance teaching, learning, and assessment practices. However, the integration of AI in higher education is still evolving, with gaps in student preparedness, ethical considerations, and equitable access to emerging technologies (Zawacki-Richter et al., 2019). While AI tools such as generative models offer immense potential to augment creativity and efficiency, students often struggle to understand how to apply these technologies meaningfully to real-world problems (Holmes et al., 2021). The AI in education market, estimated at US$18.92 billion in 2025 and expected to reach US$48.63 billion by 2030 at a CAGR of 20.8% (Knowledge Sourcing Intelligence LLP, 2025), as depicted in Figure 2.1, underscores the urgency of preparing students to engage with these technologies meaningfully.

At the same time, higher education institutions worldwide face persistent challenges in bridging the divide between classroom learning and the demands of real-world problem-solving. While curricula often emphasize theoretical knowledge, students have fewer opportunities to engage in interdisciplinary collaboration, empathetic design, and hands-on prototyping. This disconnect leaves graduates ill-prepared to address complex global issues such as sustainability, inclusivity, and digital equity (Luckin et al., 2016). Furthermore, many existing AI literacy initiatives focus narrowly on technical training, overlooking critical dimensions such as ethical awareness, user-centered design, and intercultural teamwork. As a result, there remains a pressing need for integrated educational models that teach students not only how to use AI but also how to design with AI for social good.

DOI: 10.1201/9781003633433-2

Addressing this gap requires educational interventions that merge AI skill building with human-centered design thinking (DT), enabling students to ideate and implement socially impactful solutions. The DT methodology—empathize, define, ideate, prototype, test—offers a structured yet flexible framework for creative problem-solving (Figure 2.2). When aligned with

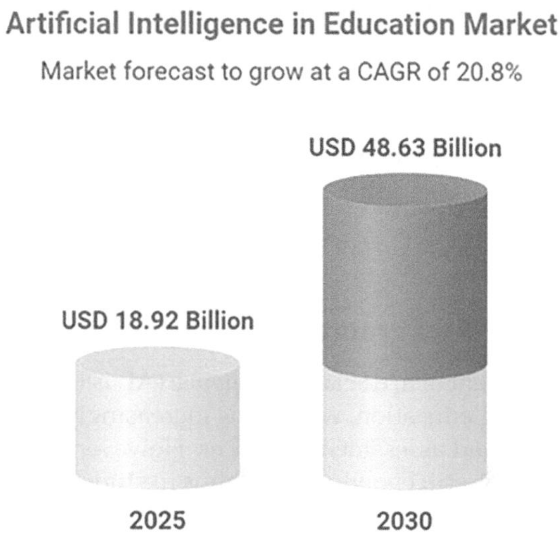

FIGURE 2.1
Global AI in education market forecast (Knowledge Sourcing Intelligence LLP, 2025).

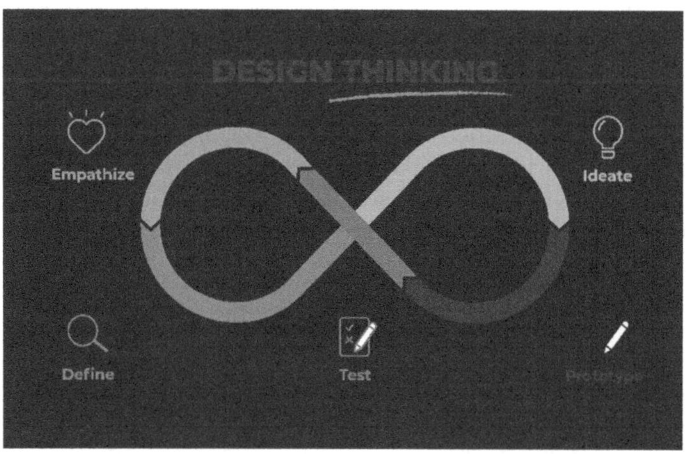

FIGURE 2.2
Design thinking process model.

(IDEO, 2023).

the United Nations Sustainable Development Goals (SDGs), it also fosters a purpose-driven mindset that connects learning outcomes to real-world challenges.

In response, the *Make a Difference Enterprise (MADE)* initiative was launched as an intercultural, interdisciplinary learning experience between Taylor's University, Malaysia, and partner institutions in India. By combining AI literacy development, structured DT pedagogy, and experiential learning activities like design challenges and prototype pitching, MADE aims to empower students as actionable changemakers capable of delivering transformative results for communities and society at large.

2.2 Literature Review

The intersection of AI, DT, and experiential learning has attracted increasing scholarly attention, particularly as higher education seeks to prepare students for the uncertainties of a rapidly changing world. Research shows that while AI adoption in education is expanding, it often remains disconnected from pedagogical frameworks that foster creativity, collaboration, and social responsibility. At the same time, DT has gained traction as a methodology that equips students with empathy-driven problem-solving skills but is rarely combined with AI literacy in structured, practice-based settings. Furthermore, the importance of intercultural collaboration and formative assessment in enhancing student outcomes is well documented, yet these elements are inconsistently embedded within technology-driven educational programs. This review synthesizes relevant strands of literature to situate the MADE initiative within existing scholarship and to highlight the unique contribution of its integrated approach.

2.2.1 AI in Higher Education

Beyond theoretical exposure, practical skill building in AI is increasingly demanded by students and employers alike. Studies note that while many universities introduce AI concepts at the curricular level, hands-on workshops and boot camps are more effective in equipping learners with applicable competencies. These workshops typically emphasize applied tools—such as natural language processing, computer vision, and generative AI—while situating them in problem-solving contexts.

Research suggests that experiential learning approaches, such as hackathons, coding sprints, and guided projects, enhance both technical proficiency and confidence in applying AI tools. For example, students trained in AI-driven prototyping report higher levels of self-efficacy and adaptability, which are critical for navigating rapidly evolving job markets (Luckin et al., 2016).

Nevertheless, AI education remains uneven across institutions. Many programs lack structured pathways that combine technical training with soft skills such as creativity, ethical reasoning, and teamwork (UNESCO, 2021). As shown in Figure 2.3, UNESCO's AI competency framework highlights this dual need for both technical and human-centered AI competencies, reinforcing the value of integrative models such as MADE. The MADE program addresses this by embedding AI skill-building within broader human-centered, collaborative contexts rather than isolating it as a purely technical competency.

2.2.2 Design Thinking in Education

Design thinking (DT) has gained momentum as a pedagogical framework that cultivates creativity, problem-solving, and empathy in learners. Originating from product and service innovation practices (Brown, 2009), DT has been adapted for education as a human-centered, iterative problem-solving process that emphasizes empathy, ideation, prototyping, and testing.

Empirical studies show that DT in classrooms can significantly improve students' ability to manage ambiguity, collaborate effectively in teams, and generate innovative solutions to real-world problems (Scheer et al., 2012). For instance, Henriksen et al. (2017) highlight how DT fosters "creative confidence," enabling students to approach challenges without fear of failure. Moreover, DT aligns with 21st-century competencies—such as critical thinking, collaboration, and adaptability—that are increasingly emphasized in global education agendas (Trilling & Fadel, 2009).

However, scholars point out challenges in scaling DT across higher education. A lack of trained facilitators, inconsistent curricular integration, and the risk of superficial adoption ("design thinking theater") can limit its effectiveness. Furthermore, while DT excels in fostering ideation and creativity, its potential synergy with technological competencies such as AI remains underexplored.

2.2.3 Intercultural Collaboration and Global Competence

In an increasingly interconnected world, intercultural competence is recognized as a core graduate attribute. Deardorff (2006) defines it as the ability to communicate effectively and appropriately with people from other cultures, based on intercultural knowledge, skills, and attitudes. Studies show that intercultural collaboration improves teamwork, empathy, and adaptability, making students better prepared for globalized workplaces.

Virtual exchange programs and international workshops have demonstrated success in fostering intercultural skills. For example, O'Dowd (2018)

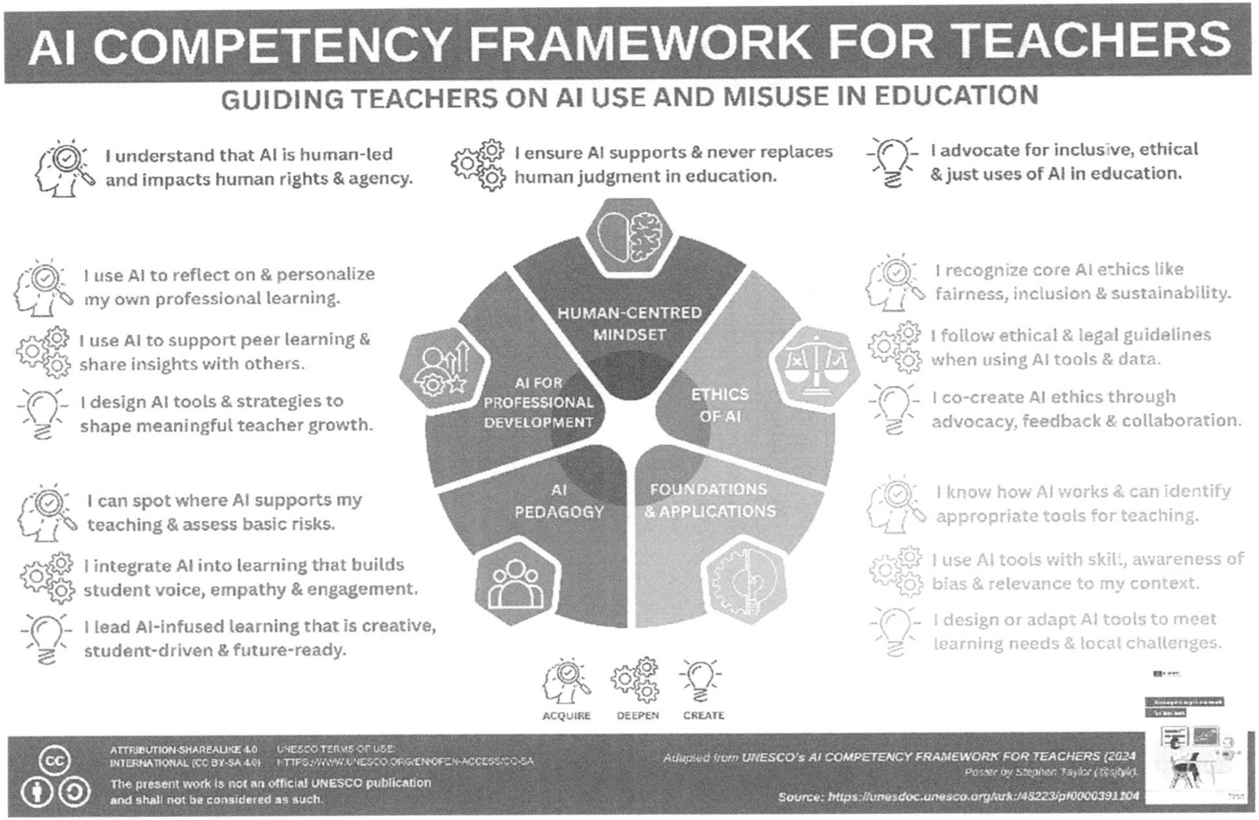

FIGURE 2.3
AI competency framework for higher education (UNESCO, 2021).

highlights how collaborative online international learning (COIL) promotes cross-cultural dialogue and joint problem-solving. Yet these initiatives often remain limited to language learning or cultural exchange rather than being embedded in STEM and innovative contexts.

MADE leverages this by situating intercultural teams within DT and AI-driven problem-solving frameworks. Early findings indicate that this approach not only strengthens collaboration but also accelerates the transfer of skills across cultural boundaries. The key themes emerging from the literature are summarized in Table 2.1, which highlights the contributions and gaps in DT, AI skill-building, intercultural collaboration, and assessment approaches. These gaps provide the rationale for the integrated MADE framework.

TABLE 2.1

Summary of Literature Review Themes

Theme	Focus on Literature	Key Findings	Identified Gaps	References
Design thinking in education	Human-centered, iterative process for problem-solving and creativity	Improves collaboration, ambiguity management, and creative confidence; aligns with 21st-century skills	Limited trained facilitators; risk of superficial adoption; little integration with AI skill development	Brown (2009), Razzouk and Shute (2012), Scheer et al. (2012), Henriksen et al. (2017), Trilling and Fadel (2009)
AI skill-building workshops	Practical, hands-on training in AI tools and methods	Workshops, hackathons, and projects enhance technical proficiency, and adaptability	Often isolated from creativity, ethics, and teamwork; uneven institutional adoption	Chou et al. (2021), Zhang and Aslan (2021), Luckin et al. (2016)
Intercultural collaboration	Development of intercultural competence through authentic, collaborative tasks	Enhances teamwork, empathy, adaptability, and global competence	Often limited to language/ cultural exchange; underexplored in STEM/ innovation contexts	Deardorff (2006), Byram (1997), Leask (2015), O'Dowd (2018)
MADE initiative	Integration of DT, AI skill building, intercultural collaboration, and innovative assessment	Students engage in cocreation, gain AI competencies, and enhance teamwork and intercultural fluency; outcomes are validated through survey-based assessments	Demonstrates a scalable, practice-based model for AI-enabled, human-centered learning across institutions	Current study

2.3 Methodology

This study employed a mixed-method approach to evaluate the effectiveness of the MADE program as an educational innovation integrating AI skills and DT. The methodology was designed to capture both measurable improvements in student competencies and the nuanced experiences of participants in a collaborative, intercultural learning environment. Quantitative data provided insights into shifts in confidence, problem-solving ability, and teamwork, while qualitative reflections highlighted the contextual and transformative aspects of learning. The following sections outline the research design, study context, participants, intervention, data-collection methods, instruments, and data-analysis strategies adopted.

2.3.1 Research Design

The study adopted a mixed-methods design, combining quantitative surveys with qualitative reflections to holistically assess the outcomes of the MADE program. The quantitative component measured changes in student competencies through pre- and post-program surveys using a 5-point Likert scale, focusing on AI confidence, problem-solving, teamwork, and intercultural collaboration. The qualitative component involved reflective journals and focus group discussions, which provided deeper insights into students' perceptions, challenges, and growth throughout the program. This design ensured both the breadth of numerical trends and the depth of lived experiences were captured, aligning with Creswell and Creswell's (2014) recommendation for integrating methods to enhance validity and reliability in educational research.

2.3.2 Context of Study

The MADE program was conducted as a seven-day international collaborative workshop co-organized by Taylor's University, Malaysia, and two Indian partner institutions: Kumaraguru College of Technology and Periyar Maniammai Institute. The program was designed to integrate DT methodologies with practical AI skill-building workshops, enabling students to apply emerging technologies to real-world community challenges.

A total of 51 students (41 from India and 10 from Malaysia) participated, forming intercultural teams of six members each. They were supported by ten academic mentors (five from each country), who facilitated learning and guided project development. At the conclusion of the program, students presented their prototypes and pitches before a panel of academics, business leaders, and industry practitioners in the *Pitch4Fund* session, where selected projects received seed funding for further development. Figure 2.4 shows some pictures taken during the MADE program.

FIGURE 2.4
Pictures taken during the MADE program.

2.3.3 imPACT Framework

The MADE initiative was grounded in the imPACT framework, which served as its guiding pedagogical philosophy. The framework emphasizes six interconnected dimensions—innovation, mobilization, partnership, action, cocreation, and transformation—that collectively support holistic student learning and meaningful knowledge application. Within MADE, these dimensions were operationalized as follows:

- **Innovation**: Encouraging students to adopt creative, future-oriented mindsets to address complex, real-world challenges.
- **Mobilization**: Leveraging resources, mentors, and tools across institutions in Malaysia and India to maximize impact.
- **Partnership**: Building cross-cultural and interdisciplinary teams that foster diversity in perspectives and approaches.
- **Action**: Guiding students from ideation to tangible solution building within a structured timeline.
- **Cocreation**: Emphasizing collaborative problem-solving, where students, mentors, and stakeholders co-design solutions.
- **Transformation**: Empowering students as changemakers, capable of applying AI and DT to transform their communities.

Figure 2.5. shows the imPACT framework created for the MADE initiative.

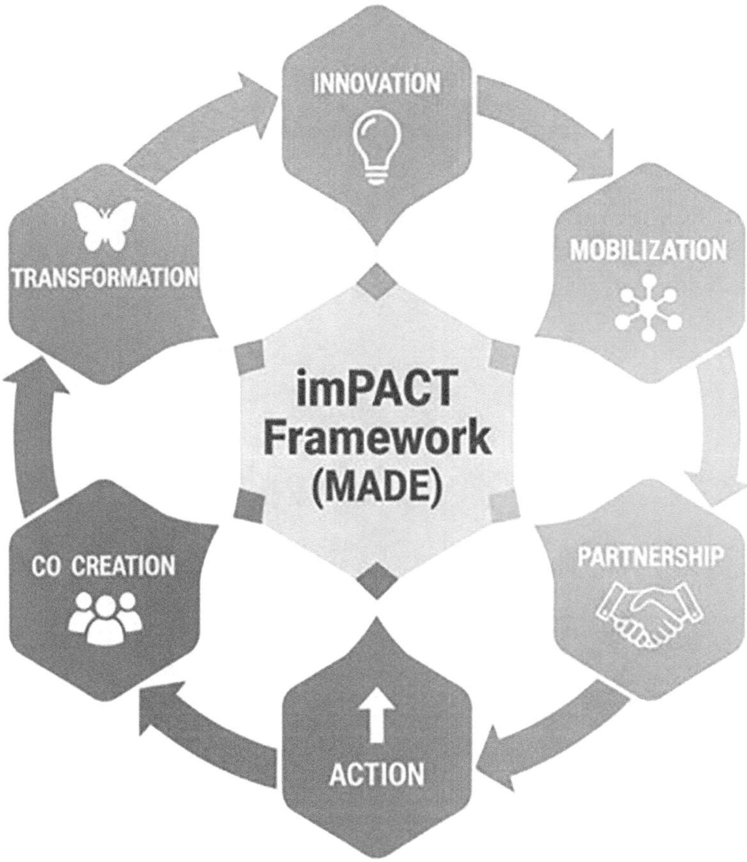

FIGURE 2.5
imPACT framework for MADE.

2.3.4 MADE Framework

The intervention was operationalized through the MADE framework, which blends the human-centered philosophy of DT with AI literacy and skill development. The goal was not only to expose students to emerging technologies but to embed these tools within a problem-solving paradigm that emphasizes empathy, creativity, and social impact.

The workshop was conducted across seven days, with each stage carefully scaffolded to reflect a progressive learning cycle (see Figure 2.6).

- **Day 1–2:** Foundations of DT. Students were immersed in the fundamentals of DT through interactive exercises such as empathy mapping, persona creation, and problem framing. These sessions emphasized understanding users' pain points and defining clear

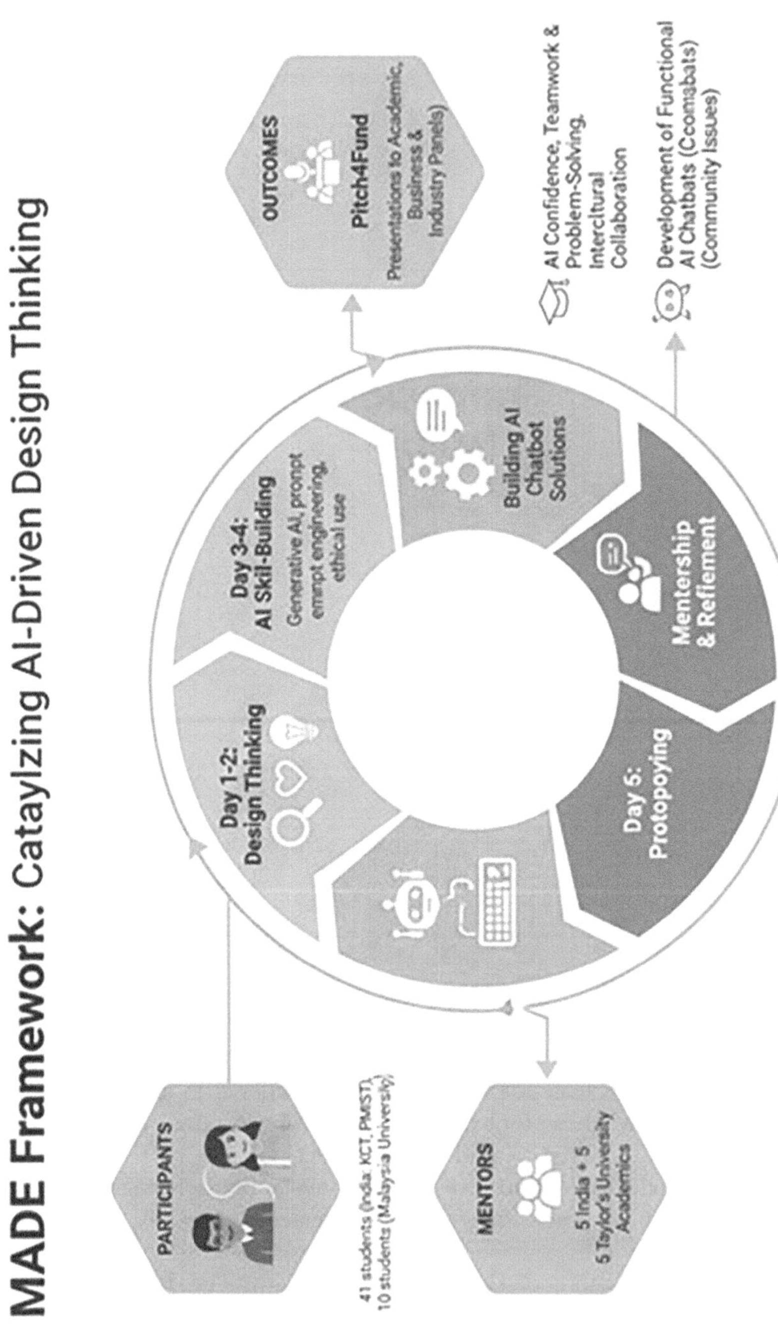

FIGURE 2.6
MADE framework and event flow.

problem statements, preparing participants to ground their AI projects in real-world relevance.

- **Day 3–4**: AI Skills and Digital Fluency. Building on the identified problem areas, students engaged in hands-on AI workshops covering generative AI, natural language processing, and prompt engineering. The emphasis was placed on practical experimentation, allowing students to prototype AI-driven solutions aligned with their chosen problem domains.
- **Day 5–6**: Prototyping and Integration. Interdisciplinary teams consolidated their DT insights with AI tools to create functional prototypes. Mentors provided iterative feedback through design critiques and checkpoint reviews, ensuring that solutions demonstrated both technical feasibility and user-centered value.
- **Day 7**: Pitch4Fund Showcase. The workshop culminated in the Pitch4Fund event, where student teams presented their prototypes to a panel of academics, business leaders, and industry partners. This final stage simulated a start-up pitching environment, providing students with authentic exposure to entrepreneurial communication, stakeholder engagement, and potential funding opportunities.

Together, this intervention fostered an experiential learning environment where students advanced through ideation → skill acquisition → prototyping → dissemination, mirroring innovation cycles in real-world practice (Figure 2.6). The MADE framework thus acted as both a curricular model and a platform for intercultural collaboration, positioning students as change makers capable of leveraging AI for societal good.

2.4 Impact and Discussions

The findings of the MADE initiative demonstrated clear evidence of student growth in both technical and soft-skill domains. Survey responses revealed significant improvements across three core competencies:

- AI Confidence: Eighty-eight percent of participants reported higher confidence in applying AI tools to practical problem-solving. Students noted that hands-on experimentation with generative AI and prompt engineering directly enhanced their ability to integrate technology with human-centered solutions.
- Problem-Solving and Teamwork: Seventy-five percent indicated improved collaboration and problem-solving skills. Interdisciplinary

grouping and mentor guidance were particularly cited as enablers of creative ideation and effective task distribution.

- Intercultural Collaboration: Ninety-two percent of participants agreed that their ability to work in cross-cultural contexts had strengthened. Exposure to peers from different cultural and academic backgrounds was perceived as a unique advantage of the program.

2.4.1 Quantitative Findings

Figures 2.7–2.9 illustrate the upward trends in student-reported competencies. These results align with prior studies that emphasize the value of experiential, collaborative learning in fostering digital fluency and intercultural awareness.

For AI confidence, responses clustered heavily around values 4 (Agree) and 5 (Strongly Agree), with relatively few students expressing neutral or negative ratings. This finding reinforces the effectiveness of immersive, hands-on workshops in building technical self-efficacy. Prior studies (Schunk & DiBenedetto, 2020) emphasize that experiential practice is a key driver of confidence development, particularly in technology-enabled learning. The MADE workshops appear to have followed this trajectory, as students directly applied AI tools in contexts they codesigned.

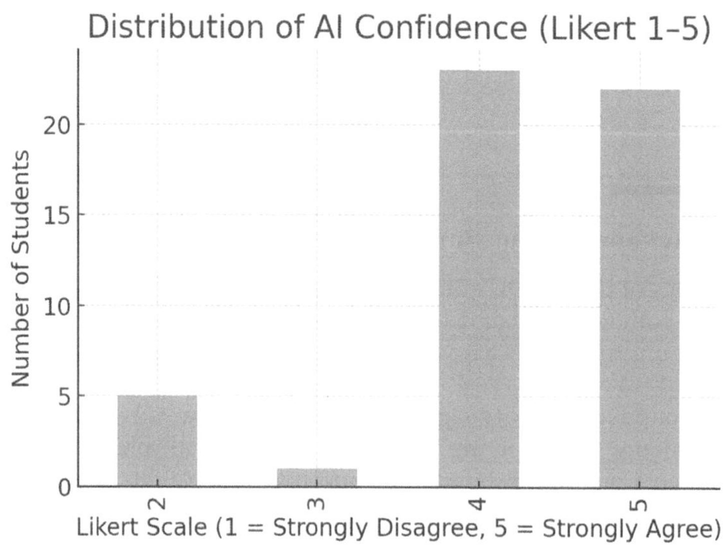

FIGURE 2.7
Survey results on AI confidence.

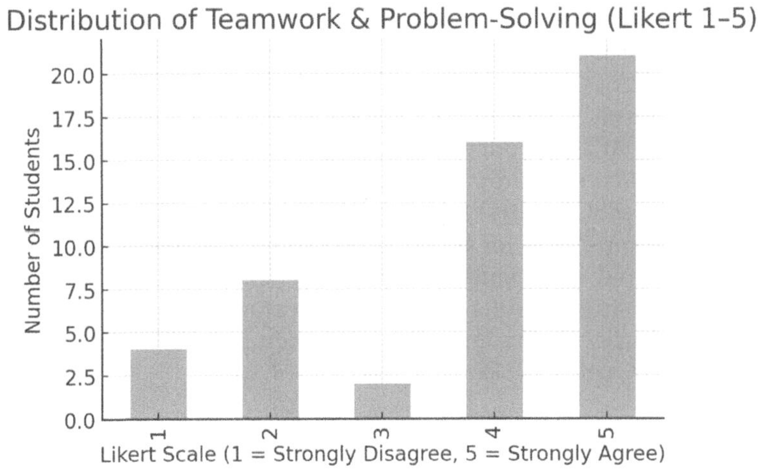

FIGURE 2.8
Survey results on teamwork and problem-solving.

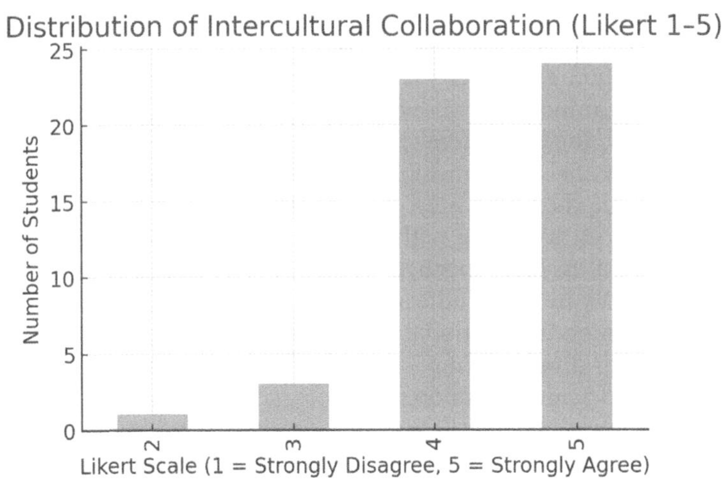

FIGURE 2.9
Survey results on intercultural collaboration.

For teamwork and problem-solving, a majority of participants indicated stronger collaboration and collective ideation skills. The intercultural groupings challenged students to reconcile different viewpoints, mirroring the dynamics of professional, interdisciplinary teams. Research supports the notion that cooperative learning structures enhance critical thinking and creativity (Gokhale, 1995; Salas et al., 2015). MADE's design, which deliberately paired students across cultures and disciplines, validated these outcomes by fostering constructive dialogue, negotiation, and shared ownership of solutions.

For intercultural collaboration, the responses were overwhelmingly positive, with over 90% of students selecting 4 or 5 on the scale. This reflects the program's success in promoting cross-cultural understanding and global competence. UNESCO (2019) highlights intercultural collaboration as a core 21st-century competency for higher education graduates, and MADE provided a structured environment where such skills could be practiced and reinforced. The strong results also align with studies showing that international partnerships enhance empathy, tolerance, and adaptability among students (Leask & Carroll, 2011).

2.4.2 Qualitative Insights

Analysis of the surveys revealed recurring themes of empowerment, creativity, and responsibility, which were consistently echoed across student groups. A significant number of participants reported that the MADE workshop provided them with an environment where they could actively cocreate solutions rather than passively receive knowledge. For example, one student noted, "I never imagined AI could be applied to improve daily lifestyle this way," reflecting both the novelty of the experience and the expansion of their problem-solving mindset.

Another emerging theme was cross-cultural learning. Since the workshop included participants from multiple disciplines and countries, students frequently commented on the value of diversity in team collaboration. As one participant shared, "Working with students from another country and university gave me a fresh perspective on teamwork," underscoring the importance of inclusivity in global education contexts. This finding resonates with previous studies on international collaborative learning, which highlights how exposure to diverse perspectives can enhance empathy, adaptability, and intercultural communication skills.

The convergence of quantitative and qualitative evidence suggests that MADE not only improved technical competencies but also supported the development of soft skills essential for future-ready graduates. By embedding AI literacy within the human-centered framework of DT, MADE bridged the gap between technical fluency and social responsibility. Moreover, the Pitch4Fund component served as an authentic assessment mechanism, validating student learning outcomes against the expectations of external stakeholders.

These findings position MADE as a scalable model for integrating AI-driven experiential learning into higher education curricula, particularly in contexts that aim to combine technological innovation with intercultural collaboration.

2.5 Conclusion

This chapter has demonstrated the potential of integrating AI, DT, and the UN SDGs within higher education through the MADE workshop. By leveraging the imPACT framework and a problem-based, collaborative learning environment, students were not only introduced to the technical foundations of AI but also challenged to apply these skills to real-world sustainability problems.

The results highlight two key outcomes. First, students developed practical competencies in AI application and DT methodologies, equipping them with tools that are directly transferable to their future professional contexts. Second, and equally significant, students reported a stronger sense of social responsibility, creativity, and intercultural collaboration, reinforcing the idea that education must go beyond skill acquisition to nurture socially conscious innovators.

Despite these positive outcomes, the study acknowledges certain limitations, including the short duration of the workshop and the limited sample size, which may constrain the generalizability of the findings. Future iterations of MADE will address these limitations by expanding participant diversity, extending the program duration, and incorporating longitudinal tracking to assess the sustainability of student learning outcomes.

In conclusion, this initiative illustrates how AI-driven, inclusive, and sustainability-focused pedagogical models can prepare students to thrive in an increasingly complex world. As higher education continues to evolve, frameworks like MADE provide a pathway to embedding innovation, inclusivity, and social impact into the heart of the learning experience.

References

Brown, T. (2009). *Change by design: How design thinking creates new alternatives for business and society*. Harper Business.

Byram, M. (1997). *Teaching and assessing intercultural communicative competence*. Multilingual Matters.

Creswell, J. W., & Creswell, J. D. (2014). *Research design: Qualitative, quantitative, and mixed methods approaches* (4th ed.). Sage Publications.

Deardorff, D. K. (2006). Identification and assessment of intercultural competence as a student outcome of internationalization. *Journal of Studies in International Education*, *10*(3), 241–266. https://doi.org/10.1177/1028315306287002

Henriksen, D., Richardson, C., & Mehta, R. (2017). Design thinking: A creative approach to educational problems of practice. *Thinking Skills and Creativity*, *26*, 140-153.

Holmes, W., Tuomi, I., & Luckin, R. (2021). AI, skills and the future of work. In *OECD education working papers* (No. 241). OECD Publishing.

IDEO. (2023). *Design thinking process.* Retrieved from https://www.ideo.com/pages/design-thinking

Knowledge Sourcing Intelligence LLP. (2025). *Artificial intelligence in education market analysis and forecasts from 2025 to 2030* (Report Code KSI061612924). Knowledge-Sourcing.com.

Leask, B., & Carroll, J. (2011). Moving beyond 'wishing and hoping': Internationalisation and student experiences of learning. In *The British Council's higher education series.* Routledge.

Luckin, R., Holmes, W., Griffiths, M., & Forcier, L. B. (2016). *Intelligence unleashed: An argument for AI in education.* Pearson Education.

O'Dowd, R. (2018). From telecollaboration to virtual exchange: State-of-the-art and the role of UNICollaboration in moving forward. *Journal of Virtual Exchange, 1,* 1–23.

Organisation for Economic Co-operation and Development (OECD). (2019). *OECD learning compass 2030: A series of concept notes.* OECD Publishing.

Scheer, A., Noweski, C., & Meinel, C. (2012). Transforming constructivist learning into action: Design thinking in education. *Design and Technology Education: An International Journal, 17*(3).

Schunk, D. H., & DiBenedetto, M. K. (2020). Motivation and social-emotional learning: Theory, research, and practice. In R. J. Sternberg, S. B. Kaufman, & L. R. S. Kaiser (Eds.), *The Cambridge handbook of applied school psychology* (pp. 222–245). Cambridge University Press.

Trilling, B., & Fadel, C. (2009). *21st century skills: Learning for life in our times.* Jossey-Bass.

United Nations Educational, Scientific and Cultural Organization (UNESCO). (2019). *Artificial intelligence in education: Challenges and opportunities for sustainable development.* UNESCO.

United Nations Educational, Scientific and Cultural Organization (UNESCO). (2021). *AI and education: Guidance for policy-makers.* UNESCO.

Zawacki-Richter, O., Marín, V. I., Bond, M., & Gouverneur, F. (2019). Systematic review of research on artificial intelligence applications in higher education—Where are the educators? *International Journal of Educational Technology in Higher Education, 16*(39), 1–27.

3

Student Engagement and Motivation toward Education 4.0

Asokan Narayanasamy

3.1 Introduction

Education is one of the fundamental human rights, and delivering knowledge to learners effectively has been a success metric for many centuries. From formal and mainstream education systems, marking an authoritarian transfer of knowledge or information and skill from a teacher to a passive student, to slightly interacting with teachers and peers using basic instructional mediums, and going on to a student-centric teaching-learning process where the teacher is more a facilitator than a teacher, and now to one where learning can happen anywhere, anytime, with technology firmly embedded in our current education systems.

Throughout history, inventions, innovations, and discoveries have consistently driven global progress and interconnectedness. Whenever novel mindsets, imaginative leaps, and innovative actions emerged, humanity witnessed transformative paradigm shifts and industrial revolutions that reshaped the world.

We are currently witnessing an unprecedented acceleration of innovation, transformation, and technological progress, radically redefining the human experience. The convergence of globalization, liberalization, and technological revolution is profoundly transforming every facet of life, yielding distinct and far-reaching impacts.

Over the past three centuries, our world has undergone four transformative industrial revolutions:

1. **Mechanization**: Steam engines and water-powered systems pioneered the first revolution.
2. **Mass Production**: The second revolution leveraged the division of labor for scaled manufacturing.
3. **Automation**: The third revolution harnessed electronics, IT, and automation to reshape production.
4. **Digital Convergence**: The current fourth revolution is driven by artificial intelligence, blurring the lines between physical and digital realities.

DOI: 10.1201/9781003633433-3

According to Peter Fisk (2017), as the concept of living a "100-year life" becomes the standard norm, the majority of that time will be spent studying and working. This means that learning will become significantly more important and fundamentally different for future generations. Most people will experience at least six different careers throughout their lives, requiring them to undergo substantial unlearning, relearning, and upskilling. As innovation continually advances at a breakneck pace, it will persistently require a new set of competencies, which include skills, knowledge, talent, attitude, and a growth mindset to keep pace with transformations.

The futurist Peter Diamandis says, think of all the progress humanity made between 1900 and 2000. The airplane, the moon landing, the transistor, the internet—all of it happened in a single century. Now here's the crazy part: the same level of technological progress we achieved in those 100 years is now being compressed into a few decades.

Peter went on:

> Between 2000 and 2016, we saw the rise of Facebook, YouTube, Tesla, and the iPhone. But the pace of change is accelerating. From 2016 to 2022, we saw just as much innovation. And between 2022 and 2026? The same amount of progress will happen again compressed into just four years.

Amid this breakneck speed of progress, students need competencies such as problem-identifying skills, problem-solving skills, creative thinking, critical thinking, analytical thinking, agile learning, continuous self-learning, and agile adaptability. In addition to these skills, students need to be comfortable with developing technology and able to use it to their advantage for their growth and development, and apply it to solve their personal, workplace, and societal problems.

This is where Education 4.0 comes in. Education 4.0 has emerged as a ubiquitous concept in contemporary educational discourse.

3.2 Education 4.0

The rapid evolution of technology has revolutionized manufacturing sectors and transformed various sectors of production and services. Education is one of the utility sectors that have reaped the greatest advantage in terms of the teaching-learning process and active student engagement. Miranda et al. (2021) pointed out that the implementation of current and emerging technologies combined with innovative pedagogical procedures and best practices is known as Education 4.0, which is synchronized with the key stages of the four industrial revolutions, exploring connections to higher education.

Education 4.0 is a forward-thinking approach to teaching and learning that aligns with the fast growing Fourth Industrial Revolution. This era combines intelligent and sustainable technologies such as cloud computing, artificial intelligence (AI), big data and AI analytics, horizontal and vertical integration, the Industrial Internet of Things (IIoT), additive manufacturing/3D printing, autonomous robots, simulation/digital twins, sensors, and cybersecurity. These technologies are increasingly incorporated into our daily lives, influencing the future of education and beyond.

According to Costan et al. (2021), Education 4.0 is "a pedagogical approach that aligns with the fourth industrial revolution (4IR). It answers to the demands of the 4IR, in which the convergence of science and technology is utilized in augmenting manual processes for improved effectiveness and efficiency."

Academicians, educationalists, education administrators, and educational leaders debate the various ways in which the curriculum, teaching-learning, student engagement, and student motivation, at all levels, will need to transform now and in the near future to facilitate Education 4.0. Disruptive innovation guru Clay Christiansen pointed to the dramatic unpacking of education from its present structure so that it can be personalized to meet student expectations, re-bundled, peer to peer, and continuous for active student engagement. Learning is poised to transcend traditional boundaries in the years ahead, unhindered by conventional constraints such as physical spaces (classrooms, workplaces), formats (online, offline), structures (structured, unstructured), delivery methods (taught, self-directed), standards (standardized, nonstandardized), and credentials (certificated, non-certificated).

3.3 Higher Education in the Era of Education 4.0

Weaving Education 4.0 into the fabric of the education system has permitted teachers and students to leverage state-of-the-art infrastructure and advancing technologies to improve the quality of the higher education curriculum, the teaching-learning process, assessment and evaluation techniques, and pedagogical procedures, which improve student engagement. In this regard, teaching-learning-evaluation strategies are also evolving and reorienting through innovation to meet the needs of continuously evolving technological advancements.

Education 4.0 addresses the needs of a continuously evolving technological landscape. The process of knowledge creation in Education 4.0 goes beyond traditional pedagogy and andragogy to encompass heutagogy, peeragogy, and cybergogy. Heutagogy emphasizes self-directed learning based on humanist and constructivist principles, focusing on the learner.

Additionally, metacognition, which involves understanding one's own learning and thinking processes through self-reflection, is highly encouraged.

Education 4.0 revitalized a timeless concept, Peeragogy, which empowers collaborative learning by fostering a shared foundation for knowledge exchange and collective growth. It refers to the set of teaching techniques that promote learning among peers (Ouhrir et al., 2019). W. Daud et al. (2019) defined cybergogy as ICT-enabled learning methodologies that provide learning experiences that transcend time and geography. The rapid evolution of technology and the internet has given rise to cybergogy, a transformative approach that leverages digital advancements to enhance and expand Educational 4.0 opportunities.

Motivating and actively engaging students beyond getting their degree, building their life and career for the next 30 years after graduation, and making them realize they are lifelong self-learners are the present challenges and opportunities in higher education, along with localized educational and social issues. Students need to be motivated to involve themselves to actively engage to develop higher-order thinking skills, learn how to learn, practice metacognition, and understand transdisciplinary subjects to solve societal problems, like aging populations, climate change, disruptive technologies, and mental health and well-being.

The bestselling author and renowned global thought leader, Professor Peter Fisk (2017), identifies nine pivotal trends shaping the future of Education 4.0.

1. E-learning tools offer great opportunities for remote, self-paced learning; the learning process can take place anytime, anywhere.
2. Personalized learning: The teacher need not instruct every student with the same instructions or topics. The teacher facilitates each student's journey on the what, when, how, and where of learning to meet each student's strengths and learning style.
3. Free choice: Students can choose between classroom learning, blended learning, the flipped classroom, and the Bring Your Own Device approach to decide how they want to learn.
4. Project-based learning: Students can work on a project for a period between one month and six months to solve a local community problem. They need to ensure the solution is accepted by the stakeholders. Students can develop problem identification and problem-solving skills. They understand the complexity of the problem and unleash their maximum energy to solve it.
5. Field experience. Field experience plays an important role in students' educational journey. It's an excellent opportunity to apply theoretical knowledge to real-world known and unknown situations. It helps students improve their retention and retrieval of factual knowledge and understand the conceptual knowledge needed to apply in given situations.

6. Data interpretation. The ability to take data, understand it, process it, extract value from it, visualize it, and communicate it is a hugely important skill students must develop in order to succeed in Education 4.0.
7. Exams will change completely. No more evaluation of rote learning. Evaluation of lower-order thinking skills and higher-order thinking skills can be measured through continuous assessment rather than summative assessment at each step of the learning process.
8. Student ownership. There is no blame game. When students take more responsibility for their own learning, they are motivated and engaged. They develop self-discipline and decision-making skills and become independent thinkers.
9. Mentoring is poised to become increasingly vital. While distance education appears to be the future, the guidance and instruction provided by teachers, along with the presence of educational institutions, remain fundamental to academic performance and the success of the educational process.

3.4 Motivation

Since the dawn of time, humans have been motivated by an intrinsic need to understand the purpose of their existence and lead meaningful lives (Ohlsson, 2011). Although exploratory goals have inevitably changed over time, they have always contributed to learning in some way. The objectives that drive education at a given time take on new dimensions with each generation (Bruner, 2009). In ancient civilizations, education was mostly accomplished via apprenticeship, in which people learned skills and information from their elders (Collins & Halverson, 2009). As societies grew and became more complex, schools and universities emerged and became the main sources of education. With the development of the printing press, knowledge and information were more readily communicated and propagated, resulting in the construction of libraries and a demand for knowledge (Gaines, 2013). The Industrial Revolution resulted in discoveries and breakthroughs, as well as a stronger focus on science and mathematics in education and the establishment of public education institutions (Bekar & Lipsey, 2004).

The 20th century witnessed a surge in mass education as technology advanced, with radio, television, and film (Kirby, 2016). The learners of the 21st century, often referred to as the "Internet Generation," are distinct from those of the past (Oblinger & Oblinger, 2005), and the internet has given a new means for individuals to access knowledge and learn. The digital revolution has profoundly impacted how people live and work (Ghobakhloo, 2020).

In today's fast-changing world, the technologies of Industry 4.0 have made an impact and triggered a seismic shift across all sectors (Philbeck & Davis, 2019), which includes improved connectivity, intelligent data processing/analytics, and computing capacity (Lee et al., 2015). Future forecasts indicate that in the coming years, employment growth will be driven by technology; hence, it is becoming more necessary to train individuals accordingly (The Future of Jobs Report, 2020).

Students bring unique perspectives and meaningful connections to academic pursuits, infusing them with personal significance that drives their energy and focus in diverse ways. This energy and focus are called motivation, or motivation to learn.

Differences in motivation are an important source of diversity in classrooms, comparable in importance to differences in prior knowledge, skill, talent, or developmental readiness. When it comes to learning, students' motivations and active engagement are important because students' physical presence in the classroom will ensure no learning, rote learning, or meaningful learning, depending on their motivation.

Students' motivations are shaped by an intricate array of factors, including the types of goals they set, their personal interests, and their attributions about learning and development.

3.4.1 Motivation as Goals

Students' motivation as a goal can be classified into three categories, namely mastery goals, performance goals, and performance-avoidance goals, which exist in combination among students.

Mastery goals are associated with intrinsic motivation, which focuses on learning for a purpose and enjoyment and leads to constructive learning.

According to Harzckiewicz et al. (2002) and Wolters (2004), students who primarily have mastery orientations toward a course tend to not only show greater interest in the course but also continue to maintain their interest well beyond the course's official end. Additionally, these students are more likely to enroll in further courses in the same subject.

Performance goal is associated with extrinsic motivation, needs external validation, helps students move to the next level of study, and leads to rote learning, which helps students get higher grades than those who choose mastery goals. Achieving a performance goal does not help students handle new situations. They find it difficult to apply their learning in unknown situations. Learning by mastery goals helps students handle any new and unknown situations. Midgley et al. (2001) cite evidence that performance-oriented students do not learn as deeply or permanently as students who are more mastery oriented.

Failure-avoidant goals can paradoxically hinder academic success. Urdan (2004) says failure-avoidant goals are usually an undesirable outcome of pressure to compete with performance goals.

3.4.2 Motives as Interests

Interest is associated with intrinsic motivation, the energy, effort, drive, and time that come from within. Hidi and Renninger (2006) stated that when students learn from interest, they typically allocate greater focus to the subject content than when they learn from effort. Effort and interest are interwoven because situational and personal interests blend into students' personal learning experiences.

Situational interests arise in response to immediate, specific environmental factors, which are temporary. Personal interests are stable and persistent, manifesting in a student's behavior and choices across various situations.

3.4.3 Attribution-Driven Motives

Attributions encompass the beliefs about the factors that contribute to success and failure and their sources. They typically influence motivation in different ways, depending on the nature of the attributions (Weiner, 2005).

The attributions students make about their learning outcomes significantly influence their motivation and engagement. Self-efficacy, the belief in one's ability to carry out a specific activity or attain specific goals, is a critical factor in motivation. Self-efficacy beliefs can be influenced by prior experiences, observing others, messages from others, and emotions related to stress and discomfort.

In Bandura's self-efficacy (1977, 1986, 1997) theory, the beliefs become a primary, explicit explanation for motivation.

Pajares and Schunk (2001, 2002) studied self-efficacy and identified the following four major sources of self-efficacy beliefs: (1) prior experiences of mastering tasks, (2) watching others master tasks, (3) messages or "persuasion" from others, and (4) emotions related to stress and discomfort.

3.5 Students' Engagement

In today's fast-paced, technology-driven world, traditional teaching methods alone may not suffice. To truly connect with students, educators must employ dynamic strategies that cater to diverse learning styles and interests.

The basic principles of student engagement are foundational to stimulating academic achievement. Xu et al. (2023) have identified that the key principles revolve around behavioral, cognitive, and emotional dimensions of engagement.

Hong et al. (2020) suggest that behavioral engagement involves students' involvement and active participation in academic and extracurricular activities, adherence to rules, and the effort put into learning activities. Engaged participation in classroom discussions, attending classes regularly, and sincerely submitting assignments are markers of behavioral engagement. Sá (2023) found that high behavioral engagement contributes to better academic outcomes and retention.

A study by Fredricks et al. (2016) found that behavioral engagement refers to the visible actions that students take to participate in their learning process, which lead to higher academic performance. This includes attending classes regularly, participating in discussions, completing assignments on time, and engaging in extracurricular activities.

According to Sesmiyanti (2018), cognitive engagement refers to students' involvement in their learning journey, including the use of meaningful learning strategies and the desire to understand complex concepts. Sá (2023) study found that students leverage cognitive abilities to navigate challenges, fostering grit and perseverance, and achieving subject matter mastery. Research by Estévez et al. (2021) shows that cognitive engagement refers to the level of intellectual investment students put into learning. It includes the use of deep learning strategies, such as critical thinking, problem-solving, and the willingness to persevere through challenges.

A cognitively engaged student, for example, will not only complete assignments but also seek to understand underlying concepts and think critically about the material. Cognitive engagement is crucial for long-term learning and academic growth, as it reflects students' efforts to connect, apply, and integrate knowledge (Fredricks et al., 2016).

According to Senior et al. (2018), emotional engagement reflects students' feelings of belonging, interest, and enthusiasm. Students who feel connected and emotionally supported by their institution are actively engaged and committed to their studies. Emotional engagement involves the feelings and attitudes students have toward their school, peers, teachers, and learning tasks (Li & Lerner, 2013). Students who feel a sense of belonging and attachment to their school are emotionally engaged. Emotional engagement also involves enthusiasm and interest in school-related activities, which may include clubs, societies, sports, and academic teams. This type of engagement is closely related to motivation and is key to fostering long-term academic persistence (Trowler, 2010).

Increasing student engagement promotes learning, retention, and academic success (Carini et al., 2006).

3.6 Technology

Miranda et al.'s (2021) analysis suggests that Education 4.0 can be classified into two types of technologies:

First, technology-based solutions such as AI-driven insights, data-driven decisioning, virtual process automation, predictive maintenance, data visualization, real-time analytics, and so on.

Second, the tools and platforms that combine different technologies for educational, administrative, and management purposes (Zoom, Google Meet, Webex, Microsoft Teams), including learning management systems (LMS).

Bonfield et al. (2020) and Hong and Ma (2020) find Education 4.0 relies on a differentiating element from Education 1.0, 2.0, and 3.0 based on the application of existing information and communication technology (ICT) tools, including engaged participation of students, bilateral integration and cooperation among the different educational agencies, and opportunities to create learning content under the concept of "learning by doing."

González-Pérez et al. (2022) pointed out six technological 4.0 enablers that guide educational actors to enhance educational innovation and open education:

1. Transparent technologies
2. Technology-integrated teaching methods
3. Enabling technologies
4. Intelligent technologies
5. Innovative technological models
6. Radical technologies

Motivation drives learning and academic achievement, which explains the reasons behind students' active engagement and performance in the learning environment and is explained by three important theories.

1. The expectancy-value theory explains that students' motivation is determined by their belief in their own achievement (expectancy) and the value they attach to the assignment (value).
2. The achievement goal theory classifies motivation into two main goal orientations, namely mastery goals and performance goals. Students with a mastery goal focus on gaining competence and understanding the content, which is associated with intrinsic motivation.
3. The self-determination theory explains the role of autonomy, competence, and relatedness in nurturing intrinsic motivation. Students are more self-motivated to learn when they feel that their learning activities are decided by them (autonomy), when they are confident of completing a task (competence), and when they feel connected to others in the learning environment (relatedness). This theory suggests that fulfilling these three basic psychological needs—autonomy, competence, and relatedness—is essential for cultivating in-depth, enduring motivation for learning.

3.7 Transformations

"The pace of transformation is accelerating." "People say it's been happening throughout human history, but that's actually not true. When we draw a logarithmic scale of transformation over the last 10,000 years, it shows that the pace of change in the last 15 years is faster than in the first 9,000. Students need to understand that today's world is very different from even three years ago." Students need to achieve "homeostasis," which is the developing competency to maintain conditions for survival in a continually transforming environment.

Three types of transformations identified by the author to enhance student engagement and motivation toward Education 4.0 are discussed in the following section.

3.7.1 Technological Transformation

Digital technologies have transformed numerous manufacturing and service industries, including education. Iivari et al. (2020) state that digital transformation has significantly influenced classrooms and the teaching strategies used by primary as well as higher education educators. Sharlovych et al. (2012) reveal that digital technology plays a significant role in students' academic activities, intellectual abilities, and creative expression while providing a platform to practice the best teaching methodologies based on an Education 4.0 background.

Technological transformation refers to the integration of digital tools, digital platforms, and resources to enhance the curriculum, teaching-learning process, and assessment and evaluation.

The existing and future technological transitions, for education to embrace, thinking and execution approaches need to shift from age-old, rigid, outdated, piecemeal, and tech-first to holistic, systems- and technology-oriented, and human-centered.

Technological transformation in terms of digital applications and educational technology assists students in obtaining grades in exams, accelerating their learning process, understanding complex concepts, applying these concepts in known and unknown situations, promoting their inquisitiveness toward research, managing their time with respect to different courses, earning diplomas and degrees, and finding dream jobs.

The state-of-the-art technologies—gaming and gamification, e-learning, video-assisted learning, and immersive learning with virtual and artificial realities—improve student learning and retention competencies.

AI has gone from being a futuristic technological concept to one that's transforming everyday activities in our lives. And here's what's truly mind-blowing: we're just getting started.

Artificial general intelligence (AGI) matches human intelligence.

Superintelligence exceeds it, unlocking unimaginable possibilities.
Both have the potential to redefine our world.
We are moving toward this faster than we think.

3.7.1.1 E-Resources

Electronic resources refer to information and resource materials in digital form, accessed and utilized through different electronic devices such as computers, smartphones, tablets, and electronic readers. These resources include e-books, e-journals, e-newspapers, electronic theses and dissertations (ETDs), e-standards and patents, online academic databases, multimedia materials, video lectures, interlinked hypertext documents, digital repositories, search engines, websites, blogs, online magazines, and other forms of digital content. As technology continues to advance, electronic resources will play an important role in Education 4.0, transforming how we access and use information for meaningful learning.

The COVID-19 pandemic has underscored the importance of e-resources in education, with blended learning (Garrison & Kanuka, 2004), flipped classrooms (Strayer, 2012), and the addition of Massive Open Online Courses (MOOCs) to higher education (Ahmad et al., 2018) becoming more mainstream. Libraries, as pivotal enablers of hybrid online education and research models (Maidment-Otlet, 2021), play an important part in accomplishing sustainable development objectives (Msauki, 2021) and must adapt to disruptive changes while ensuring inclusivity for special-needs users. Technical innovations (Salleh et al., 2020) are key to advancing sustainable digital library solutions that accommodate diverse accessibility needs (Iroeze & Owate, 2021).

Students are encouraged to leverage e-resources to supplement their academic journey. E-resources offer a wealth of benefits. They are an invaluable tool for students, offering a flexible, convenient, and accessible way to learn and grow toward Education 4.0.

3.7.1.2 Gamification

Greipl et al. (2020) argued that gamification is emerging as an innovative teaching methodology that is rarely used in higher education. Almalki (2022) says the gamification methodology uses games to acquire educational competencies through directed self-learning and provides a hands-on experience for students.

Noroozi et al. (2020) find that the activity theory supports gamification, which offers a dynamic and dialectical view of the educational process. The gradual internalization of learning occurs through tasks within a virtual environment that organizes them to positively guarantee conceptual advances while simultaneously establishing optimal communication, collaboration, and reflection formulas.

Gris and Bengtson (2021) and Wang et al. (2022) studied the effectiveness of digital game-based learning in students compared with other instructional methods, taking as variables the subjects, the different educational levels, the game design, and the duration of the intervention.

Dabbous et al. (2022) investigated the effectiveness of game-based learning in experiential pharmacy education and found that it can enhance student engagement, motivation, and ultimately learning outcomes. A study by Pons-Valladares et al. (2022) investigated the effectiveness of active learning strategies in the Architecture 360 project, revealing that the use of interactive simulations, case studies, and gamification enhanced student learning outcomes and teacher-provided didactic materials.

Arias-Calderón et al. (2022) and Willis and Bryant (2022) investigated the impact of serious games on online teaching and found that this gamification approach can foster increased motivation and engagement among students, leading to a more immersive learning experience.

Using an educational board game to review the key concepts of a subject during class represents a gamification intervention, while using a points system or badges (i.e., game elements) to reward students in a classroom for their performance on an exam is an example of gamification. It has been demonstrated that these are attractive and motivating methodologies, with a positive impact on student learning and feedback (Bawa, 2022; Coleman & Money, 2020).

Interactive mobile quizzes have revolutionized the way we learn, making the process more engaging and enjoyable. By incorporating gamification techniques into mobile quizzes, learners are motivated to actively participate, leading to better knowledge retention and a more immersive learning experience.

Gamification enhances extrinsic motivation, student engagement, knowledge acquisition, knowledge creation, and knowledge sharing by leveraging the inherent human desire for competition, achievement, and rewards.

At Sona Medical College of Naturopathy & Yoga, India, we applied gamification to learning, transforming the traditional approach into a dynamic and interactive experience. It creates a thrill of challenge, urgency, and accomplishment, encouraging learners to actively seek knowledge to improve their performance. By making learning fun and enjoyable, gamification increases learner motivation and promotes a growth mindset.

Students are encouraged to harness the power of gamification to elevate their academic experience. Gamification involves applying game design elements and mechanics to nongame contexts, such as active learning, to increase student engagement, extrinsic motivation, and active participation. By incorporating gamification into their academic curriculum, students can experience a more engaging, interactive, and enjoyable learning environment.

3.7.1.3 Open Education

Open educational resources (OER) offer opportunities for sustainable growth in improving access and quality of education by enabling the use of learning materials that are free and easily accessible and hold high quality. The use of eContent has become an essential component of the teaching and learning processes due to the diverse needs of learners.

The open education closes the gap between educational systems operated with a fundamental disconnect between practices left over from the analog world and the internet to support more affordable, effective teaching and learning. Open education encompasses course materials, modules, textbooks, streaming videos, tests, software, and any other tools, practices, or techniques that are free of legal, financial, and technical barriers and can be fully used, shared, and adapted in the digital environment to support access to knowledge.

Popular OER repositories are as follows:

- OpenStax is a provider of interactive learning technologies and education research, and a nonprofit organization that provides free and peer-reviewed open textbooks.
- MIT OpenCourseWare is a web-based publication of MIT course materials, freely and openly licensed, and available to anyone, anywhere.
- Khan Academy is a nonprofit organization that provides free and openly licensed educational videos and resources to anyone, anywhere.
- MERLOT: A curated collection of OER, including textbooks, course materials, and software.

Students are encouraged to take advantage of OER to access high-quality learning materials while reducing educational costs, leading to better learning outcomes.

3.7.1.4 Smart Education

Zhu and He (2012) defined smart education as

> the essence of smarter education is to create intelligent environments by using smart technologies, so that smart pedagogies can be facilitated as to provide personalized learning services and empower learners to develop talents of wisdom that have better value orientation, higher thinking quality, and stronger conduct ability.

Jang (2014) defined smart education as "an educational system that allows students to learn by using up-to-date technology and it enables students to study with various materials based on their aptitudes and intellectual levels." Bajaj and Sharma (2018) defined smart education as "about providing personalized learning, anywhere and anytime. Moreover, they state that smart education is about taking learning outside the traditional classrooms; and is an activity that can be done anywhere and anytime." According to Demir (2021), smart education is the "effective and coherent use of information and communication technologies to reach a learning outcome using a suitable pedagogical approach."

Uskov et al. (2015) say that smart education is considered a growing and emerging field of research that represents the integration of smart systems and environments, smart technologies, state-of-the-art educational programs and tools, and innovative pedagogies, teaching strategies, and learning methodologies based on advanced technology. According to Darsham-Singh and Hassan (2017), a smart learning environment "features the use of innovative technologies and elements that allow greater flexibility, effectiveness, adaptation, engagement, motivation, and feedback for the learner."

Ghallabi et al. (2022) propose an architecture with reusable components to create a personalized learning system that generates courses adapted to learners' characteristics. Personalized, individualized, adaptive, interactive, ubiquitous, collaborative, flipped, blended, case-based, and challenge-based learning are the learning approaches that form the basis for smart education systems.

Smart classrooms, interactive boards, e-books, learning analytics, academic tubes, virtual reality, augmented reality, cloud computing, mobile devices, Web 3.0, and social networks are used in smart education systems.

ICT, combined with new learning and teaching methodologies, will help realize the concept of smart education.

3.7.2 Strategic Transformation

Learning outcomes have shifted from acquiring subject knowledge and practicing skills to developing competencies in today's education system. If knowledge is acquired consistently along with practicing skills, then competencies will develop in a complex manner. Competencies are difficult to develop in one course of study, so we can discuss the "learning strategies" practiced over the duration of the program. The learning strategies integrate both approaches and principles, the direction of development, and the methods and types of instruction, able to move back and forth with ease along a continuum of teaching models that ranges from teacher-centered at one end to student-centered at the other end, but they are always subject-centered no matter how teachers are teaching.

The more comprehensive the strategies, the greater the impact, yielding more significant results, better motivating the students' cognitive ability, evolving the practical experience of solving problems, and enhancing in-depth understanding.

3.7.2.1 Teacher–Student Relationship

It is important for students to develop cordial relationships with their teachers as well as with their peers. McFarland et al. (2016) find that when students begin formal schooling, they need to develop quality relationships, as interpersonal relationships in the school setting influence children's development and positively impact student outcomes, which include their motivation to learn, behavior, and cognitive skills.

3.7.2.2 Swap Seating

Modify the physical learning environment. The traditional model of students sitting in rows is not the only way to facilitate learning; innovative seating arrangements can foster engagement and motivation. Classroom layouts can be tailored to promote collaboration, creativity, and comfort rather than adhering to rigid, traditional structures. Classrooms can be designed to accommodate diverse learning styles, promoting flexibility and autonomy for students.

According to Cole et al. (2021), consider flexible seating for a more dynamic classroom. By providing comfortable seating options, educators can promote student engagement, motivation, and academic success. Alter seating arrangements of students frequently inside the classroom. Change the classroom for every subject or every period to encourage students to move around, refreshing their minds and reducing monotony, and foster a sense of transition and separation between subjects, helping students mentally prepare for the next class. Research shows that students who are comfortable in their seating are more likely to participate, pay attention, and retain information.

3.7.2.3 Questioning

Kippers et al. (2018) say that classroom engagement, classroom conversation, and asking questions play a critical role in gathering evidence concerning student learning.

Asking questions demonstrates that students are thinking about their learning and are engaged. They are actively filling the knowledge gap. Questioning is most frequently employed in scheduled discussions about assigned material, but it can be used daily by incorporating the questioning process into your interactions with students.

Doğan and Yücel-Toy (2020) put forward as follows:

> The process of asking questions helps students understand the new topic, realize others' ideas, evaluate their own progress, monitor learning processes, and increase their motivation and interest on the topic by arousing curiosity.

Socratic questioning

> is a systematic method of disciplined questioning that can be used to explore complex ideas, to get to the truth of things, to open up issues and problems, to uncover assumptions, to analyse concepts, to distinguish what we know from what we don't know, and to follow out logical implications of thought.
>
> (Paul & Elder 2006)

3.7.2.4 Student Autonomy

According to Schunk and DiBenedetto (2020), "[m]otivational processes are personal/internal influences that lead to outcomes such as choice, effort, persistence, achievement, and environmental regulation." Intrinsic and extrinsic motivations are two types of motivation.

Ryan and Deci (2020) define intrinsic motivation as congruous with higher performance and predictive of student performance and higher achievement and define extrinsic motivation as derived from an external source and involving a contingent reward. Intrinsic motivation refers to the internal desire to learn and achieve, driven by personal interest, curiosity, and satisfaction.

Perhaps no single phenomenon reflects the positive potential of human nature as much as intrinsic motivation, the inherent tendency to seek out novelty and challenges, to extend and exercise one's capacities, to explore, and to learn (Ryan & Deci, 2000).

Autotelic tasks (Csikszentmihalyi, 1990), which are intrinsically motivating, have the potential to lift us into a state of flow, marked by deep engagement, energized focus, and a warped sense of time. Mihaly Csikszentmihalyi recognized the significance of "flow" and coined the term accordingly.

> The autotelic experience, or flow, lifts the course of life to a different level. Alienation gives way to involvement, enjoyment replaces boredom, helplessness turns into a feeling of control, and psychic energy works to reinforce the sense of self, instead of being lost in the service of external goals. When experience is intrinsically rewarding life is justified in the present, instead of being held hostage to a hypothetical future gain.

Self-determination theory (Sheehan et al., 2018) addresses the reason for behavior and asserts that different motivations, including external motivation, internal motivation, and amotivation, lie on a continuum. Student autonomy enables students to exercise control over their learning, making informed decisions, and developing a sense of ownership and accountability.

Autonomy refers to the sense that one's actions flow from one's desires and not merely from external demands. Autonomy has been proven to have many positive motivational, well-being (Deci & Ryan, 2012), and educational benefits (Patall et al., 2008). Black and Deci (2000) found that in classes where teachers support autonomy, students' engagement is higher, their academic performance is better, and they experience more clarity. Both laboratory studies by Grolnick and Ryan (1987) and field studies by Soenens and Vansteenkiste (2005) have shown that tasks that support autonomy considerably increase students' interest in and mastery of courses. These effects of autonomy have been demonstrated across cultures, as stated by Chirkov (2009) and Levesque-Bristol et al. (2018), across programs ranging from STEM education, as stated by Lavigne et al. (2007), to foreign languages, as stated by Noels et al. (2001).

Research shows that the secret to excellent performance is not due to our biological drive or our reward-and-punishment drive but to one of our three drives:

1. our deep-seated desire to direct our own lives
2. to extend and expand our abilities
3. to live a life of purpose

Daniel Pink, in his book *Drive*, argues that the approach to motivation has three essential elements, which are as follows:

1. Autonomy—the desire to direct our own lives
2. Mastery—the urge to get better and better at something that matters
3. Purpose—a deep-seated desire to contribute to something greater than ourselves, driving us to make a meaningful impact.

3.7.2.5 Experimentation and Innovation

There's no innovation without experimentation; experimentation is a critical part of innovation. Innovation is not about new ideas. Innovation is "[t]he process of translating an idea or invention into a good or service that creates value." The prime focus is on the process and value creation, not ideas. Experimentation is fundamental to gaining insights and new knowledge and can be viewed as a "search for new value," a pathway to innovation, says Zevae M. Zaheer, Director of Innovation at Collider Studio.

Multiple methodologies support experimentation, including opportunity identification, feedback collection, idea testing, RCTs, prototyping, MVPs, and design thinking, all centered on human needs.

Experimentation is like innovation but involves trying things out on a miniature level. We can spend ages brainstorming good (or bad) ideas, but without testing them, they are just concepts without any evidence to prove that they would work. So the question to ask is not "what's your idea?" but "how have you tried to test it?"

Experimentation is about learning, answering questions, testing assumptions, and gathering data. By testing assumptions and gathering feedback, experimentation helps innovators make informed decisions and confidently navigate uncertain terrain. We should be free to experiment to gather the necessary information to become more certain.

Failure is part and parcel of experimentation and innovation, but there should be a recognition of how one fails, and the size of the failure matters. Failures cost time and money; "the key is to fail quickly and cheaply, spend a little to learn a lot," says Prof. Vijay Govindarajan of the Tuck School of Business.

3.7.3 Learner Characteristics Transformation

"Learners" means both teachers and students. Focusing on understanding and addressing the diverse needs, preferences, and competencies of learners helps them navigate various learning environments, adapt to new situations, and achieve their academic and personal goals. "The student's responsibility is to help world and solve the societal problems, see beyond what the world is now to what it could become." While developing the following learner characteristics, students are actively engaged and motivated intrinsically, which helps them fulfill and succeed in Education 4.0 and beyond.

3.7.3.1 Purpose-Driven Students

Purpose-driven students are individuals who have a clear sense of direction, motivation, and passion for their academic pursuits. They are driven by a desire to achieve specific goals and make a meaningful impact in their chosen field. They are able to overcome obstacles and setbacks and learn from failures. They take ownership of their learning and are accountable for their progress.

3.7.3.2 Strength-Based Goal

A strength-based goal is focused on positive outcomes and is created to cater to students' natural inborn characteristics, called talents. During adversity, they remain mastery oriented. They welcome efforts to improve performance and facilitate lifelong self-learning. It's effective for applications in new situations. Students need to set their strength-based goals that stretch them, excite them, and complement their natural talents. Focus on strength-based goals instead of learning goals and performance goals.

3.7.3.3 Growth Mindset

Mindset is the way students think about their competence. A growth mindset is changing the way students think to fulfill their potential. Dweck, in her book *Mindset*, presents evidence that students who hold a growth mindset are more likely to excel academically than those with a fixed mindset. These students relish challenges, understand the value of effort, and view failure as an opportunity to learn. She says students who, instead of being limited by a fear of not being smart enough, were able to improve their grades and their enjoyment of school by adopting a growth mindset.

3.7.3.4 Fanatic Discipline

Jim Collins and Morten Hansen's extensive research reveals that, in their book *Great by Choice*, discipline is "consistency of action." They do not mean regimentation, measurement, hierarchical obedience, or adherence to bureaucratic rules. "For a 10xer, the only legitimate form of discipline is self-discipline, having the inner will to do whatever it takes to create a great outcome, no matter how difficult." Legitimate discipline is self-discipline. Self-discipline involves deliberately cultivating habits, controls, and restraints to meet the demands of one's profession and achieve personal excellence. Fanatic discipline is about being clear on performance measurements, methods, values, goals, and standards for achieving success.

3.7.3.5 Learning Agility

Learning agility is our ability to learn, unlearn, and relearn rapidly in response to the demands of situations and apply the relearned knowledge to new situations. Learning agility is a continuous thirst to learn, pivot, and contribute to any endeavor. It describes how naturally learning new things comes to each individual student. It's a set of complex competencies consisting of mental agility, people agility, change agility, results agility, and self-awareness that enable students to learn from one place and apply that learning in every other new situation.

3.7.3.6 Resilience

Resilience is the capacity to recover mental toughness and composure when facing uncertainty, volatility, complexity, and ambiguity. Resilience is the capacity to remain flexible and adaptable while facing life's challenges. It is a complex concept involving characteristics, environmental milieu, and a learned capacity that comes from experience.

Psychological research demonstrates that the resources and skills associated with greater resilience can be practiced and cultivated. Three essential elements form the foundation of resilience:

1. Self-Awareness: Understanding and valuing oneself
2. Mental Flexibility: Adapting to challenges and shifting focus
3. Emotional Regulation: Managing and navigating emotional experiences

3.7.3.7 Reading Different Genres of Books

Books are packed with priceless insights, be it for your personal or professional life. Each book packs a punch of wisdom and motivation, tackling different aspects of personal growth. Each book presents a rich, detailed environment, inviting readers to engage fully and explore its depths. Those who settle for a cursory understanding, rather than embracing the complexity of the narrative, deny themselves a truly transformative experience.

Education extends far beyond the classroom, and individuals must take ownership of their learning journey. By recognizing the limitations of traditional schooling, we can empower ourselves to seek knowledge and growth through self-directed learning. Rather than relying solely on the education system, we can cultivate a love for reading and learning, unlocking a world of possibilities.

Reading books is an investment in yourself—investments that come in many forms: novels, nonfiction, self-help, how-to, poetry, fantasy, classics, memoirs, and biographies. They are a way to learn about history and what happened in the past and to observe what is happening presently.

Reading books is a way for you to learn about people, how the world works, and human nature. Books help you think more clearly as a whole, be kinder, visualize the bigger picture, and improve at the things that matter to you in your personal life and career.

Reading books is a tradition of thousands of years old and stretches forward to the day after tomorrow.

3.8 Conclusion

These three types of transformations—technological transformation, strategic transformation, and learner characteristics transformation—are interconnected and can have a significant impact on the educational landscape.

References

Ahmad, I., Jasola, S., & Anupriya, A. (2018). Supplementing higher education with MOOCs: A case study [Paper presentation]. *2017 international conference on emerging trends in computing and communication technologies, ICETCCT 2017, 2018-Janua*. https://doi.org/10.1109/ICETCCT.2017.8280346

Almalki, M. E. M. (2022). Didactic games and gamification in education. *International Journal of Computer Science and Network Security*, *22*(4), 417–419. https://doi.org/10.22937/IJCSNS.2022.22.4.49

Arias-Calderón, M., Castro, J., & Gayol, S. (2022). Serious games as a method for enhancing learning engagement: Student perception on online higher education during COVID-19. *Frontiers in Psychology*. https://doi.org/10.3389/fpsyg.2022.889975

Bajaj, R., & Sharma, V. (2018). Smart education with artificial intelligence based determination of learning styles. *Procedia Computer Science, 132*, 834–842. https://doi.org/10.1016/j.procs.2018.05.095

Bandura, A. (1977). Self-efficacy: Toward a unifying theory of behavioral change. *Psychological Review, 84*, 191–215.

Bandura, A. (1986). *Social foundations of thought and action: A social cognitive theory*. Englewood Cliffs, NJ: Prentice Hall.

Bandura, A. (1997). *Self-efficacy: The exercise of control*. New York: Freeman.

Bawa, P. (2022). Game on!: Investigating digital game-based versus gamified learning in higher education. In Information Resources Management Association (Ed.), *Research anthology on developments in gamification and game-based learning* (pp. 957–991). IGI Global. https://doi.org/10.4018/978-1-6684-3710-0.ch044

Bekar, C., & Lipsey, R. (2004). Science institutions and the industrial revolution. *Journal of European Economic History, 33*(3), 709–753.

Black, A. E., & Deci, E. L. (2000). The effects of instructors' autonomy support and students' autonomous motivation on learning organic chemistry: A self-determination theory perspective. *Science Education, 84*, 740–756.

Bonfield, C. A., Salter, M., Longmuir, A., Benson, M., & Adachi, C. (2020). Transformation or evolution? Education 4.0, teaching and learning in the digital age. *Higher Education Pedagogies, 5*(1), 223–246. https://doi.org/10.1080/23752696.2020.1816847

Bruner, J. S. (2009). *The process of education*. Harvard University Press.

Carini, R. M., Kuh, G. D., & Klein, S. P. (2006). Student engagement and student learning: Testing the linkages. *Research in Higher Education, 47*(1), 1–32. http://doi.org/10.1007/s11162-005-8150-9

Chirkov, V. I. (2009). A cross-cultural analysis of autonomy in education. *Theory and Research in Education, 7*, 253–262.

Cole, K., Schroeder, K., Bataineh, M., & Al-Bataineh, A. (2021). Flexible seating impact on classroom environment. *Turkish Online Journal of Educational Technology-TOJET, 20*(2), 62–74.

Coleman, T. E., & Money, A. G. (2020). Student-centred digital game-based learning: A conceptual framework and survey of the state of the art. *Higher Education, 79*(3), 415–457. https://doi.org/10.1007/s10734-019-00417-0

Collins, A., & Halverson, R. (2009). *Rethinking education in the age of technology: The digital revolution and schooling in America*. Teachers College Press. https://doi.org/10.5555/1803829

Costan, Emily, et al. (2021). Education 4.0 in developing economies: A systematic literature review of implementation barriers and future research agenda. *Sustainability (Switzerland), 13*(22).

Csikszentmihalyi, M. (1990). *Flow: The psychology of optimal experience*. Harper Perennial.

Dabbous, M., Kawtharani, A., Fahs, I., Hallal, Z., Shouman, D., Akel, M., & Sakr, F. (2022). The role of game-based learning in experiential education: Tool validation, motivation assessment, and outcomes evaluation among a sample of pharmacy students. *Education Sciences*. https://doi.org/10.3390/educsci12070434

Darsham-Singh, A., & Hassan, M. (2017). *In pursuit of smart learning environments for the 21st century* (Núm. 12; Current and Critical Issues in UNESCO International Bureau of Education. Curriculum, Learning and Assessment, p. 20). https://unesdoc.unesco.org/ark:/48223/pf0000252335
Daud, W. A. A. W., Teck, W. K., Ghani, M. T. A., & Ramli, S. (2019). The needs analysis of developing mobile learning application for cybergogical teaching and learning of Arabic language proficiency. *International Journal of Research in Business and Social Science*, *9*(8), 33–46.
Deci, E. L., & Ryan, R. M. (2012). Self-determination theory. In P. A. M. Van Lange, A. W. Kruglanski, & E. T. Higgins (Eds.), *Handbook of theories of social psychology* (Vol. 1, pp. 416–436). Sage.
Demir, K. A. (2021). Smart education framework. *Smart Learning Environments*, *8*, 29. https://doi.org/10.1186/s40561-021-00170-x
Doğan, F., & Yücel-Toy, B. (2020). Development of an attitude scale towards asking questions for elementary education students. *Ilkogretim Online*, *19*(4), 2237–2248.
Estévez, I., Rodríguez-Llorente, C., Piñeiro, I., González-Suárez, R., & Valle, A. (2021). School engagement, academic achievement, and self-regulated learning. *Sustainability*, *13*(6), 3011. https://doi.org/10.3390/su13063011
Fisk, P. (2017). *Education 4.0 . . . the future of learning will be dramatically different, in school and throughout life.* https://www.peterfisk.com/2017/01/future-education-young-everyone-taught-together/
Fredricks, J. A., Filsecker, M., & Lawson, M. A. (2016). Student engagement, context, and adjustment: Addressing definitional, measurement, and methodological issues. *Learning and Instruction*, *43*, 1–4. https://doi.org/10.1016/j.learninstruc.2016.02.002
The Future of Jobs Report. (2020). https://www3.weforum.org/docs/WEF_Future_of_Jobs_2020.pdf
Gaines, B. R. (2013). Knowledge acquisition: Past, present and future. *International Journal of Human-Computer Studies*, *71*(2), 135–156. https://doi.org/10.1016/j.ijhcs.2012.10.010
Garrison, D. R., & Kanuka, H. (2004). Blended learning: Uncovering its transformative potential in higher education. *The Internet and Higher Education*, *7*(2), 95–105. https://doi.org/10.1016/j.iheduc.2004.02.001
Ghallabi, S., Essalmi, F., Jemni, M., & Kinshuk. (2022). Reuse of e-learning personalization components. *Smart Learning Environments*, *9*(1), 32. https://doi.org/10.1186/s40561-022-00214-w
Ghobakhloo, M. (2020). Industry 4.0, digitization, and opportunities for sustainability. *Journal of Cleaner Production*, *252*, 119869. https://doi.org/10.1016/j.jclepro.2019.119869
González-Pérez, L.-I., Ramírez Montoya, M. S., & García-Peñalvo, F. J. (2022). Habilitadores tecnológicos 4.0 para impulsar la educación abierta: Aportaciones para las recomendaciones de la UNESCO. *RIED-Revista Iberoamericana De Educación a Distancia*. https://doi.org/10.5944/ried.25.2.33088
Greipl, S., Moeller, K., & Ninaus, M. (2020). Potential and limits of game-based learning. *International Journal of Technology Enhanced Learning*, *12*(4), 363. https://doi.org/10.1504/IJTEL.2020.110047
Gris, G., & Bengtson, C. (2021). Assessment measures in game-based learning research: A systematic review. *International Journal of Serious Games*, *8*(1), 3–26. https://doi.org/10.17083/ijsg.v8i1.383

Grolnick, W. S., & Ryan, R. M. (1987). Autonomy in children's learning: An experimental and individual difference investigation. *Journal of Personality and Social Psychology*, *52*, 890–898.

Harzckiewicz, J., Barron, K., Tauer, J., & Elliot, A. (2002). Short-term and long-term consequences of achievement goals. *Journal of Educational Psychology*, *92*, 316–320.

Hidi, S., & Renninger, A. (2006). A four-phase model of interest development. *Educational Psychology*, *41*, 111–127.

Hong, C., & Ma, W. W. K. (2020). Introduction: Education 4.0: Applied degree education and the future of work. In C. Hong & W. W. K. Ma (Eds.), *Applied degree education and the future of work* (pp. 1–13). Singapore: Springer. https://doi.org/10.1007/978-981-15-3142-2_1

Hong, W., Zhen, R., Liu, R., Wang, M., Ding, Y., & Wang, J. (2020). The longitudinal linkages among Chinese children's behavioural, cognitive, and emotional engagement within a mathematics context. *Educational Psychology*, *40*(6), 666–680. https://doi.org/10.1080/01443410.2020.1719981

Iivari, N., Sharma, S., & Ventä-Olkkonen, L. (2020). Digital transformation of everyday life—How COVID-19 pandemic transformed the basic education of the young generation and why information management research should care? *International Journal of Information Management*, *55*, 102183. https://doi.org/10.1016/j.ijinfomgt.2020.102183

Iroeze, P., & Owate, C. N. (2021). Application of industry 4.0 in delivering library services to special need library users. In *Examining the impact of industry 4.0 on academic libraries* (pp. 55–62). Emerald Publishing Limited. https://doi.org/10.1108/978-1-80043-656-520201014

Jang, S. (2014). Study on service models of digital textbooks in cloud computing environment for SMART education. *International Journal of u- and e-Service, Science and Technology*, *7*(1), 73–82. https://doi.org/10.14257/ijunesst.2014.7.1.07

Kippers, W. B., Wolterinck, C. H., Schildkamp, K., Poortman, C. L., & Visscher, A. J. (2018). Teachers' views on the use of assessment for learning and data-based decision making in classroom practice. *Teaching and Teacher Education*, *75*, 199–213. https://doi.org/10.1016/j.tate.2018.06.015

Kirby, D. A. (2016). Film, radio, and television. In *A companion to the history of science* (pp. 428–441). Wiley. https://doi.org/10.1002/9781118620762.ch30

Lavigne, G. L., Vallerand, R. J., & Miquelon, P. (2007). A motivational model of persistence in science education: A self-determination theory approach. *European Journal of Psychology of Education*, *22*, 351–369.

Lee, J., Bagheri, B., & Kao, H.-A. (2015). A cyber-physical systems architecture for industry4.0-based manufacturing systems. *Manufacturing Letters*, *3*, 18–23. https://doi.org/10.1016/j.mfglet.2014.12.001

Levesque-Bristol, S., Yu, C., & Maeda, Y. (2018). General need for autonomy and subjective well-being: A meta-analysis of studies in the US and East Asia. *Journal of Happiness Studies*, *19*, 1863–1882.

Li, Y., & Lerner, R. (2013). Interrelations of behavioral, emotional, and cognitive school engagement in high school students. *Journal of Youth and Adolescence*, *42*, 20–32. https://doi.org/10.1007/s10964-012-9857-5

Maidment-Otlet, R. (2021). Digital-first approaches and the library brand in a post-pandemic world. In *Libraries, Digital Information, and COVID* (pp. 103–110). Elsevier. https://doi.org/10.1016/B978-0-323-88493-8.00016-1

McFarland, L., Murray, E., & Phillipson, S. (2016). Student–teacher relationships and student self-concept: Relations with teacher and student gender. *Australian Journal of Education*, *60*(1), 5–25. https://doi.org/10.1177/0004944115626426

Midgley, C., Kaplan, A., & Middleton, M. (2001). Performance-approach goals: Good for what, for whom, and under what conditions, and at what cost? *Journal of Educational Psychology*, *93*, 77–86.

Miranda, J., Navarrete, C., Noguez, J., Molina-Espinosa, J.-M., Ramírez-Montoya, M.-S., Navarro-Tuch, S. A., Bustamante-Bello, M.-R., Rosas-Fernández, J.-B., & Molina, A. (2021). The core components of education 4.0 in higher education: Three case studies in engineering education. *Computers & Electrical Engineering*, *93*, 107278. https://doi.org/10.1016/j.compeleceng.2021.107278

Msauki, G. (2021). Library 4.0 and sustainable development: Opportunities and challenges. In *Examining the impact of industry 4.0 on academic libraries* (pp. 31–44). Emerald Publishing Limited. https://doi.org/10.1108/978-1-80043-656-520201012

Noels, K., Clément, R., & Pelletier, L. (2001). Intrinsic, extrinsic, and integrative orientations of French Canadian learners of English. *The Canadian Modern Language Review*, *57*, 424–442.

Noroozi, O., Dehghanzadeh, H., & Talaee, E. (2020). A systematic review on the impacts of game-based learning on argumentation skills. *Entertainment Computing*, *35*, 100369. https://doi.org/10.1016/j.entcom.2020.100369

Oblinger, D., & Oblinger, J. (2005). Is it age or IT: First steps towards understanding the net generation. In *Educating the net generation* (pp. 2.1–2.20). EDUCAUSE. http://www.educause.edu/educatingthenetgen

Ohlsson, S. (2011). *Deep learning*. Cambridge University Press. https://doi.org/10.1017/CBO9780511780295

Ouhrir, S., Lotfi, S., & Talbi, M. (2019). Online peeragogy: Effects of videos developed by students on peer learning and their impact on academic results. *International Journal for Research in Engineering and Emerging Trends*, *7*(11), 576–583.

Pajares, F., & Schunk, D. (2001). Self-beliefs and school success: Self-efficacy, self-concept, and school achievement. In R. Riding & S. Rayner (Eds.), *Perception* (pp. 239–266). London: Ablex Publishing.

Pajares, F., & Schunk, D. (2002). Self-beliefs in psychology and education: An historical perspective. In J. Aronson (Ed.), *Improving academic achievement* (pp. 3–21). New York: Academic Press.

Patall, E. A., Cooper, H., & Robinson, J. C. (2008). The effects of choice on intrinsic motivation and related outcomes: A meta-analysis of research findings. *Psychological Bulletin*, *134*, 270–300.

Paul, R., & Elder, L. (2006). *Critical thinking: Learn the tools the best thinkers use*. Pearson Prentice Hall.

Philbeck, T., & Davis, N. (2019). The fourth industrial revolution shaping a new era. *Journal of International Affairs*, *72*(1), 17–22. https://www.jstor.org/stable/26588339

Pons-Valladares, O., Hosseini, S. M. A., & Franquesa, J. (2022). Innovative approach to assist architecture teachers in choosing practical sessions. *Sustainability (Switzerland)*. https://doi.org/10.3390/su14127081

Ryan, R. M., & Deci, E. L. (2000). Self-determination theory and the facilitation of intrinsic motivation, social development, and well-being. *The American Psychologist*, *55*(1), 68–78. https://doi.org/10.1037/0003-066X.55.1.68

Ryan, R. M., & Deci, E. L. (2020). Intrinsic and extrinsic motivation from a self-determination theory perspective: Definitions, theory, practices, and future directions. *Contemporary Educational Psychology, 61,* 101860. https://doi.org/10.1016/j.cedpsych.2020.101860

Sá, M. J. (2023). Student academic and social engagement in the life of the academy—A lever for retention and persistence in higher education. *Education Sciences, 13*(3), Article 269. https://doi.org/10.3390/educsci13030269

Salleh, M. A., Bahari, M., & Ismail, W. (2020). Exploring the software quality criteria and sustainable development targets. A case study of digital library in Malaysian higher learning institution. In (pp. 1076–1086). https://doi.org/10.1007/978-3-030-33582-3_101

Schunk, D. H., & DiBenedetto, M. K. (2020). Motivation and social cognitive theory. *Contemporary Educational Psychology, 60,* 101832. https://doi.org/10.1016/j.cedpsych.2019.101832

Senior, R. M., Bartholomew, P., Soor, A., Shepperd, D., Bartholomew, N., & Senior, C. (2018). "The rules of engagement": Student engagement and motivation to improve the quality of undergraduate learning. *Frontiers in Education, 3,* Article 32. https://doi.org/10.3389/feduc.2018.00032

Sesmiyanti, S. (2018). Student's cognitive engagement in learning process. *Polingua, 5*(2), 48–51. http://doi.org/10.30630/polingua.v5i2.34

Sharlovych, Z., Vilchynska, L., Danylyuk, S., Huba, B., & Zadilska, H. (2023). Digital technologies as a means of improving the efficiency of higher education. *International Journal of Information and Education Technology, 13*(8), 1214–1221. https://doi.org/10.18178/ijiet.2023.13.8.1923

Sharlovych, Z., Vilchynska, L., Danylyuk, S., Huba, B., Zadilska, H., Zhu, Z. T., & He, B. (2012). Smart education: New frontier of educational informatization. *E-Education Research, 12,* 1–13.

Sheehan, R. B., Herring, M. P., & Campbell, M. J. (2018). Associations between motivation and mental health in sport: A test of the hierarchical model of intrinsic and extrinsic motivation. *Frontiers in Psychology, 9,* 707. https://doi.org/10.3389/fpsyg.2018.00707

Soenens, B., & Vansteenkiste, M. (2005). Antecedents and outcomes of self-determination in 3 life domains: The role of parents' and teachers' autonomy support. *Journal of Youth and Adolescence, 34,* 589–604.

Strayer, J. F. (2012). How learning in an inverted classroom influences cooperation, innovation and task orientation. *Learning Environments Research, 15*(2), 171–193. https://doi.org/10.1007/s10984-012-9108-4

Trowler, V. (2010). Student engagement literature review. *Higher Education Academy.*

Urdan, T. (2004). Predictors of self-handicapping and achievement: Examining achievement goals, classroom goal structures, and culture. *Journal of Educational Psychology, 96,* 251–254.

Uskov, V., Howlett, R. J., & Jain, L. C. (Eds.). (2015). *Smart education and smart e-learning* (1st ed.). Springer.

Wang, L.-H., Chen, B., Hwang, G.-J., Guan, J.-Q., & Wang, Y.-Q. (2022). Effects of digital game-based STEM education on students' learning achievement: A meta-analysis. *International Journal of STEM Education, 9*(1), 26. https://doi.org/10.1186/s40594-022-00344-0

Weiner, B. (2005). Motivation from an attribution perspective and the social psychology of perceived competence. In A. Elliot & C. Dweck (Eds.), *Handbook of competence and motivation* (pp. 73–84). New York: Guilford Press.

Willis, T., & Bryant, V. (2022). Harry potter and the osteopathic medical school part 2: Creating a virtual harry potter-themed day as a high-yield review for final examinations. *Medical Science Educator*, *32*(1), 39–42. https://doi.org/10.1007/s40670-022-01501-4

Wolters, C. (2004). Advancing achievement goal theory: Using goal structures and goal orientations to predict students' motivation, cognition, and achievement. *Journal of Educational Psychology*, *96*, 236–250.

Xu, X., Shi, Z., Bos, N., & Wu, H. (2023). Student engagement and learning outcomes: An empirical study applying a four-dimensional framework. *Medical Education Online*, *28*(1), Article 2268347. https://doi.org/10.1080/10872981.2023.2268347

Zhu, Z. T., & He, B. (2012). Smart education: New frontier of educational informatization. *E-Education Research*, *12*, 1–13.

4

Determinants of Successful Integration and Adoption of AI in Education: A Structural Equation Modeling Approach

Kingsley Ofosu-Ampong, Priscilla Pomaa Annor, Samuel Owusu-Ansah, Dharel P. Acut, Chockalingam Aravind Vaithilingam, Ari Happonen, and Manuel B. Garcia

4.1 Introduction

Among the emerging technologies, artificial intelligence (AI) plays an increasingly pivotal role in helping modern educational institutions meet the diverse needs of both online and offline learners, even though it is a challenging time for navigating the opportunities and challenges of AI, especially when we would like to make this transition in a sustainable way (Abulibdeh et al., 2024). Advances in educational technology have facilitated a paradigm shift from traditional teaching methods to AI-powered virtual learning environments, particularly in response to the growing preference for online education (Ofosu-Ampong et al., 2023). These innovations enable institutions to provide personalized, high-quality education tailored to students' preferred pace and location. The impact of the COVID-19 pandemic, the advent of generative AI, and the subsequent surge in technological adoption have further accelerated this modern digitalization and a shift in society's operational models. This transition, especially because of COVID-19, prompted student-centered institutions to embrace online teaching and AI-driven solutions and has pushed new lines of thinking in educational units to maintain competitiveness in an increasingly demanding educational landscape (Wang et al., 2021). In developing countries like Ghana, institutions have been adopting AI-powered learning systems and formulating digital learning policies to enhance support for both students and faculty. The rapid adoption of these tools has been bolstered by high internet penetration rates, which facilitate virtual learning. As of March 2021, mobile data penetration in Ghana stood at approximately 73.48%, with 22,763,483 mobile data subscriptions recorded (National Communication Authority, 2021). This

DOI: 10.1201/9781003633433-4

widespread internet access has enabled institutions to deploy AI-powered educational resources, providing students and educators with innovative tools to enhance teaching and learning experiences.

Despite the advancements and potential benefits, evidence indicates that many educators remain hesitant to adopt AI technologies. A significant factor is that many educators themselves lack proficiency in AI; after all, you cannot teach AI skills if you are not AI-literate yourself (Velander et al., 2023). Concerns such as reduced human interaction, fear of technological displacement, and resistance to change hinder the widespread acceptance of AI in education (Alhumaid et al., 2023). Moreover, institutions in developing countries often face additional barriers, including limited resources, inadequate training, and institutional reluctance to fully embrace AI-enabled learning solutions (Ofosu-Ampong et al., 2023). These challenges underscore the need for a nuanced understanding of the factors influencing AI adoption in education, particularly in post-COVID-19 contexts, where traditional teaching methods are no longer sufficient to meet evolving educational demands. While extensive research has examined AI integration and adoption in developed countries, there remains a significant gap in understanding how these technologies are adopted in developing economies (McElheran et al., 2024). Ghana, as a developing country with increasing digital adoption, offers a compelling context to explore these dynamics. Unlike developed economies, where AI adoption is well documented, educational institutions in Ghana face unique challenges that require tailored strategies for successful implementation. Furthermore, the ethical complexities and operational challenges associated with AI systems—such as their application in assessment and evaluation—highlight the need for educators to adapt their teaching practices to integrate these technologies effectively (Ali et al., 2023; Chan, 2023).

This study aims to bridge the knowledge gap by systematically examining the critical factors influencing AI integration and adoption in Ghana's educational system. Specifically, it explores how technological, institutional, and human factors shape the acceptance and implementation of AI in higher education. To ensure a comprehensive analysis, the research is grounded in the diffusion of innovation theory (DIT; Rogers, 2003) and the unified theory of acceptance and use of technology 2 (UTAUT2; Venkatesh et al., 2012), which serve as theoretical frameworks for understanding technology adoption. With these theoretical lenses, the study aims to provide valuable insights into how institutions in developing economies can overcome barriers to AI adoption and leverage these technologies to enhance educational outcomes. To provide a clear roadmap for the study, the structure of this chapter is as follows: The next section presents a review of the relevant literature and outlines the conceptual model. This is followed by a detailed discussion of the research methodology and the presentation of the study results. Finally, the chapter concludes with a discussion of the findings, their implications, and recommendations for future research.

4.2 Literature Review

4.2.1 Theoretical Perspectives on Technology Adoption

Technology adoption has been examined from different perspectives and continues to form a significant part of information systems (IS) literature (Venkatesh et al., 2012). Theoretically, a number of factors have been investigated and approved as important determining factors of student and faculty technology adoption. These factors have mostly been examined through various theoretical lenses, such as the technology acceptance model (TAM), the DIT (Rogers, 2003), UTAUT, and its extended version, UTAUT2 (Venkatesh et al., 2012). The UTAUT2 posits that the intention to use technology is influenced by behavioral factors such as relative advantage, trust, and habit (i.e., spontaneous behaviors) (Venkatesh et al., 2012). As technology adoption has been extensively examined from the diffusion of innovation perspective and shown to have positive influences, this study examines AI integration and adoption from an extended pedagogical perspective, focusing on adoption constructs such as relative advantage, interoperability, and trust. Specifically, as Ghanaian universities are slowly integrating AI into their teaching and learning modalities, it is important to examine the critical factors influencing their adoption needs.

4.2.2 Diffusion of Innovation and Technology Adoption

Among other related IS theories, the DIT also explains better the levels of technology adoption (Rahi & Ghani, 2018). The DIT posits that the decision to adopt a technology is influenced by its relative advantage (perceived usefulness) and interoperability (consistency with one's experience or existing values). However, because AI is still an emerging technology, many educators lack a deep understanding of what it can do, why it matters, where and how it should be implemented, and the potential costs involved, further affecting their willingness to adopt it. System integration characteristics such as relative advantage, compatibility, trialability, and observability have been recognized as key determinants of technology adoption. However, many researchers have examined technology adoption from different perspectives, particularly using the diffusion of innovation framework (Oliveira & Martins, 2011; Rahi & Ghani, 2018). For instance, Okour et al. (2021) found that decision-makers' use of knowledge management systems is significantly influenced by relative advantage and complexity but not compatibility.

That said, technology adoption is not solely a rational process driven by system characteristics. There are various motivational drivers behind why individuals invest their time in learning or contributing to a particular technological context. Many people do not always approach adoption in a purely logical or structured manner, as implied by traditional models. Factors such as personal curiosity, social influence, intrinsic motivation, or even external pressures can play significant roles in shaping adoption behaviors, making the process more complex than a straightforward cost-benefit analysis (Palacin et al., 2020).

4.2.3 Factors Influencing AI Integration in Education

The adoption and integration of AI in education are influenced by several interconnected factors, including accessibility, affordability, interoperability, trust, ethical considerations, relative advantage, and pedagogy (Ofosu-Ampong, 2024b). Each of these factors contributes uniquely to how AI tools are perceived and utilized within educational systems, with their impacts often intertwined.

First, accessibility is a critical consideration, as AI can significantly enhance learning by accommodating diverse learner needs. For instance, AI-powered tools such as translation systems, speech recognition, and lip-reading apps can help individuals with disabilities by breaking down barriers to education. These tools are capable of customizing content for students with visual, auditory, or cognitive impairments, thereby fostering inclusion (Phillips-Wren, 2012). However, affordability remains a significant challenge for widespread AI adoption. The high development and implementation costs associated with AI tools can limit access, especially in underfunded educational systems (Muranga et al., 2023). That said, the current AI boom has pushed many companies to offer generative AI tools with free-access models, such as limited daily usage or free-tier tokens, making AI more accessible than before. In many cases, if a student needs an AI tool for a specific task, they can likely find a free version that meets their needs (Hornberger et al., 2023). As a result, the real barrier to AI adoption is not necessarily the cost but rather the awareness, digital literacy, and ability to navigate and maximize these freely available AI tools effectively—especially in the early stages of learning (Yang et al., 2024). To address this challenge, efforts to make AI solutions more cost-effective, such as the use of open-source AI platforms, have been suggested as a means to expand AI usage in low-resource settings (Hongli & Leong, 2024; Pedro et al., 2019; Ghioni et al., 2024).

In addition to accessibility and affordability, interoperability plays a crucial role in AI adoption. Successful AI integration in education benefits from interoperability with existing technologies, such as learning management systems (LMS) and other digital infrastructures. While some tools, like MS Word, function effectively as standalone applications, AI-driven systems often rely on seamless integration to enable automation, real-time feedback, and personalized learning. Ensuring compatibility enhances efficiency and maximizes the potential of AI in educational settings. Interoperability ensures that AI tools can communicate effectively with these platforms, enhancing their functionality and user experience. For example, a chatbot designed to assist with student queries should be able to integrate with the institution's database to provide accurate and relevant information. However, robust access controls, authentication mechanisms, and data governance policies must be in place to ensure that the chatbot retrieves only the information appropriate for a specific user (Yang et al., 2023). Institutions must implement strict role-based access and compliance measures to prevent unauthorized data exposure. Poor interoperability can lead to technical bottlenecks, reducing efficiency and discouraging adoption (Perisic et al., 2023; Krauss et al., 2023). Alongside interoperability, trust is foundational to AI adoption in education. Educators and learners must be assured of the technology's reliability, transparency, and ethical use of data. Trust can be established through consistent performance, robust data privacy safeguards, and clear communication regarding AI's limitations (Ofosu-Ampong et al., 2023).

Moreover, ethical considerations are paramount when integrating AI into education (Usmani et al., 2023). These considerations involve addressing potential biases in AI algorithms and ensuring equitable access to resources, which are essential for fostering confidence in AI technologies. Additionally, it is crucial to ensure that AI systems remain neutral and do not promote any political or religious agendas (Díaz-Rodríguez et al., 2023). If users can ask questions or engage with content related to these topics, the selection of data sources must be handled with extreme care to prevent misinformation, bias, or undue influence. Ethical frameworks provide guidance for the development and implementation of AI systems, assisting educational institutions in managing complex moral challenges while promoting fair and responsible use. Addressing these ethical concerns fosters trust and supports broader acceptance among users (Zhu et al., 2024; Tatineni, 2019; Lim et al., 2023).

4.2.4 Pedagogical Implications of AI

The perceived benefits of AI significantly influence its adoption in education (Kim, 2020). For educators, AI tools such as automated grading systems and adaptive learning platforms offer significant time savings and enhanced teaching efficiency. However, the suitability of AI for grading depends on the nature of the task (Swiecki et al., 2022). For objective, deterministic assessments (e.g., multiple-choice quizzes), AI can provide accurate and immediate feedback (Nazari et al., 2021). For subjective tasks, such as essay grading, ensuring neutrality and fairness remains a challenge, as AI models are not deterministic and may evolve over time (Chai et al., 2024). To address this, robust validation processes, transparency in scoring criteria, and human oversight are essential to mitigate bias and ensure reliable evaluations. For students, AI has the potential to provide personalized learning paths and instant feedback, which can improve engagement and learning outcomes. Beyond this, AI-powered personal learning assistants can act as intelligent tutors, guiding students through their learning journey by helping them identify what to focus on next and why. Rather than merely supplying answers, these AI systems can foster critical thinking and problem-solving, prompting students to participate meaningfully in the learning experience. However, these advantages must outweigh potential drawbacks, such as the loss of human interaction or an overdependence on technology. To drive adoption, it is crucial to demonstrate clear, measurable improvements in educational performance (Abdaljaleel et al., 2024).

AI adoption in education represents a paradigm shift from traditional teaching approaches to more personalized, adaptive learning environments (Zogheib & Zogheib, 2024). While teacher-centered approaches remain prevalent, especially in technical fields like engineering, AI integration offers opportunities to transform educational delivery and student engagement (Zhou & Kim, 2024). In conventional settings, students often remain passive recipients of information, lacking critical engagement and reflective commitment (Grubb & Cox, 2005). In contrast, AI-enabled learning environments can facilitate a more dynamic, student-centered approach that addresses individual student needs and learning styles (Hussain & Anwar, 2024).

In order for AI to be successfully integrated into education, it must align with pedagogical goals. AI tools that support active learning, critical thinking, and collaboration are more likely to be embraced by both educators and students. For example, AI-driven simulations can enhance experiential learning, while chatbots can support inquiry-based approaches (Saihi et al., 2024). The challenge lies in ensuring that AI complements, rather than blindly replaces, traditional teaching methods. While traditional methods have been refined over time for their effectiveness, AI should be integrated where it demonstrably enhances learning outcomes. If AI tools prove to be more effective in certain aspects, they may naturally replace some conventional approaches. However, preserving the human element remains essential, as aspects like mentorship, ethical reasoning, and emotional intelligence cannot be easily replicated by AI (Bozkurt et al., 2024). This balance is crucial for preserving the human element, which remains central to effective pedagogy (Almogren et al., 2024).

Moreover, AI's integration has transformative potential in assessment practices. While accessibility and affordability are foundational for AI's reach, their impact is limited without interoperability and trust (Dahri et al., 2024). Ethical considerations also play a pivotal role in shaping trust, influencing AI perceptions and acceptance (Zhu et al., 2024). In this context, relative advantage provides a tangible value proposition that justifies the adoption of AI. Additionally, the role of pedagogy is essential in ensuring that AI tools not only integrate into educational systems but also effectively enhance teaching and learning processes (Ding et al., 2024). However, large-scale integration requires institutional support, policy frameworks, and professional development initiatives (Domorenok et al., 2021). While individual educators who are well versed in AI may incorporate these tools into their teaching, systematic adoption depends on administrative backing, curriculum alignment, and teacher training programs to bridge the gap between familiarity and full-scale implementation. By addressing these factors holistically, AI can foster a robust and innovative ecosystem in education, one that maintains both equity and quality (Ofosu-Ampong, 2023; Sun et al., 2024).

4.2.5 Overcoming Assessment Limitations and Preparing Educators for AI Integration

AI integration in education addresses the limitations of traditional assessment methods while also requiring significant shifts in pedagogical approaches and educator readiness. Traditional assessments, such as summative evaluations and discrete testing, often fail to provide real-time insights and personalized support (Justıno & Rafael, 2019). AI-powered continuous assessment systems can overcome these limitations by providing ongoing feedback, tracking student progress, and identifying learning gaps, which allow for timely interventions and personalized support (Bakhadirov & Alasgarova, 2024). Additionally, AI can address the challenge of disconnected course units by identifying cross-disciplinary connections and supporting the development of transversal skills. Intelligent content recommendation systems and adaptive learning platforms further enhance learning by creating cohesive experiences that reinforce both technical and soft skills (Ofosu-Ampong, 2024a; Ma, 2024). However, transitioning to AI-enhanced education requires educators to embrace significant changes in their roles. More importantly, successful adoption depends not only on individual willingness but also on institutional commitment. Educational organizations must provide structured training and establish a unified, coherent approach to AI integration, ensuring that all stakeholders are aligned in effectively utilizing AI for teaching and learning. Success in this shift depends on several key actions (Ma, 2024):

- redesigning curriculum delivery to leverage AI capabilities;
- developing new assessment strategies that utilize AI analytics;
- building educator capacity for AI-enhanced instruction;
- providing comprehensive student and teacher orientation, including training on planning, implementing, and effectively using AI-powered systems;
- ensuring equity in access to AI-powered learning tools;
- maintaining a balance between technological innovation and human interaction.

Although these challenges may be daunting, especially for pioneers who navigate uncharted territory, late adopters can benefit from established best practices and proven AI models. Nonetheless, the integration of AI offers unprecedented opportunities to create more engaging, effective, and personalized learning environments that better prepare students for the demands of the modern economy (Van et al., 2024).

4.3 Conceptual Model

As shown in Figure 4.1, six determinants—namely interoperability, relative advantage, pedagogical alignment, accessibility and affordability, and ethical consideration and trust—form the proposed conceptual model. To be precise, relative advantage and interoperability form part of Venkatesh et al.'s (2012) UTAUT2 to address technology adoption. Similarly, pedagogical alignment, ethical consideration and trust, and accessibility and affordability were proposed in Ofosu-Ampong et al.'s (2023) work and inspired by Rogers' (2003) DIT to predict individuals' adoption or intention toward an emerging trend or system. Further, AI integration and adoption has been a widely researched area and noted in the IS literature as an important determinant of technologies (Siau & Wang, 2020; Ofosu-Ampong et al., 2024). The following section discusses the hypotheses development and justification of the constructs.

4.3.1 Interoperability

Interoperability—the ability of different systems to work together seamlessly—is a critical factor in the successful integration and adoption of AI in education. It ensures that AI tools can effectively communicate and exchange data with existing educational systems and platforms, enhancing their functionality and usability (Rehm et al., 2020). Furthermore, interoperability enables AI systems to access and utilize data from various sources such as student records, LMS, and assessment platforms. This rich data is essential for training AI models and providing personalized learning experiences.

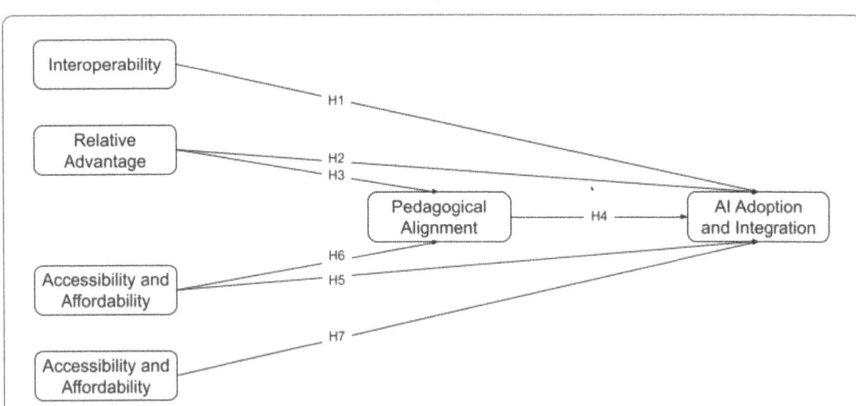

FIGURE 4.1
Conceptual model of AI integration and adoption.

Thus, interoperability is essential for the successful integration and adoption of AI in education. By ensuring seamless communication and data exchange between AI tools and existing systems, interoperability can enhance the functionality, scalability, and user experience of AI applications, ultimately leading to improved student outcomes (Rehm et al., 2020). Therefore, it is hypothesized as follows:

H1: Interoperability influences AI integration and adoption.

4.3.2 Relative Advantage

Relative advantage is defined as "the degree to which an innovation is perceived as being better than the idea it supersedes" (Ofosu-Ampong & Acheampong, 2022). Relative advantage in Rogers' DIT is equivalent to Davis et al.'s (1989) perceived usefulness. Students are more likely to adopt new technology for learning and research if it enhances their performance and significantly benefits the institution. Prior studies (Hester, 2011) have found a positive influence of relative advantage on IS usage. In AI integration in education, the relative advantage is expressed in terms of increased productivity, flexibility, and scalability to meet the growing demand for education (Alasmari, 2024). Thus, the primary benefits of relative advantage involve improved productivity, better learning outcomes, and the ability to complete tasks more efficiently without requiring extra effort compared to traditional methods. Furthermore, there are several advantages associated with the relative advantage of AI integration in education. Thus, the greater the perceived relative advantage of AI technology, the more likely it is to be adopted by individuals and organizations. However, these advantages must be clearly demonstrated and communicated to potential adopters through a well-planned and well-implemented orientation process, ensuring that educators and stakeholders understand how AI can enhance teaching and learning while addressing their concerns (Kemp, 2024). As a result, relative advantage is essential in the adoption of AI. Hence, it is hypothesized as follows:

H2: Relative advantage influences AI integration and adoption.

H3: Relative advantage of AI integration and adoption influences the pedagogical alignment of educational institutions.

4.3.3 Pedagogical Alignment

Pedagogical alignment significantly influences the successful adoption and integration of AI in educational settings by ensuring that technology supports rather than disrupts teaching and learning objectives (Ofosu-Ampong, 2024b). This alignment manifests through four key dimensions: instructional design compatibility, learning objectives alignment, teacher-technology fit, and student learning experience enhancement.

Effective AI integration requires compatibility with existing pedagogical frameworks while supporting various learning styles and curriculum goals (Wang & Tahir, 2020). Tools must complement teachers' pedagogical beliefs and practices, facilitating professional development that bridges the gap between AI capabilities and instructional needs (Nazaretsky et al., 2022). However, challenges exist in achieving this alignment, including technical integration issues, teacher preparation requirements, assessment consistency, and curriculum-integration needs. Success requires strategic planning, stakeholder involvement, continuous assessment, and robust professional development programs (Ofosu-Ampong & Adu-Ntim, 2025).

To overcome these challenges, institutions should develop clear implementation guidelines aligned with pedagogical goals, engage teachers in the selection process, regularly evaluate tool effectiveness, and provide ongoing training programs. Xu (2024) emphasize that, when properly aligned, AI tools can enhance both teaching efficiency and student learning outcomes, leading to more meaningful educational experiences and improved academic performance. Therefore, it is hypothesized as follows:

H4: Pedagogical alignment influences AI integration and adoption

4.3.4 Accessibility and Affordability

Accessibility and affordability significantly impact AI adoption and integration in educational settings. Digital infrastructure limitations, including poor internet connectivity and inadequate hardware resources, particularly in rural areas and developing nations, create substantial barriers to AI implementation (Aderibigbe et al., 2023). The "digital divide" is further widened by varying levels of technical literacy among teachers and students, necessitating continuous professional development (Ofosu-Ampong, 2023).

From an affordability perspective, high initial investment costs for AI infrastructure, software licenses, and ongoing maintenance present significant challenges. However, AI adoption does not need to happen all at once. A phased approach—starting with free or low-cost tools that require minimal infrastructure—can help institutions gradually integrate AI while maximizing benefits without overwhelming resources (Goralski & Tan, 2020). Economic disparities between institutions and regions lead to uneven adoption rates, with wealthy schools able to afford more sophisticated AI tools while under-resourced institutions struggle with basic implementation (Maggo & Maggo, 2025). To address these challenges, stakeholders must focus on developing sustainable and scalable solutions. This includes establishing public–private partnerships, creating resource-sharing networks, and implementing policies for the equitable distribution of AI resources. Additionally, focusing on cost-effective solutions and building local capacity for AI implementation can help bridge the accessibility gap. Success requires coordinated efforts from policymakers, educators, and technology providers to create inclusive and sustainable AI integration strategies in education. Therefore, it is hypothesized as follows:

H5: Accessibility and affordability influence AI integration and adoption.

H6: Accessibility and affordability of AI integration and adoption influence the pedagogical alignment of educational institutions.

4.3.5 Ethical Consideration

Ethical considerations play a crucial role in shaping the integration and adoption of AI in various fields, including education. These considerations ensure that AI technologies are developed and deployed in a responsible and beneficial manner (Ofosu-Ampong, 2024a). AI algorithms can inadvertently perpetuate existing biases present in data, leading to discriminatory outcomes. It is essential to develop and use AI systems that are fair and unbiased, ensuring equitable treatment for all individuals. AI models can be complex and difficult to understand, making it challenging to explain their decision-making processes. Ensuring transparency and explainability helps build trust and accountability in AI systems. Notwithstanding, AI adoption in education hinges on ethical considerations. Privacy, bias, transparency, and human–AI collaboration are key ethical concerns (Eitel-Porter, 2021). Building trust in AI systems, institutions, and educators is vital. Transparent practices, reliable systems, and clear explanations foster trust. Therefore, it is hypothesized as follows:

H7: Ethical consideration influences AI integration and adoption.

4.4 Methodology

4.4.1 Research Design

This study employs a quantitative, survey-based approach to examine the factors influencing AI integration and adoption in Ghanaian higher education institutions. A cross-sectional design was chosen, as it allows for the systematic collection of empirical data at a single point in time, enabling the identification of adoption patterns and key determinants. Grounded in the DIT (Rogers, 2003) and the UTAUT2 (Venkatesh et al., 2012), this approach provides a structured framework to assess the adoption behaviors of teaching and non-teaching staff. The use of a survey ensures objective measurement and statistical analysis, making it an effective method for testing relationships between key adoption factors and AI implementation in universities.

4.4.2 Participants and Setting

The study was conducted in Accra, Ghana, targeting both teaching and non-teaching staff across various universities. A total of 300 questionnaires were distributed across 34 universities, ensuring a representative sample. The sample selection aimed to reflect diversity in institutional types, covering both public and private universities. The University of Ghana, the country's oldest public university, and Valley View University, the oldest private university in Accra, were included in the study. Notably, over 70% of universities in Accra are private institutions, making them a significant focus of the research. Participants included faculty members, administrators, IT personnel, and educational policymakers with direct or indirect experience in AI adoption for teaching, learning, or administrative purposes. The inclusion criteria required participants to have some level of familiarity with AI-based technologies in their institutions. This approach ensured that responses were drawn from individuals with relevant exposure and insights into AI integration in higher education.

4.4.3 Data Collection

Data collection was carried out between September and October 2024 using a combination of electronic and paper-based surveys. This period coincided with the gradual return of university staff from academic breaks, ensuring adequate participation. The survey was designed to capture participants' perceptions of AI integration, their level of engagement with AI-powered learning environments, and the factors influencing adoption decisions. The questionnaire items were adapted from well-established scales in prior studies. The measurement items were adapted from previous studies (see Appendix A). In all, 18 scale items were adapted to measure the conceptual model. Specifically, the main items of pedagogical alignment were adapted from Grubb and Cox (2005); AI integration and adoption, ethical consideration, and trust were adapted from Ofosu-Ampong et al. (2023, 2024) and Venkatesh et al. (2012). The relative advantage scales were taken from Venkatesh et al. (2012), while the accessibility and affordability as innovation items were taken from Goel (2020). The items were measured on a 7-point Likert scale, which ranged from (1) strongly disagree to (7) strongly agree.

4.4.4 Data Analysis

The collected data was analyzed using structural equation modeling (SEM) to examine relationships among key adoption factors. Descriptive statistics (mean, standard deviation, frequencies, and percentages) were computed to summarize participant demographics and general trends in AI adoption. The partial least squares structural equation modeling (PLS-SEM) approach was employed using SmartPLS 4.0 to test the research hypotheses. This method was chosen due to its suitability for predictive modeling and exploratory research, especially when analyzing complex relationships between multiple independent and dependent variables. The measurement model was assessed for construct reliability, validity, and discriminant validity, while the structural model evaluated the significance of the hypothesized relationships.

4.5 Results

4.5.1 Demographics of Respondents Profile

Out of the 300 questionnaires allocated to the respondents, 230 (representing 76.7%) responses were received for further analysis. The majority of the respondents were male (63%, n = 145), and females represented 37%. The public universities recorded the highest percentage of respondents with 74.3% (n = 171), followed by the private universities in Ghana with 25.7% (n = 59). Concerning the participants' ages, most of them were in the age group of 34–45 (87%), and 13% were between 46 and 59; while 82.6% (n = 190) of them had a doctoral degree qualification, and 17.4% (n = 40) had a master's degree.

The evaluation of the model followed a two-step approach. The first was the assessment of the measurement model to examine the variables' psychometric properties. The second was to assess the structural model for collinearity issues and to examine the relationships among the constructs (Saihi et al., 2024).

4.5.2 Measurement Model Assessment

The examination of the reliability of the variables was estimated through Cronbach's alpha (CA), composite reliability, and average variance extracted (AVE). According to Hair et al. (2016), the acceptable range of internal consistency is between 0.60 and 0.70. Similarly, convergent validity estimated via the AVE with a value of 0.50 indicates that the constructs explain 50% of the indicator variance. Table 4.1 shows the reliability and validity of the constructs. Also, all the rho_A values are higher than 0.70, indicating a good alternative measure of indicator reliability.

Using the Heterotrait-Monotrait ratio of correlations (HTMT), the discriminant validity of the constructs was examined. According to Henseler et al. (2015), HTMT values below 0.90 indicate that discriminant validity has been established. As shown in Table 4.2, most of the values were equal to or below the 0.90 HTMT threshold.

The model's goodness of fit (explanatory power) was also assessed. The most widely used criterion for assessing the GOF is the R^2 determination coefficient (R^2) (Hair et al., 2016). As a rule of thumb rule, R^2 values of 0.25, 0.50, and 0.75 can be classified as weak, moderate, and substantial (Henseler et al., 2015). As shown in Table 4.3, the R^2 value of the model is 0.773, indicating substantial

TABLE 4.1

Construct Reliability and Validity

Construct	CA (α)	rho_A	CR	AVE
Interoperability	0.729	0.809	0.845	0.648
Ethical consideration and trust	0.777	0.786	0.871	0.694
Accessibility and affordability	0.722	0.729	0.842	0.640
Relative advantage	0.701	0.833	0.855	0.747
Pedagogical alignment	0.728	0.754	0.847	0.650
AI integration and adoption	0.849	0.849	0.909	0.768

TABLE 4.2

Discriminant Validity

	1	2	3	4	5	6
Interoperability	—					
Ethical consideration and trust	0.426	—				
Accessibility and affordability	0.272	0.671	—			
Relative advantage	0.367	0.901	0.735	—		
Pedagogical alignment	0.280	0.747	0.879	0.893	—	
AI integration and adoption	0.260	0.900	0.869	0.899	0.893	—

TABLE 4.3

R-squared

Dependent Constructs	R^2	R^2 Adjusted
AI integration and adoption	0.773	0.763
Pedagogical alignment	0.664	0.655

explanatory value. This implies that the exogenous latent variables account for 77.3% of higher education's intention to adopt AI integration.

4.5.3 Structural Model Assessment

This section examines collinearity assessment using the variance inflation factor (VIF) and the effect size (F^2) to evaluate the structural model. Collinearity was assessed using VIF statistics, where values below 5 indicate the absence of multicollinearity issues (Hair et al., 2016). As shown in Table 4.4, the VIF values in this study range from 1.037 to 2.786, confirming that multicollinearity is not a concern.

Additionally, the effect size (F^2) of each path was assessed using Cohen's F^2 (Cohen, 1988), where values below 0.02 indicate no effect, 0.15 represents a medium effect, and 0.35 indicates a large effect. As presented in Table 4.5,

TABLE 4.4

Collinearity Statistics (VIF)

	VIF 1	VIF 2
Interoperability	1.037	—
Ethical consideration and trust	2.457	—
Accessibility and affordability	1.810	1.373
Relative advantage	2.786	1.373
Pedagogical alignment	—	—
AI integration and adoption	2.753	—

TABLE 4.5

Hypothesis Confirmation and Effect Sizes

Hypothesis	Construct	Path Coefficient (β)	F^2	Significance	Interpretation
H1	Interoperability → AI integration and adoption	0.234	0.005	0.001	Supported
H2	Relative advantage → AI integration and adoption	0.188	0.043	0.011	Supported
H3	Relative advantage → Pedagogical alignment	0.544	0.434	0.000	Supported
H4	Pedagogical alignment → AI integration and adoption	0.483	0.305	0.000	Supported
H5	Accessibility and affordability → AI integration and adoption	0.366	0.370	0.000	Supported
H6	Accessibility and affordability → Pedagogical alignment	0.343	0.212	0.000	Supported
H7	Ethical considerations → AI integration and adoption	0.150	0.005	0.004	Supported

the F^2 values range from 0.005 to 0.434, highlighting variations in effect sizes across the model.

The hypothesis testing and the level of confidence for each independent variable are performed using the path coefficient and the significance level (p-value) (Hair et al., 2016). As shown in Table 4.5, the significant estimates indicate that all seven proposed hypothetical paths were significant determinants of AI integration and adoption in the higher education context. Thus, all the critical behavioral factors had p-values less than the 0.05 threshold, indicating a significant relationship with AI integration and adoption.

Relative advantage recorded the highest estimate value among the estimated paths, followed by pedagogical alignment and accessibility and affordability. This implies that the two most important determinants of AI integration and alignment in Ghana—a developing country—are relative advantage and pedagogical alignment.

4.6 Discussion

Interoperability significantly enhances the adoption and integration of AI in education by fostering seamless collaboration between various technologies and systems, which is critical in diverse educational settings. One key advantage is improved efficiency. Interoperable systems ensure that AI tools can connect with existing educational platforms such as LMS or student information systems (SIS). This compatibility reduces redundancy and allows educators to access insights, like performance analytics or personalized recommendations, from a single interface, simplifying implementation and use. Such integration minimizes disruptions in teaching workflows, encouraging broader adoption among educators and institutions (Păvăloaia & Necula, 2023). Another positive influence is accessibility and scalability. Interoperability ensures that AI-powered tools can be easily deployed across institutions with varying technical infrastructures. This inclusivity enables equitable access to AI's benefits, such as personalized learning or adaptive assessments, even in under-resourced schools. Moreover, by allowing different systems to "speak the same language," educators can utilize diverse AI tools without being locked into a single vendor's ecosystem, fostering innovation and competition (Perisic et al., 2023). Trust and transparency are also enhanced through interoperability. When AI tools integrate seamlessly with existing systems, they provide educators and administrators with a holistic view of data flow and decision-making processes, thereby increasing confidence in the technology. This transparency is crucial for addressing ethical concerns related to data privacy and the fairness of AI-driven decisions in educational settings (Chaudhry et al., 2022). Additionally, interoperability drives cost-effectiveness. Institutions can adopt AI solutions incrementally, integrating them with legacy systems rather than overhauling their infrastructure entirely. This modular approach reduces initial investment barriers, making AI adoption more feasible for a broader range of educational institutions. Also, interoperability supports long-term sustainability in AI integration by enabling systems to adapt to future technological advancements. As new AI tools emerge, interoperable systems can incorporate these innovations without extensive reconfiguration, ensuring that educational environments remain cutting-edge and responsive to changing needs (Chaudhry et al., 2022). In short, interoperability is a cornerstone for effectively embedding

AI in education, enhancing usability, equity, and trust while reducing costs and supporting sustainable growth. By prioritizing interoperable solutions, educational institutions can maximize the potential of AI to transform teaching and learning.

Relative advantage—the perception that a new technology offers significant benefits compared to existing alternatives—positively influences the adoption and integration of AI in education. This concept aligns with frameworks like the TAM and the DIT, which emphasize that innovations perceived as advantageous are more likely to be adopted (Davis et al., 1989). AI tools enhance education by automating routine administrative tasks, such as grading and scheduling, which allow educators to focus on core teaching activities. For instance, AI-powered systems can analyze student performance and provide personalized learning pathways, improving both teaching effectiveness and learning outcomes. Teachers can use insights from AI tools to identify and address individual learning gaps, enhancing student engagement and success rates. These advantages make AI adoption appealing to educators striving for efficiency and better outcomes in their classrooms (Ofosu-Ampong, 2024b; Kemp, 2024).

From a student perspective, we have realized that AI in higher education offers transformative, personalized learning experiences for individual needs. Through adaptive platforms that adjust content delivery based on learner progress, AI fosters enhanced engagement and retention. The technology addresses broader educational challenges by reducing digital divides through automated support systems like chatbots and streamlined curriculum planning (Pedro et al., 2019). This ensures accessibility for diverse student populations while simplifying existing workflows for educators. The integration of AI also enables 24/7 learning support, real-time feedback, and intelligent content recommendations, maximizing resource utilization. AI enhances inclusivity in learning environments by automating routine tasks and providing multilingual support. However, a potential risk lies in the standardization of guidance, where students may receive only AI-driven perspectives on routine tasks rather than benefit from diverse viewpoints offered by multiple educators. Compared to traditional systems that expose students to varied instructional approaches, AI integration should be designed to complement rather than replace human input. Ensuring a balance between automation and diverse teaching perspectives can help educators adopt AI technologies while preserving the richness of instructional diversity (Pedro et al., 2019).

Overall, the relative advantage of AI in education, spanning efficiency, personalization, and inclusivity, drives its adoption and integration. This perspective aligns with theories like TAM and innovation diffusion theory, demonstrating how perceived benefits outweigh initial barriers, ensuring widespread acceptance in educational contexts.

Pedagogical alignment plays a critical role in the successful adoption and integration of AI in education. When educators strategically integrate

AI tools to complement established teaching objectives and methods, the impact on learning outcomes is significantly enhanced. This alignment ensures that AI applications are not merely technological add-ons but integral elements of the educational process. First, pedagogical alignment ensures relevance and coherence. AI tools, such as adaptive learning systems or intelligent tutoring systems, can be effectively utilized to address specific educational goals, such as personalized learning pathways or immediate feedback on assignments. By aligning these tools with curriculum standards and instructional strategies, educators can ensure that AI enhances rather than disrupts the learning process. For example, AI-based language-learning applications have demonstrated improved outcomes in pronunciation and grammar skills when used in structured lesson plans.

Moreover, alignment encourages teacher buy-in and confidence. Teachers are more likely to adopt AI when its integration aligns with their pedagogical values and practices. Training programs that connect AI capabilities to familiar teaching scenarios have been shown to alleviate concerns about complexity or irrelevance (Garcia et al., 2026). For instance, in language education, AI tools are often embraced for their ability to simulate real-world interactions, enhancing both teaching efficacy and student engagement. Pedagogical alignment also mitigates ethical and practical challenges. When AI is deployed with clear educational intentions, concerns about data privacy, accessibility, and equity can be proactively addressed. For example, AI tools in public and private schools exhibit similar adoption rates when aligned with universally accessible teaching practices (Alasmari, 2024). This demonstrates that alignment supports equitable integration across diverse educational contexts. Finally, pedagogical alignment fosters innovation. Embedding AI within established educational frameworks enables teachers to explore innovative instructional methods, such as gamification or collaborative AI-driven projects, that enhance student engagement and motivation. However, effective implementation requires teachers to have a clear understanding of these approaches, including the principles of gamification and how AI can support interactive learning experiences. Providing professional development and training on these concepts ensures that educators can effectively integrate AI-driven strategies into their teaching practices. In conclusion, pedagogical alignment transforms AI from a technological novelty into a transformative educational tool. This alignment ensures that AI serves the broader goals of education—enhancing learning outcomes, supporting teacher efforts, and addressing ethical considerations—ultimately making AI integration a seamless and impactful endeavor in education (Garcia te al., 2026).

Similarly, we found that the accessibility and affordability of AI technologies play a pivotal role in their widespread adoption and integration into education, profoundly transforming teaching and learning experiences. Thus, accessibility ensures that AI tools are available to educators and students regardless of geographic or socioeconomic barriers. For instance, initiatives such as AI-driven digital textbooks and virtual tutors have been shown to enhance personalized learning experiences and improve academic outcomes in diverse settings (Garcia et al., 2025). These tools help address the digital divide by offering tailored resources that meet various needs, including for students with disabilities or those in underserved communities. In Brazil and West Africa, programs like Letrus and Kabakoo Academies exemplify how AI can provide inclusive education and prepare learners for future opportunities (Elhussein et al., 2024). Affordability, on the other hand, democratizes access to these technologies by lowering costs for schools and governments. AI-driven platforms reduce expenses related to creating and distributing educational content such as textbooks and lesson plans. Additionally, automating administrative tasks like grading and attendance tracking alleviates teacher workloads, allowing them to focus on student engagement and personalized instruction. This cost-effectiveness makes AI a sustainable solution for improving education in both high-income and developing regions (Elhussein et al., 2024). Furthermore, affordable and accessible AI fosters innovation by enabling institutions to experiment with cutting-edge tools. For instance, AI translators and adaptive learning platforms have shown promise in bridging linguistic and cultural gaps in education, especially in multilingual societies. Such innovations ensure that educational resources are relevant and impactful across different contexts. However, to fully leverage these benefits, challenges like digital infrastructure gaps and data privacy concerns must be addressed. Policymakers and educators need to collaborate with AI developers to ensure that the tools are equitable, secure, and aligned with pedagogical goals. Thus, the positive influence of accessibility and affordability in AI adoption is evident in its capacity to enhance equity, efficiency, and engagement in education. By prioritizing these factors, educational systems worldwide can harness AI to create a more inclusive and effective learning environment.

Moreover, we found that ethical considerations and trust are pivotal in fostering the adoption and integration of AI in education. Addressing ethical concerns such as data privacy, transparency, and inclusivity builds confidence among educators, students, and parents. These elements ensure that AI systems are designed and implemented to prioritize safety, equity, and respect for individuals' rights, which are critical in educational contexts (Eitel-Porter, 2021). Trust in AI is essential for its adoption, as educators must feel assured that these technologies enhance teaching without compromising pedagogical integrity. Trust is cultivated through clear communication about AI's capabilities and limitations, as well as through involving stakeholders in its development and deployment. When stakeholders believe that AI tools are secure, unbiased, and beneficial, they are more likely to embrace them. For instance, the U.S. Department of Education highlights frameworks emphasizing ethical integration to maximize AI's positive impact while minimizing risks. Moreover, embedding ethical practices through game-like elements (Ofosu-Ampong, 2020) in AI design ensures responsible AI use and strengthens trust. This approach can lead to increased acceptance, as evidenced by systems that enhance personalized learning while safeguarding sensitive information. Educators, when supported with ethical guidelines and transparent AI functionalities, can confidently incorporate AI into teaching strategies, thereby enhancing learning outcomes and fostering innovation (Siau & Wang, 2020). In sum, ethical principles and trust play intertwined roles in driving AI's success in education. Aligning AI tools with ethical standards and promoting trust through transparency and inclusivity helps remove certain ethical and trust-based barriers, making AI adoption more acceptable in educational settings. However, while this approach enhances stakeholder confidence, it does not eliminate all challenges related to AI implementation. Continuous monitoring, policy refinement, and stakeholder engagement remain essential to addressing persistent concerns and ensuring responsible AI integration.

Similarly, we found that the relative advantage of AI in education positively influences pedagogical alignment by highlighting its ability to enhance learning outcomes and streamline teaching processes. When educators perceive AI as more effective than traditional methods—offering personalized feedback, automating routine tasks, or supporting diverse learning styles—they are more likely to align their teaching strategies with AI integration (Kakhkharova & Tuychieva, 2024). This alignment fosters a cohesive framework where pedagogical goals and technology adoption mutually reinforce each other, improving overall educational effectiveness.

On the other hand, accessibility and affordability in AI adoption positively influence pedagogical alignment by fostering inclusivity and equitable learning opportunities. Affordable AI tools enable widespread implementation, ensuring that institutions across the economic spectrum can enhance teaching and learning practices (Goel, 2020). Accessibility features like adaptive learning platforms and speech recognition support diverse learner needs, including those with disabilities. These capabilities align with personalized and competency-based education approaches, enhancing engagement and outcomes (Ofosu-Ampong, 2020). For instance, AI has been pivotal in bridging gaps for remote learners and those with specific challenges, transforming traditional educational barriers into tailored support systems.

Furthermore, the five explanatory variables successfully predicted 77.3% of AI integration and adoption variance in higher education contexts in developing countries. The predicted value accounted for in the conceptual model is higher than that of Venkatesh et al. (2012), who estimated 74%. In this regard, higher education institutions should promote innovative AI integration environments based on these five predicting factors, which help explain the tendency to adopt AI in developing countries. As AI continues to grow and expand its networks in developing countries and gain prominence, higher education institutions may prioritize these critical success factors at the adoption stage.

4.6.1 AI Maturity Model

The study findings reveal a trend of increasing AI maturity in Ghanaian higher education institutions, driven by the growing reliance on data to advance AI applications in education (Ofosu-Ampong, 2024a). Universities in Ghana demonstrate strong performance in ensuring the accessibility and affordability of AI tools while progressively integrating and adopting AI-driven solutions to enhance teaching and learning. As institutions move from the initial awareness phase toward full-scale optimization, they establish structured strategies for AI adoption, reinforcing its relative advantages and effectiveness in pedagogical contexts.

Despite these advancements, ethical considerations and trust remain critical challenges that must be proactively addressed. Institutional leadership plays a key role in ensuring transparency, fairness, and data privacy, particularly as AI becomes more embedded in educational decision-making processes. To facilitate a seamless transition, universities are aligning AI initiatives with curriculum objectives, ensuring pedagogical coherence rather than disruption.

Interoperability has also emerged as a strategic priority, with staff advocating for robust ICT-driven initiatives that enable seamless integration across platforms and systems. The maturity model (Figure 4.2) maps AI development across six key dimensions—interoperability, relative advantage, pedagogical alignment, accessibility and affordability, integration, and ethical considerations—illustrating a structured progression from foundational awareness to full-scale AI optimization in higher education.

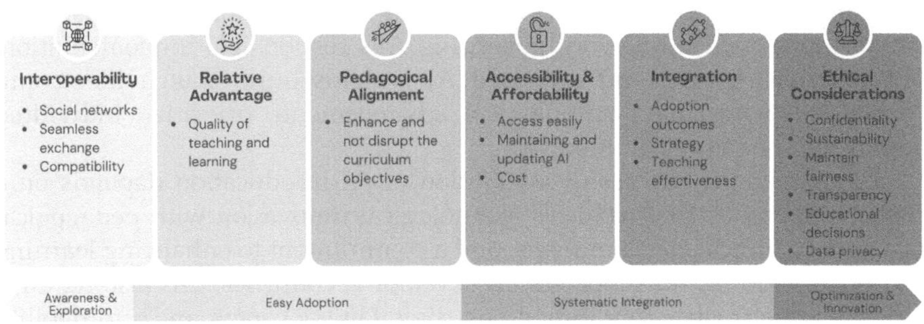

FIGURE 4.2
AI maturity model in higher education institutions in Ghana.

4.7 Conclusion

Interoperability, relative advantage, pedagogical alignment, accessibility, affordability, and ethical considerations are critical determinants in the successful integration of AI in educational contexts. These interconnected factors collectively shape the adoption of AI technologies, transforming traditional educational landscapes into dynamic, personalized, and efficient learning environments. Interoperability emerges as a cornerstone, enabling seamless technological integration across diverse educational platforms. By facilitating compatibility between different systems, it reduces implementation barriers, enhances efficiency, and supports long-term technological sustainability. This approach ensures that educational institutions can leverage AI tools without extensive infrastructure overhauls.

The perceived relative advantage of AI drives its adoption by demonstrating tangible benefits over conventional methods. AI's ability to automate administrative tasks, provide personalized learning pathways, and support diverse student populations makes it an attractive technological solution. Educators and students alike recognize its potential to enhance engagement, improve learning outcomes, and address educational challenges more effectively. Pedagogical alignment further solidifies AI's educational integration by ensuring that technological tools complement rather than disrupt established teaching objectives. When AI applications are strategically incorporated into curriculum frameworks, they become integral learning components that enhance rather than replace traditional instructional methods. Accessibility and affordability democratize AI's educational potential, making advanced technologies available across socioeconomic spectrums. Reducing implementation costs and offering inclusive tools make AI more accessible to a wider range of educational institutions. As these technologies become more widely available, they have the potential to bridge digital divides and create equitable learning opportunities. However, ensuring long-term adoption also requires building trust among educators and stakeholders through transparent policies and reliable support systems. Ethical considerations and trust form the foundational framework governing AI's responsible implementation. Transparent, secure, and unbiased AI systems build stakeholder confidence, ensuring that technological advancements prioritize individual rights and pedagogical integrity.

Ultimately, the successful integration of AI in education depends on a holistic approach that balances technological innovation with pedagogical sensitivity, ethical considerations, and a commitment to enhancing learning experiences for all stakeholders. In developing countries, this also requires addressing infrastructure limitations, digital literacy gaps, and affordability concerns to ensure equitable access to and meaningful adoption of AI-driven educational solutions.

1. Develop comprehensive national guidelines for AI integration in educational institutions, emphasizing interoperability standards and ethical frameworks.
2. Create funding mechanisms to support AI technology adoption, particularly in under-resourced schools and developing regions.
3. Introduce low-cost, entry-level AI adoption strategies that allow institutions to gradually integrate AI tools without significant financial or infrastructure burdens.
4. Mandate professional development programs for educators to build AI literacy and pedagogical alignment skills.
5. Establish robust data privacy regulations specific to educational AI technologies.
6. Promote collaborative partnerships between educational institutions, technology developers, and policymakers to ensure responsible AI implementation.
7. Design inclusive AI adoption strategies that address accessibility barriers and support diverse learning needs.

4.7.1 Implications for Future Research

Future research should investigate the long-term impacts of AI integration on student learning outcomes across diverse educational contexts while developing robust methodologies to assess AI tools' pedagogical effectiveness and alignment. Researchers must collaborate with industry partners to develop comprehensive ethical frameworks for AI implementation that consider varied cultural and socioeconomic settings. Additionally, research should explore the psychological and cognitive impacts of AI-powered personalized learning to promote its responsible and effective implementation. Additionally, critical research should focus on analyzing AI's potential to bridge educational inequities, support learners with specific challenges, and examine the evolving role of educators within increasingly AI-enhanced learning environments. These diverse research avenues will offer a thorough understanding of AI's impact on education, supporting its responsible, equitable, and effective implementation worldwide.

References

Abdaljaleel, M., Barakat, M., Alsanafi, M., Salim, N. A., Abazid, H., Malaeb, D., Mohammed, A. H., Hassan, B. A., Wayyes, A. M., Farhan, S. S., Khatib, S. E., & Sallam, M. (2024). A multinational study on the factors influencing university students' attitudes and usage of ChatGPT. *Scientific Reports*, *14*(1), 1983.

Abulibdeh, A., Zaidan, E., & Abulibdeh, R. (2024). Navigating the confluence of artificial intelligence and education for sustainable development in the era of industry 4.0: Challenges, opportunities, and ethical dimensions. *Journal of Cleaner Production*, *437*, 140527. https://doi.org/10.1016/j.jclepro.2023.140527

Aderibigbe, A. O., Ohenhen, P. E., Nwaobia, N. K., Gidiagba, J. O., & Ani, E. C. (2023). Artificial intelligence in developing countries: Bridging the gap between potential and implementation. *Computer Science & IT Research Journal*, *4*(3), 185–199.

Alasmari, T. (2024). Acceptance factors of generative AI in EFL teaching: A pedagogical perspective. *JETL (Journal of Education, Teaching and Learning)*, *9*(2), 196–211.

Alhumaid, K., Naqbi, S., Elsori, D., & Mansoori, M. (2023). The adoption of artificial intelligence applications in education. *International Journal of Data and Network Science*, *7*(1), 457–466.

Ali, M. S., Suchiang, T., Saikia, T. P., & Gulzar, D. (2024). Perceived benefits and concerns of AI integration in higher education: Insights from India. *Educational Administration: Theory and Practice*, *30*(5), 656–668.

Almogren, A. S., Al-Rahmi, W. M., & Dahri, N. A. (2024). Exploring factors influencing the acceptance of ChatGPT in higher education: A smart education perspective. *Heliyon*, *10*(11).

Bakhadirov, M., & Alasgarova, R. (2024). Factors influencing teachers' use of artificial intelligence for instructional purposes. *IAFOR Journal of Education*, *12*(2), 9–32.

Bozkurt, A., Xiao, J., Farrow, R., Bai, J. Y. H., Nerantzi, C., Moore, S., Dron, J., Stracke, C. M., Singh, L., Crompton, H., Koutropoulos, A., Terentev, E., Pazurek, A., Nichols, M., Sidorkin, A. M., Costello, E., Watson, S., Mulligan, D., Honeychurch, S., . . . Asino, T. I. (2024). The manifesto for teaching and learning in a time of generative AI: A critical collective stance to better navigate the future. *Open Praxis*, *16*(4), 487–513. https://doi.org/10.55982/openpraxis.16.4.777

Chai, F., Ma, J., Wang, Y., Zhu, J., & Han, T. (2024). Grading by AI makes me feel fairer? How different evaluators affect college students' perception of fairness. *Frontiers in Psychology*, *15*. https://doi.org/10.3389/fpsyg.2024.1221177

Chan, C. K. Y. (2023). A comprehensive AI policy education framework for university teaching and learning. *International Journal of Educational Technology in Higher Education*, *20*(1). https://doi.org/10.1186/s41239-023-00408-3

Chaudhry, M. A., Cukurova, M., & Luckin, R. (2022). A transparency index framework for AI in education. In *International conference on artificial intelligence in education* (pp. 195–198). Cham: Springer International Publishing.

Cohen, J. (1988). *Statistical power analysis for the behavioral sciences* (2nd ed.). Lawrence Erlbaum Associates.

Dahri, N. A., Yahaya, N., & Al-Rahmi, W. M. (2024). Exploring the influence of ChatGPT on student academic success and career readiness. *Education and Information Technologies*, 1–45.

Davis, F. D., Bagozzi, R. P., & Warshaw, P. R. (1989). Technology acceptance model. *Journal of Management Science*, *35*(8), 982–1003.

Díaz-Rodríguez, N., Del Ser, J., Coeckelbergh, M., De Prado, M. L., Herrera-Viedma, E., & Herrera, F. (2023). Connecting the dots in trustworthy artificial intelligence: From AI principles, ethics, and key requirements to responsible AI systems and regulation. *Information Fusion*, *99*, 101896. https://doi.org/10.1016/j.inffus.2023.101896

Ding, A. E., Shi, L., Yang, H., & Choi, I. (2024). Enhancing teacher AI literacy and integration through different types of cases in teacher professional development. *Computers and Education Open, 6*, 100178. https://doi.org/10.1016/j.caeo.2024.100178

Domorenok, E., Graziano, P., & Polverari, L. (2021). Introduction: Policy integration and institutional capacity: Theoretical, conceptual and empirical challenges. *Policy and Society, 40*(1), 1–18. https://doi.org/10.1080/14494035.2021.1902058

Eitel-Porter, R. (2021). Beyond the promise: Implementing ethical AI. *AI and Ethics, 1*(1), 73–80.

Elhussein, G., Hasselaar, E., & Lutsyshyn, O. (2024). *Shaping the future of learning: The role of AI in education 4.0*. World Economic Forum.

Garcia, M. B., Metwally, A. H. S., Wang, T., Alasgarova, R., Nerantzi, C., & Bozkurt, A. (2026). Psychological and developmental repercussions of pervasive AI usage in schools: A review of educational benefits and challenges. *Responsible AI Integration in Education*, 87–118.

Garcia, M. B., Rosak-Szyrocka, J., Yılmaz, R., Metwally, A. H. S., Acut, D. P., & Bozkurt, A. (2025). Rethinking educational assessment in the age of generative AI: Actionable strategies to mitigate academic dishonesty. In *Pitfalls of AI integration in education: Skill obsolescence, misuse, and bias* (pp. 1–24). IGI Global Scientific Publishing.

Ghioni, R., Taddeo, M., & Floridi, L. (2024). Open source intelligence and AI: A systematic review of the GELSI literature. *AI & Society, 39*(4), 1827–1842.

Goel, A. (2020). AI-powered learning: Making education accessible, affordable, and achievable. *arXiv preprint arXiv:2006.01908*.

Goralski, M. A., & Tan, T. K. (2020). Artificial intelligence and sustainable development. *The International Journal of Management Education, 18*(1), 100330.

Grubb, W. N., & Cox, R. D. (2005). Pedagogical alignment and curricular consistency: The challenges for developmental education. *New Directions for Community Colleges, 2005*(129), 93–103.

Hair, J. F., Hult, G. T. M., Ringle, C. M., & Sarstedt, M. (2016). *A primer on partial least squares structural equation modeling (PLS-SEM)*. Sage Publications.

Henseler, J., Ringle, C. M., & Sarstedt, M. (2015). A new criterion for assessing discriminant validity in variance-based structural equation modeling. *Journal of the Academy of Marketing Science, 43*(1), 115–135.

Hester, A. J. (2011). A comparative analysis of the usage and infusion of wiki and non-wiki-based knowledge management systems. *Information Technology and Management, 12*(4), 335–355.

Hongli, Z., & Leong, W. Y. (2024). AI solutions for accessible education in underserved communities. *Journal of Innovation and Technology, 2024*.

Hornberger, M., Bewersdorff, A., & Nerdel, C. (2023). What do university students know about Artificial Intelligence? Development and validation of an AI literacy test. *Computers and Education Artificial Intelligence, 5*, 100165. https://doi.org/10.1016/j.caeai.2023.100165

Hussain, F., & Anwar, M. A. (2024). Towards informed policy decisions: Assessing student perceptions and intentions to use ChatGPT for academic performance in higher education. *Journal of Asian Public Policy*, 1–28.

Justıno, J., & Rafael, S. (2019). The expansion of pedagogical alignment—a step for the learning success. *The Eurasia Proceedings of Educational and Social Sciences, 12*, 32–36.

Kakhkharova, M., & Tuychieva, S. (2024). AI-enhanced pedagogy in higher education: Redefining teaching-learning paradigms. In *2024 international conference on knowledge engineering and communication systems (ICKECS)* (Vol. 1, pp. 1–6). IEEE.

Kemp, A. (2024). Competitive advantage through artificial intelligence: Toward a theory of situated AI. *Academy of Management Review, 49*(3), 618–635.

Kim, J. (2020). The influence of perceived costs and perceived benefits on AI-driven interactive recommendation agent value. *Journal of Global Scholars of Marketing Science, 30*(3), 319–333.

Krauss, C., Streicher, A., Poxleitner, E., Altun, D., Mueller, J., An, T. S., & Mueller, C. (2023). Best-of-breed: Service-oriented integration of artificial intelligence in interoperable educational ecosystems. In *International workshop on learning technology for education challenges* (pp. 267–283). Cham: Springer Nature Switzerland.

Lim, T., Gottipati, S., & Cheong, M. L. (2023). Ethical considerations for artificial intelligence in educational assessments. In *Creative AI tools and ethical implications in teaching and learning* (pp. 32–79). IGI Global.

Ma, M. (2024). Exploring the acceptance of generative artificial intelligence for language learning among EFL postgraduate students: An extended TAM approach. *International Journal of Applied Linguistics, 35*(1), 91–108.

Maggo, J., & Maggo, T. (2025). Disparities in educational opportunities between urban and rural regions across the globe and the potential of AI to bridge the divide. *International Journal of Business Analytics & Intelligence (IJBAI), 13*(1).

McElheran, K., Li, J. F., Brynjolfsson, E., Kroff, Z., Dinlersoz, E., Foster, L., & Zolas, N. (2024). AI adoption in America: Who, what, and where. *Journal of Economics & Management Strategy, 33*(2), 375–415.

Muranga, K., Muse, I. S., Köroğlu, E. N., & Yildirim, Y. (2023). Artificial intelligence and underfunded education. *London Journal of Social Sciences, 6*, 56–68. https://doi.org/10.31039/ljss.2023.6.105

Nazaretsky, T., Ariely, M., Cukurova, M., & Alexandron, G. (2022). Teachers' trust in AI-powered educational technology and a professional development program to improve it. *British Journal of Educational Technology, 53*(4), 914–931.

Nazari, N., Shabbir, M. S., & Setiawan, R. (2021). Application of artificial intelligence powered digital writing assistant in higher education: Randomized controlled trial. *Heliyon, 7*(5), e07014. https://doi.org/10.1016/j.heliyon.2021.e07014

Ofosu-Ampong, K. (2020). The shift to gamification in education: A review on dominant issues. *Journal of Educational Technology Systems, 49*(1), 113–137.

Ofosu-Ampong, K. (2023). Gender differences in perception of artificial intelligence-based tools. *Journal of Digital Art & Humanities, 4*(2), 52–56.

Ofosu-Ampong, K. (2024a). Artificial intelligence research: A review on dominant themes, methods, frameworks and future research direction. *Telematics and Informatics Reports, 13*, 100127.

Ofosu-Ampong, K. (2024b). Beyond the hype: Exploring faculty perceptions and acceptability of AI in teaching practices. *Discover Education, 3*(1), 38.

Ofosu-Ampong, K., & Acheampong, B. (2022). Adoption of contactless technologies for remote work in Ghana post-COVID-19: Insights from technology-organisation-environment framework. *Digital Business, 2*(2), 100023.

Ofosu-Ampong, K., Acheampong, B., Kevor, M. O., & Amankwah-Sarfo, F. (2023). Acceptance of artificial intelligence (ChatGPT) in education: Trust, innovativeness and psychological need of students. *Information and Knowledge Management, 13*(4), 37–47.

Ofosu-Ampong, K., & Adu-Ntim, J. (2025). Transformational leadership, AI competitiveness, and project performance: A moderation analysis. *International Journal of Global Business and Competitiveness*, *20*(2), 67–79.

Ofosu-Ampong, K., Atebawone, E., Mustafa, A. S., & Koomson, A. (2024). The shift to artificial intelligence, ChatGPT, and emerging technologies in education: A review on dominant issues. In *Empowering digital education with ChatGPT* (pp. 17–39). Taylor and Francis.

Okour, M. K., Chong, C. W., & Fattah, F. A. M. A. (2021). Knowledge management systems usage: Application of diffusion of innovation theory. *Global Knowledge, Memory and Communication*. https://doi.org/10.1108/GKMC-08-2020-0117

Oliveira, T., & Martins, M. F. (2011). Literature review of information technology adoption models at firm level. *Electronic Journal of Information Systems Evaluation*, *14*(1), 110–121.

Palacin, V., Gilbert, S., Orchard, S., Eaton, A., Ferrario, M. A., & Happonen, A. (2020). Drivers of participation in digital citizen science: Case studies on Järviwiki and Safecast. *Citizen Science Theory and Practice*, *5*(1), 22. https://doi.org/10.5334/cstp.290

Păvăloaia, V. D., & Necula, S. C. (2023). Artificial intelligence as a disruptive technology—a systematic literature review. *Electronics*, *12*(5), 1102.

Pedro, F., Subosa, M., Rivas, A., & Valverde, P. (2019). *Artificial intelligence in education: Challenges and opportunities for sustainable development*. ESCO Working Papers on Education Policy. https://en.unesco.org/themes/education-policy-planning/Designed

Perisic, A., Perisic, I., Lazic, M., & Perisic, B. (2023). The foundation for future education, teaching, training, learning, and performing infrastructure: The open interoperability conceptual framework approach. *Heliyon*, *9*(6).

Phillips-Wren, G. (2012). AI tools in decision making support systems: A review. *International Journal on Artificial Intelligence Tools*, *21*(02), 1240005.

Rahi, S., & Ghani, M. A. (2018). The role of UTAUT, DOI, perceived technology security and game elements in internet banking adoption. *World Journal of Science, Technology and Sustainable Development*, *15*(4), 338–356.

Rehm, G., Galanis, D., Labropoulou, P., Piperidis, S., Welß, M., Usbeck, R., . . . Lagzdiņš, A. (2020). Towards an interoperable ecosystem of AI and LT platforms: A roadmap for the implementation of different levels of interoperability. *arXiv preprint arXiv:2004.08355*.

Rogers, E. M. (2003). *Diffusion of innovations* (5th ed.). New York: Free Press.

Saihi, A., Ben-Daya, M., Hariga, M., & As' ad, R. (2024). A Structural equation modeling analysis of generative AI chatbots adoption among students and educators in higher education. *Computers and Education: Artificial Intelligence*, *7*, 100274.

Siau, K., & Wang, W. (2020). Artificial intelligence (AI) ethics: Ethics of AI and ethical AI. *Journal of Database Management (JDM)*, *31*(2), 74–87.

Sun, D., Boudouaia, A., Yang, J., & Xu, J. (2024). Investigating students' programming behaviors, interaction qualities and perceptions through prompt-based learning in ChatGPT. *Humanities and Social Sciences Communications*, *11*(1), 1–14.

Swiecki, Z., Khosravi, H., Chen, G., Martinez-Maldonado, R., Lodge, J. M., Milligan, S., Selwyn, N., & Gašević, D. (2022). Assessment in the age of artificial intelligence. *Computers and Education Artificial Intelligence*, *3*, 100075. https://doi.org/10.1016/j.caeai.2022.100075

Tatineni, S. (2019). Ethical considerations in AI and data science: Bias, fairness, and accountability. *International Journal of Information Technology and Management Information Systems (IJITMIS)*, *10*(1), 11–21.

Usmani, U. A., Happonen, A., & Watada, J. (2023). Human-centered artificial intelligence: Designing for user empowerment and ethical considerations. *2023 5th international congress on human-computer interaction, optimization and robotic applications (HORA)* (pp. 1–7). https://doi.org/10.1109/HORA58378.2023.10156761

Van, N. T., Mohd Daril, M. A., Ali, M., & Korejo, M. S. (2024). Enhancing psychological well-being in higher education post-COVID-19 pandemic. The role of AI-based support systems-bibliometric reviews. *International Journal of Online & Biomedical Engineering, 20*(6).

Velander, J., Taiye, M. A., Otero, N., & Milrad, M. (2023). Artificial Intelligence in K-12 Education: Eliciting and reflecting on Swedish teachers' understanding of AI and its implications for teaching & learning. *Education and Information Technologies, 29*(4), 4085–4105. https://doi.org/10.1007/s10639-023-11990-4

Venkatesh, V., Thong, J. Y., & Xu, X. (2012). Consumer acceptance and use of information technology: Extending the unified theory of acceptance and use of technology. *MIS Quarterly*, 157–178.

Wang, A. I., & Tahir, R. (2020). The effect of using Kahoot! for learning—A literature review. *Computers & Education, 149*, 103818.

Wang, Y., Liu, C., & Tu, Y. F. (2021). Factors affecting the adoption of AI-based applications in higher education. *Educational Technology & Society, 24*(3), 116–129.

Xu, Z. (2024). AI in education: Enhancing learning experiences and student outcomes. *Applied and Computational Engineering, 51*(1), 104–111.

Yang, J., Blount, Y., & Amrollahi, A. (2024). Artificial intelligence adoption in a professional service industry: A multiple case study. *Technological Forecasting and Social Change, 201*, 123251. https://doi.org/10.1016/j.techfore.2024.123251

Yang, J., Chen, Y., Por, L. Y., & Ku, C. S. (2023). A systematic literature review of information security in Chatbots. *Applied Sciences, 13*(11), 6355. https://doi.org/10.3390/app13116355

Zhou, W., & Kim, Y. (2024). Innovative music education: An empirical assessment of ChatGPT-4's impact on student learning experiences. *Education and Information Technologies*, 1–27.

Zhu, W., Huang, L., Zhou, X., Li, X., Shi, G., Ying, J., & Wang, C. (2024). Could AI ethical anxiety, perceived ethical risks and ethical awareness about AI influence university students' use of generative AI products? An ethical perspective. *International Journal of Human–Computer Interaction*, 1–23.

Zogheib, S., & Zogheib, B. (2024). Understanding university students' adoption of ChatGPT: Insights from TAM, SDT, and beyond. *Journal of Information Technology Education: Research, 23*, 025.

APPENDIX A

Constructs and Measurement Item Questions

Constructs	Measurement Items	References
Interoperability	The AI educational tools we use can seamlessly exchange data with our existing learning management systems. AI tools can effectively integrate with other educational software platforms we currently use. The AI systems in our institution are compatible with different devices and operating systems.	Rehm et al. (2020)
Ethical Consideration and Trust	I trust that the AI tools protect student data privacy and confidentiality. The AI systems we use maintain fairness and avoid bias in student assessment. I believe the AI tools are transparent about how they make educational decisions.	Eden et al. (2024), Eitel-Porter (2021)
Accessibility and Affordability	The AI educational tools are financially accessible for our institution. Students can easily access the AI learning systems regardless of their economic background. The cost of maintaining and updating AI tools is reasonable for our educational budget.	Ofosu-Ampong (2024b)
Relative Advantage	Using AI tools improves the quality of teaching and learning compared to traditional methods. AI systems help me accomplish teaching tasks more efficiently than before. The benefits of using AI in education outweigh the effort required to implement it.	Alasmari (2024)
Pedagogical Alignment	The AI tools effectively support our existing teaching methodologies and approaches. AI systems align well with our curriculum objectives and learning outcomes. The AI tools enhance rather than disrupt our established pedagogical practices.	Ofosu-Ampong (2024b)
AI integration and adoption	AI tools enhance my teaching effectiveness. AI integration improves student learning outcomes. AI adoption reduces my administrative workload. AI integration makes assessment more efficient.	Eden et al. (2024), Ofosu-Ampong (2024b)

5

Artificial Intelligence for Equitable and Sustainable Assessment

Sook Jhee Yoon and Lydia Yoke Yean Foong

5.1 Introduction

Artificial intelligence (AI) is transforming assessment in various ways that challenge academics' current designs and practices. While AI brings several benefits to learning, such as enabling personalized learning and serving as a "tutor" who can provide formative assessment tasks, AI also seems to impact how academics gather valid evidence of students' learning, as academics can no longer be sure that the work assessed is based solely on authentic human input. There is a need to critically evaluate the impact of AI in assessment to ensure validity, reliability, and fairness. AI may also cause further education disparities, as students from certain demographics have better access to AI and better opportunities to develop AI literacy, or face challenges due to cultural bias in AI (OECD, 2024). Thus, assessment needs to be equitable to ensure that all students have access to AI when demonstrating their competencies. As AI becomes more important, the skill sets expected of our students may also change along with technological advancements. Designing sustainable assessment (Boud, 2000) can ensure that academics assess students' current competencies and prepare them for lifelong learning. The chapter aims to provide an overview of the concepts of equitable and sustainable assessment in the age of AI. The chapter also aims to share the experience of how a private university in Malaysia promotes assessment integrated with AI while ensuring that assessments are equitable and sustainable. The chapter begins with an intersection between assessment in the age of AI and equitable and sustainable assessments. It examines how universities worldwide have responded to the impact of AI in assessment thus far. The chapter then presents a case of promoting assessment integrated with AI at a Malaysian university. Reflecting on our experience, this chapter can provide policymakers and academics with insights into guiding principles and considerations in designing assessments integrated with AI.

DOI: 10.1201/9781003633433-5

5.2 Foundation Underpinning AI in Assessment

To unpack the role of AI in assessment, there is a need to understand two key concepts: AI in education and assessment design. Since AI has become more available to the public in recent years, several educational organizations have published principles and frameworks to guide academics on the purposeful integration of AI. These guidelines help educators implement AI-enhanced assessment practices while maintaining validity, reliability, and inclusivity. UNESCO proposed an AI competency framework for educators and learners (UNESCO, 2021), which aims to support teachers and students in developing the competencies needed in the age of AI. At the higher education level, the Russell Group (2023) suggested five principles to guide its universities on the use of AI. These principles focus on AI literacy, students' effective use of AI, ethical AI adoption in teaching and learning, ensuring academic rigor and academic integrity, and the collaborative sharing of best practices in the use of AI (Russell Group, 2023). The Quality Assurance Agency for Higher Education (QAA) publishes a set of resources, including advice, examples, and guidance for the ethical use of AI in education. In Australia, the Tertiary Education Quality and Standards Agency (TEQSA) published a document urging academics to reform their assessment practices (TEQSA, 2023). In the document, TEQSA proposes two principles and five propositions, along with insights on how AI may impact assessment practices. A year later, TEQSA (2024) released another document with an analysis of policies and practices from all Australian universities. This document has a section dedicated to assessment security, highlighting important issues including short-term and medium- to long-term measures, and AI detection, among others. Assessment design, as a core component to gather valid evidence of students' learning, warrants more discussion to support academics in aligning assessment to learning outcomes, designing assessment, implementing, and monitoring.

At the university level, universities worldwide also saw the need for more focused discussion on AI in assessment. In a review by Moorhouse et al. (2023) on highly ranked universities, they reported that the universities have guidelines on academic integrity and AI in assessment, covering pertinent areas such as plagiarism, acknowledgment of the use of AI, and detection of AI use. In the same review, the authors also pointed out the need to examine current assessment design and practices. In another review done by Jin et al. (2025) on 40 universities across the continents, they highlighted that universities emphasized academic integrity and the ethical use of AI while encouraging academics to leverage AI to promote critical evaluation and human-centric competencies. To facilitate practice, most universities and researchers established boundaries on how students can or cannot use AI in assessments (Corbin et al., 2025). For example, one notable guidance published is the two-lane approach by Liu (2024), who recommends assessments that are essential for verifying students' learning attainment as Lane 1, while assessments that are likely to involve AI outside of controlled environment as Lane 2. This two-lane approach has been well received by academics as a starting point to review and redesign assessment. The rise of cases breaching academic integrity also prompted Perkins et al. (2024) to propose the AI assessment scale, which consists of five categories of AI integration. This scale was further enhanced in 2024, in which the categories are now: No AI, AI planning, AI collaboration, Full AI, and AI exploration. In a similar vein, universities such as University College London (UCL) and the University of New South Wales (UNSW) introduced categories on the use of AI. UCL has included three categories, namely AI cannot be used, AI can be used in an assistive role, and AI has an integral role, while UNSW introduced six categories indicating different uses of AI, including one category where AI is not allowed. Further analysis of policies published by several universities across the globe also shows similar practices, with one category in which AI is not applicable due to the purpose or format of assessment, and varying categories for the use of AI. Some universities (e.g., Harvard University and the National University of Singapore) encourage academics to promote different uses of AI with students while keeping them informed of the advantages and risks of AI, instead of having an institutional category of use. This practice seems to be in line with the work of Corbin and his colleagues (2025), who argued that practices for establishing boundaries on how students can or cannot use AI may be more complex than just categories of varying degrees of permissible use. They proposed moving away from examining AI in assessment from a fixed-boundary perspective and embracing the need for negotiated spaces to meet ever-changing technologies and educational needs (Corbin et al., 2025).

Turning our attention now to assessment design, academics' understanding of principles of good assessment design has become more important than ever in the age of AI. The QAA (2018) outlined 10 guiding principles for assessment design in higher education. Academics needed to internalize these principles even before the pre-AI age. Similar to other emerging technologies, when academics integrate any technological advances such as mobile devices, smartboards, or virtual reality (VR) glasses, a firm understanding of the core principles of assessment design ensures they integrate AI when it aligns with pedagogical intent, not as a response to technological trends alone. Assessment design without consideration of AI may pose risks to the validity, reliability, and fairness of assessment (Yeo, 2023). For instance, Farazouli and colleagues (2024) argued that AI can perform well in assessment, including providing argumentation considered creative and novel. It may also omit references and generate irrelevant content for assessment tasks. These findings underscore the need for careful assessment task design, particularly as students increasingly engage with AI in academic, professional, and societal settings. As such, assessment design in a digital world proposed by Bearman et al. (2023), a framework for assessment in a digital world, emphasizes three purposes: using digital tools for better assessment, building and credentialing digital literacies, and building and credentialing human capabilities for a digital world (Bearman et al., 2023, p. 301). As assessments need to allow students to demonstrate current competencies and prepare them for future needs, it is timely for academics to give serious consideration to designing assessments.

A final perspective on AI in assessment is constructive alignment. According to Biggs and Tang (2011), assessment needs to constructively align with learning outcomes and teaching and learning activities. Constructive alignment is built on two core principles. The first is constructivist learning theory, which asserts that students actively construct knowledge through their learning experiences rather than passively receiving information. The second is the alignment principle, which emphasizes that teaching and learning activities and assessment tasks are aligned to ensure students achieve the intended learning outcomes. Academics need to consider whether students should be assessed on knowledge and skills from the pre-AI age or if there are new learning outcomes that are more relevant in preparing students to navigate an AI-driven world. Weng et al. (2024) argue that learning outcomes in the age of AI are expected to address career-driven competencies and lifelong learning skills, which traditional assessment approaches may fail to assess also argued that there is an urgency in developing students' evaluative judgment. Students need to be able to make a judgment of the quality of work generated by AI, themselves, or others. Making a judgment of quality includes not only determining if the information is hallucinated (Bearman et al., 2024). When incorporating these new learning outcomes, constructive alignment can serve as the theoretical framework that underpins the redesign and evaluation of AI-integrated assessments. Constructive alignment can also ensure that AI-driven assessment solutions do not undermine but rather enhance academic integrity, equity, and sustainability in education. Academics can leverage AI to enhance students' engagement with the learning materials, promote higher-order thinking and evaluative judgment, and support reflective learning, reinforcing deep learning rather than rote memorization. For example, AI-generated feedback can be aligned with formative assessment strategies to provide real-time, tailored support for students. Similarly, AI-assisted adaptive learning systems can ensure assessments remain aligned with students' evolving competencies. Nevertheless, AI in assessment also presents risks such as students becoming overly reliant on AI-generated responses or facing challenges in maintaining academic integrity. Institutions must ensure that AI integration aligns with sound pedagogical objectives and preserves the core principles of constructive alignment. Constructively aligning learning outcomes with assessment ensures that AI tools are facilitators of learning rather than shortcuts that bypass critical learning processes.

5.3 AI and Equitable Assessment

Traditional assessment methods, such as standardized exams and manually graded assignments, provided structured evaluation frameworks but often suffered from grading inconsistencies, unconscious biases, and scalability issues (OECD, 2019). AI-driven assessment introduces opportunities to improve equity and sustainability by enabling adaptive learning experiences, real-time formative feedback, and automated grading, addressing persistent biases and disparities in access (Agostini & Picasso, 2024). These features can support more equitable learning environments, particularly for diverse student populations. However, AI tools cannot independently determine which fairness test or ethical standard applies in different assessment contexts. Decisions about what constitutes fairness, inclusivity, and appropriate use still rest with educators and institutions. Universities must remain critically reflective about how AI is used: Are efficiency gains undermining deeper educational values? Are AI tools being deployed in ways that reinforce or reduce inequities? AI should be viewed as a tool to enhance human judgment, not replace it (Ajjawi et al., 2023). Hence, having an understanding of inclusive and equitable pedagogical principles is imperative.

Equity in assessment refers to the principle that all students, regardless of their backgrounds, abilities, or access to resources, should have an equal opportunity to demonstrate their learning outcomes in a fair and just manner (Montenegro & Jankowski, 2020). In terms of assessment design, inclusive assessment emphasizes using fair and effective assessment to allow students to showcase their skills, knowledge, and comprehension (Hockings, 2010). Tai et al. (2023) argue that assessment should go beyond procedural notions of fairness that treat all students the same and reconsider traditional assessment assumptions so that diverse students are not disadvantaged by design choices. They emphasize that assessment should interact meaningfully with curriculum, learning processes, and the varied contexts in which students operate. Similarly, equitable assessment should also go beyond the fair use of methods and the measurement of learning to one that supports students' long-term development, employability, and self-efficacy.

In the age of AI, it is imperative that the design of assessment does not assume that all students start from the same position or ignore structural barriers such as digital access, cultural biases in AI training datasets, or systemic disadvantages faced by marginalized students. Jin et al. (2025) called for more equitable use of AI to avoid further educational divides. Thus, an ethical and equitable assessment framework must address these disparities by embedding inclusivity into assessment design rather than merely adapting existing models. This includes designing assessments that promote fairness, transparency, and inclusivity (Montenegro & Jankowski, 2020). Academics need to design and implement ways for students to use AI tools to reflect diverse learners, including those from underrepresented backgrounds, students with disabilities, and non-native speakers. Institutions need to ensure that all students, regardless of socioeconomic status, have access to AI-enabled learning resources to minimize disparities in technological access and digital literacy (OECD, 2019). Institutions should conduct regular audits of AI-assisted grading and feedback systems to ensure fairness and reliability in assessment outcomes. AI tools must undergo continuous evaluation to ensure they do not reinforce systemic biases. Algorithmic bias occurs when AI models reflect and reinforce existing inequalities in the data they are trained on (QAA, 2023). Institutions must implement robust testing and auditing procedures to identify and mitigate biases in AI-driven assessment tools. Strategies such as explainable AI models, regular algorithmic evaluations, and human oversight in grading can ensure that AI systems do not disproportionately disadvantage specific student groups. It is important for universities to establish policies that define the role of AI in assessment and grading and ensure that human evaluators review AI-generated scores to prevent errors or biases. AI should augment rather than replace human judgment in assessment (Ajjawi et al., 2023).

Second, for an inclusive assessment design, AI-driven or integrated assessments must take into consideration cultural and linguistic inclusivity. AI models often perform better in certain languages and cultural contexts, which can lead to disparities in assessment outcomes for non-native speakers (Montenegro & Jankowski, 2020). To address this, AI-driven assessments should incorporate language adaptation features, offer multilingual support, and allow for culturally relevant assessment design. Additionally, institutions should ensure that students receive guidance on how AI-generated feedback aligns with their specific learning environments and expectations. One key strategy is the provision of institutional support and infrastructure to guarantee equal access to AI tools. Universities should offer AI training programs, access to AI-powered assessment platforms, and guidelines on ethical AI use to prevent biases in assessment outcomes. Universal design principles that accommodate diverse learners, including those with disabilities and non-native speakers, with features such as real-time speech-to-text transcription and adaptive learning tools, can make assessments more accessible (Archer et al., 2014).

However, it is important to note that the boundary of the ethical use of AI in assessment is unclear. Corbin et al. (2025) argue that defining the acceptable boundaries of AI use is challenging, as both students and faculty struggle to determine the ethical "line" for AI-generated work. The lack of institutional clarity will lead to self-defined ethical AI use among students, who often equate AI-assisted work with traditional tools like spellcheckers. To address this, institutions should establish clear guidelines that balance the benefits of AI with concerns over academic integrity. In addition, to support academics who face ethical dilemmas in enforcing AI policies, with many experiencing emotional burdens and uncertainty in assessing AI-assisted work, Corbin et al. (2025) propose a dynamic educational boundaries model (DEBM) that emphasizes discipline-specific ethical AI policies, assessment-embedded boundaries, and educator support. For instance, instead of outright bans, assessment design should guide students on when and how AI can be used. More efforts are required to design equitable pedagogical structures rather than relying on restrictive policies.

5.4 AI and Sustainable Assessment

Sustainable assessment refers to assessment practices that not only meet the immediate educational needs but also extend beyond immediate certification, equipping students with the ability to continue learning autonomously throughout their lives, equipping them with the skills needed for future learning (Boud, 2000; Boud & Soler, 2016). This perspective shifts assessment from being a mechanism for grading to an essential part of fostering lifelong learning capabilities. Boud and Soler (2016) highlight that sustainable assessment must focus on self-regulation, informed judgment, and long-term capability development. Traditional assessment models, which primarily focus on measuring students' immediate knowledge, often fail to equip learners for future challenges. Instead, sustainable assessment integrates authentic tasks, formative feedback loops, and student involvement in assessment design to ensure learners develop critical evaluative skills applicable beyond formal education.

This notion of current and future needs becomes more important now than ever as tasks are increasingly AI-related. Tasks that can be automated are being automated. As reported by the World Economic Forum (2025), jobs such as clerical workers, administrative assistants, accountants, auditors, executive secretaries, and printing workers are declining. As such, skill sets related to those jobs will soon be obsolete. On the other hand, by 2030, jobs fueled by technological advancements such as robotics and AI are expected to have higher demand. The most sought-after skills by employers currently are analytical skills, resilience, flexibility and agility, leadership and social influence, creative thinking, motivation, and self-awareness. In the next five years, the same report forecasted the most sought-after skills to be AI and big data, networks and cybersecurity, technological literacy, creative thinking, resilience, flexibility, and agility. As universities prepare for the future workforce, they need to align their practices to ensure that students are prepared for immediate needs while also ensuring that they can continue to contribute to the workforce in the coming decades. The skills they learn may not all be useful, as some may become obsolete as the world advances. By developing students to have the skills to continuously self-assess their needs and pursue learning, their contribution as a productive workforce can be sustainable. Nevertheless, assessment integrated with AI presents both opportunities and challenges for sustainable assessment. On one hand, AI can provide personalized feedback, scalability, and efficiency in formative assessments, helping students engage in continuous learning. On the other hand, if not carefully designed, AI assessments risk reinforcing narrow, standardized measures of learning that undermine self-regulation and reflective practice (Boud & Soler, 2016). Hence, the design of sustainable assessments must be flexible and future-focused, ensuring that students develop the skills necessary to navigate an AI-enhanced academic and professional landscape.

5.5 The Experience at Taylor's University

As professionals supporting AI-integrated assessment reform at Taylor's University, the authors collaborated with over 200 academics across various disciplines. This section draws on practical insights from these engagements, outlining key challenges, institutional responses, and implications for higher education institutions navigating AI adoption. Taylor's University is a private university located in Malaysia. When AI became more widely accessible with ChatGPT in 2023, the university published a position paper affirming its stance to embrace AI through a whole-community approach. A generative AI task force was established to explore AI's impact on teaching, learning, assessment, and academic integrity. The authors led a series of workshops to support academics in adopting AI ethically and responsibly in assessment. The authors co-curated the workshop with academics, listening to their opinions on students' (mis)use of AI, academics' challenges and knowledge gaps, and their aspirations for how AI can be leveraged to further elevate the quality of assessment practices. Co-curating materials brought several advantages. First, academics can contribute discipline-specific knowledge as they emphasize the importance of seeing AI from a disciplinary lens. Second, academics gain a sense of ownership as they see their concerns being addressed in the workshops. The final and arguably most crucial advantage of involving academics is that they become advocates for promoting the design of assessments with AI in mind. We also benchmarked several universities, including Monash University, University College London, and the National University of Singapore, to identify good practices.

A total of nine workshops were conducted, involving more than 200 academics from various disciplines. The workshops covered several topics, including introducing trends in assessment in the age of AI, principles of good assessment design from the lens of AI, revisiting learning outcomes, designing assessment tasks, and grading. Academics worked in groups and presented their ideas on how they would design their assessments. Some academics implemented their assessment design. In the designing process, academics revisited their assessment design through the lens of equitable and sustainable assessment. Table 5.1 highlights considerations for equitable assessment integrated with AI, while Table 5.2 lists considerations for sustainable assessment integrated with AI.

TABLE 5.1

Considerations on Equitable Assessment Integrated with AI

Assessment Design Stages	Considerations
Planning	a) Prepare students with the skills and knowledge to use Gen AI effectively in academic, professional, and societal contexts. b) Ensure students understand the significance, strengths, and limitations of Gen AI in their learning.
Designing	a) Determine AI tools that meet the specific needs of assessment tasks or disciplines. b) Ensure students have access to the recommended AI tools. c) Provide resources for students to use AI tools before attempting the assessment tasks. d) Ensure adequate opportunities for feedback throughout their learning. e) Diversify assessment formats to allow students to demonstrate learning through different modes of expression.
Implementing and monitoring	a) Provide clear communication on how students can or cannot use AI in completing assessment tasks. b) Provide opportunities for students to reflect in action as they complete the assessment tasks. c) Discuss the concerns and challenges that arise to build trust and shared understanding and expectations regarding the use of AI for assessment tasks and disciplines. d) Ensure that students are informed of the risks, biases, and data privacy issues in using AI tools.

TABLE 5.2

Considerations in Sustainability When Designing Assessment Integrated with AI

Assessment Design Stages	Considerations
Planning	a) Ensure that the assessment plan promotes lifelong learning. b) Identify the unassisted human abilities that students need to demonstrate. c) Determine the skills and knowledge that can be achieved collaboratively with other students or Gen AI. d) Determine the relevance of learning outcomes in the age of AI.
Designing	a) Design assessment tasks to highlight authentic human knowledge, skill demonstrations, and critical engagement. b) Emphasize on skills that prepare students for future work. c) Provide opportunities for students to reflect on their joint human and AI interaction. d) Ensure assessment tasks are meaningful and reflect real-world needs. e) Emphasize assessing learning processes rather than final products.
Implementing and monitoring	a) Communicate explicitly how students should document, acknowledge, and reference their use of AI. b) Monitor students' use of AI whenever possible to ensure that they are not overly reliant on AI.

5.6 Principles of Designing Sustainable and Equitable Assessments in the Age of AI

Based on the consolidated literature on AI in assessment and insights gained from institutional practice, including workshops conducted on AI in assessment at Taylor's University, the authors established six guiding principles for designing assessments integrated with AI. These principles complement principles of assessment design for higher education (QAA, 2018) and explicitly consider equity and sustainability. The six principles are intended to support academics across the full assessment process at the planning, designing, implementing, and monitoring stages when integrating AI into assessment practices. Figure 5.1 shows an overview of these six principles.

Principle 1: Ethical and authentic engagement with AI: Promote student engagement in AI through assessments to uphold ethical standards and demonstrate practical, real-world applications relevant to their field of study.

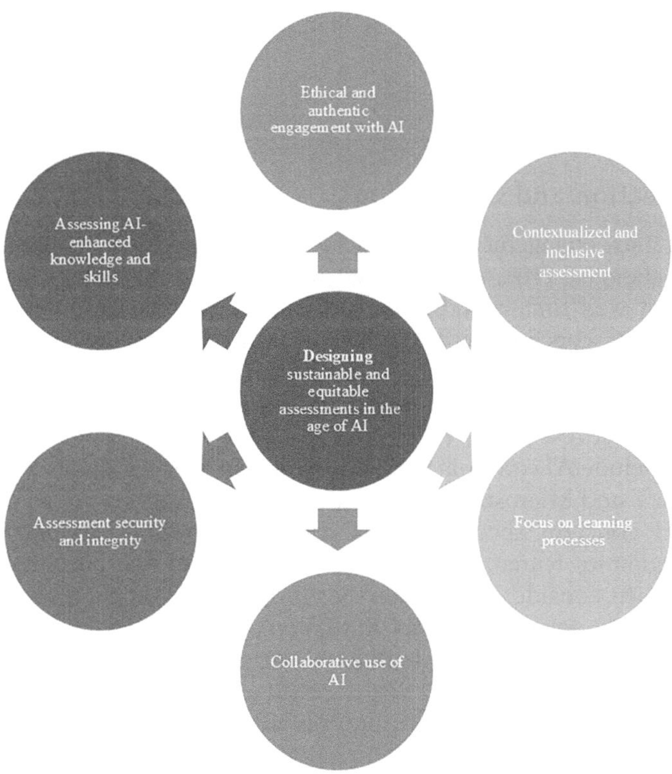

FIGURE 5.1
Principles of designing equitable and sustainable assessment in the age of AI.

Principle 2: Contextualized and inclusive assessment: Create tasks that are inclusive of diverse learner backgrounds, discipline-specific, and aligned with program learning outcomes, ensuring assessments are meaningful and reflective of diverse learning contexts.

Principle 3: Focus on learning processes: Design assessments that evaluate the process of learning, encouraging students to critically analyze and thoughtfully use AI as part of their development processes.

Principle 4: Collaborative use of AI: Incorporate opportunities for students to work collaboratively with peers and AI, fostering teamwork and critical engagement in assessment tasks.

Principle 5: Assessment security and integrity: Implement rigorous and robust security measures at key stages to verify the authenticity of student submissions and ensure fairness in evaluation and academic progression.

Principle 6: Assessing AI-enhanced knowledge and skills: Evaluate students on their ability to navigate an AI-driven world, focusing on competencies such as critical thinking, the ethical use of AI, and the contextual application of AI-generated work.

5.7 Reflection and Conclusion

Through our engagement with academics, the authors identified three major challenges. First, many lacked foundational AI literacy when AI in assessment was first introduced. Although seminars were conducted for academics, misconceptions and a lack of awareness of how AI may impact assessment practices hindered academics from experimenting with AI. Technological literacy among academics varies; with some requiring more support. To address this, we reflected and adjusted the content of the workshops to include AI concepts and hands-on activities using AI chatbots such as ChatGPT and Microsoft CoPilot.

Second, concerns about academic dishonesty among students emerged. Some academics feared AI use would compromise the fairness of assessments. Hence, considerable time in the workshop was spent discussing practices around AI detection and the limitations of AI detection software.

Third, academics expressed anxiety over skill loss among students, particularly critical thinking and writing skills, if they depend on AI to complete assessment tasks. Concerning critical thinking, students may accept content generated by AI without critically examining if there are any biases or hallucinations. In writing skills, overdependence on AI may lessen students' voice in the final piece.

These three challenges point to the need for increased AI literacy as well as strengthening the principles of equitable and sustainable assessment design.

Our experience in promoting AI in assessment, supported by the body of knowledge present in the literature point to two major implications. First, there is a need to support academic-led, evidence-based practices to ensure AI integration is relevant to the local context, practical, inclusive, and effective. As the integration of AI in assessment is highly contextualized, considering interpretations of equitable and sustainable assessment that fit local narratives is crucial. For instance, a private university with a high number of international students may have a different take on equitable and sustainable assessment compared to public universities in Malaysia that cater mainly to local students. Second, working closely with academics in revising relevant policies and conducting professional development programs is important, as they are the practitioners of AI in assessment. Involving academics from the early stages builds shared commitment and trust, enabling open, transparent, and progressive communication within the university community. Given that AI is fast evolving, institutions must create adaptive policies and professional development ecosystems that evolve with technological advancements, ensuring higher education remains responsive, equitable, and future-ready.

References

Agostini, D., & Picasso, F. (2024). Large language models for sustainable assessment and feedback in higher education: Towards a pedagogical and technological framework. *Intelligenza Artificiale, 18*(2024), 121–138.

Ajjawi, R., Tai, J., Boud, D., & Jorre de St Jorre, T. (Eds.). (2023). *Assessment for Inclusion in Higher Education: Promoting Equity and Social Justice in Assessment* (1st ed.). Routledge. https://doi.org/10.4324/9781003293101

Archer, E., Chetty, Y. B., & Prinsloo, P. (2014). Benchmarking the habitus of equitable assessment in higher education: A social realist perspective. *Higher Education Research & Development, 33*(5), 1024–1037.

Bearman, M., Nieminen, J. H., & Ajjawi, R. (2023). Designing assessment in a digital world: An organising framework. *Assessment & Evaluation in Higher Education, 48*(3), 291–304. https://doi.org/10.1080/02602938.2022.2069674

Bearman, M., Tai, J., Dawson, P., Boud, D., & Ajjawi, R. (2024). Developing evaluative judgement for a time of generative artificial intelligence. *Assessment & Evaluation in Higher Education, 49*(6), 893–905. https://doi.org/10.1080/02602938.2024.2335321

Biggs, J., & Tang, C. (2011). *Teaching for Quality Learning at University*. McGraw-Hill Education.

Boud, D. (2000). Sustainable assessment: Rethinking assessment for the learning society. *Studies in Continuing Education, 22*(2), 151–167.

Boud, D., & Soler, R. (2016). Sustainable assessment revisited. *Assessment & Evaluation in Higher Education, 41*(3), 400–413.

Corbin, L., et al. (2025). Where's the line? It's an absurd line: Towards a framework for acceptable uses of AI in assessment. *Journal of Assessment Ethics, 12*(1), 56–78.

Farazouli, A., Cerratto-Pargman, T., Bolander-Laksov, K., & McGrath, C. (2024). Hello GPT! Goodbye home examination? An exploratory study of AI chatbots impact on university teachers' assessment practices. *Assessment & Evaluation in Higher Education, 49*(3), 363–375. https://doi.org/10.1080/02602938.2023.2241676

Hockings, C. (2010). *Inclusive Learning and Teaching in Higher Education: A Synthesis of Research*. Higher Education Academy.

Jin, Y., Yan, L., Echeverria, V., Gašević, D., & Martinez-Maldonado, R. (2025). Generative AI in higher education: A global perspective of institutional adoption policies and guidelines. *Computers and Education: Artificial Intelligence, 8*, 100348. https://doi.org/10.1016/j.caeai.2024.100348

Liu, D. (2024, September 12). *Program Level Assessment Design and the Two-Lane Approach—Teaching@Sydney*. https://educational-innovation.sydney.edu.au/teaching@sydney/program-level-assessment-two-lane/

Montenegro, E., & Jankowski, N. (2020). *Equity and assessment: Moving towards culturally responsive assessment*. National Institute for Learning Outcomes Assessment (NILOA).

Moorhouse, B. L., Yeo, M. A., & Wan, Y. (2023). Generative AI tools and assessment: Guidelines of the world's top-ranking universities. *Computers and Education Open, 5*, 100151. https://doi.org/10.1016/j.caeo.2023.100151

OECD. (2019). *Measuring equity in education: Meeting the challenge of accountability in a globalized world*. Organisation for Economic Co-operation and Development.

OECD. (2024, August 13). *The potential impact of Artificial Intelligence on equity and inclusion in education*. OECD. https://www.oecd.org/en/publications/the-potential-impact-of-artificial-intelligence-on-equity-and-inclusion-in-education_15df715b-en.html

Perkins, M., Furze, L., Roe, J., & MacVaugh, J. (2024). The Artificial Intelligence Assessment Scale (AIAS): A framework for ethical integration of generative AI in educational assessment. *Journal of University Teaching and Learning Practice, 21*(06), Article 06. https://doi.org/10.53761/q3azde36

QAA. (2018). *UK quality code, advice and guidance: Assessment*. https://www.qaa.ac.uk/the-quality-code/2018/advice-and-guidance-18/assessment

Quality Assurance Agency for Higher Education (QAA). (2023). *Guidance on the use of AI in higher education assessments*. QAA.

Russell Group. (2023). *New principles on use of AI in education*. https://russellgroup.ac.uk/news/new-principles-on-use-of-ai-in-education

Tai, J., Ajjawi, R., Bearman, M., Boud, D., Dawson, P., & Jorre, T. J. de S. (2023). Assessment for inclusion: Rethinking contemporary strategies in assessment design. *Higher Education Research & Development*. https://www.tandfonline.com/doi/abs/10.1080/07294360.2022.2057451

TEQSA. (2024). *Gen AI strategies for Australian higher education: Emerging practice*. https://www.teqsa.gov.au/sites/default/files/2024-11/Gen-AI-strategies-emerging-practice-toolkit.pdf

Tertiary Education Quality and Standards Agency. (2023). *Assessment reform for the age of artificial intelligence*. https://www.teqsa.gov.au/guides-resources/resources/corporate-publications/assessment-reform-age-artificial-intelligence

UNESCO. (2021). *AI competency framework for educators and learners*. United Nations Educational, Scientific and Cultural Organization.

Weng, X., Xia, Q., Gu, M., Rajaram, K., & Chiu, T. K. F. (2024). Assessment and learning outcomes for generative AI in higher education: A scoping review on current research status and trends. *Australasian Journal of Educational Technology, 40*(6), Article 6. https://doi.org/10.14742/ajet.9540

World Economic Forum. (2025). *The future of jobs report 2025*. https://www.weforum.org/publications/the-future-of-jobs-report-2025/

Yeo, M. A. (2023). Academic integrity in the age of Artificial Intelligence (AI) authoring apps. *TESOL Journal, 14*(3), e716. https://doi.org/10.1002/tesj.716

6

AI Ethics in Education

Wai Leong Pang, Hui Hwang Goh, Yee Wei Sim,
Intan Izafina Idrus, Hafisoh Ahmad,
Kah Yoong Chan, and Gwo Chin Chung

6.1 Introduction: AI's Role in Education

Artificial intelligence (AI) is implemented in various solutions, such as in health, agriculture, communications, and so on (Barakat et al., 2023, 2024; You et al., 2022). AI leverages existing data to simulate human intelligence, enabling the rapid execution of diverse tasks. AI is widely used in image generation, problem-solving, script drafting, proofreading, learning, decision-making, providing data-driven suggestions, image and video generation, and so on. AI has impacted conventional education and offered educators tools like ChatGPT, Co-pilot, Gemini, and DeepSeek to carry out various tasks, such as preparing teaching materials, publications, proposals, plans, solutions, examination questions, data analyses, and reports (Stolpe & Hallström, 2024). Figure 6.1 illustrates the use of generative AI in education. Similarly, image generation AI tools like DALL-E and Midjourney are widely used to produce high-quality, professional images for various purposes according to the requirements given (Bond et al., 2024). As shown in Figure 6.2, video generation AI tools like Pictory and Vyond are highly popular for producing videos according to preset requirements within a short period.

Generative AI tools are widely adopted, particularly by learners who utilize them for homework, assignments, and reports. AI has transformed conventional education (Peters & Green, 2024). Generative AI that is good at content creation allows educators and learners to prepare teaching materials, plans, proposals, reports, data analyses, image processing, image generation, and technical reports. AI makes things run smoother and improves how learners learn. One of the big pluses is how it can create personalized learning paths, adapting to different needs and learning styles.

Learners with disabilities can utilize generative AI to strengthen their studies. Functions like text-to-speech, real-time translation, and data analysis can help the learners study at their own pace (Bond et al., 2024).

 DOI: 10.1201/9781003633433-6

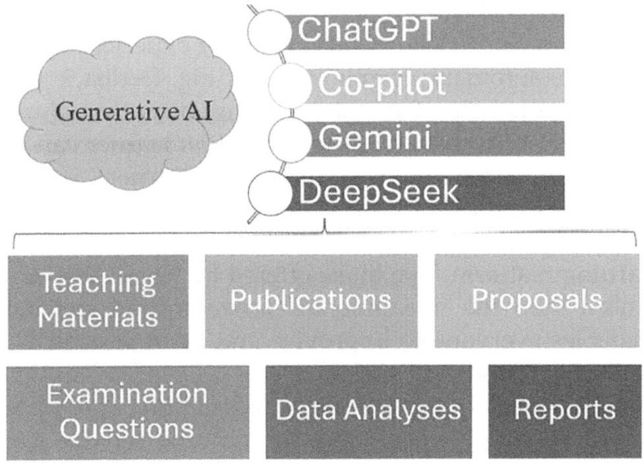

FIGURE 6.1
The usage of generative AI in education.

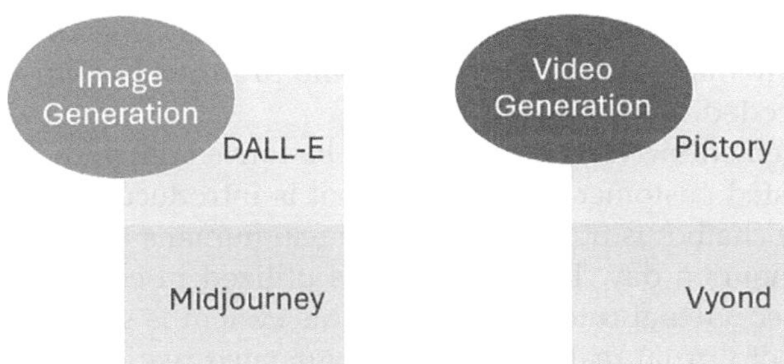

FIGURE 6.2
The AI tools for image and video generation.

Furthermore, educators can utilize AI to assist in grading assignments and practical reports. AI can be used to analyze the learners' performance, track their attendance and coursework submission status, and generate a report on the strengths and weaknesses of their learners. Educators can give immediate support to weak learners to strengthen their learning progress and ensure they receive a personalized learning experience that will benefit them in their study progress (Ayeni et al., 2024).

Various online learning platforms are created to allow learners to progress and learn at their own pace. Smart digital tools that use machine learning (ML) and AI algorithms are integrated to assist learners in accessing and harvesting knowledge. Instant assessments and feedback can be given to the learners in order to have a personalized learning experience. Various administrative tasks like automatic enrollment, grading, feedback, and comments can be done with the help of AI. This can significantly reduce the burden on educators. The performance of the individual learner can be monitored closely with the advancement of AI. Individual learners' performances can be analyzed, and personalized learning plans can be custom-made accordingly (Ayeni et al., 2024). AI enables smart tutoring systems to be deployed on the e-learning platform, like those offered by Khan Academy, which are more advanced than the conventional classroom and suited for working adults. AI enables everyone to improvise and learn effectively at any time and progress daily (Bond et al., 2024).

There are drawbacks to using AI in education. The system requires continuous enhancement to ensure a smooth and reliable learning experience for the learners, despite the high implementation cost. Extensive training is needed for all training providers and educators to master these AI systems (Ayeni et al., 2024). The relationship between the learners and training providers is lost due to a lack of close interaction. This unhealthy relationship limits the development of the learners' soft skills. The care and warm relationship between the educators and learners is easier to cultivate through existing physical lessons in the classroom. An enhanced framework to integrate AI in education and preserve human interaction is urgently needed.

Automated online virtual tutoring can be carried out with AI technology. The automated customer feedback chatbot is introduced through AI technology. The chatbot is utilized to replace real humans to provide customer service 24 hours a day. The same idea is utilized in education to provide an automated virtual tutoring system. This system is strengthened by the integration of virtual reality (VR) and augmented reality (AR). The knowledge transfer process can be delivered effectively with VR or AR. These significantly enhance learners' interest in harvesting knowledge. It also benefits the part-time learner who is working; they can learn at any time during their free time. However, the learner needs to invest in AR and VR tools and remain connected in order to carry out the learning activities. The learner also needs to carry out the learning activities alone without communicating with educators and course mates.

6.2 Current Applications of AI in Education

Ethics is important in deploying AI in education. Educators and system developers need to integrate AI into education ethically. The protection of the learners' information and privacy and the fairness of the decisions made by the AI education system are gaining extensive attention nowadays. Extra effort is needed to deploy AI with minimal negative impact on ethics, higher trust, and fairness and, at the same time, demonstrate its full capability and potential in education. The system administrators are responsible for protecting the learners' data and carrying out the e-learning safely with the help of AI. Educators are expected to use AI wisely and with high ethics in building the content, carrying out the learning activities, and evaluating the assessment components. Learners are also expected to do the same in carrying out the learning activities and preparing their assignments and learning tasks ethically when using AI (Castelló-Sirvent et al., 2024). Sufficient effort should be given by the academics and learners in learning, instead of blindly using the content generated by AI tools without ethics. The use of AI in education should strengthen the learning experiences, assist in learning activities, and provide insightful ideas for completing the assignments assigned to the learners. Figure 6.3 shows the various online tools, such as Turnitin, Scribbr, QuillBot, and ZeroGPT, that are used to detect the contents generated by the AI tools (Castelló-Sirvent et al., 2024). However, the accuracy of these tools in detecting AI-generated content is not promising. The educators should use AI ethically in preparing the learning content, assessment components, marking, and assessment, with the ultimate goal of enhancing the learning experience and ensuring fair learning opportunities for the learners.

The major ethical concern in implementing AI in education is data privacy protection. Extra effort is needed to protect sensitive learners' information

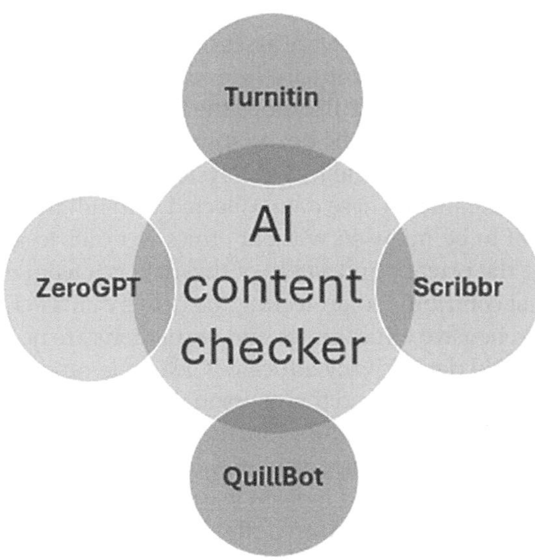

FIGURE 6.3
The tools used to detect the content generated by the AI tools.

from unauthorized access by illegal parties. Another challenging issue is ensuring fairness when performing data analyses using AI, which is still considered a "black box" (Khreisat, 2024). The decision or conclusion made by the AI system through the data analyses relies heavily on the amount of data fed to train the AI system. The training data used should be real without any modification or changes in order to preserve the true and raw data, which has a direct impact on the accuracy of the decision or conclusion in real deployment. This is to ensure that the AI system can generate a transparent, accurate, and understandable decision or conclusion. The AI system fails to generate fair and accurate decisions or conclusions if edited data is used during the training process.

A balance between AI and educators is needed to enable trust in the results analyzed by the AI system and to study these data to improve the learning experience of the learners (Ayeni et al., 2024). Educators should learn and master the operational logic of the AI system in order to appreciate and utilize the reports generated by the AI system. The educators should have control of the AI system to rectify abnormal or unreasonable operations. The reports generated by the AI system should be verified and approved by the educators to prevent them from fully depending on the AI system and losing the ability to evaluate the learners' performance in the long run. This also ensures that the learning activities can be carried out without interruption if the AI system is malfunctioning or down for maintenance.

Due to the limitations and mutuality of the AI system in education, wrong diagnostics may be generated in the learners' assignment work. A creative and out-of-the-normal model solution may be graded wrongly and unfairly by the AI grading system due to the absence of the preset model answers. Furthermore, the AI grading system will update the assessment outcome automatically without interference from the academics in the e-learning system, which causes the unfair grading to be captured. It also stops the learners from providing creative solutions and thinking outside the box to solve the problems.

Furthermore, the data collected by AI systems has significant commercial value to all tech companies. These data collected through the education system have the potential to be misused without ethics in order to gain valuable fortunes. Protecting the privacy and safety of this data is a team effort, and all the stakeholders must contribute to protecting the data by cross-checking the team members. Comprehensive ethical rules and regulations are needed for learning institutions to uphold data privacy ethically. Clear rules and regulations enable all the stakeholders to understand their personal responsibility and follow them strictly without compromising ethics (Burriss et al., 2024). All the stakeholders should be well trained on the responsibilities of each personnel member to protect data ethically when using AI tools in learning activities. All parties should sign a nondisclosure agreement to strengthen the protection through law.

The system developer should design AI solutions with stringent data protection in the first place to guarantee data privacy. The system owner also needs to emphasize the importance of providing data protection and fairness in the AI-integrated education system to the system developer. The system owner is required to carry out an extensive evaluation of the AI-integrated education system delivered in various conditions and scenarios in order to ensure the reliability of the AI-embedded education system. The system owner also needs to carry out audits and monitor the AI system closely when it is live and online to ensure the system protects the data and operates ethically without bias as designed. Early rectification can be done if there is any violation of data security, ethics, and fairness. This is a necessary effort to uphold the ethical use of AI in education.

The integration and usage of AI in education are unavoidable, and ethical protection is urgently needed (Al-Zahrani & Alasmari, 2024). Cooperation among stakeholders is needed in order to deploy an ethical AI-powered education solution. Continued effort, research, and investment are needed to strengthen AI solutions. Stakeholders can benefit from technological evolution and significantly motivate learners to pursue knowledge. This is a quantum-leap transformation in education, and all stakeholders will benefit from it.

6.3 Ethical Considerations for AI Deployment in Education

The major ethical issues of AI integration in education are data protection and privacy (Yu, 2024). Learners may misuse the generative AI tools to prepare the assignments, lab reports, and theses, which breaches plagiarism standards and diverts from the learning purposes (Castelló-Sirvent et al., 2024). Various personal data are protected under the Personal Data Protection Act (PDPA) such as personal data, learning records, examination results, and individual learner learning progress and trends. Educational institutions need to protect these data from any abuse and illegal usage according to the PDPA. Actions should be taken strictly by the authorities against any organization that breaches the PDPA. The parties that fail to obey the PDPA are subject to penalties and are accountable for their misconduct.

The Institute for Ethical AI in Education has identified the risks of using AI in education. The institute has proposed a framework to address the ethical concerns in deploying AI in education. A clear guideline is proposed for application decisions and procurement processes made by the stakeholders to uphold the ethical usage of AI. The government and civil servants should be cultivated with the implication of ethical usage of AI solutions. The institute also stated the importance of blending AI in education in order to provide sustainable, high-quality lifelong learning. Collaborative effort is needed globally from all to enhance AI solutions and long-term strategies in promoting the ethical use of AI in education.

Figure 6.4 shows the risks identified by the institute, which are the obstacles to AI integration in education. Discrimination may happen to some

FIGURE 6.4
The risks of using AI in education.

learners due to the preexisting bias in the training data collected, which contributes to the inaccurate outcomes produced by AI solutions. The massive amount of information in the system poses high risks to data privacy and security, with a high potential for cyberattacks and security lapses from the viruses or hacker attacks. Most of the stakeholders have limited knowledge of the complicated AI operations that create transparency and accountability challenges. Furthermore, the deployment of AI solutions has significantly reduced human involvement in decision-making, data analysis, critical thinking, and problem-solving skills. The major challenge is to uphold the ethical use of AI among the stakeholders without plagiarism violations in carrying out various learning activities in education.

Figure 6.5 shows a network architecture with high security and reliability for AI in education to protect the valuable data collected by AI solutions from hackers or cyberattacks. All users are connected to the internal firewall through the network switch. The internal firewall is responsible for screening and filtering the harmful traffic from accessing the servers. The internal firewall will protect the servers from internal network attacks. The servers are accessible through the server switch and are protected by the second

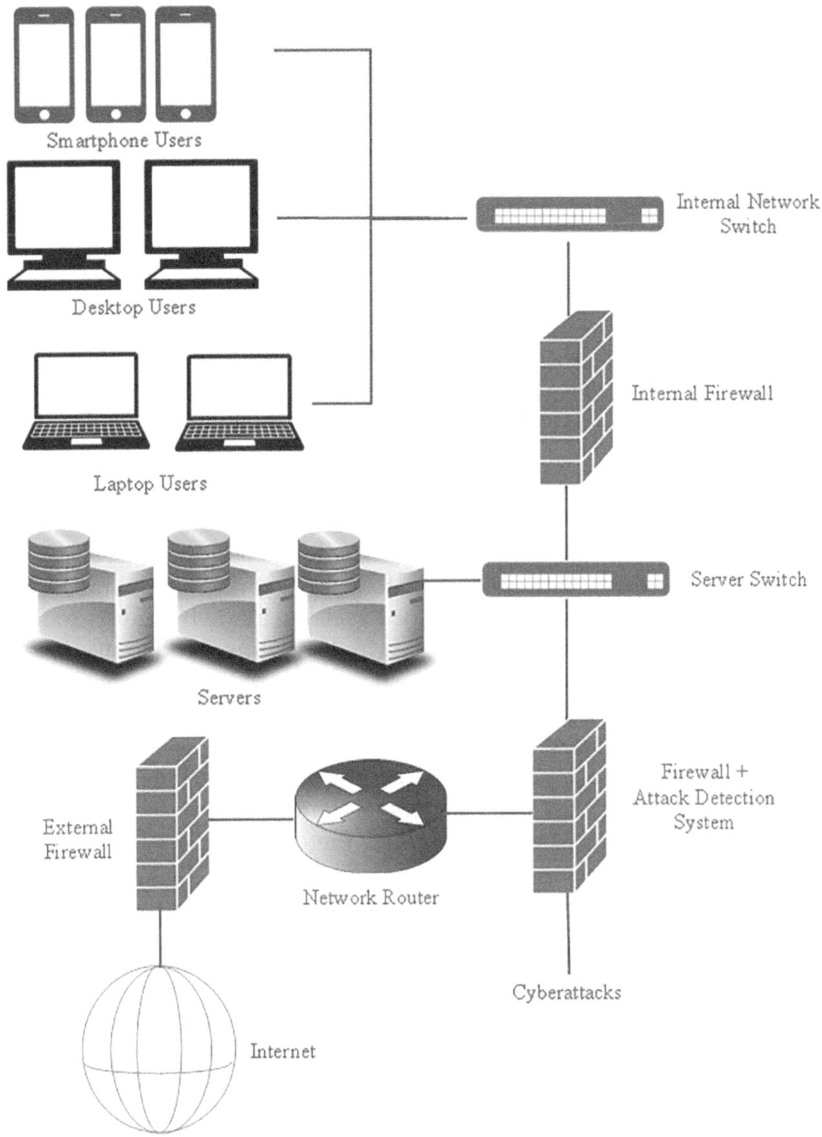

FIGURE 6.5
The block diagram of a secure and reliable network architecture.

firewall that comes with the attack detection system. It will protect the servers and internal networks from unfriendly external cyberattacks. The last firewall will protect the network from any suspicious or malicious cyberattacks that escape the external firewall in order to strengthen the network security (Chuan et al., 2021, 2023).

The immature AI education solutions have a high possibility of operating with bias and unfairness (Ayeni et al., 2024). The data may be wrongly analyzed based on the raw data collected. For example, wrong analytics may happen due to the learners' information, such as gender, race, address, and socioeconomic status used in AI analyses. The AI solutions may recommend the wrong recipients for the scholarships, make inappropriate course recommendations, or produce biased recruitment of the learners into the program due to their particulars.

Another hot topic is the accountability and responsibility of AI solutions once any mistake or misconduct happens. For example, the AI misevaluated the performance of the applicant, which caused the rejection of the scholarship application and contributed to the delay in his study. A clear accountability framework is urgently needed (Stolpe & Hallström, 2024). The system owner and developer are accountable and responsible for any misconduct and data leaks (Khreisat, 2024). They are required to protect the data as required by the PDPA.

The data processing must be performed transparently to gain the trust of the stakeholders. The stakeholders will lose confidence in the results generated by AI tools without transparency. All stakeholders must be able to examine and evaluate the results or decisions made by the AI tools. For example, educators should be able to verify the recommendations or results generated by the AI tools based on the data collected. The learners can also do the same to verify the results accordingly in order to make the AI system trustworthy and traceable.

As shown in Figure 6.6, the AI systems should grant administrative rights and permissions to the system owners, system administrators, and educators. These people can evaluate or update the outputs, decisions, results, or conclusions made by the AI systems. Learners and parents have the right to check and verify these outputs, decisions, results, or conclusions (Nguyen

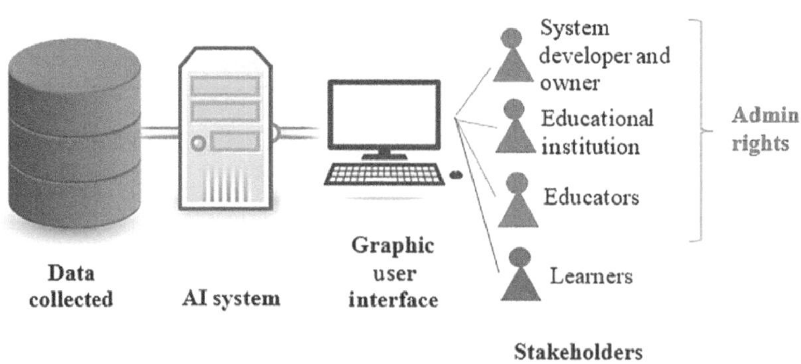

FIGURE 6.6
The architecture of the AI system in education.

et al., 2023). The learners are allowed to review the results and reports generated by AI with their educators. Extra attention and guidance should be given by educators to junior or weak learners to enhance their learning progress. It is important to maintain conventional physical learning activities for the junior learners who need more care and assistance at the early stage. Regular review and discussion between the learners and educators are necessary to ensure the effectiveness of the AI learning system and that all the learners achieve the learning outcomes. Extra effort and guidance are needed for the learners who struggle to achieve the learning outcomes in order to make sure these groups of learners progress through the extra physical learning activities. Table 6.1 shows the roles of the stakeholders in deploying AI in education.

Educators should engage the learners to discuss and review the reports generated by the AI systems with them in order to ensure that the AI education system can never replace the existing education system with its personal touch and care. Weak and junior learners who require extra care and attention will benefit from the physical learning activities.

TABLE 6.1

The Roles of the Stakeholders in Deploying AI in Education

Stakeholders	Roles and Responsibilities
System Developers	• Develop AI tools with high data privacy and security for education. • Provide technical support and training for educators and learners. • Work closely with educational institutions and stakeholders to improve AI solutions in fairness, security, and reliability.
Educational Institutions	• Monitor closely the implementation progress of AI ethics in education. • Enforce the policies and procedures for the implementation of AI in education. • Conduct regular audits to ensure the ethical use of AI in education. • Work closely with various stakeholders to improve the security and performance of the AI solutions.
Educators	• Work closely with the stakeholders to design ethical AI systems for education. • Deploy the AI solutions in the learning activities and the curriculum. • Cultivate the learners to utilize the AI solutions ethically and effectively.
Learners	• Practice the ethical use of the AI solutions in education. • Work closely with the stakeholders to provide feedback on the impact of the AI solutions deployed. • Monitor closely the results and analyses generated by AI solutions.
Policymakers	• Work closely with the stakeholders to design a holistic policy for the deployment of AI in education. • Promote the equitable opportunities to access the AI solutions. • Cultivate the ethical use and promote the research and development of AI in education.

6.4 Recommendations for Ethical AI Policies

The deployment of AI in education has advanced the education system. The world recognizes the importance of implementing AI in education, and various research efforts have been carried out to develop comprehensive policies to govern the rise of AI (Bond et al., 2024). However, the risks of the AI system include unethical misuse, data privacy issues, and inaccurate results. A holistic policy is urgently needed to govern the ethical use of AI systems in education to ensure fairness, transparency, accountability, and data privacy (Ayeni et al., 2024). As shown in Figure 6.7, policymakers must establish comprehensive rules and regulations that cover intensive accountability, transparency, and justice for all AI solutions. They will serve as clear guidelines for all stakeholders to safeguard the ethical deployment of AI in education. Data transparency and security are protected by the AI education system. Penalties for data misconduct and misuse are clearly outlined in the policy. Regular audits are needed to ensure all AI solutions operate according to the policies.

All stakeholders must have a sufficient understanding of the operations and fundamental processes of the AI system in generating the results and outputs to verify the fairness of the AI system. Comprehensive documentation and system access are required to allow the related stakeholders to examine and analyze the outputs generated by the AI system. The AI-generated reports are transparent, accessible, and explainable. The AI system owners are accountable for any data misconduct or unfair outcomes generated, and they need to strictly follow the legal procedures for data collection. They also need to implement a tight AI system security for data protection. All learners should be able to access the AI system to carry out their learning, especially those who are underprivileged.

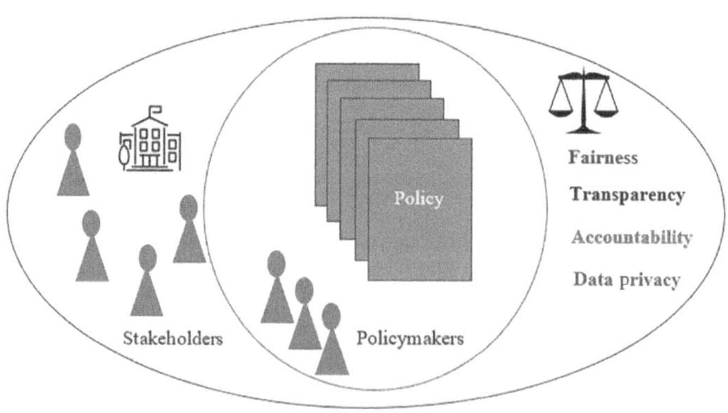

FIGURE 6.7
The policy for the deployment of AI in education.

The AI system developers should prioritize the ethical criteria and AI policies during the initial development process. Right from the beginning of development, we need to prioritize security and transparency. As shown in Figure 6.8, the goal is to build AI systems that are inherently secure, transparent, and fair. AI developers need to collaborate closely with everyone, such as educational institutions, educators, learners, policymakers, and ethicists (Khreisat, 2024). This collaboration will ensure we create ethical, reliable, and high-performing AI solutions that truly meet the specific needs of each educational institution, as they have a crucial responsibility to ensure ethical usage and compliance with all relevant AI policies. Regular workshops and discussions about the ethical implications of AI tools in education should be held for both educators and learners to raise awareness of the ethical usage of AI systems (Bond et al., 2024).

All data collected must be encrypted to keep the information safe. The data collection and storage methods are designed with strong security measures to protect this valuable information (Al-Zahrani & Alasmari, 2024). AI developers should provide clear and comprehensive documentation explaining exactly how the AI system works. This documentation will allow system administrators to easily monitor and check the system's performance. It is also important to have a user-friendly interface that allows the stakeholders to easily access and understand the information generated by the AI. Finally, educational institutions, as system owners, should regularly conduct ethical audits to ensure the system is performing reliably and ethically.

The core values of any good AI policy are fairness, transparency, and accountability. These values are crucial for ensuring AI is used ethically in education. All stakeholders, that is, AI developers, educational institutions, policymakers, and learners, need to work together to prioritize ethical AI

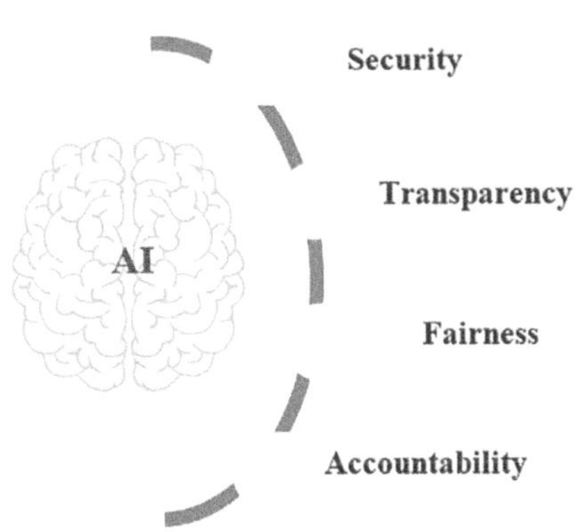

FIGURE 6.8
The ethical criteria of the AI system for education.

use and uphold strong moral principles. Ultimately, the AI systems we use in education must be trustworthy, transparent, and accessible to everyone.

6.5 Conclusion

The integration of AI in education has revolutionized traditional learning methodologies, offering powerful tools for both educators and learners. From personalized learning pathways to automated grading and administrative assistance, AI-driven solutions significantly enhance efficiency, accessibility, and engagement. The ability of AI to provide real-time feedback, adaptive learning, and smart tutoring has transformed the educational landscape, making learning more interactive, inclusive, and data driven. Despite its vast potential, AI implementation in education comes with ethical, financial, and social challenges. The high cost of deployment, continuous system enhancements, and the need for extensive training pose significant barriers. Additionally, concerns regarding data privacy, bias in AI-driven assessments, and the diminishing human interaction between educators and learners must be critically addressed. While AI can automate various aspects of education, it cannot replace the nuanced guidance, emotional support, and mentorship that human educators provide. A well-defined ethical framework and regulatory policies are essential to fully harness the benefits of AI while mitigating its risks. Transparent AI operations, accountability measures, and stringent data protection policies must be in place to ensure fairness, accuracy, and trust in AI-driven educational systems. Educators and learners must be equipped with the knowledge and skills to use AI responsibly, balancing its advantages with critical thinking and ethical considerations. Ultimately, AI should be seen as a complementary tool rather than a replacement for human educators. A well-balanced integration of AI that enhances learning efficiency while firmly upholding core educational values such as mentorship, collaboration, and critical thinking will be essential in shaping an ethical, sustainable, and transformative future for AI-driven education. Continuous research, stakeholder engagement, and policy refinement are necessary to ensure AI serves as an enabler of equitable, ethical, and effective learning experiences for all.

Acknowledgment

This research was supported by Taylor's University, Malaysia, through Taylor's Internal Research Grant Scheme—Impact Lab Grant (TIRGS-ILG/1/2024/SOE/001).

References

Al-Zahrani, A. M., & Alasmari, T. M. (2024). Exploring the impact of artificial intelligence on higher education: The dynamics of ethical, social, and educational implications. *Humanities and Social Sciences Communications*, *11*(1), 912. https://doi.org/10.1057/s41599-024-03432-4

Ayeni, O. O., Al Hamad, N. M., Chisom, O. N., Osawaru, B., & Adewusi, O. E. (2024). AI in education: A review of personalized learning and educational technology. *GSC Advanced Research and Reviews*, *18*(2), 261–271. https://doi.org/10.30574/gscarr.2024.18.2.0062

Barakat, M., Chung, G. C., Lee, I. E., Pang, W. L., & Chan, K. Y. (2023). Detection and sizing of durian using zero-shot deep learning models. *International Journal of Technology*, *14*(6), 1206–1215. https://doi.org/10.14716/ijtech.v14i6.6640

Barakat, M. E. H. A., Chung, G. C., Pang, W. L., Prasetio, M. D., Roslee, M. bin, & Chan, K. Y. (2024). *Exploration of Wi-Fi-Based Indoor Positioning System Using Linear Regression and K-Nearest Neighbour* (pp. 383–392). https://doi.org/10.1007/978-981-97-0142-1_38

Bond, M., Khosravi, H., De Laat, M., Bergdahl, N., Negrea, V., Oxley, E., Pham, P., Chong, S. W., & Siemens, G. (2024). A meta systematic review of artificial intelligence in higher education: A call for increased ethics, collaboration, and rigour. *International Journal of Educational Technology in Higher Education*, *21*(1). Springer Science and Business Media Deutschland GmbH. https://doi.org/10.1186/s41239-023-00436-z

Burriss, S. K., Hutchins, N., Conley, Z., Deweese, M. M., Doe, Y. J., Eeds, A., Villanueva, A., Ziegler, H., & Oliver, K. (2024). Redesigning an AI bill of rights with/for young people: Principles for exploring AI ethics with middle and high school students. *Computers and Education: Artificial Intelligence*, *7*. https://doi.org/10.1016/j.caeai.2024.100317

Castelló-Sirvent, F., Roger-Monzó, V., & Gouveia-Rodrigues, R. (2024). Quo vadis, university? A roadmap for AI and ethics in higher education. *Electronic Journal of E-Learning*, *22*(6), 34–51. https://doi.org/10.34190/ejel.22.6.3267

Chuan, L. L., Roslee, M., Anuar, K., & Leong, P. W. (2021). Investigation of the algorithm of attack on the data center in an IoT network. In *2021 IEEE 15th Malaysia International Conference on Communication (MICC)* (pp. 13–18). https://doi.org/10.1109/MICC53484.2021.9642105

Chuan, L. L., Roslee, M., Leong, P. W., & Irawati, I. D. (2023). Analysis of security threats on data centre in Internet of Things. In *Proceedings of the Multimedia University Engineering Conference (MECON 2022)* (pp. 377–389). Atlantis Press International BV. https://doi.org/10.2991/978-94-6463-082-4_33

Khreisat, M. N. (2024). Ethical implications of AI integration in educational decision making: Systematic review. *Educational Administration Theory and Practice*, 8521–8527. https://doi.org/10.53555/kuey.v30i5.4406

Nguyen, A., Ngo, H. N., Hong, Y., Dang, B., & Nguyen, B. P. T. (2023). Ethical principles for artificial intelligence in education. *Education and Information Technologies*, *28*(4), 4221–4241. https://doi.org/10.1007/s10639-022-11316-w

Peters, M. A., & Green, B. J. (2024). Wisdom in the age of AI education. *Postdigital Science and Education*. https://doi.org/10.1007/s42438-024-00460-w

Stolpe, K., & Hallström, J. (2024). Artificial intelligence literacy for technology education. *Computers and Education Open*, *6*, 100159. https://doi.org/10.1016/j.caeo.2024.100159

You, C. E., Pang, W. L., & Chan, K. Y. (2022). AI-based low-cost real-time face mask detection and health status monitoring system for COVID-19 prevention. *WSEAS Transactions on Information Science and Applications*, *19*, 264–271. https://doi.org/10.37394/23209.2022.19.26

Yu, H. (2024). The application and challenges of ChatGPT in educational transformation: New demands for teachers' roles. *Heliyon*, *10*(2). Elsevier Ltd. https://doi.org/10.1016/j.heliyon.2024.e24289

7

A Job-Based Course Recommender System Using Unsupervised Machine Learning for Text Clustering to Promote a Multidisciplinary Curriculum

Mohd Aftar Abu Bakar, Noratiqah Mohd Ariff, Alia Muhammad Radzi, Sarmela Nadarajan, Muhammed Haziq Muhammed Nor, and Sarani Zakaria

7.1 Introduction

The Fourth Industrial Revolution (4IR) refers to the rapid development of technologies that have inherently changed the way humans live and conduct business. It is characterized by increased digitalization and automation across diverse sectors around the world such as transportation, health, biotechnology, manufacturing, and education. Higher education plays a vital role in preparing for the societal transitions fundamental for people to adapt well to the 4IR. However, the current higher education system was designed to accommodate the demands of the previous industrial revolution (Gleason, 2018). Many programs offered by higher education institutions today do not expose students to multiple disciplines, which widens the gap between education and employment. The higher education curriculum should accommodate more flexibility, nonformal learning, and better collaboration between diverse cultural and social experiences in order for the curriculum to adapt faster to real scenarios and introduce more diverse learning paths (Murad et al., 2021). Furthermore, fostering a multidisciplinary approach in higher education enables students to acquire the skills necessary for solving complex real-world problems (Drake & Reid, 2020).

A multidisciplinary curriculum is an integrated curriculum in which a topic or issue is studied from the perspective of more than one discipline, allowing students to cross traditional boundaries between disciplines (UNESCO International Bureau of Education [IBE], 2022). Students learn how to blend knowledge and ideas from different fields of study and apply them to tackling industrial problems (Kgari-Masondo & Ngwenya, 2020). Thus, a multidisciplinary approach results in cognitive advancement that would

DOI: 10.1201/9781003633433-7

have been unlikely with a single-disciplinary approach. Although the concept is not new within the education community, it is still widely discussed, as institutions have not widely adopted the concept and its most effective implementation method is still debated.

Despite the lack of multidisciplinary programs, higher education institutions, particularly universities, offer a diverse range of courses that can be leveraged by students to acquire a multidisciplinary learning experience. However, course selection can be onerous for students due to the abundance of options when aligning courses with their career interests. Courses from different disciplines may not seem to possess similarities, but they can produce synergy and enhance students' learning experience when integrated cohesively. Since the current structure of courses offered by each faculty is confined within the borders of respective disciplines, the connection between courses might not be apparent.

This research addresses this issue by developing a course recommender system (RS) framework to facilitate multidisciplinary curriculum planning among students. The contributions of this chapter are as follows: (1) This study integrates different clustering algorithms, namely *k*-means, *k*-medoids, and agglomerative hierarchical clustering in a content-based course RS framework to recommend courses with a multidisciplinary outlook. (2) This study supplies users with course recommendations according to their job interests or needs. (3) This study compares the performance of recommendations generated by integrating each of the three clustering algorithms into the course RS framework.

The remainder of this chapter is organized as follows. Section 7.2 summarizes the benefits and challenges of multidisciplinary education and reviews existing studies on course RSs and document clustering. In Section 7.3, we describe the data and framework for building the course RS. Section 7.4 presents the results and evaluations from testing the RS, while Section 7.5 discusses the evaluation outcomes. Finally, conclusions, limitations, and future recommendations are presented in Section 7.6.

7.2 Related Works

7.2.1 Multidisciplinary Education: Benefits and Challenges

Multidisciplinary education cultivates critical thinking, which leads to the birth of new knowledge, the creation of joint solutions, and scientific innovations (Akkerman & Bakker, 2011; Klaassen, 2018). According to Richter et al. (2009), a multidisciplinary approach to engineering education aids students in acquiring cross-disciplinary skills and learning how to integrate techniques and knowledge from different disciplines to solve complex issues in a working environment. Besides, multidisciplinary education offers students the flexibility to determine their career goals, as they will be exposed to broader knowledge and skills.

While multidisciplinary education offers multiple benefits, it is not without its challenges. Despite being faculties at the same university, the amount and type of effort needed to design courses vary among faculties. This contrast is due to the differences in students' interests and expectations and is a concern in outlining multidisciplinary curricula. For example, engineering education often requires deterministic, precise, and thorough analysis, while marketing or architecture may emphasize more on individuality and spontaneity (Badurdeen et al., 2014). For this reason, when designing multidisciplinary curricula, tertiary institutions should be cognizant of the wide-ranging academic interests among students to duly select the topics and depth to be covered from each discipline. Additionally, multidisciplinary curricula might necessitate students to take more credit hours due to the requirement of a broad scientific foundation from multiple disciplines. There is also a risk of students being pulled in different directions, particularly when there is a lack of collaboration and communication between faculties (Kriegel et al., 2011). Therefore, the process of designing a multidisciplinary curriculum is exacting, and significant efforts are required before students can reap the benefits.

7.2.2 Course Recommender Systems

An RS applies filtering techniques and uses different sources of information to effectively provide users with personalized recommendations. The main purpose of an RS is to help people who lack information and experience to choose from a broad spectrum of options (Mettouris & Papadopoulos, 2014, Zhang et al., 2021). The principal approaches for building RSs are collaborative filtering (CF), content-based filtering (CBF), and hybrid recommendation, which combines CF and CBF approaches (Ariff et al., 2018a; Li & Kim, 2021; Mettouris & Papadopoulos, 2014).

Course RSs can be more complex than typical RSs such as book, movie, or music RSs. A course RS in a university environment suffers more severely from the cold-start problem due to the absence of historical course enrollment information for newly enrolled students. Hence, the commonly used CF approach will not have sufficient information to provide meaningful recommendations (Jing & Tang, 2017). Moreover, the opportunity cost of making incorrect course recommendations is also greater than conventional movie or music recommendations, as university courses consume more time (Ma et al., 2021). One way of solving the cold-start problem is by using the CBF approach (Lops et al., 2011; Zhang et al., 2021).

CBF recommends items that are similar to the items liked by a target user previously (Li & Kim, 2021; Magara et al., 2018; Ricci et al., 2015; Shoval et al., 2008; Zhang et al., 2021). In this filtering technique, each item and user profile is represented by a feature vector or embedding. The similarities between the items and user representations are computed and collated to provide a list of recommendations to the end user. Morsomme and Alferez (2019) developed a content-based course RS to gauge the appropriateness of a course for a student by considering the student's eligibility and interests. The RS, however, requires students to select keywords from a predetermined list to infer their academic interests before suggesting courses using a latent Dirichlet allocation (LDA) topic model. According to Gulzar et al. (2018), an RS was proposed using information retrieval techniques and ontology relations to select courses based on students' interests. The RS expands a query by finding synonyms to retrieve more courses, thereby increasing the accuracy of recommendations. Additional relevant courses were also extracted using ontology support.

Although the aforementioned studies recommended courses according to students' interests, our work differs by using skills extracted directly from users' job interests to provide course recommendations that cross-disciplinary boundaries. This was done by integrating clustering algorithms into the course RS framework, detailed in Section 7.3, to ensure multidisciplinary course recommendations. In addition, instead of requesting users to input keywords, the course RS allows users to obtain course suggestions by inputting a description of their desired job.

7.2.3 Document Clustering

Document clustering is the unsupervised classification of textual documents into the most relevant groups, called clusters, based on homogeneity or heterogeneity attributes (Mohemad et al., 2022). Document clustering allows the possibility of improving information retrieval systems, organizing and understanding large documents, detecting duplicate content, and providing recommendations (Selvaraj & Choi, 2021).

Al-Badarenah and Alsakran (2016) presented an RS that suggests university elective courses to students based on the affinity between courses taken by similar students. The *k*-means clustering was used to group similar students, and then association rules mining was applied to each cluster for recommending courses. A similar approach was also adopted by Asadi et al. (2019) to design a course RS for undergraduates. Lin et al. (2015) applied another partitioning method, namely the *k*-medoids algorithm, to cluster content features of resources in a CF RS to solve the data sparsity problem. When compared with a normal CF RS, the proposed method performed better. Meanwhile, Wang et al. (2017) clustered job skills from computer science–related employment data using agglomerative hierarchical clustering for recommending online courses according to students' desired jobs.

In this research, *k*-means, *k*-medoids, and hierarchical algorithms were used to cluster skills from employment data of multiple disciplines as an integral component of the course RS to generate recommendations that align with multidisciplinary curricula.

7.3 Research Methodology

7.3.1 Data Collection and Processing

Three different databases were used in the course RS framework: the jobs, skills, and courses databases. The jobs database consists of job postings and their descriptions scraped from jobstreet.com.my. Only job positions that call for multidisciplinary skills were scraped. The skills database is comprised of hard skills obtained from the Emsi Skills Library, while the courses database is a course catalog containing all postgraduate courses and their descriptions from a public university in Malaysia.

7.3.1.1 Jobs and Skills Database

In this study, job descriptions for various multidisciplinary job positions were scraped from the job postings available on jobstreet.com.my to train different clustering models. Web scraping involves parsing website hypertext markup language (HTML) to extract data using HTML tags in an automated manner with only a certain degree of human intervention (Dongo et al., 2021; Krotov et al., 2020). The Requests and Beautiful Soup libraries from Python were used to scrape job data from the website.

A list of job positions with cross-disciplinary skill requirements was compiled in alignment with the objective of creating multidisciplinary recommendations. For each job position, a total of six pages, each listing 30 job postings, was scraped. However, not all job positions had postings up to six pages, and for such positions, the number of postings scraped was limited to the maximum number of available job postings on the website. The web scraping process is illustrated in Figure 7.1. First, the web scraping pipeline accepts the list of job positions as input. The URL and HTML structure of jobstreet.com.my were observed and found to be standardized. Thus, the URL for each job position and page was generated via looping. Then, an HTTP GET request was sent for each URL to scrape the job titles, company names, and job descriptions on the respective page. Time delays were added between the requests to prevent the server from being overloaded with too many requests in a very short period. The entire scraped data was compiled into a data frame that consists of information on 6,124 job postings.

Furthermore, a collection of 28,956 hard skills was obtained from the Emsi Skills Library using their API to form the skills database. The skills for each job description were then extracted by filtering through the skills database and grouped by job positions. Unigrams, bigrams, and trigrams were generated for every job description to preserve the multiple-word skills found in them. Unique skills were collated for every job posting to indicate the importance of a skill for a job position based on the frequency of the skill's appearances in the job position.

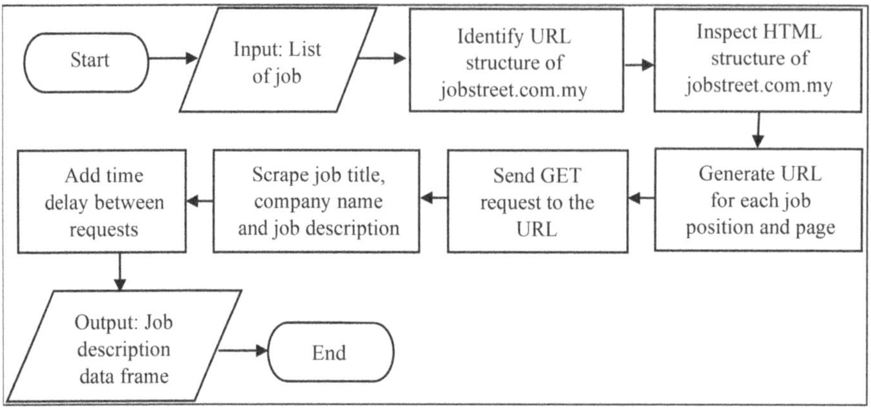

FIGURE 7.1
Illustration of the web scraping process.

7.3.1.2 Courses Database

The course data is from the university's postgraduate course catalog. The course catalog in the Malay language was translated into English and inspected for missing values, discrepancies, and duplicates. The data contains three attributes, representing course code, course name, and course description, and a total of 1,162 unique observations. Then, the course description was cleaned by removing all punctuation, extra white spaces, and digits. Next, the course descriptions were converted to lowercase and tokenized. Stop words were also removed in the cleaning process.

7.3.2 System Architecture

The course RS was built with an underlying job skills cluster prediction element to generate serendipitous recommendations with multidisciplinary coverage. The courses recommended by the system are from the university's postgraduate course catalog, based on the job description or skills entered by the user or student. Figure 7.2 shows the course RS framework. The RS works by first extracting skills from job descriptions given by a user and matching them to the course descriptions in the course catalog using cosine similarity. Prior to that, *k*-means, *k*-medoids, and agglomerative hierarchical clustering models were constructed using skills extracted from the job descriptions in the jobs database. Then, the cluster of skills extracted from user input is predicted, and courses are recommended based on the top 25 skills in the cluster. This step is significant to ensure that the course recommendations are multidisciplinary. The combination of courses recommended allows students to explore courses that cross-disciplinary boundaries. Recommendations

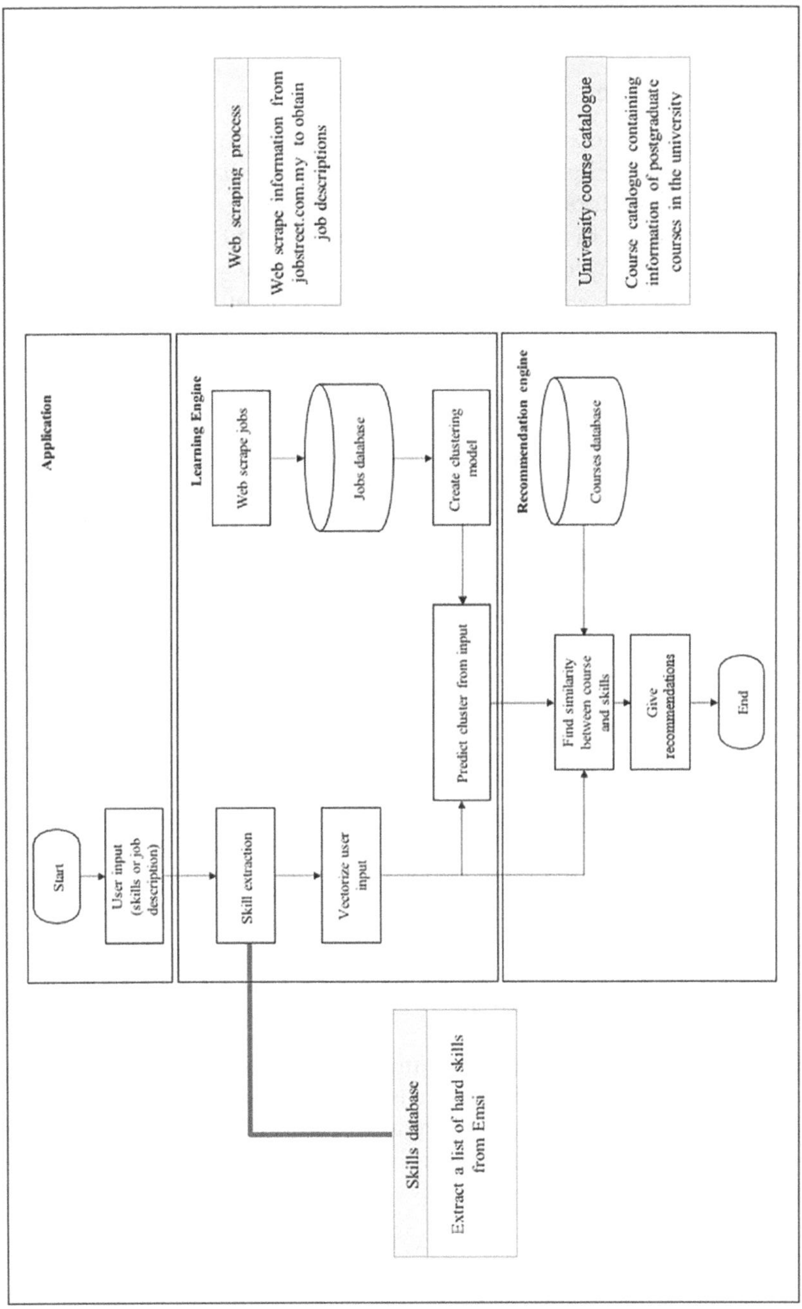

FIGURE 7.2
Course recommender system framework.

generated using the *k*-means, *k*-medoids, and agglomerative hierarchical clustering models are then compared to observe which algorithm leads to more consistent and relevant recommendations.

7.3.3 Text Vectorization

The skills extracted and cleaned course descriptions are vectorized using word embedding, as clustering algorithms and similarity computations require numerical vectors as input. Word embedding allows for a more efficient representation of words by preserving the contextual similarity of words and constructing lower-dimensional numerical vectors (Naili et al., 2017). Many pretrained word embeddings have a default representation of 300-dimensional word vectors. Some popular word embedding algorithms include word2vec, fastText, and GloVe. The *fasttext-wiki-news-subwords-300* pretrained model is found to be effective for vectorizing text data in this study. The pretrained *fasttext-wiki-news-subwords-300* uses the continuous bag-of-words model, which combines representations of surrounding words to predict the word in the middle. The datasets used to build the pretrained model include English Wikipedia from 2017, all news data from statmt.org from 2007 to 2016, and the UMBC webBase corpus (Mikolov et al., 2013; Mikolov et al., 2019). The pretrained *fastText-wiki-news-subwords-300* model can be downloaded directly and loaded into memory using Python's *Gensim* library for use.

7.3.4 Document Clustering

This study applies *k*-means, *k*-medoids, and agglomerative hierarchical clustering to cluster vectorized skills data from the jobs database using the Euclidean distance metric. The elbow method and silhouette analysis were used to determine the optimal number of clusters for *k*-means and *k*-medoids clustering, while the dendrogram and silhouette analysis were used for agglomerative hierarchical clustering.

7.3.4.1 k-means Clustering

The *k*-means clustering method is a common and popular algorithm in cluster analysis due to its simplicity and ease of implementation (Ariff et al., 2020). The *k*-means clustering algorithm aims to minimize the intra-cluster distance or, in other words, the within-cluster sum of squares, as defined below:

$$WCSS = \sum_{j=1}^{k} \sum_{i=1}^{n} x_i^{(j)} - c_j^2 \tag{7.1}$$

where WCSS is the within-cluster sum of squares, k is the number of clusters, n is the number of documents, is the document i, is the centroid of cluster j, and is the distance function.

The number of clusters is first determined. Based on the chosen number of clusters, k documents are initialized as centroids. Then, all other documents are assigned to the nearest cluster centroid based on Euclidean distance, and new cluster centroids are computed. The document's cluster assignment and centroid recalculation are repeated until there is no change in the cluster members and centroids or the maximum number of iterations is reached.

One of the methods for determining the optimal number of clusters for the k-means clustering model is the elbow method. The within-cluster sum of squares was plotted against the varying number of clusters. The optimal number of clusters was then identified by observing the elbow of the plot. Silhouette analysis was also used for selecting the optimal number of clusters and is detailed in Section 7.3.4.4.

7.3.4.2 k*-medoids Clustering*

The k-medoids clustering algorithm is a variant of the k-means clustering algorithm. The centroids are replaced by medoids, and the aim is to minimize the sum of distances between each document and the medoid of its cluster. A medoid is a document or data point with the minimum total distance to the other documents in its cluster (Ariff et al., 2018b).

The k-medoids clustering algorithm also requires the number of clusters to be predetermined. Based on the chosen number of clusters, k documents are selected as medoids. Next, each document is assigned to the closest medoid based on Euclidean distance, and the new medoid for each cluster is identified by minimizing the total distance to other documents in the cluster. The document's cluster assignment and medoid recalculation are repeated until there is no change in the medoids or the maximum number of iterations is reached.

7.3.4.3 Agglomerative Hierarchical Clustering

One advantage of hierarchical clustering is that it does not require the number of clusters to be predetermined, unlike k-means and k-medoids clustering. Hierarchical clustering can be conducted using two approaches, namely the divisive and agglomerative approaches. This study uses the complete linkage method, an agglomerative approach. This approach begins by representing each document as an individual cluster, which is combined if the distances between documents are small. The combining process is repeated until the selected number of clusters is obtained or until all the documents are combined into one large cluster. A dendrogram is a tree diagram that shows how documents are clustered and, in this research, it was used to determine the appropriate number of clusters. Besides, silhouette analysis was also conducted for selecting the optimal number of clusters.

7.3.4.4 Silhouette Analysis

The silhouette coefficient takes a value within the closed interval [–1, 1]. A positive coefficient with a value close to 1 indicates that the document is distant from its neighboring cluster, a value of 0 shows that the document is on or very close to the decision boundary of two neighboring clusters, and a negative coefficient with a value close to –1 suggests that the document might have been assigned to the wrong cluster. The silhouette coefficients of all documents are averaged to obtain the silhouette score. The silhouette coefficient for a single document is defined below:

$$S_i = \frac{b_i - a_i}{\max(a_i, b_i)} \tag{7.2}$$

where is the silhouette coefficient for document *i*, is the mean distance between document *i* and other documents in the same cluster, and is the mean distance between document *i* and other documents in the neighboring cluster.

7.3.5 Recommendation Strategy

This section describes how the course RS produces a final set of course recommendations for a particular user. Cosine similarity was used as the similarity measure. It measures the similarity between two vectors in an inner-product space, in this case, between the vectorized skill and the vectorized course description. Cosine similarity ranges from 0 to 1, with a value closer to 1 indicating higher similarity. The formula for cosine similarity is shown below:

$$cosine\,similarity(\vec{d_1}, \vec{d_2}) = \frac{\vec{d_1}\ \vec{d_2}}{|\vec{d_1}|\ |\vec{d_2}|} = \frac{\sum_{i=1}^{n} d_1 d_2}{\sum_{i=1}^{n} {d_1}^2 \sum_{i=1}^{n} {d_2}^2} \tag{7.3}$$

where is the vectorized skill and is the vectorized course description.

The cosine similarity was used in two different stages: first, when matching the skills extracted directly from the job description to the course description in the course database, and second, when matching the top 25 skills from the predicted cluster with the course description. In the first stage, for every skill extracted, three courses with the highest cosine similarity and a minimum similarity value of 0.7 were recommended. In the second stage, for every top 25 skills, three courses with the highest cosine similarity were gathered. Among those gathered courses, 20 courses with the highest cosine similarity and a minimum similarity value of 0.85 were recommended. The courses that were recommended in the first stage were excluded from being recommended in the second stage to avoid redundancy. Figure 7.3 depicts the course recommendation process detailed in this section.

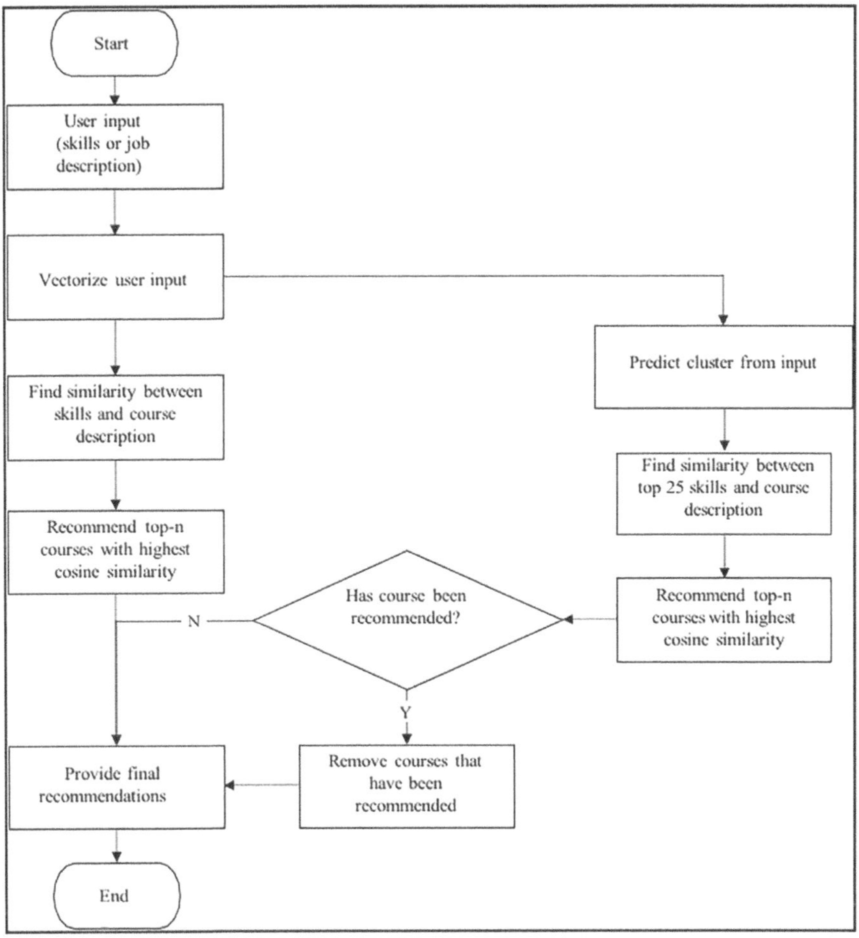

FIGURE 7.3
Process of recommending courses.

7.4 Results

7.4.1 Selection of Clustering Models

7.4.1.1 k-means Clustering

The graph of the within-cluster sum of squares against the experimental number of clusters, *k*, between 2 and 48 for *k*-means clustering is shown in Figure 7.4. An elbow is a point beyond which adding more clusters will not contribute significantly to improving the quality of the clusters and thus was used to infer the optimal number of clusters. In Figure 7.4, the elbow seemed to occur at $k = 11$. The silhouette scores from $k = 10$ to $k = 15$ are presented in Table 7.1. The *k*-means clustering model with 10 clusters has the maximum silhouette score. The silhouette scores for 11, 13, and 14 clusters are also high. Thence, the silhouette plots for 10, 11, 13, and 14 clusters were observed, as displayed in Figure 7.5.

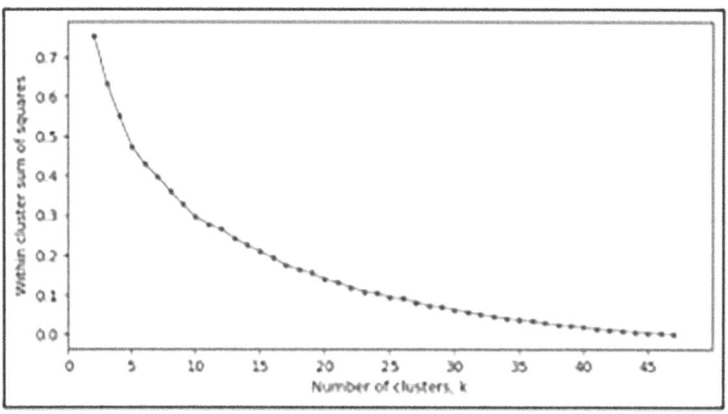

FIGURE 7.4
Elbow method for *k*-means clustering.

TABLE 7.1
Silhouette Scores for k-Means Clustering.

Number of Clusters	Silhouette Score
10	0.2208
11	0.2106
12	0.1719
13	0.1974
14	0.2083
15	0.1606

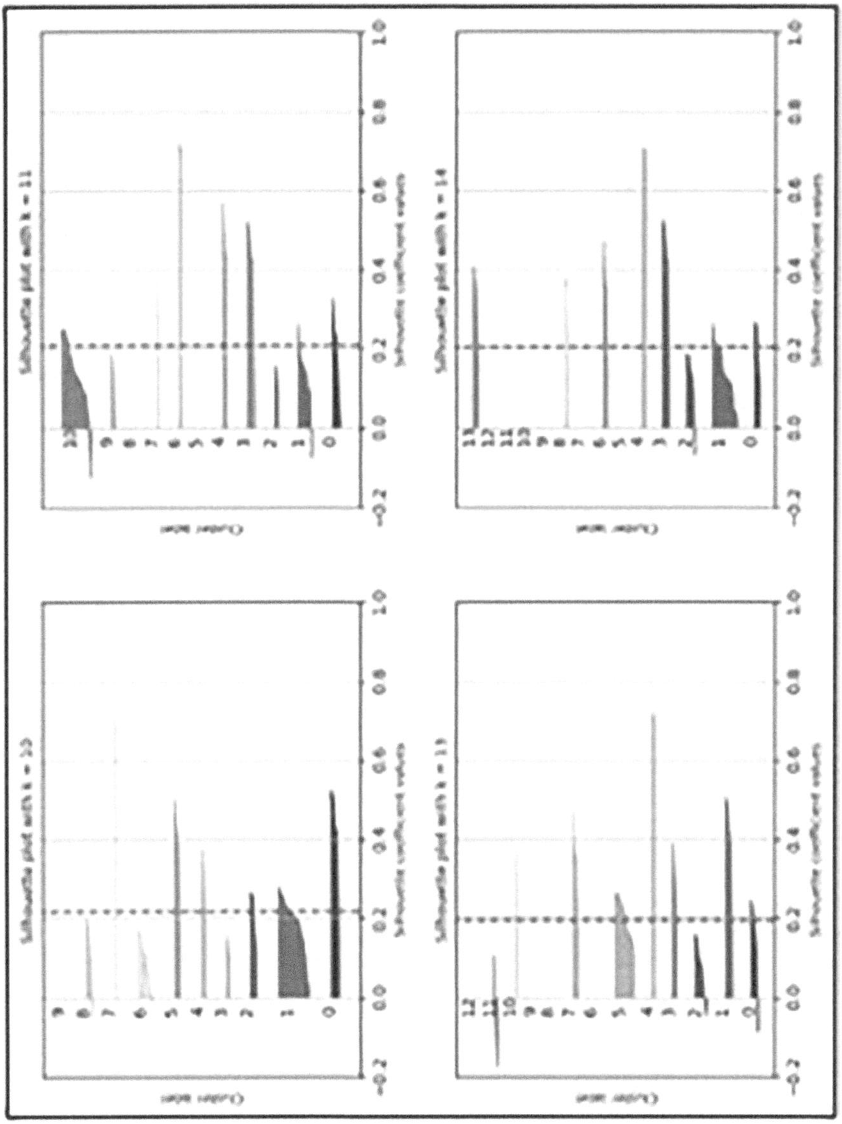

FIGURE 7.5
Silhouette plots for *k*-means clustering.

Silhouette plot for ten clusters appears to have the fewest documents with a negative silhouette coefficient, and more than half of the clusters have above-average silhouette scores, as indicated by the dotted red line. Meanwhile, silhouette plots for a higher number of clusters do not show obvious improvement in terms of cluster distribution. Therefore, the model with 10 clusters was chosen to cluster the skills extracted from job descriptions.

7.4.1.2 k-medoids Clustering

Figure 7.6 displays the plot of within-cluster sum of squares against the experimental number of clusters, *k*, between 2 and 48 for *k*-medoids clustering. Based on Figure 7.6, the determination of the elbow point is ambiguous, as elbows appear to exist at two points, $k = 11$ and $k = 14$. The silhouette scores from $k = 10$ to $k = 15$ are shown in Table 7.2. The models with 10, 11, 12, and 14 clusters have more promising silhouette scores, and so the silhouette plots for 10, 11, 12, and 14 clusters were compared to select the appropriate number of clusters for *k*-medoids clustering. These plots are shown in Figure 7.7.

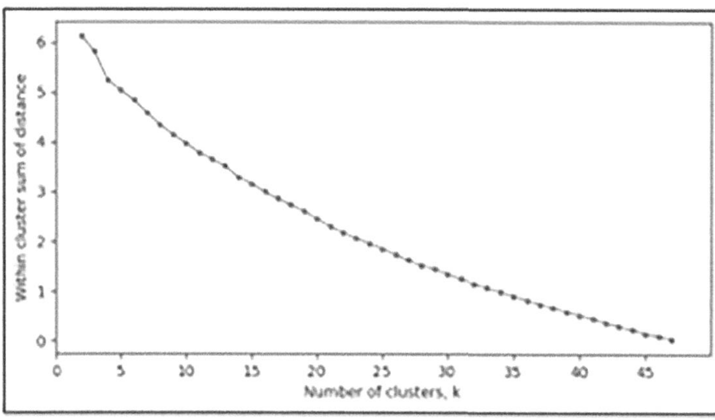

FIGURE 7.6
Elbow method for *k*-medoids clustering.

TABLE 7.2
Silhouette Scores for k-Medoids Clustering

Number of Clusters	Silhouette Score
10	0.1833
11	0.1818
12	0.1607
13	0.1497
14	0.1647
15	0.1596

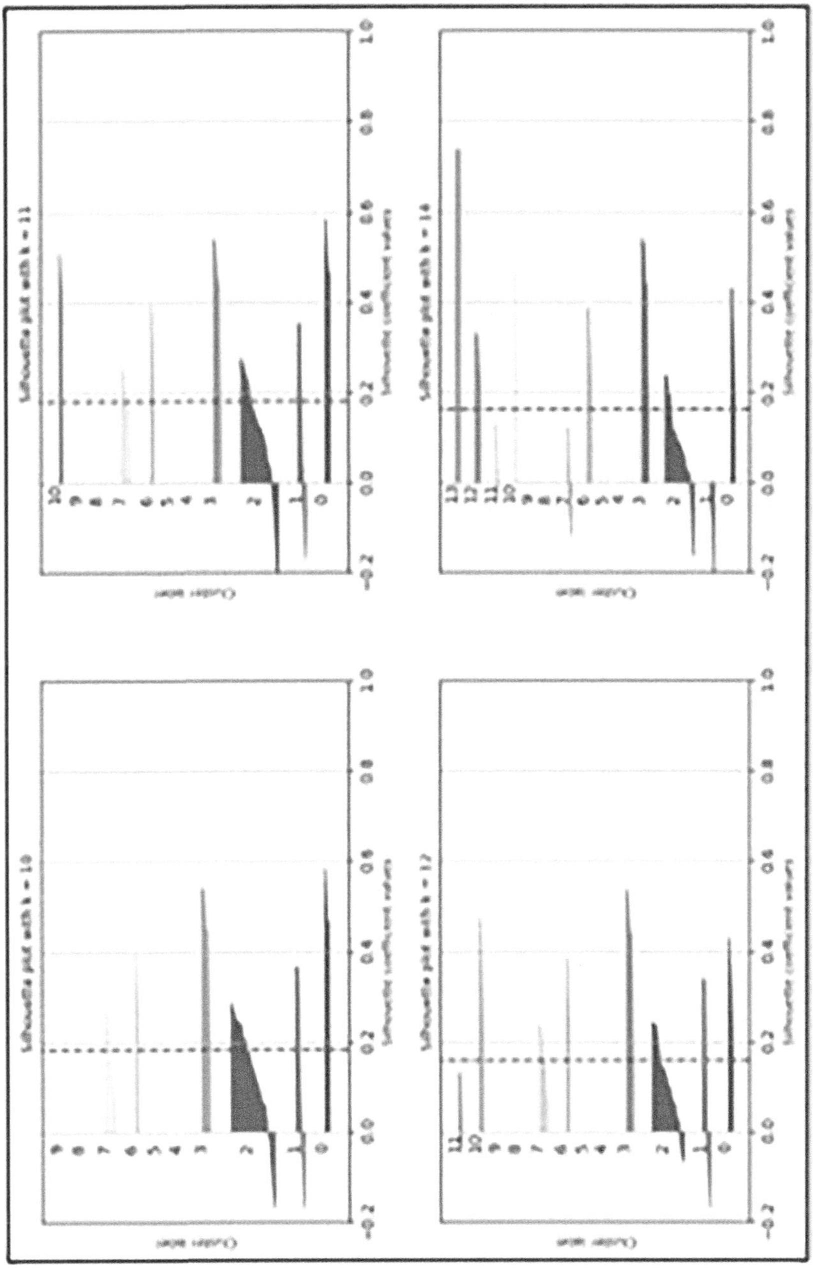

FIGURE 7.7
Silhouette plots for *k*-medoids clustering.

All the silhouette plots in Figure 7.7 have documents with negative silhouette coefficient values, which indicates that some of the skill lists might have been assigned to the wrong clusters. Although the *k*-medoids model with 10 clusters has the highest score in Table 7.2, the silhouette plot with 12 clusters has more uniformly distributed cluster sizes and lower values for documents with negative silhouette coefficients. Thus, the model with 12 clusters was selected.

7.4.1.3 Agglomerative Hierarchical Clustering

Figure 7.8 shows the dendrogram of the complete linkage hierarchical clustering model. The vertical axis of the dendrogram reflects the distance between clusters. The higher the height of the branch, the greater the difference between clusters. This characteristic of the dendrogram was utilized to determine the suitable number of clusters. The dendrogram was cut horizontally at a 0.18 distance, as the heights of most branches below it are short. Cutting the dendrogram at a lower height might result in pairs of clusters that are similar to one another. Thirteen clusters were produced by cutting the dendrogram at a 0.18 distance. The silhouette scores for complete linkage hierarchical clustering from k = 10 to k = 15 can be seen in Table 7.3. The hierarchical clustering model with 12 clusters has the highest silhouette score, while the models with 11, 13, and 14 clusters show silhouette scores above 0.19. The silhouette plots for 11, 12, 13, and 14 clusters are displayed in Figure 7.9.

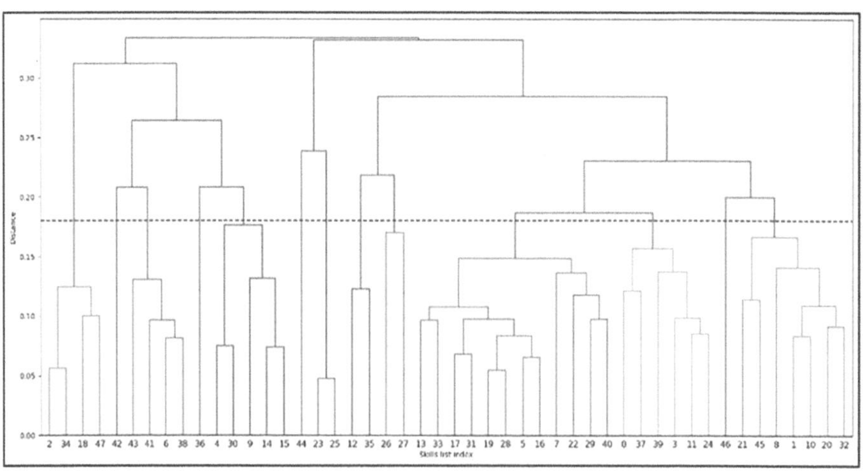

FIGURE 7.8
Dendrogram for complete linkage hierarchical clustering.

TABLE 7.3
Silhouette Scores for Complete Linkage Hierarchical Clustering

Number of Clusters	Silhouette Score
10	0.1882
11	0.1985
12	0.1987
13	0.1934
14	0.1924
15	0.1875

Silhouette plot of complete linkage hierarchical clustering with 12 clusters has the lowest number of documents with negative silhouette coefficients and, hence, has the lowest likelihood of assigning skills lists to the wrong clusters. Although the models with 13 and 14 clusters show lower fluctuations in cluster sizes than the model with 12 clusters, both models have more observations with higher negative coefficient values. Thus, the model with 12 clusters also has a slightly better distribution of cluster sizes than the model with 11 clusters. Therefore, the model with 12 clusters was chosen.

7.4.2 Evaluation of Recommendations

Two different methods were devised to measure and compare the appropriateness of recommendations. First, the recommendations generated by the RS using the *k*-means, *k*-medoids, and hierarchical clustering algorithms were compared with the course curricula of multidisciplinary postgraduate programs in other universities. Second, the relevance of skills attached to the courses recommended by the RS was examined. This is possible because the course RS also recommends skills that might align with multidisciplinary education.

7.4.2.1 Comparison between Courses Recommended and Course Curricula

The comparison was conducted for four distinct multidisciplinary fields or industries, namely finance, food science, human resources (HR), and information security. One job description from each industry was input into the RS to produce course recommendations for each clustering method. Table 7.4 shows the percentage of recommendations that matched the curricula of the master of science (MSc) in Islamic banking and finance from two public

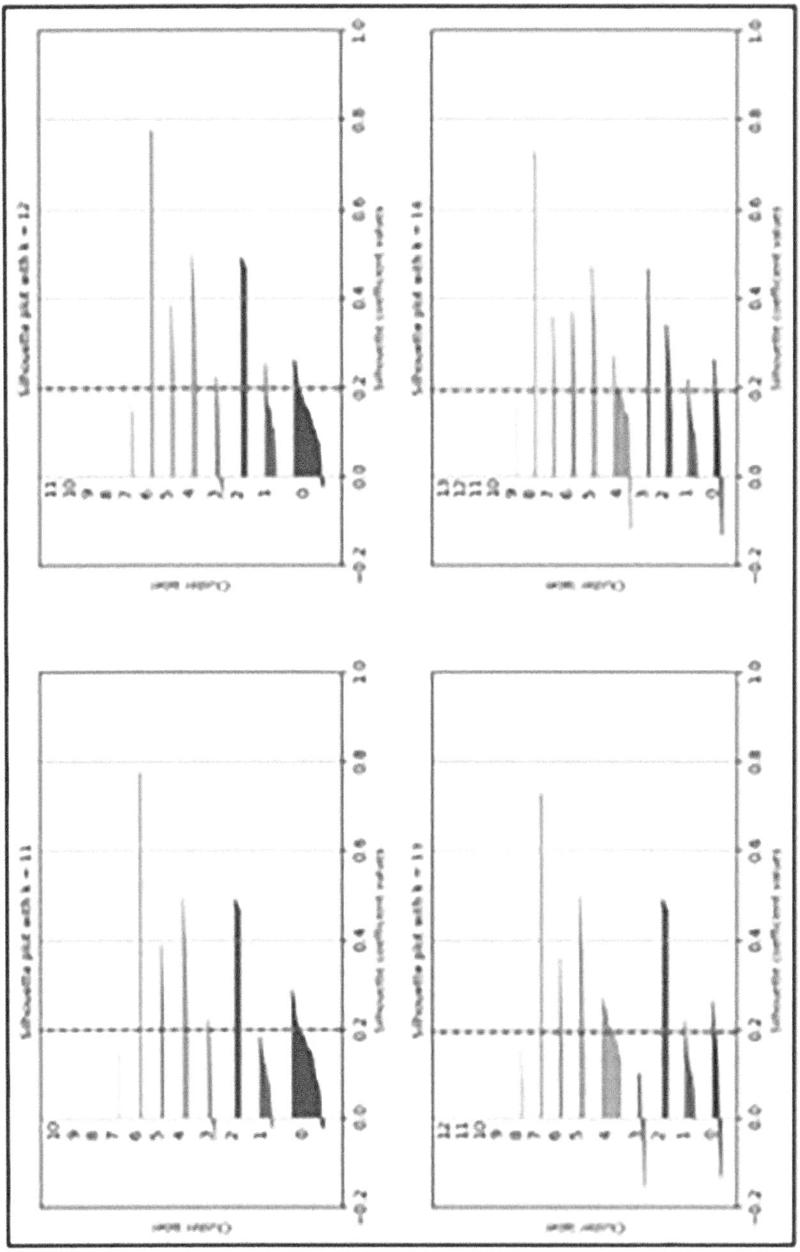

FIGURE 7.9
Silhouette plots for complete linkage hierarchical clustering.

TABLE 7.4

Percentage of course Recommendations That Matched Finance-Related Curricula.

Clustering Method	Percentage of Recommendations That Matched the Curriculum (%)			Mean Percentage of Courses Recommended That Matched the Curriculum (%)
	MSc in Islamic Banking and Finance (UniA)	Master in Islamic Finance and Banking (UniB)	Masters in Islamic Finance Practice (UniC)	
k-means	46.67	50.00	41.18	45.95
k-medoids	46.67	50.00	41.18	45.95
Hierarchical	46.67	50.00	41.18	45.95

universities (UniA and UniB) and the master in Islamic practice from the International Centre for Education in Islamic Finance at a private university (UniC) in Malaysia.

Based on Table 7.4, the RS recommended more than 40% of the courses listed in each university's curriculum, with an average of 46%. Although the percentages are the same across all clustering methods, this does not necessarily imply that the recommendations are the same, but rather that the number of matched recommendations is the same. The recommended courses that matched the courses in the curricula are almost the same, revealing similarity between the curricula. Also, the recommendations matched half of the courses listed in the master in Islamic finance and banking of UniB. In this case, the course RS has the same level of recommendation performance, regardless of the clustering method used. One instance that keeps the RS from yielding higher percentages of matched recommendations is that the RS failed to recommend courses on Islamic jurisprudence, which are listed in all the curricula. This is because the job description had no statements related to Islamic jurisprudence.

Table 7.5 shows the percentage of courses recommended that matched the food science–related curricula. The programs considered are the MSc in food science and technology and the MSc in food science with business management from two private universities in Malaysia (UniD and UniE). The RS using the *k*-means clustering method provided better recommendations than the other two methods, with an average of 41% matched recommendations. The courses listed in the curriculum from UniD and UniE are quite different, as the former is more concentrated on the practices of food science and technology, while the latter includes some business, management, and marketing courses. Despite that, the RS using the *k*-means clustering method matched more than 40% of the courses listed in both curricula. This shows that it can capture distinct sets of courses within the food science field, even though not extensively.

TABLE 7.5

Percentage of Course Recommendations That Matched Food Science-Related Curricula

Clustering Method	Percentage of Recommendations That Matched the Curriculum (%)		Mean Percentage of Courses Recommended That Matched the Curriculum (%)
	MSc in Food Science and Technology (UniD)	MSc in Food Science with Business Management (UniE)	
k-means	40.91	41.18	41.04
k-medoids	22.73	23.53	23.13
Hierarchical	22.73	23.53	23.13

TABLE 7.6

Percentage of Course Recommendations That Matched Human Resource-Related Curricula

Clustering Method	Percentage of Recommendations That Matched the Curriculum (%)		Mean Percentage of Courses Recommended That Matched the Curriculum (%)
	Master of Human Resource Management (UniF)	Master in Strategic Human Resource Management (UniG)	
k-means	60.00	64.29	62.14
k-medoids	60.00	64.29	62.14
Hierarchical	60.00	64.29	62.14

Next, the course recommendations for a job in the HR field were compared with the course curriculum of the master of human resource management from a public university (UniF) and the master in strategic human resource management from a private university (UniG) in Malaysia. Table 7.6 presents the percentage of course recommendations that matched the human resource-related curricula. For any clustering method, on average, the RS matched 62% of courses listed in human resource-related curricula. More than half of the courses in both were recommended. Some courses were not recommended because terms closely related to such courses had zero or low occurrence in the job description.

Lastly, the percentage of recommendations that matched the information security-related curricula can be seen in Table 7.7. The programs considered are the master of information security from a public university (UniH) and the MSc in information security from a private university (UniI). Half of the courses listed in both curricula were recommended by the RS using any of the clustering methods.

TABLE 7.7

Percentage of Course Recommendations That Matched Information Security–Related Curricula

Clustering Method	Percentage of Recommendations That Matched the Curriculum (%)		Mean Percentage of Courses Recommended That Matched the Curriculum (%)
	Master of Information Security (UniH)	MSc in Information Security (UniI)	
k-means	50.00	50.00	50.00
k-medoids	50.00	50.00	50.00
Hierarchical	50.00	50.00	50.00

TABLE 7.8

Percentage of Course Recommendations Correctly Matched to Skills

Clustering Method	Percentage of Courses Correctly Matched to Skills (%) by Job Title—Industry					Mean Percentage of Courses Correctly Matched to Skills (%)
	Business Development Manager—Banking	Compliance Manager—Consumer Goods	Business Research Analyst—Urban Planning	Environment Engineer—Environmental	Marketing Executive—Property Development	
k-means	93.55	84.85	90.32	84.62	89.47	88.56
k-medoids	89.66	86.21	90.32	80.00	89.47	87.13
Hierarchical	93.55	84.85	93.55	84.62	86.67	88.65

7.4.2.2 Review of the Relevance of Skills Recommended

Five job descriptions, each from a different industry, were given to the RS to obtain five sets of skills along with the matched courses. For every course recommended, the relevance of skills attached to the courses is inspected. Table 7.8 illustrates the percentage of course recommendations correctly matched to skills for five different industries according to the clustering method used in the RS.

The percentages of correct matches between skills and the courses recommended range from 80% to 94% across different industries, revealing that the RS is generally effective in matching skills to the right courses. The high percentages indicate that the pretrained fastText word embedding and cosine similarity measure are effective at detecting relevant courses based on skills. Although some skills might be irrelevant to a job description, this evaluation still showcases the model's competency from a semantic perspective.

When compared across the clustering methods, the average percentage of course recommendations correctly matched to skills is highest for RS using the hierarchical clustering method, followed very closely by the *k*-means clustering method, while it is lowest using *k*-medoids clustering. Since the difference in the mean percentage of courses matched correctly to skills between *k*-means and hierarchical clustering is trivial, only 0.09%, the performances of both methods from the skills perspective are considered equally good. This indicates that the top 25 skills within the predicted cluster using *k*-means and hierarchical clustering are more accurately matched to the courses provided as recommendations.

7.5 Discussion

The two types of evaluation were done to highlight the performance of the RS from two perspectives. The first is a measure of how the RS recommends courses when compared to the established curricula offered by universities. The second mainly demonstrates the effectiveness of the text vectorization technique and the similarity measure.

The percentages of course recommendations that matched the established curricula ranged from 41% to 64% when using *k*-means clustering and from 23% to 64% when using *k*-medoids and hierarchical clustering. This reveals that the RS performs better in terms of recommending courses that match the existing curricula using *k*-means clustering. Yet the performance is still average. The sets of courses recommended by the RS are not completely identical to the list of courses in programs from other universities that are publicized as multidisciplinary. One of the reasons is that the courses in the multidisciplinary programs from other universities are still contained within the boundaries of two or three disciplines. Second, the curricula from other universities are designed based on the expertise available in those universities. As a result, some of the course equivalents are not facsimiles of the courses from the original university. Moreover, the RS is meant to give serendipitous recommendations, but some recommendations might deviate far from the principal subject matter.

Besides, there is no standardized measurement to define a good course combination. Additionally, the recommendations depend on the skills detailed in the job description inputted by a user. If the job description does not include an elaborated set of skills, the recommendations might be less comprehensive for a multidisciplinary curriculum in the field. This is because the skills extracted from the job description might be assigned to the wrong cluster due to being situated near cluster boundaries. Consequently, the top skills in the predicted cluster and the courses matched might not be the most relevant to the field. Finally, with the course recommendations anchored to skills, the RS suggests multidisciplinary courses by emphasizing the skills required for a job in a specific industry instead of a one-size-fits-all multidisciplinary curriculum.

However, when examined from the perspective of courses correctly matched to the respective skills, the RS performed relatively well. Specifically, at least 80% of the courses recommended are correctly matched to the respective skills, regardless of the clustering method adopted in the RS across different industries. This reveals that the course RS is effective in generating semantically appropriate results. There are two main techniques for evaluating word embedding. These are extrinsic evaluators that use word embeddings as input features for a downstream task and intrinsic evaluators that test the quality of an independent natural language processing (NLP) task (Wang et al., 2019). Based on an absolute intrinsic evaluation, the pretrained word embedding model executes the task well. In addition, it proves the compatibility of the similarity measure used. Nevertheless, from the standpoint of extrinsic evaluation, although the courses are largely matched correctly to skills, they may not produce recommendations that are most suitable for the inputted job description. In this evaluation, the RS performed equally using *k*-means and hierarchical clustering.

7.6 Conclusions and Future Directions

As the 4IR advances, employers demand an amalgamation of skills. Multidisciplinary education allows students to acquire skills and knowledge from distinct disciplines, thus improving their adaptability and meeting industry demands. To automate the process of course selection for a multidisciplinary curriculum, this study presents a course RS framework that assists users, particularly students, by suggesting a combination of multidisciplinary courses. This involves integrating a clustering component into the RS framework. The course RS accepts users' job interests as input to return a certain degree of personalized recommendations. Based on the evaluations, the performance of the RS using *k*-means clustering is more consistent across distinct industries than the other methods. As this work is still in the preliminary stage, the performance of the course RS, especially using *k*-means clustering, is satisfactory and can be improved for better results in the future.

There are some limitations that should be noted for future studies. First, the course RS only considers the skills in a user-given job description to prevent information overload and an increase in computation time. Inevitably, this causes the RS to disregard other important contextual information that might be present within the job description. Future research could integrate other contexts of job descriptions into the RS pipeline, for example, by adding another filtration for company background. Second, the jobs database consists of only over 6,000 unique jobs scraped from a single employment website. The RS relies on the jobs database to form skill clusters. Less exhaustive representations of job positions could skew the resulting clusters toward undesirable results. Future studies should maximize the number of job postings scraped from different employment websites for exhaustive representations of job positions. Third, the clustering algorithms tested were not extensive. Other algorithms such as density-based or graph-based clustering can be tested. Fourth, the evaluations were based only on the results obtained using job descriptions from several selected fields. Future research ought to evaluate recommendations across more industries and job positions.

References

Akkerman, S. F., & Bakker, A. (2011). Boundary crossing and boundary objects. *Review of Educational Research, 81*(2), 132–169. https://doi.org/10.3102/0034654311404435

Al-Badarenah, A., & Alsakran, J. (2016). An automated recommender system for course selection. *International Journal of Advanced Computer Science and Applications (IJACSA), 7*(3), 166–175. https://doi.org/10.14569/ijacsa.2016.070323

Ariff, N. M., Bakar, M. A. A., & Rahim, N. F. (2018a). Comparison between content-based and collaborative filtering recommendation system for movie suggestions. *AIP Conference Proceedings, 2013*(1), 020057. https://doi.org/10.1063/1.5054256

Ariff, N. M., Bakar, M. A. A., & Rahmad, M. I. (2018b). Comparative study of document clustering algorithms. *International Journal of Engineering & Technology, 7*(4), 246–251. https://doi.org/10.14419/ijet.v7i4.11.20816

Ariff, N. M., Bakar, M. A. A., & Zamzuri, Z. H. (2020). Academic preference based on students' personality analysis through *k*-means clustering. *Malaysian Journal of Fundamental and Applied Sciences, 16*(3), 328–333. https://doi.org/10.11113/mjfas.v16n3.1640

Asadi, S., Jafari, S. M., & Shokrollahi, Z. (2019). Developing a course recommender by combining clustering and fuzzy association rules. *Journal of AI and Data Mining, 7*(2), 249–262. https://doi.org/10.22044/JADM.2018.6260.1739

Badurdeen, F., Sekulic, D., Gregory, B., Brown, A., & Fu, H. (2014). Developing and teaching a multidisciplinary course in systems thinking for sustainability: Lessons learned through two iterations. In *2014 ASEE Annual Conference & Exposition* (24.392.1–24.392.22). http://doi.org/10.18260/1-2-20283

Dongo, I., Cardinale, Y., Aguilera, A., Martinez, F., Quintero, Y., Robayo, G., & Cabeza, D. (2021). A qualitative and quantitative comparison between web scraping and API methods for Twitter credibility analysis. *International Journal of Web Information Systems, 17*(6), 580–606. https://doi.org/10.1108/IJWIS-03-2021-0037

Drake, S. M., & Reid, J. L. (2020). 21st century competencies in light of the history of integrated curriculum. *Froniers Education, 5*, 122. https://doi.org/10.3389/feduc.2020.00122

Gleason, N. W. (2018). *Higher Education in the Era of the Fourth Industrial Revolution*. Palgrave Macmillan. https://doi.org/10.1007/978-981-13-0194-0

Gulzar, Z., Leema, A. A., & Deepak, G. (2018). PCRS: Personalized course recommender system based on hybrid approach. *Procedia Computer Science, 125*, 518–524. https://doi.org/10.1016/j.procs.2017.12.067

International Bureau of Education (IBE) UNESCO, UNESCO International Bureau of Education. (2013). *Glossary of Curriculum Terminology*. Retrieved December 9, 2022, from https://unesdoc.unesco.org/ark:/48223/pf0000223059/PDF/223059eng.pdf.multi

Jing, X., & Tang, J. (2017). Guess you like: Course recommendation in MOOCs. In *Proceedings of the International Conference on Web Intelligence* (pp. 783–789). https://doi.org/10.1145/3106426.3106478

Kgari-Masondo, C., & Ngwenya, J. (2020). Lecturers' reflections on the teaching of social sciences in a multidisciplinary context at a university in South Africa. *Reflective Practice, 21*(2), 198–209. https://doi.org/10.1080/14623943.2020.1732332

Klaassen, R. G. (2018). Interdisciplinary education: A case study. *European Journal of Engineering Education, 43*, 842–859. https://doi.org/10.1080/03043797.2018.1442417

Kriegel, C., Koehne, J., Tinkle, S., Maynard, A. D., & Hill, R. A. (2011). Challenges of trainees in a multidisciplinary research program: nano-biotechnology. *Journal of Chemical Education, 88*(1), 53–55. https://doi.org/10.1021/ed1001174

Krotov, V., Johnson, L., & Silva, L. (2020). Tutorial: Legality and ethics of web scraping. *Communications of the Association for Information Systems, 47*, 539–563. https://doi.org/10.17705/1CAIS.04724

Li, Q., & Kim, J. (2021). A deep learning-based course recommender system for sustainable development in education. *Applied Sciences, 11*(19), 8993. https://doi.org/10.3390/app11198993

Lin, Z., Ni, W., Zhang, H., Zhao, M., & Yang, Y. (2015) A k-medoids algorithm based method to alleviate the data sparsity in collaborative filtering. In *2015 34th Chinese Control Conference (CCC)* (pp. 4974–4979). https://doi.org/10.1109/ChiCC.2015.7260413

Lops, P., De Gemmis, M., & Semeraro, G. (2011). Content-based recommender systems: State of the art and trends. In P. Ricci, F. Rokach, L. Shapira, & B. Kantor (Eds.), *Recommender Systems Handbook* (pp. 73–105). Springer. https://doi.org/10.1007/978-0-387-85820-3

Ma, B., Lu, M., Taniguchi, Y., & Konomi, S. (2021). CourseQ: The impact of visual and interactive course recommendation in university environments. *Research and Practice in Technology Enhanced Learning, 16*, Article 18. https://doi.org/10.1186/s41039-021-00167-7

Magara, M. B., Ojo, S. O., & Zuva, T. (2018). A comparative analysis of text similarity measures and algorithms in research paper recommender systems. In *2018 Conference on Information Communications Technology and Society (ICTAS)* (pp. 1–5). https://doi.org/10.1109/ICTAS.2018.8368766

Mettouris, C., & Papadopoulos, G. A. (2014). Ubiquitous recommender systems. *Computing, 96*, 223–257. https://doi.org/10.1007/s00607-013-0351-z

Mikolov, T., Grave, E., Bojanowski, P., Puhrsch, C., & Joulin, A. (2019). Advances in pre-training distributed word representations. *arXiv preprint*. https://doi.org/10.48550/arXiv.1712.09405

Mikolov, T., Le, Q. V., & Sutskever, I. (2013). Exploiting similarities among languages for machine translation. *arXiv preprint*. https://doi.org/10.48550/arXiv.1309.4168

Mohemad, R., Muhait, N. N. M., Noor, N. M. M., & Othman, Z. A. (2022). Performance analysis in text clustering using k-means and k-medoids algorithms for Malay crime documents. *International Journal of Electrical and Computer Engineering, 12*(5), 5014–5026. https://doi.org/10.11591/ijece.v12i5.pp5014–5026

Morsomme, R., & Alferez, S. V. (2019). Content-based course recommender system for liberal arts education. In C. F. Lynch, A. Merceron, M. Desmarais, & R. Nkambou (Eds.), *EDM 2019—Proceedings of the 12th International Conference on Educational Data Mining* (pp. 748–753). International Educational Data Mining Society.

Murad, D. F., Hassam, R., Heryadi, Y., Wijanarko, B. D., & Titan. (2021). Recommendation system based on recognition of prior learning to support curriculum design in online higher education. In *2021 International Conference on Information Management and Technology (ICIMTech)* (Vol. 1, pp. 413–417). https://doi.org/10.1109/ICIMTech53080.2021.9535012

Naili, M., Chaibi, A. H., & Ghezala, H. H. B. (2017). Comparative study of word embedding methods in topic segmentation. *Procedia Computer Science, 112*, 340–349. https://doi.org/10.1016/j.procs.2017.08.009

Ricci, F., Shapira, B., & Rokach, L. (2015). Recommender systems: Introduction and challenges. In F. Ricci, L. Rokach, & B. Shapira (Eds.), *Recommender Systems Handbook* (pp. 1–34). Springer. https://doi.org/10.1007/978-1-4899-7637-6_1

Richter, D. M., Paretti, M. C., & McNair, L. D. (2009). Teaching interdisciplinary collaboration: learning barriers and classroom strategies. In *2009 ASEE Southeast Section Conference* (pp. 1–6). https://vtechworks.lib.vt.edu/server/api/core/bitstreams/a11b135e-69e7-40fc-a80a-ed5b3e86e022/content

Selvaraj, S., & Choi, E. (2021). Swarm intelligence algorithms in text document clustering with various benchmarks. *Sensors, 21*(9), 3196. https://doi.org/10.3390/s21093196

Shoval, P., Maidel, V., & Shapira, B. (2008). An ontology-content-based filtering method. *International Journal Information Theories & Applications, 15*, 303–314.

Wang, B., Wang, A., Chen, F., Wang, Y., & Kuo, C. C. J. (2019). Evaluating word embedding models: methods and experimental results. *APSIPA Transactions on Signal and Information Processing, 8*, e19. https://doi.org/10.1017/ATSIP.2019.12

Wang, H. H., Chootong, C., Ochirbat, A., Sommool, W., Gunarathn, W. K. T. M., & Shih, T. K. (2017). Online courses recommendation system based on industry occupation skills requirements. In *2017 10th International Conference on Ubi-Media Computing and Workshops (Ubi-Media)* (pp. 1–6). https://doi.org/10.1109/UMEDIA.2017.8074083

Zhang, Q., Lu, J., & Jin, Y. (2021). Artificial intelligence in recommender systems. *Complex & Intelligent Systems, 7*, 439–457. https://doi.org/10.1007/s40747-020-00212-w

8

The Integration of Artificial Intelligence in Education: A Systematic Review of Pedagogical, Ethical, and Systemic Dimensions

Jia Qi Cheong, Wong Hock Tsen, Chong Shyue Chuan, and Sing Yun Wong

8.1 Introduction: Background and Driving Forces

Artificial intelligence (AI) has become a pivotal force in the education sector, transforming instructional methods, administrative procedures, and student participation globally. Progress in machine learning, natural language processing, and data analytics has facilitated the creation of ITS, adaptive learning platforms, and conversational agents that customize educational experiences on a large scale (Chen et al., 2020a; Wang et al., 2024). The increasing incorporation of AI in formal and informal education highlights its capacity to tackle enduring issues, including educational disparities, resource constraints, and the necessity for adaptable, student-focused methodologies (Dwivedi et al., 2021; Dogan et al., 2023).

The importance of AI in education (AIED) is found not only in technological advancement but also in its capacity to transform the dynamics among educators, learners, and educational institutions. While conventional methods of technology-enhanced learning focused on delivering static content, AI facilitates systems that dynamically adjust to learners' requirements, thus fostering more individualized and inclusive learning paths (Garito, 1991; Ahmad et al., 2021). Recent research on human–AI hybrid adaptivity has emphasized the necessity of reconciling computational accuracy with educator discretion, enabling AI to function as a collaborative ally rather than a substitute for human teachers (Holstein et al., 2020). This viewpoint aligns with the overarching transition toward human-centered AIED, which prioritizes accountability, transparency, and equity in implementation (Li & Gu, 2023).

Despite these benefits, the literature has recognized numerous problems with AI. Ethical challenges are especially prominent in K-12 environments,

DOI: 10.1201/9781003633433-8

as privacy, bias, and autonomy difficulties converge with the susceptibility of younger students (Akgun & Greenhow, 2022; Floridi et al., 2018). Researchers have observed that confidence in AI-driven educational technologies is inconsistent, frequently influenced by educators' professional growth and institutional support (Nazaretsky et al., 2022). In the absence of meticulous regulation, AI may exacerbate disparities by favoring pupils with superior access to digital resources while marginalizing those from underprivileged backgrounds (Cain, 2023; Ahmad et al., 2021). These discussions emphasize that AI is not a neutral instrument but a sociotechnical system whose effects are influenced by governmental frameworks, cultural contexts, and educational decisions.

The body of literature about AIED is growing swiftly, with systematic studies examining many applications, including chatbots (Wollny et al., 2021; Kuhail et al., 2023), distance learning (Jamalova et al., 2022; Dogan et al., 2023), and learning analytics (Alfredo et al., 2024). Chatbots have been thoroughly examined for their capacity to improve student engagement and deliver prompt feedback, with findings indicating both advantages and drawbacks contingent on design and execution (Hwang & Chang, 2021; Lai & Lee, 2024). Nevertheless, a significant portion of the current research is disjointed, with several studies concentrating exclusively on technological efficacy while neglecting pedagogical and ethical considerations (Chen et al., 2020b; Bhutoria, 2022). Although Bayesian network methodologies and data-mining techniques have shown promise in forecasting learning outcomes (García et al., 2007; Costa et al., 2017), concerns persist regarding their interpretability and equity in practical classroom environments.

An additional concern pertains to the contextual diversity of AI adoption. Studies conducted in developed nations, including the United States, China, and European countries, frequently highlight sophisticated personalization systems, multimodal analytics, and AI-driven assessment (Bhutoria, 2022; Alfredo et al., 2024). In contrast, research in emerging economies emphasizes infrastructural challenges, digital divides, and policy gaps that impede effective implementation (Knox, 2020; Ahmad et al., 2021). This disparity highlights wider socioeconomic inequalities and emphasizes the necessity of comparative analyses that incorporate findings from various contexts. Furthermore, although higher education has received significant attention in AI research, K-12 and vocational education are still inadequately examined despite their importance for achieving long-term educational equity (Akgun & Greenhow, 2022; Goçen & Doger, 2025).

Academic discussions highlight theoretical and methodological deficiencies. Chen et al. (2020b) noted that a significant portion of the literature on AIED experiences an "application–theory gap," where empirical studies progress swiftly while conceptual frameworks remain underdeveloped. This disjunction has constrained researchers' capacity to formulate integrated models for assessing the long-term effects of AI on pedagogy and learning outcomes. Reviews of empirical studies indicate a prevalence of small-scale pilot projects, frequently characterized by insufficiently rigorous comparative designs or longitudinal perspectives (Wang et al., 2024; Dogan et al., 2023). The identified limitations restrict the generalizability of findings and underscore the necessity for systematic reviews to integrate fragmented evidence into a unified body of knowledge.

The significance of trust, transparency, and teacher agency has become a prominent theme. Teachers' perceptions of AI tools are crucial for successful adoption; however, many report feeling unprepared to integrate these systems into their practice (Nazaretsky et al., 2022; Jinhee Kim, 2023). Initiatives for professional development that improve teachers' confidence and critical engagement with AI are essential. Research indicates that AI can enhance motivation and self-regulated learning among students when it is designed with suitable scaffolding and feedback (Chiu et al., 2023; Winkler et al., 2020). Nonetheless, excessive dependence on AI can raise issues related to academic integrity, highlighted by the ongoing discourse surrounding generative AI tools such as ChatGPT and their effects on plagiarism and evaluation (Cotton et al., 2023; Cooper, 2023).

In conclusion, the literature indicates the increasing potential of AI to transform education; however, it also highlights a fragmented and uneven landscape characterized by ethical dilemmas, methodological limitations, and contextual disparities. Current reviews offer important insights into particular facets of AIED; however, there is a scarcity of comprehensive syntheses that encompass applications, ethical discussions, pedagogical results, and governance frameworks.

In response to these gaps, this systematic review provides a comprehensive synthesis of research on artificial intelligence in the education sector. The study pursues three core objectives: (1) to integrate findings across pedagogical, ethical, and systemic domains, (2) to critically assess methodological rigor and contextual generalizability, and (3) to identify future research directions that align AI innovation with educational equity, teacher agency, and ethical governance. By bridging fragmented strands of scholarship and highlighting convergences across diverse approaches, this review contributes a structured evidence base for educators, policymakers, and researchers navigating AI's evolving role in education. The chapter is organized as follows: Section 8.2 presents the literature review, including an overview of the topic and scope, as well as focused discussions on chatbots and conversational agents; Section 8.3 outlines the methodology guided by preferred reporting items for systematic reviews and meta-analyses (PRISMA) protocols; Section 8.4 discusses the synthesized findings in relation to theoretical and practical implications; and Section 8.5 concludes with contributions, limitations, and recommendations for future research.

8.2 Literature Reviews

8.2.1 Introduction to the Topic and Scope

AI has become a fundamental element of digital transformation in education, altering teaching methods, institutional administration, and overarching policy frameworks. Rapid advancements in machine learning, natural language processing, and adaptive algorithms have led to the increasing integration of AI in various tools, including personalized tutoring systems and predictive analytics for student retention. Researchers frequently categorize AI applications in education into two interrelated domains: (i) pedagogical applications that influence teaching, learning, and assessment, and (ii) systemic functions that pertain to administration, policy, and institutional decision-making (Wang et al., 2024; Ahmad et al., 2021).

The increasing interest in AI signifies both potential and concern. AI offers scalable personalization, improved accessibility, and enhanced institutional efficiency. Conversely, it prompts concerns regarding ethics, equity, teacher autonomy, and the potential for excessive dependence on automated systems (Ali et al., 2024; Akgun & Greenhow, 2022). The United Nations Educational, Scientific, and Cultural Organization (UNESCO, 2021) and **Organisation for Economic Co-operation and Development** (OECD, 2025) underscore the necessity for AI to be human-centered, accountable, and equitable in the context of global policy discussions. However, a significant portion of the literature is fragmented, with various strands concentrating exclusively on technological affordances, pedagogical outcomes, or ethical challenges.

This review organizes the current research into four thematic clusters: (i) pedagogical personalization and hybrid adaptivity, (ii) chatbots and conversational agents, (iii) trust, ethics, and governance, and (iv) institutional adoption and systemic challenges. The purpose is to map converging trends, critically examine methodological strengths and weaknesses, and identify research gaps requiring integrative frameworks.

The integration of AI into education also reflects broader societal and economic transformations. The Fourth Industrial Revolution has accelerated demand for digital skills, data-driven decision-making, and lifelong learning pathways, positioning AI not just as a tool for instructional support but as a driver of systemic reform (Dwivedi et al., 2021). As Garito (1991) noted early in the evolution of educational technology, shifts in the teaching–learning relationship often follow technological breakthroughs, and AI represents the latest and perhaps most disruptive iteration. This transformation places new responsibilities on educators, institutions, and governments to balance innovation with inclusivity, ensuring that technological progress does not exacerbate existing inequities (Bhutoria, 2022).

Recent systematic reviews demonstrate that research on AIED has grown exponentially yet remains methodologically fragmented (Alfredo et al., 2024;

Moreno-Guerrero et al., 2020). For example, bibliometric studies reveal clusters of publications on learning analytics, intelligent tutoring, and chatbots, but far fewer studies connect these domains under a unified theoretical framework (Chen et al., 2019). Chen et al. (2020b) emphasized the persistent gap between the development of AI applications and their theoretical grounding in educational psychology or pedagogy. This gap may lead to the perception of AI as merely a technological intervention rather than an integral component of a comprehensive educational ecosystem.

Policy frameworks underscore this fragmentation. The European Union and the UNESCO have issued ethical guidelines for AI adoption; however, numerous national governments tend to implement a fragmented strategy, frequently emphasizing innovation rather than regulation (Kim, 2023). Conversely, nations like China have made substantial investments in AI-driven educational reforms, thereby enhancing their national competitiveness (Knox, 2020). The global variation in strategies highlights the necessity of cross-contextual analysis to prevent excessively Western-centric interpretations of AI's role in education. According to Baker and Smith (2019), the future of AI in educational institutions depends on the establishment of governance models that balance swift technological advancement with ethical considerations and pedagogical integrity.

8.2.2 Thematic Organization

8.2.2.1 Pedagogical Personalization and Hybrid Adaptivity

For over two decades, personalized learning has been a primary goal of artificial intelligence in the field of education. Initial experimental research employed Bayesian networks and clustering algorithms to identify learner styles and forecast academic trajectories (García et al., 2007; Costa et al., 2017). Subsequently, ubiquitous learning environments like UTiLearn demonstrated the capacity of mobile and adaptive platforms to provide education that is accessible "anytime, anywhere" (Mehmood et al., 2017). Early initiatives were predominantly focused on technology, frequently overlooking pedagogical subtleties and the role of teacher agency.

Recent scholarship reinterprets personalization as a collaboration between humans and AI rather than a substitute for teachers. Holstein et al. (2020) proposed orchestration systems in which AI supports teachers in managing diverse learners instead of prescribing pedagogical methods. Chine et al. (2022) empirically demonstrated that hybrid personalization, in which AI adapts resources while teachers offer context-sensitive support, can enhance equity outcomes. However, these findings frequently originate from limited pilot studies or controlled settings, which raises concerns regarding their scalability.

Another methodological issue is the *measurement of learning outcomes.* While some studies rely on performance metrics (grades, test scores), others use self-reported motivation or engagement. This inconsistency complicates cross-study comparisons (Qiu et al., 2025). Furthermore, personalization research remains heavily skewed toward higher education, with limited exploration of K-12 or vocational settings, where developmental differences and institutional constraints matter significantly (Akgun & Greenhow, 2022).

Critics contend that personalization could unintentionally weaken collaborative learning and standardize student trajectories through algorithmic recommendations. The potential risk is that AI systems may prioritize efficiency over creativity, serendipity, and social learning (Cain, 2023). This tension highlights the necessity of integrative frameworks that balance personalization and collective pedagogies.

A significant aspect of the literature challenges the assumption that technological advancement automatically results in pedagogical enhancement, reflecting a form of technological determinism (Knox, 2020). Early AIED systems frequently emphasized computational feasibility at the expense of pedagogical effectiveness, resulting in adaptations that were more superficial than transformative (Chen et al., 2020b). This mindset has established a legacy in which certain educators perceive AI as an imposed technical solution rather than a pedagogical tool that can be integrated effectively. The transition to "hybrid adaptivity" signifies an essential adjustment, redirecting the conversation from the capabilities of AI to the requirements of education. This reframing positions AI as a resource within a broader, teacher-guided pedagogical ecosystem rather than the central authority on learning, thereby addressing concerns regarding the erosion of professional expertise.

The implementation of personalization relies heavily on the comprehensive gathering and examination of student data, which raises important issues regarding privacy and the "datafication" of learning (Akgun & Greenhow, 2022; Floridi et al., 2018). Adaptive systems must continuously collect data on student interactions, performance, and behavioral patterns to function effectively. This data is essential for algorithmic personalization; however, it generates a conflict between the advantages of individualized learning and the surveillance of students. The literature indicates a notable deficiency in the mechanisms through which these systems communicate data usage to users and secure informed consent, especially concerning minors in K-12 environments. This oversight presents a significant risk to student autonomy and privacy, indicating that ethical data governance should be an integral aspect of personalization frameworks rather than a secondary consideration.

Ultimately, a significant challenge remains in the creation of AI systems that possess genuine context awareness. Many personalization algorithms rely on decontextualized data points, such as quiz scores and time on task, and face challenges in addressing the intricate, contextual realities of a classroom, including peer dynamics, off-task behaviors, and a student's emotional state on specific days (Cukurova et al., 2019). Alfredo et al. (2024) emphasize that human-centered AI design is essential for bridging this gap. In the absence of this context, AI recommendations may lack sensitivity or relevance, which could jeopardize the trust of educators. Future research should concentrate on multimodal AI capable of interpreting a broader range of contextual signals and on developing interfaces that clearly convey the algorithm's reasoning to educators, ensuring that its adaptations are transparent and actionable.

8.2.2.2 Chatbots and Conversational Agents

Recent research examines the impact of a chatbot's personality and rapport-building capabilities on educational outcomes, extending beyond mere functionality. Huang et al. (2022) demonstrated that chatbots exhibiting a supportive and empathetic style are more effective in facilitating language learning and maintaining student engagement compared to those that are purely transactional. This indicates that the emotional aspect of human-chatbot interaction is a critical success factor, akin to the significance of teacher-student relationships in human learning. Still, creating genuine empathy and culturally appropriate rapport is a tough technical and ethical challenge, with the risk of creating interactions that feel manipulative or uncanny if done poorly (Li & Gu, 2023). This alters the criterion for success from mere utility to a more nuanced assessment of social and emotional impact.

Conversational agents are often advocated as instruments for scalable and equitable education. Nonetheless, their advantages are not inherently universal. Kuhail et al. (2023) indicate that the effectiveness of chatbots may be influenced by variables including students' language proficiency, digital literacy, and cultural background. Students who are less familiar with the formal register typically employed by chatbots may encounter difficulties in effective interaction, which could exacerbate achievement gaps rather than mitigate them. The infrastructure necessary for advanced generative chatbots, such as reliable high-speed internet and capable devices, is not uniformly accessible worldwide (Bhutoria, 2022). The equity potential of chatbots depends on deliberate design for inclusivity and a critical understanding of the digital divides they may worsen.

The emergence of generative AI is prompting a conceptual transformation in the function of chatbots, evolving from intelligent tutors to collaborative learning partners or "co-learners." ChatGPT and similar tools facilitate idea generation, argument critique, and debate simulation, providing students with an interactive platform to evaluate and enhance their reasoning (Chiu et al., 2023). This shifts the chatbot from merely providing answers to serving as a catalyst for cognitive conflict and deeper inquiry. This presents a significant opportunity to enhance critical thinking skills while also introducing complexities for assessment and pedagogy. Educators are required to create activities that utilize collaborative potential while reducing the risk of intellectual outsourcing. The focus should shift toward evaluating the learning process and critical engagement with AI-generated outputs, rather than solely assessing the final product.

8.2.2.3 Trust, Ethics, and Governance

Explainability is fundamental to establishing trust, as it enables an AI system to articulate its recommendations in a manner comprehensible to both educators and students. Vereschak et al. (2021) emphasize that the absence of explainability renders AI a "black box," undermining trust and hindering teachers' ability to validate, critique, or properly contextualize its recommendations. If an AI identifies a student as at risk, it is essential for the teacher to understand the rationale to implement effective interventions. Nazaretsky et al. (2022) found that professional development that demystifies AI's functioning significantly increases teachers' trust and willingness to adopt it. Therefore, the development of Explainable AI (XAI) tailored to educational contexts is not a luxury but an ethical prerequisite for meaningful and accountable implementation.

Perhaps the most severe ethical risk is the perpetuation or amplification of societal biases through algorithmic systems. AI models trained on historical educational data can inherit biases present in that data such as those related to gender, socioeconomic status, or race (Akgun & Greenhow, 2022). This could lead to systems that systematically lower expectations for certain student groups, recommend less challenging pathways, or misidentify dialectical differences as errors. The literature calls for rigorous algorithmic auditing and the development of "debiasing" techniques specific to educational datasets. However, as Li and Gu (2023) argue, technical solutions are insufficient without a concurrent commitment to diversifying development teams and incorporating critical perspectives from sociology and ethics into the design process.

The current governance landscape is characterized by a significant gap between high-level ethical principles (e.g., those from UNESCO) and enforceable policy at the national or institutional level (Kim, 2023). This vacuum is often filled by commercial entities whose primary incentives may be market share and profit, not pedagogical efficacy, or equity. The reliance on third-party, proprietary platforms raises concerns about who owns educational data, how it is used for commercial purposes, and the long-term sustainability of building education on corporate infrastructure. This underscores the urgent need for robust public policy and institutional frameworks that assert educational values—such as equity, privacy, and pedagogical autonomy—over commercial interests in the adoption of AI.

8.2.2.4 Institutional Adoption and Systemic Challenges

Technology proponents frequently characterize AI as a disruptive force; however, the adoption of such technologies within institutions is fundamentally a matter of integrating them into established cultures, curricula, and assessment frameworks (Granic, 2022). This frequently results in a "pilot paradox," wherein small-scale experiments show potential yet do not scale effectively due to the neglect of fundamental institutional structures such as timetables, funding models, or accountability measures (Dogan et al., 2023). Sustainable adoption necessitates the transition from isolated projects to comprehensive, institution-wide digital transformation strategies that integrate AI initiatives with fundamental educational missions and values.

The successful adoption of initiatives is closely associated with effective leadership and change management practices. Studies demonstrate that institutional leaders frequently lack the necessary technical and strategic acumen to critically assess AI technologies or advocate for their deliberate integration (Jamalova et al., 2022). In the absence of a definitive vision from leadership that considers both the opportunities and challenges, AI projects may become disjointed and influenced by departmental zeal or vendor promotion rather than educational strategy. This underscores the necessity for professional development not just for educators but also for administrators and policymakers, enabling them to pose pertinent inquiries regarding efficacy, ethics, cost, and long-term sustainability before making purchase decisions.

The economic aspect of AI implementation poses a significant threat to intensifying global educational disparity. The expenses related to licensing sophisticated AI platforms, sustaining infrastructure, and educating workers are considerable (Bhutoria, 2022). Dogan et al. (2023) observed that the COVID-19 pandemic revealed and exacerbated digital disparities. The incorporation of AI poses the risk of establishing a new "AI divide," wherein affluent institutions and governments exploit technology to enhance learning, while under-resourced counterparts lag further behind. This prompts critical inquiries regarding the advancement of open-source educational AI alternatives, equitable funding frameworks, and international collaboration to guarantee that AI functions as an instrument for diminishing, rather than exacerbating, global educational inequalities.

8.2.2.5 Chatbots and Conversational Agents

Chatbots are a prominent application of AIED, experiencing significant growth in adoption within higher education and online learning platforms. Systematic reviews (Kuhail et al., 2023; Wollny et al., 2021; Lai & Lee, 2024) consistently emphasize their applications in language learning (Huang et al., 2022), intelligent tutoring (Latham et al., 2011), and course scaffolding (Winkler et al., 2020).

Research indicates that effectively designed chatbots can improve motivation, self-regulated learning, and retention. Chiu et al. (2023) demonstrated that the combination of chatbots and teacher scaffolding enhanced metacognitive awareness in undergraduates. Qiu et al. (2025) identified quantifiable learning improvements in experimental contexts where students engaged with conversational agents for problem-solving.

Nevertheless, the findings exhibit considerable variability. Certain studies indicate a limited impact, citing inadequate natural language processing, scripted dialogues, or insufficient contextual relevance as contributing factors (Hwang & Chang, 2021). Janati et al. (2020) observed that students' trust in chatbots is influenced by cultural and disciplinary contexts, indicating that adoption is not universally applicable.

The emergence of generative AI chatbots, such as ChatGPT, has heightened discussions. Although capable of generating advanced responses, they also obscure the distinctions between appropriate assistance and academic dishonesty (Cotton et al., 2023). Cooper (2023) cautioned against "plagiarism by proxy," a phenomenon in which students delegate cognitive tasks to machines. Institutions face challenges in revising assessment designs to incorporate these capabilities. Methodologically, there is a paucity of studies investigating generative chatbots within controlled educational environments, resulting in a notable deficiency in empirical validation.

Chatbot research demonstrates the dual nature of AI: while these technologies can enhance engagement, they also pose a threat to academic integrity and profound learning if improperly utilized. In addition to functionality, recent studies examine how a chatbot's personality design and rapport-building capabilities affect educational results. Huang et al. (2022) discovered that chatbots employing a supportive and sympathetic conversation style were more efficacious in fostering language acquisition and perseverance compared to solely transactional agents. This indicates that the emotional aspect of human-chatbot interaction is a crucial determinant of success, mirroring findings in human learning where teacher-student connections are essential. However, engineering genuine empathy and culturally appropriate rapport remains a significant technical and ethical challenge, risking the creation of manipulative or uncanny interactions if poorly executed (Li & Gu, 2023). This shifts the evaluation metric from simple utility to a more nuanced measure of social-emotional efficacy.

Conversational agents are frequently promoted as tools for scalable, equitable education. However, their benefits are not automatically universal. Kuhail et al. (2023) note that chatbot effectiveness can be mediated by factors such as students' language proficiency, digital literacy, and cultural background. For instance, students less familiar with the formal register often used by chatbots may struggle to interact effectively, potentially widening rather than narrowing achievement gaps. Furthermore, the infrastructure required for advanced generative chatbots (e.g., reliable high-speed internet, capable devices) is not equally accessible globally (Bhutoria, 2022). Therefore, the equity promise of chatbots is contingent on intentional design for inclusivity and critical awareness of the digital divides they might exacerbate.

The advent of generative AI is catalyzing a conceptual shift in the role of chatbots from intelligent tutors to collaborative learning partners or "co-learners." Tools like ChatGPT can generate ideas, critique arguments, and simulate debates, offering students a dynamic platform to test and refine their thinking (Chiu et al., 2023). Such an approach converts the chatbot from a mere provider of answers into a trigger for cognitive dissonance and profound exploration. Such an approach offers a significant chance to enhance critical thinking skills, but it also adds complexity for assessment and instruction. Educators must now create activities that harness collaborative potential while reducing the risk of intellectual outsourcing, focusing on evaluating the learning process and critical interaction with AI-generated outputs rather than solely the finished product.

8.2.2.6 Trust, Ethics, and Governance

The integration of AIED depends not solely on technical efficacy but also on the trust established among educators, students, and policymakers. The readiness of educators to include AI is significantly influenced by their judgments of transparency, reliability, and congruence with professional responsibilities (Nazaretsky et al., 2022; Shen et al., 2025).

Research constantly highlights ethical issues: data privacy, algorithmic bias, student autonomy, and accountability (Akgun & Greenhow, 2022; Floridi et al., 2018). Li and Gu (2023) introduced a risk paradigm that emphasizes the distribution of responsibility among developers, educators, and institutions. However, implementing such frameworks in actual classrooms continues to be challenging.

Evaluation approaches demonstrate significant variability. Evaluation practices vary widely. Vereschak et al. (2021) found inconsistent methods for assessing AI-assisted decision-making, undermining comparability. Some frameworks emphasize fairness metrics, while others focus on usability or pedagogical alignment. This methodological pluralism reflects a lack of consensus on what "trustworthy AI in education" entails.

A further debate concerns the role of AI relative to teachers. Cukurova et al. (2020) and Cain (2023) warn against framing AI as a potential replacement, advocating instead for AI as a co-pilot that augments teacher expertise. However, techno-optimist perspectives often underplay the risk of teacher deskilling or reduced professional autonomy. The ethical challenge lies in designing systems that empower rather than displace educators.

Internationally, governance remains fragmented. While the EU has advanced regulations on "high-risk AI," most national education systems lack clear policies. As a result, adoption often proceeds in an ad hoc manner without robust ethical safeguards (Kim, 2023).

A cornerstone of building trust is explainability—the ability of an AI system to justify its recommendations in a way that educators and students can understand. Vereschak et al. (2021) highlight that without explainability, AI becomes a "black box," eroding trust and making it impossible for teachers to validate, critique, or appropriately contextualize its suggestions. For example, if an AI flags a student as being at risk, the teacher needs to understand the reason *in order* to take meaningful action. Nazaretsky et al. (2022) found that professional development that demystifies AI's functioning significantly increases teachers' trust and willingness to adopt it. Therefore, the development of Explainable AI (XAI) tailored to educational contexts is not a luxury but an ethical prerequisite for meaningful and accountable implementation.

Perhaps the most severe ethical risk is the perpetuation or amplification of societal biases through algorithmic systems. AI models trained on historical educational data can inherit biases present in that data, such as those related to gender, socioeconomic status, or race (Akgun & Greenhow, 2022). This could lead to systems that systematically lower expectations for certain student groups, recommend less challenging pathways, or misidentify dialectical differences as errors. The literature calls for rigorous algorithmic auditing and the development of "debiasing" techniques specific to educational datasets. However, as Li and Gu (2023) argue, technical solutions are insufficient without a concurrent commitment to diversifying development teams and incorporating critical perspectives from sociology and ethics into the design process.

The current governance landscape is characterized by a significant gap between high-level ethical principles (e.g., those from UNESCO) and enforceable policy at the national or institutional level (Kim, 2023). This vacuum is often filled by commercial entities whose primary incentives may be market share and profit, not necessarily pedagogical efficacy or equity. The reliance on third-party, proprietary platforms raises concerns about who owns educational data, how it is used for commercial purposes, and the long-term sustainability of building education on corporate infrastructure. This underscores the urgent need for robust public policy and institutional frameworks that assert educational values—such as equity, privacy, and pedagogical autonomy—over commercial interests in the adoption of AI.

8.2.2.7 Institutional Adoption and Systemic Challenges

Beyond classrooms, AI influences institutional management, online learning ecosystems, and national education strategies. The COVID-19 pandemic accelerated reliance on AI-enabled platforms, enabling continuity but also exposing inequities in access (Dwivedi et al., 2020; Dogan et al., 2023).

Systematic mapping studies (Jamalova et al., 2022) note that while AI holds promise for scaling education, most implementations remain experimental. Granic (2022) identified recurring adoption barriers: cost, expertise deficits, infrastructure gaps, and resistance from stakeholders. Comparative research highlights international inequalities. China and the United States are at the forefront of innovation, whereas numerous developing regions face limitations due to inadequate bandwidth, devices, and policy support (Knox, 2020; Bhutoria, 2022).

Institutional adoption is hindered by deficiencies in professional development. Educators often lack the necessary training to effectively utilize AI tools (Goçen & Doger, 2025). In the absence of capacity-building, AI may transform into a technological imposition instead of serving as a pedagogical enhancement. Policy frameworks at the systemic level are inadequately developed. UNESCO (2023) advocates for the inclusive adoption of AI; however, the scope and enforceability of national policies differ significantly. Some focus on innovation and competitiveness, whereas others highlight the importance of ethical safeguards. This divergence results in a heterogeneous array of practices that yield inconsistent effects on equity and quality.

A notable systemic issue is the disparity between the swift advancement of AI technology and the gradual, methodical evolution within educational institutions. Technology advocates frequently characterize AI as a disruptive force; however, institutional adoption is fundamentally a process of integrating it into established cultures, curricula, and assessment frameworks (Granic, 2022). This process frequently results in a "pilot paradox," wherein small-scale experiments show potential yet do not scale effectively due to a failure to engage fundamental institutional structures such as timetables, funding models, or accountability measures (Dogan et al., 2023). Sustainable adoption necessitates transitioning from isolated projects to comprehensive, institution-wide digital transformation strategies that integrate AI initiatives with fundamental educational missions and values.

The successful adoption of initiatives is closely associated with effective leadership and change management practices. This suggests that institutional leaders frequently do not possess the necessary technical and strategic literacy to critically assess AI tools or to advocate for their careful integration (Jamalova et al., 2022). In the absence of a coherent vision from leadership that considers both the opportunities and challenges, AI initiatives risk becoming disjointed and influenced more by departmental interests or vendor promotions than by educational strategy. This underscores the necessity for professional development for both educators and administrators, enabling them to pose pertinent inquiries regarding efficacy, ethics, cost, and long-term sustainability prior to procurement decisions.

The economic aspect of AI adoption poses a significant risk of worsening global educational inequality. The expenses related to licensing advanced AI platforms, sustaining infrastructure, and training personnel are significant (Bhutoria, 2022). Dogan et al. (2023) observe that the COVID-19 pandemic has both revealed and intensified existing digital divides. The integration of AI poses the risk of establishing a new "AI divide," wherein affluent institutions and nations utilize technology to enhance learning, while those with limited resources increasingly lag behind. This prompts critical inquiries regarding the advancement of open-source educational AI alternatives, equitable funding frameworks, and international collaboration to guarantee that AI functions as a mechanism for diminishing, rather than exacerbating, global educational inequalities.

8.2.3 Critical Analysis

The literature identifies persistent limitations across these themes that hinder the cumulative advancement of knowledge regarding AIED. A primary issue is methodological narrowness, with numerous studies depending on small-scale pilots or short-term experimental designs that offer restricted generalizability (Holstein et al., 2020; Winkler et al., 2020). Longitudinal and cross-cultural research is infrequent, limiting the ability to comprehend enduring effects across various learning contexts. Conceptual fragmentation presents a significant challenge. Research on personalization often overlooks ethical considerations, while studies on governance frequently disregard pedagogical aspects, resulting in parallel discourses with limited integration. The absence of cross-cutting frameworks diminishes the potential for both theoretical development and practical implementation. Furthermore, evaluation methods are inconsistent, with outcomes assessed through performance improvements, engagement metrics, or teacher satisfaction, complicating comparative analysis and leading to inconclusive results (Huang et al., 2022; Qiu et al., 2025). A notable limitation is the ongoing bias toward higher education. Universities frequently function as experimental sites for AI tools; however, K-12, vocational, and lifelong learning environments are less examined in scholarly discourse, despite their critical role in promoting equitable access to education. The restricted incorporation of student and teacher viewpoints indicates a top-down approach in much of the discourse, favoring institutional or technological narratives at the expense of lived experiences. These shortcomings indicate that although the field is dynamic and growing quickly, it is still fragmented and lacks cohesive frameworks for integration.

The literature is increasingly shaped by commercial interests, leading to potential conflicts of interest and distortion in research focus, in addition to methodological and conceptual challenges. A substantial number of studies receive funding from, or are conducted in collaboration with, EdTech companies (Knox, 2020; Baker & Smith, 2019). Such an arrangement results in a publication bias favoring positive outcomes, an emphasis on commercially viable products over fundamental pedagogical inquiries, and a propensity to view educational contexts as uniform markets instead of culturally distinct ecosystems. The commercial influence may align the AIED research agenda with corporate priorities—such as scalability, user engagement, and data capture—rather than with fundamental educational values like equity, critical thinking, and teacher agency, which could undermine the field's academic independence and critical rigor.

A significant philosophical limitation exists in the field's tendency to depend on a restricted, instrumentalist conception of learning. The emphasis on measurable "learning gains," as indicated by test scores or completion rates (Qiu et al., 2025; Huang et al., 2022), frequently overlooks more intricate, human-centered educational results. Research on AI's influence on the development of metacognition, creativity, collaboration, and critical thinking skills is notably insufficient—skills that are increasingly essential in the 21st century (Funke et al., 2018). Accepting performance metrics as the primary valid evidence may lead the literature to inadvertently optimize AI systems for efficient training instead of transformative education, thereby neglecting the broader purpose of schooling within a democratic society.

Finally, the critical analysis must highlight a profound lack of *ecological validity* in much of the research. The controlled, often short-term conditions under which AI tools are tested (e.g., a single-semester course in a university setting) bear little resemblance to the messy, complex, and resource-constrained reality of most educational environments (Granic, 2022; Dogan et al., 2023). These studies fail to account for how teachers creatively adapt (or abandon) technologies, how students use them in unintended ways, or how the tools perform under the strain of outdated infrastructure or limited bandwidth. This creates a validity gap, where tools deemed "effective" in research settings may prove dysfunctional or even harmful when integrated into the dynamic social ecosystem of a real classroom, further widening the divide between research and practice.

8.2.4 Identification of the Research Gap

The current literature illustrates AI's revolutionary capacity in education; yet, the body of work is fragmented and unevenly distributed across topic areas. Pedagogical research frequently emphasizes personalization and adaptive learning as fundamental advantages of AI; yet these studies generally proceed independently of wider systemic and governance issues. Research on chatbots and intelligent tutoring systems has predominantly focused on interaction design and user engagement, frequently neglecting the institutional or regulatory factors that influence their long-term efficacy. This conceptual division has generated competing lines of investigation that rarely coalesce into a comprehensive understanding of AI's role in education.

A disparity exists between theoretical and empirical contributions. Although numerous ethical and governance models have been suggested, they often lack empirical validation in practical learning situations, especially in non-Western cultures. In contrast, studies on institutional adoption mostly emphasize infrastructural preparation, financial capability, and digital infrastructure, frequently neglecting the necessary pedagogical integration to guarantee that AI tools enrich educational practices rather than merely digitizing them. The disparity between technological acceptance and pedagogical reform indicates that essential aspects of teaching and learning are being eclipsed by operational issues.

Collectively, these limitations highlight the lack of comprehensive, interdisciplinary assessments that integrate educational, ethical, and systemic aspects into a unified analytical framework. Furthermore, there exists a significant deficiency in the consideration of global disparities and contextual variability. Limited research explicitly examines how AI adoption may either intensify or mitigate educational disparities across socioeconomic, cultural, and geographical contexts. This absence is notably noteworthy, as AI's effects are expected to be unevenly distributed, with marginalized populations and under-resourced organizations encountering increased risks of exclusion. To address this research gap, it is essential to employ integrative techniques that emphasize equity, inclusion, and global perspectives, ensuring that AIED evolves in a manner that is both contextually relevant and socially equitable.

The disunity in the literature results in a significant implementation gap. Although pedagogical studies innovate in customization and chatbot research enhances interface design, they frequently function in isolation, detached from the systemic realities of institutional acceptance, regulatory limitations, and teacher preparedness (Goçen & Doger, 2025; Jamalova et al., 2022). In contrast, institutional studies emphasize infrastructure and expenses, lacking a sophisticated comprehension of the most successful or ethically appropriate pedagogical applications. This disjunction indicates that educators and policymakers face either innovative tools that are unfeasible for widespread implementation or extensive infrastructure proposals devoid of educational guidance. The gap needs not merely additional research but research that effectively integrates these disparate silos to offer practical avenues for application.

Contemporary research is primarily reactive, examining existing instruments and their immediate effects. A notable deficiency exists in anticipatory and forward-looking research that predicts forthcoming advancements in AI capabilities and their prospective effects on education (Dwivedi et al., 2021; Cain, 2023). The rapid emergence of generative AI exemplifies this; the literature was largely caught off guard, scrambling to address issues of academic integrity after the fact. There is an urgent necessity for research utilizing foresight methodologies to model prospective scenarios, foresee ethical dilemmas (e.g., AI-generated synthetic students, emotion-sensing environments), and establish resilient governance frameworks that can adapt to rapid technological advancements rather than consistently trailing behind.

The bias in the field toward higher education in developed nations (Bhutoria, 2022; Chen et al., 2020b) has resulted in a significant oversight concerning the global majority. The research gap extends beyond the absence of studies in low-income or Global South contexts; it encompasses a deficiency in contextually relevant frameworks that recognize varying infrastructural realities, cultural values pertaining to education, pedagogical traditions, and economic models. The belief that AIED models created in affluent Western universities can be universally applied represents a form of academic neocolonialism, potentially worsening global inequities. Thus, there exists a significant need for research that transcends mere documentation of the "digital divide" to engage in the co-design and evaluation of context-sensitive, sustainable, and equitable AIED approaches that cater to diverse populations without imposing external technocentric paradigms.

8.2.5 Link to the Research Question

In response to these identified gaps, this systematic review is designed to provide a comprehensive and integrative analysis of AIED. Specifically, the study seeks to synthesize findings across pedagogical, ethical, and systemic domains, thereby addressing the fragmented nature of existing scholarship. It also critically evaluates the methodological robustness and contextual generalizability of prior studies, highlighting both the strengths and limitations of current evidence. Furthermore, the review identifies future research directions that align AI innovation with educational equity, teacher agency, and ethical governance, ensuring that technological adoption remains grounded in inclusive and sustainable principles. By bridging these fragmented literatures, this work provides a comprehensive foundation for educators, policymakers, and researchers seeking to navigate AI's evolving role in education.

Directly addressing these gaps, this review will consciously adopt a systemic and interdisciplinary lens. It will move beyond a technocentric analysis to examine AIED through integrated dimensions: the pedagogical (what happens in the classroom), the ethical (what values are embedded and at risk), and the sociotechnical (how institutions and policies shape adoption). This review synthesizes insights from computer science, education, sociology, ethics, and policy studies to address the conceptual fragmentation identified in the critical analysis. This approach is essential for creating a comprehensive map of the field, recognizing the complexity of educational change, in which technology interacts with human and systemic factors.

This review will prioritize equity and agency as central evaluative criteria in response to the identified biases and gaps. This analysis will evaluate the literature based on reported efficacy and its consideration of how AI applications may affect socioeconomic disparities (Bhutoria, 2022) and their impact on the agency of educators and learners (Li & Gu, 2023; Cukurova et al., 2020). This value-explicit position intentionally addresses the frequently implicit technooptimism and commercial influences in the field, redirecting the discussion toward the fundamental objectives of education. It positions the review as a critical intervention aimed at ensuring that the future of AIED is shaped by educational priorities rather than technological capabilities.

Ultimately, this systematic review seeks to provide a foundational reference point for responsible innovation in AIED. By synthesizing the current state of knowledge across disparate domains, it will offer researchers a clear understanding of robust methodologies and persistent theoretical gaps to guide future primary studies. For practitioners and policymakers, it will translate fragmented findings into a coherent set of evidence-based considerations for tool selection, implementation strategy, and ethical governance. By mapping the landscape holistically, this review aims to catalyze a more mature, critical, and impactful research agenda that ensures artificial intelligence serves to enhance rather than undermine equitable and human-centric education.

8.3 Methodology

This study employed a systematic review methodology to provide a comprehensive synthesis of research on AI in the education sector. Following the PRISMA framework, the review was structured to ensure transparency, replicability, and rigor in both the search and evaluation processes. The systematic approach was chosen to move beyond narrative reviews and to critically assess the fragmented and multidisciplinary evidence base spanning pedagogy, ethics, governance, and institutional adoption.

The search strategy was designed to capture peer-reviewed literature from leading academic databases, including Scopus, Web of Science, IEEE Xplore, and ERIC, which collectively represent education, computer science, and interdisciplinary research domains. Keywords and Boolean operators were employed to cover a broad range of relevant terms such as "artificial intelligence," "AI in education," "learning analytics," "intelligent tutoring systems," "chatbots in learning," "ethics in AI education," and "educational technology adoption." The search was limited to publications between 2010 and 2025 to reflect the most relevant technological advancements and policy debates in the sector. Only peer-reviewed journal articles and conference proceedings written in English were considered to maintain academic quality and comparability.

Clear inclusion and exclusion criteria were applied to refine the corpus. Studies were included if they explicitly addressed the use, impact, or governance of AI in educational contexts, ranging from K-12 to higher education, vocational, and lifelong learning. Articles that dealt with adjacent technologies (such as generic digital platforms or non-AI learning management systems) without an explicit AI component were excluded. Additionally, editorials, opinion papers, and nonempirical commentaries were filtered out to prioritize empirical and theoretical contributions. This process ensured that the dataset represented a balanced body of evidence across both experimental and applied domains.

The selection process proceeded in three stages: (1) title and abstract screening, (2) full-text review, and (3) quality assessment. Duplicates were removed using reference management software, after which two independent reviewers screened the articles to reduce selection bias. The quality of eligible studies was then appraised on the basis of methodological rigor, clarity of research design, and relevance to the research objectives. Discrepancies in assessments were resolved through discussion to reach a consensus.

Data extraction was carried out systematically, with each study coded for bibliographic details, educational level, AI application type, research design, and key findings. A thematic synthesis approach was then employed to integrate results across pedagogical, ethical, and systemic domains, allowing the identification of both converging patterns and gaps in the literature. Quantitative insights, such as publication trends by year and geographical distribution, were combined with qualitative thematic analysis to provide a holistic understanding of the field.

Finally, to ensure robustness and minimize bias, the entire review process was documented and validated against systematic review standards. This methodological framework allows the study not only to consolidate fragmented knowledge but also to critically evaluate the strengths and limitations of existing research, thereby laying a foundation for future scholarship and practice in AI and education.

Figure 8.1 shows the study selection process according to the Preferred Reporting Items for Systematic Reviews and Meta-Analyses (PRISMA) guidelines. A total of 1,236 records were identified through searches of the Scopus, Web of Science, IEEE Xplore, and ERIC databases. After removing 312 duplicates, 924 records were screened based on their title and abstract. From this screening, 641 records were excluded for reasons such as not being AI-focused, not being related to the education sector, or being nonempirical commentaries. The full text of the remaining 283 articles was assessed for eligibility. Of these, 191 were excluded due to insufficient methodological detail, a focus on purely technical AI without educational application, or limited relevance to the review's focus on pedagogy and ethics. Ultimately, 92 studies (comprising 72 journal articles and 20 conference papers) were included in the qualitative synthesis.

Figure 8.2 presents a bar chart illustrating the distribution of the reviewed studies across different educational levels. The data reveals a significant concentration of AI in education (AIED) research in the *higher education (Higher Ed)*

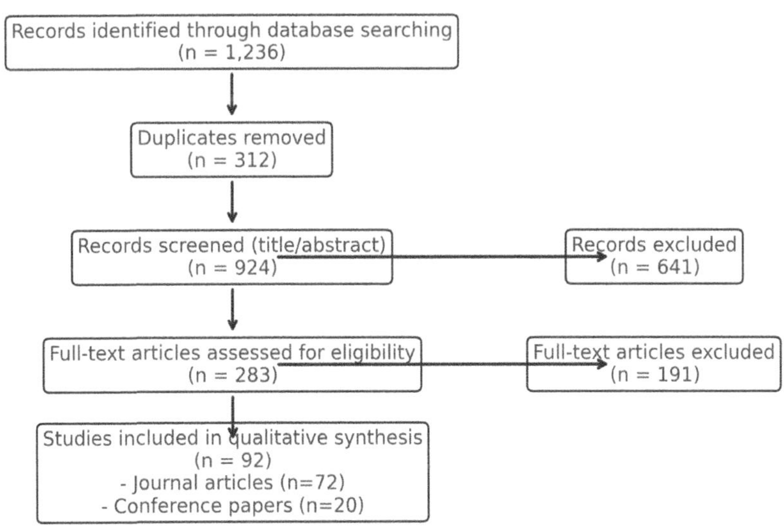

FIGURE 8.1
PRISMA flow diagram.

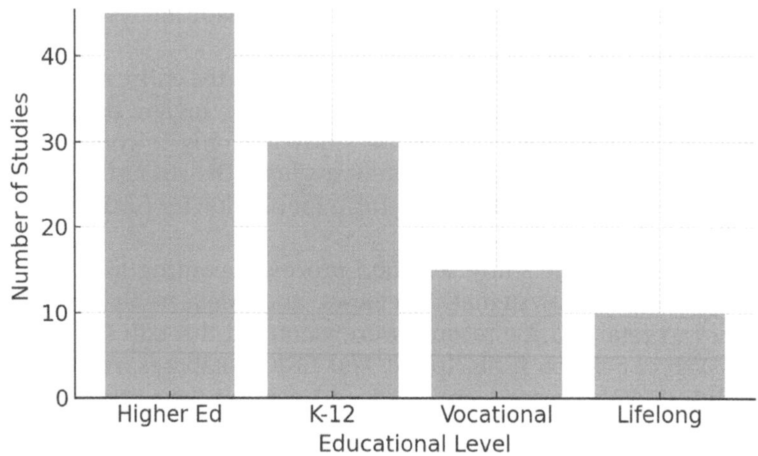

FIGURE 8.2
Distribution of studies by educational level.

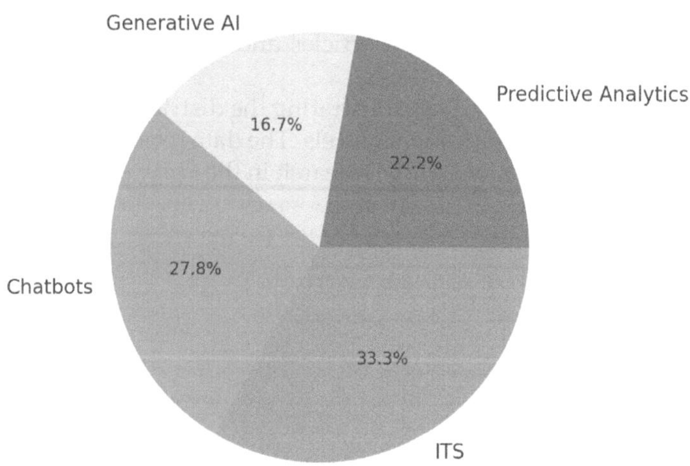

FIGURE 8.3
AI technologies studied.

sector, which is represented by the tallest bar on the chart. This is followed by research conducted in *K-12* settings. In contrast, studies focusing on *vocational* and *lifelong* learning contexts are substantially fewer.

Figure 8.3 is a pie chart that breaks down the percentage of studies focused on specific types of AI technologies within the education sector. The data shows that intelligent tutoring systems (ITS) were the most frequently studied technology, comprising 33.3% of the reviewed research. This was closely followed by research on chatbots at 27.8%. Predictive analytics and generative AI were studied less frequently, accounting for 22.2% and 16.7% of the studies, respectively.

8.4 Discussion

This systematic review synthesized findings from 92 studies to map the landscape of AI applications in the education sector, identify key themes, and critically evaluate their implications. The discussion interprets these findings, relates them to the existing body of literature, and addresses the initial research questions while also considering the practical implications and limitations of the current research.

The analysis indicated that AI applications in education primarily emphasize pedagogical personalization such as adaptive learning systems and intelligent tutoring systems, and automated assessment and feedback mechanisms, including essay grading and feedback generators, as well as educational chatbots designed for student support and query resolution (Kuhail et al., 2023; Huang et al., 2022). A significant theme that emerged is the essential role of trust, ethics, and teacher agency in the effective implementation of these technologies (Akgun & Greenhow, 2022; Nazaretsky et al., 2022). The findings indicate that the most effective implementations are those that augment human capabilities through hybrid human–AI collaboration models rather than those that aim to replace educators (Holstein et al., 2020; Chiu et al., 2023).

The analysis identified multiple interrelated themes essential for comprehending the role of AIED. The finding that hybrid human–AI models are most effective for pedagogical personalization supports contemporary posthumanist pedagogical theories, which view technology as an augmenting tool rather than a replacement for the teacher (Holstein et al., 2020). Studies, including that of Chine et al. (2022), provide evidence that combined human–AI personalization results in significant improvements in educational equity, a result seldom attained by fully automated systems alone. This suggests that future AIED development should shift from creating fully autonomous systems to developing "orchestration tools" that offer teachers actionable insights while maintaining human control over pedagogical decisions. This approach directly addresses concerns regarding teacher deskilling and upholds professional agency. This review examines the disconnect between technical innovation and ethical considerations, showing that studies incorporating ethical design principles—such as explainable AI (XAI), transparency, and fairness—consistently indicate increased levels of teacher trust and adoption (Nazaretsky et al., 2022; Vereschak et al., 2021). Li and Gu (2023) propose a risk framework that integrates ethical considerations throughout the AI lifecycle, positioning ethics as a fundamental design requirement rather than an afterthought. The challenges identified by Ali et al. (2024), including data privacy and algorithmic bias, represent not only technical obstacles but also essential barriers to adoption that require resolution through participatory design that engages educators, students, and policymakers (Alfredo et al., 2024). Third, although chatbots demonstrate potential in delivering scalable, round-the-clock support (Kuhail et al., 2023; Lai & Lee, 2024), our synthesis indicates that their effectiveness is frequently confined to lower-order cognitive tasks, such as responding to FAQs and offering basic practice drills, with a restricted capacity to promote deep, critical thinking (Hwang & Chang, 2021). The emergence of generative AI chatbots has heightened discussions regarding academic integrity (Cotton et al., 2023) and simultaneously created opportunities for enhancing creativity. This highlights the essential consideration that deploying chatbot applications should be purposefully aligned with defined learning objectives and incorporated into a comprehensive pedagogical framework that includes explicit guidelines for ethical use.

This review's findings have important implications for primary stakeholders in education. Practitioners should actively pursue and promote AI tools that provide transparency in decision-making processes, as this is essential for preserving professional agency and the capacity to intervene and contextualize AI outputs. Educators must cultivate a critical understanding of AI to effectively instruct students in its ethical application, shifting from passive consumers of technology to active co-designers of AI-enhanced learning environments. Policymakers and institutions should strategically align investments in AI infrastructure with comprehensive professional development and the collaborative establishment of clear ethical guidelines (Akgun & Greenhow, 2022). Policies must require algorithmic transparency and auditability, and institutions should implement clear protocols for data privacy to foster trust and safeguard stakeholder rights, thereby establishing a framework that facilitates responsible innovation. This review identifies significant gaps in current research, highlighting the necessity of longitudinal studies to assess the long-term effects of AI, especially in K-12 environments (Chiu et al., 2023). It also emphasizes the exploration of domain-specific applications beyond STEM and language learning, as well as the need for the development of comprehensive theoretical frameworks that elucidate the mechanisms and efficacy of AI interventions, thereby advancing the field from proof-of-concept to theory-driven, evidence-based practice (Chen et al., 2020b).

8.4.1 Critical Reflection on Limitations

The results of this review should be considered within the context of its limitations and those of the studies included. The reviewed studies exhibit a notable limitation due to their short-term pilot nature or their execution in controlled laboratory environments, thereby constraining the applicability of their findings to diverse, real-world classroom settings over longer durations (Wang et al., 2024). Moreover, a substantial dependence on self-reported data or limited sample sizes in many studies may compromise the validity and robustness of the findings. This review acknowledges certain limitations. Despite efforts to ensure comprehensiveness, its scope may be constrained by the exclusion of non-English publications and a focus on specific databases, which could result in the omission of pertinent studies from other languages or sources. The field of AIED, especially generative AI, is evolving rapidly. As a result, the search cutoff date excludes many recent breakthroughs and studies related to large language models (LLMs), posing a significant challenge for any systematic review in this fast-developing area.

This systematic review demonstrates that AI has considerable potential to transform education through personalization, automation, and support. Realizing this potential depends on transcending a technocentric perspective. The optimal approach involves human-centered AI, defined by hybrid collaboration models that enhance teacher expertise, a strong dedication to ethical and transparent design, and a research agenda focused on long-term, theory-driven studies within genuine educational settings. The success of AIED will be evaluated based on its capacity to empower educators and improve learning in an equitable and ethical manner, rather than its sophistication.

8.5 Conclusion

This systematic review aims to synthesize the existing literature on AI applications in education, mapping key applications, evaluating their efficacy, and identifying the main challenges and opportunities in this rapidly evolving field. This systematic review demonstrates that AI possesses considerable transformative potential for education, facilitating enhanced personalization, automation, and scalable support. The efficacy and successful integration of this approach depend significantly on a human-centered framework that emphasizes pedagogical integration, ethical governance, and equitable access rather than solely technological considerations (Alfredo et al., 2024; Akgun & Greenhow, 2022). Evidence suggests that the most effective models involve hybrid human–AI collaboration, wherein technology enhances teacher expertise instead of attempting to replace it (Holstein et al., 2020; Chiu et al., 2023).

This review presents a novel synthesis that transcends the mere cataloging of AI tools, critically analyzing the conditions that determine their success or failure. The main contribution is a comprehensive framework that integrates the technical aspects of AI, such as adaptive algorithms and chatbots, with essential human factors, including teacher trust (Nazaretsky et al., 2022), ethical risk (Li & Gu, 2023), and pedagogical design (Cukurova et al., 2019). This approach provides a detailed framework for researchers and practitioners, highlighting that the value of AIED is not intrinsic but is achieved through careful implementation that considers these interrelated dimensions.

This synthesis reveals several specific directions for future research based on identified gaps. There is a critical necessity to advance from short-term pilots to longitudinal studies that monitor the enduring effects of AI tools on educational outcomes and teaching practices in genuine, diverse classroom environments (Wang et al., 2024). To ensure the usability, trustworthiness, and pedagogical soundness of these technologies, a participatory, human-centered design approach is essential. This requires research that actively engages teachers and students as co-designers throughout the AI development process (Alfredo et al., 2024). Further investigation is necessary to develop and validate ethical frameworks tailored to specific contexts that can facilitate responsible AI adoption, particularly considering the distinct challenges and opportunities in low-resource environments and among underrepresented student populations (Akgun & Greenhow, 2022; Floridi et al., 2018). Ultimately, the discipline must confront its foundational theoretical gap by creating and evaluating robust models that clearly articulate the mechanisms by which AI interventions enhance learning. This shift is essential for transitioning from mere proof-of-concept demonstrations to establishing a more rigorous and principled basis for evidence-based practice (Chen et al., 2020b).

The integration of AIED represents not merely a shift toward automation, but rather an opportunity to rethink and improve human learning and teaching methodologies. The success of this endeavor will be assessed not by the complexity of the algorithms, but by our capacity to use them to create more equitable, engaging, and empowering educational experiences for all. The advancement of the field necessitates strong adherence to human-centered values, which will serve as the critical guide for its responsible and transformative future.

References

Ahmad, S.F., Rahmat, M.K., Mubarik, M.S., Alam, M.M., Hyder, S.I.: Artificial intelligence and its role in education. *Sustainability* **13**(22), 12902 (2021). https://doi.org/10.3390/su132212902

Akgun, S., Greenhow, C.: Artificial intelligence in education: Addressing ethical challenges in K-12 settings. *AI Ethics* **2**, 431–440 (2022). https://doi.org/10.1007/s43681-021-00096-7

Alfredo, R., Echeverria, V., Jin, Y., Yan, L., Swiecki, Z., Gašević, D., Martinez-Maldonado, R.: Human-centred learning analytics and AI in education: A systematic literature review. *Computers and Education: Artificial Intelligence* **5**, 100215 (2024).

Ali, O., Murray, P.A., Momin, M., Dwivedi, Y.K., Malik, T.: The effects of artificial intelligence applications in educational settings: Challenges and strategies. *Technological Forecasting and Social Change* **199**, 123076 (2024). https://doi.org/10.1016/j.techfore.2023.123076

Baker, T., Smith, L.: *Educ-AI-Tion Rebooted? Exploring the Future of Artificial Intelligence in Schools and Colleges.* (2019). https://www.nesta.org.uk/report/education-rebooted/

Bhutoria, A.: Personalized education and Artificial Intelligence in the United States, China, and India: A systematic review using a human-in-the-loop model. *Computers and Education: Artificial Intelligence* **3**, 100068 (2022).

Cain, W.: AI emergence in education: Exploring formative tensions across scholarly and popular discourse. *Journal of Interactive Learning Research* **34**(2), 239–273 (2023).

Chen, L., Chen, P., Lin, Z.: Artificial intelligence in education: A review. *IEEE Access* **8**, 75264–75278 (2020a).

Chen, X., Xie, H., Zou, D., Hwang, G.-J.: Application and theory gaps during the rise of artificial intelligence in education. *Computers and Education: Artificial Intelligence* **1**, 100002 (2020b). https://doi.org/10.1016/j.caeai.2020.100002

Chen, X., Yu, G., Cheng, G., Hao, T.: Research topics, author profiles, and collaboration networks in the top-ranked journal on educational technology over the past 40 years: A bibliometric analysis. *Journal of Computers in Education* **6**(4), 563–585 (2019).

Chine, D.R., Brentley, C., Thomas-Browne, C., Richey, J.E., Gul, A., Carvalho, P.F., . . . Koedinger, K.R.: Educational equity through combined human-AI personalization: A propensity matching evaluation. In: *International Conference on Artificial Intelligence in Education*, pp. 366–377. Springer, Cham (2022).

Chiu, T.K.F., Xia, Q., Zhou, X., Chai, C.S., Cheng, M.: Systematic literature review on opportunities, challenges, and future research recommendations of artificial intelligence in education. *Computers and Education: Artificial Intelligence* **4**, 100118 (2023).

Cooper, G.: Examining science education in ChatGPT: An exploratory study of generative artificial intelligence. *Journal of Science Education and Technology* **32**, 444–452 (2023). https://doi.org/10.1007/s10956-023-10039-y

Costa, E.B., Fonseca, B., Santana, M.A., de Araújo, F.F., Rego, J.: Evaluating the effectiveness of educational data mining techniques for early prediction of students' academic failure in introductory programming courses. *Computers in Human Behavior* **73**, 247–256 (2017).

Cotton, D.R.E., Cotton, P.A., Shipway, J.R.: Chatting and cheating: Ensuring academic integrity in the era of ChatGPT. *Innovations in Education and Teaching International* (2023). https://doi.org/10.1080/14703297.2023.2190148

Cukurova, M., Kent, C., Luckin, R.: Artificial intelligence and multimodal data in the service of human decision-making: A case study in debate tutoring. *British Journal of Educational Technology* **50**(6), 3032–3046 (2019).

Cukurova, M., Luckin, R., Kent, C.: Impact of an artificial intelligence research frame on the perceived credibility of educational research evidence. *International Journal of Artificial Intelligence in Education* **30**(2), 205–235 (2020).

Dogan, M.E., Dogan, T.G., Bozkurt, A.: The use of artificial intelligence (AI) in online learning and distance education processes: A systematic review of empirical studies. *Applied Sciences* **13**, 3056 (2023).

Dwivedi, Y.K., Hughes, D.L., Coombs, C., Constantiou, I., Duan, Y., Edwards, J.S., Gupta, B., Lal, B., Misra, S., Prashant, P., Raman, R., Rana, N.P., Sharma, S.K., Upadhyay, N.: Impact of COVID-19 pandemic on information management research and practice: Transforming education, work and life. *International Journal of Information Management* **55**, 102211 (2020).

Dwivedi, Y.K., Hughes, L., Ismagilova, E., Aarts, G., Coombs, C., Crick, T., Williams, M.D.: Artificial intelligence (AI): Multidisciplinary perspectives on emerging challenges, opportunities, and agenda for research, practice and policy. *International Journal of Information Management* **57**, 101994 (2021). https://doi.org/10.1016/j.ijinfomgt.2019.08.002

Floridi, L., Cowls, J., Beltrametti, M., Chatila, R., Chazerand, P., Dignum, V., . . . Vayena, E.: An ethical framework for a good AI society: Opportunities, risks, principles, and recommendations. *Minds and Machines* **28**, 1–24 (2018). https://doi.org/10.1007/s11023-018-9482-5

Funke, J., Fischer, A., Holt, D.V.: Competencies for complexity: Problem solving in the twenty-first century. In: Care, E., Griffin, P., Wilson, M. (eds.) *Assessment and Teaching of 21st Century Skills. Educational Assessment in an Information Age*, pp. 41–53. Springer, Cham (2018).

García, P., Amandi, A., Schiaffino, S., Campo, M.: Evaluating Bayesian networks' precision for detecting students' learning styles. *Computers & Education* **49**(3), 794–808 (2007).

Garito, M.A.: Artificial intelligence in education: Evolution of the teaching-learning relationship. *British Journal of Educational Technology* **22**(1), 41–47 (1991). https://doi.org/10.1111/j.1467-8535.1991.tb00050.x

Gocen, A., Doger, M.F.: A global perspective on artificial intelligence in educational leadership. *The Journal of Educational Research* (2025). https://doi.org/10.1080/00220671.2025.2510397

Granic, A.: Educational technology adoption: A systematic review. *Education and Information Technologies* **27**, 9725–9744 (2022). https://doi.org/10.1007/s10639-022-10951-7

Holstein, K., Aleven, V., Rummel, N.: A conceptual framework for human–AI hybrid adaptivity in education. In: Bittencourt, I.I., Cukurova, M., Muldner, K., Luckin, R., Millán, E. (eds.) *Artificial Intelligence in Education. LNCS*, vol. 12163, pp. 240–254. Springer, Cham (2020). https://doi.org/10.1007/978-3-030-52237-7_20

Huang, W., Hew, K.F., Fryer, L.K.: Chatbots for language learning—Are they really useful? A systematic review of chatbot-supported language learning. *Journal of Computer Assisted Learning* **38**(1), 237–257 (2022). https://doi.org/10.1111/jcal.12610

Hwang, G.-J., Chang, C.-Y.: A review of opportunities and challenges of chatbots in education. *Interactive Learning Environments* **31**(7), 4099–4112 (2021). https://doi.org/10.1080/10494820.2021.1952615

Jamalova, G., Aymatova, F., Ikromov, S.: The state-of-the-art applications of artificial intelligence in distance education: A systematic mapping study. In: *Proceedings of the 6th International Conference on Future Networks & Distributed Systems*, pp. 600–606. ACM, New York (2022). https://doi.org/10.1145/3584202.3584292

Janati, S.E., Maach, A., Ghanami, D.E.: Adaptive e-learning AI-powered chatbot based on multimedia indexing. *International Journal of Advanced Computer Science and Applications* **11**(12), (2020). https://doi.org/10.14569/IJACSA.2020.0111238

Kim, J.: Leading teachers' perspective on teacher-AI collaboration in education. *Education and Information Technologies* **29**(7), 8693–8724 (2023). https://doi.org/10.1007/s10639-023-12109-5

Knox, J.: Artificial intelligence and education in China. *Learning, Media and Technology* **45**(3), 298–311 (2020). https://doi.org/10.1080/17439884.2020.1754236

Kuhail, M.A., Alturki, N., Alramlawi, S., Alhejori, K.: Interacting with educational chatbots: A systematic review. *Education and Information Technologies* **28**, 973–1018 (2023). https://doi.org/10.1007/s10639-022-11177-3

Lai, W.Y.W., Lee, J.S.: A systematic review of conversational AI tools in ELT: Publication trends, tools, research methods, learning outcomes, and antecedents. *Computers and Education: Artificial Intelligence* **7**, 100291 (2024). https://doi.org/10.1016/j.caeai.2024.100291

Latham, A., Crockett, K., McLean, D., Edmonds, B.: Oscar: An intelligent adaptive conversational agent tutoring system. In: O'Shea, J., Nguyen, N.T., Crockett, K., Howlett, R.J., Jain, L.C. (eds.) *Agent and Multi-Agent Systems: Technologies and Applications. KES-AMSTA 2011. LNCS*, vol. 6682, pp. 1–10. Springer, Berlin, Heidelberg (2011). https://doi.org/10.1007/978-3-642-22000-5_58

Li, S., Gu, X.: A risk framework for human-centered artificial intelligence in education. *Educational Technology & Society* **26**(1), 187–202 (2023). https://www.jstor.org/stable/48707976

Mehmood, R., Alam, F., Albogami, N.N., Katib, I., Albeshri, A., Altowaijri, S.M.: UTiLearn: A personalised ubiquitous teaching and learning system for smart societies. *IEEE Access* **5**, 2615–2635 (2017).

Moreno-Guerrero, A.-J., Lopez-Belmonte, J., Marin-Marín, J.-A., Soler-Costa, R.: Scientific development of educational artificial intelligence in web of science. *Future Internet* **12**(8), 124 (2020). https://doi.org/10.3390/fi12080124

Nazaretsky, T., Ariely, M., Cukurova, M., Alexandron, G.: Teachers' trust in AI-powered educational technology and a professional development program to improve it. *British Journal of Educational Technology* **53**(4), 914–931 (2022). https://doi.org/10.1111/bjet.13232

Organisation for Economic Co-operation and Development (OECD). (2025). Education Policy Outlook 2025. OECD Publishing. https://www.oecd.org/en/publications/education-policy-outlook-2025_c3f402ba-en.html

Qiu, W., Su, C.L., Jamil, N.B., Thway, M., Ng, S.S.H., Zhang, L., Lim, F.S., Lai, J.W.: A systematic approach to evaluate the use of chatbots in educational contexts: Learning gains, engagements and perceptions. *Computers* **14**(7), 270 (2025). https://doi.org/10.3390/computers14070270

Shen, L., Qiu, N., Wang, Z.: Psychological safety and trust as drivers of teachers' continued use of AI tools in classrooms. *Scientific Reports* **15**(1), (2025). https://doi.org/10.1038/s41598-025-13789-4

UNESCO. (2023). *Recommendation on the Ethics of Artificial Intelligence*. United Nations Educational, Scientific and Cultural Organization. https://unesdoc.unesco.org/ark:/48223/pf0000381137

UNESCO (United Nations Educational, Scientific and Cultural Organization). (2021). *AI and Education: Guidance for Policy-makers*. UNESCO. https://www.unesco.org/en/articles/ai-and-education-guidance-policy-makers.

Vereschak, O., Bailly, G., Caramiaux, B.: How to evaluate trust in AI-assisted decision making? A survey of empirical methodologies. *Proceedings of the ACM on Human-Computer Interaction* **5**(CSCW2), 1–39 (2021). https://doi.org/10.1145/3476064

Wang, S., Wang, F., Zhu, Z., Wang, J., Tran, T., Du, Z.: Artificial intelligence in education: A systematic literature review. *Expert Systems with Applications* **252**(Part A), 124167 (2024). https://doi.org/10.1016/j.eswa.2024.124167

Winkler, R., Hobert, S., Salovaara, A., Söllner, M., Leimeister, J.M.: Sara, the lecturer: Improving learning in online education with a scaffolding-based conversational agent. In: *Proceedings of the 2020 CHI Conference on Human Factors in Computing Systems*, pp. 1–14. ACM, New York (2020). https://doi.org/10.1145/3313831.3376781

Wollny, S., Schneider, J., Di Mitri, D., Weidlich, J., Rittberger, M., Drachsler, H.: Are we there yet?—a systematic literature review on chatbots in education. *Frontiers in Artificial Intelligence* **4**, 654924 (2021). https://doi.org/10.3389/frai.2021.654924

9

Exploring the Influence of Artificial Intelligence on Education: Perceptions and Attitudes among University Students

Victoria T. Hasheela, Micheal Tuape, and Ari Happonen

9.1 Introduction

In recent years, artificial intelligence (AI) has transformed numerous societal and industrial sectors, enhancing the efficiency, sustainability, and functionality of various aspects of everyday life (Bogdanovich et al., 2025), pushing both traditional and frontline technology-area corporations' operations forward. One of the sectors being transformed is the education sector, which is being impacted significantly by tools and knowledge available for teachers and students (Vieriu & Petrea, 2025). AI-powered tools such as chatbots, intelligent tutoring systems, and other learning platforms are increasingly being integrated into the students' learning environments to enhance their learning experience (Xu, 2024). At the same time, the student engagement models keep changing, as AI tools keep evolving (Garcia et al., 2025). In this context, the well-known AI-powered ChatGPT, developed by OpenAI, as well as other current LLM-based models offering academic and educational support (Jiang et al., 2022), has become popular in providing academic support, answering student queries, and giving them instant supplementary learning support (Hwang et al., 2020). This has greatly transformed traditional educational practice by challenging, for example, educators on how to teach and test the students so that they would truly have assimilated the desired set of skills and knowledge (Fabiyi, 2025). Furthermore, the integration of AI in education raises crucial questions regarding its impact on critical thinking skills, as well as its effect on students' education (Suriano et al., 2025).

The rapid proliferation of AI-based learning systems in higher education necessitates a thorough understanding of students' perceptions of their usage and effects, as these technologies directly impact their learning experiences. They also affect their learning styles, learning skills, and motivation to learn independently. While AI's integration into education is gaining momentum (Fan et al., 2025), a notable gap exists in the empirical literature concerning university students' attitudes, usage patterns, perceived benefits, risks, and

DOI: 10.1201/9781003633433-9

concerns regarding AI tools. To fill this knowledge gap, our study examines university students' perceptions of AI-based learning systems. This study specifically focuses on students in order to provide critical insights for educators, developers, and policymakers seeking to implement AI responsibly and effectively in educational environments, considering that students are the primary beneficiaries of AI educational tools. The research seeks to provide empirical insights into the factors that influence students' adoption and utilization of AI in their studies and to identify key considerations and potential challenges that need to be addressed for the successful and responsible integration of AI-based learning systems in higher education.

Pursuant to this aim, the study will answer the following research questions:

1. How do students currently utilize AI-powered tools in their studies?
2. What are their perceptions regarding the benefits and risks associated with using AI in education?
3. What specific concerns do students have regarding the broader integration of AI into their learning experiences?

Given the limited empirical research specifically evaluating university students' perceptions and attitudes toward AI in this context, our findings are anticipated to offer novel and significant contributions to the burgeoning body of knowledge on AI-based learning, related student perceptions, and ideas on how educators could take action to positively respond to the opportunities that the proper use of AI offers for higher education institutions in improving education. Furthermore, the insights will provide valuable guidance for EdTech developers, educators, and researchers interested in AI-based learning systems by highlighting both the opportunities and potential risks of AI usage in higher education. Ultimately, this study helps in designing and implementing more effective and ethically sound AI integration strategies and in identifying key areas of research to advance the beneficial usage of AI in higher education institutions.

9.2 Literature Review

AI has become a topic of growing interest in education, and it has the potential to transform educational practices, but in reality, most universities are slowly adopting different AI-based learning systems in order to maximize their benefits in learning and educational activities. This literature review focuses on the benefits as well as the currently known and acknowledged risks and challenges of AI.

9.2.1 The Role of AI in Education

AI has been increasingly adopted in educational settings to enhance learning experiences and outcomes. One of the most significant contributions of AI is its ability to provide personalized learning experiences (Roshanaei et al., 2023). AI-driven systems can analyze students' learning patterns, strengths, and weaknesses, allowing the customization of educational content to meet individual needs (Al Nabhani et al., 2025). For example, adaptive learning platforms such as Knewton and DreamBox use AI algorithms to adjust the difficulty of tasks in real time based on student performance, ensuring that each learner is challenged at an appropriate level (Kaiser & Kaiser, 2024). Furthermore, AI-powered tools such as Grammarly help students improve their writing skills by offering real-time suggestions and editing (Tran, 2025). AI-based tools also boost students' self-regulation capabilities and enhance learner independence as well (Mohebbi, 2025).

In addition, AI can also support students with disabilities by providing assistive technologies such as text-to-speech and speech-to-text applications (Brotosaputro et al., 2024). There are also other AI tools such as basic language teaching applications (Li et al., 2025), as well as more advanced translation tools and speech recognition systems that can break down language barriers, help students from diverse linguistic backgrounds to translate educational content (Karakas, 2023), and support diverse learners while fostering inclusive educational environments (Rogahang et al., 2024).

9.2.2 Challenges and Concerns

Despite the benefits of AI integration in education, it is not without challenges. One of the significant concerns is the students' growing dependency on AI and the negative impacts AI might have on their critical thinking and problem-solving skills (Vieriu & Petrea, 2025; Zhai et al., 2024). Academic critics argue that students' overreliance on AI tools may lead to a decline in their ability to think independently and creatively (Selwyn, 2024). Like in general, too much reliance on outsourcing our own activities and thinking to technologies will undermine our daily learnings (Baron, 2021), and at the same time improper use of these tools can result in academic dishonesty (Marzuki et al., 2023). One example of dishonesty and AI dependency is the constant use of AI-powered tools such as ChatGPT, which is able to generate essays and solve complex problems. This may discourage students from paying the necessary attention and applying their own skills (Efimova & Nygren, 2024). (Zhai et al., 2024) stated that it has become common practice for students to submit AI-generated work as their own, thereby lessening their interest in taking their schoolwork seriously and being accountable. This can result in reduced metacognitive skills (Fan et al., 2025). These findings agree with (Bozkurt et al., 2024), that AI-generated solutions discourage deep learning. For linguistic students, dependency on AI translation tools can also impair vocabulary acquisition (Rapa et al., 2024). Additionally, students who use editing tools such as Grammarly can experience a decline in self-editing competence (Zawacki-Richter et al., 2019).

Another significant concern is that, despite AI's ability to provide personalized support in education, it does not offer the human interaction necessary for effective learning (Holmes et al., 2019), which can lead to feelings of social isolation and anxiety (Klimova & Pikhart, 2025). Human interaction remains valuable and should not be overlooked. Therefore, there should be a balance between AI-driven solutions and human interaction in education.

9.2.3 Student Perceptions of AI in Education

It is important to understand students' perceptions of AI-based learning systems in order to successfully integrate AI in education, as it can help educators, policymakers, and developers formulate ethical frameworks and practices (Treve, 2024). Research shows that there is a generally positive attitude toward AI among students, and they perceive AI tools as resourceful in enhancing their learning experiences, resulting in good academic performance (Vieriu & Petrea, 2025). For example, AI tools such as Grammarly and ChatGPT help in completing academic work more quickly and efficiently and also in improving students' creativity (Sosunova et al., 2024). Popenici and Kerr (2017) states that students with disabilities perceive AI tools such as speech-to-text to be transformative for inclusive education. Similarly, a survey by Luckin et al. (2016) has shown positive feedback from students regarding AI-driven platforms such as Smart Sparrow for catering to individual learning paces, especially in science and mathematics. Another survey by Zhang and Aslan (2021) reported similar results, whereby students who participated perceived AI-based learning systems to be beneficial in terms of personalized learning and were satisfied with the flexibility aspects that come with AI-based learning. A study by Siau and Wang (2020) alluded that students with more digital literacy knowledge reported a higher positive attitude toward AI-based learning in comparison to students with low levels of technology knowledge. These findings are consistent with those of Kim and Kwon (2023), which reported that students with limited digital literacy tend to utilize AI less than those who are more knowledgeable in digital literacy.

However, students also express concerns about the potential negative impacts of AI on their education. Several studies reported critiques from students regarding ethical and pedagogical issues (Holmes et al., 2019; Luckin et al., 2016; Selwyn, 2024; Williamson, 2017). Many students raised concerns about becoming overly dependent on AI tools, which they fear may hinder their ability to think critically and solve problems independently (Selwyn, 2019). Similarly, a study by Holmes and Tuomi (2022) found that AI tools such as ChatGPT have the potential to reduce independent critical thinking. A study by Williamson (2017) reported concerns that AI has the potential of creating biased learning environments, particularly when the algorithms used in the systems rely on biased data. Generative AI models are also known to produce inaccurate information, often referred to as "hallucinations," and present it as valid, which can result in misinforming the information recipient (Malik et al., 2024). There is thus a concern about accuracy in AI tools (Rudolph et al., 2023) and other related problems that can result in fake knowledge.

While the existing literature demonstrates a growing interest in the role of AI in education, highlighting its benefits in personalization, inclusivity, and improved academic outcomes, it also reveals notable concerns related to student dependency, reduced critical thinking, ethical implications, and the accuracy of generated content. These insights underline the importance of understanding, not just the technical or theoretical advantages of AI tools, but also how students perceive and engage with them in real-world academic settings. Given the increasing integration of generative AI technologies like ChatGPT and Grammarly into educational environments, it becomes imperative to explore students' actual experiences, attitudes, and concerns in depth. This study was therefore conducted to investigate university students' perceptions of AI-based learning systems, focusing on how they use these tools, the perceived impact on their learning behavior, and their views on the benefits and risks associated with AI in education.

9.3 Research Methodology

9.3.1 Data Collection

To address the research objectives, data was collected through a structured survey administered across several universities. The sample consisted of 1,014 students from seven universities. Figure 9.1 shows the demographics.

The research data was collected using a self-administered online questionnaire, which was distributed via Google Forms. The questionnaire was made available from December 2024 until April 2025. Before commencing the main survey question, consent was obtained from each of the students, and from the onset each participant was notified of the liberty to quit the survey at will. The questions comprised both closed and open-ended formats that allowed students to elaborate more on their insights into their perceptions and experiences with AI in their studies. To ensure relevance, students were first asked whether they had used AI tools in their academic work and only those who indicated usage proceeded to answer the related questions. The questionnaire consisted of four constructs, namely (a) AI tools and techniques of interest, (b) benefits of AI, (c) challenges and concerns in AI adoption, and (d) drivers that lead to AI adoption.

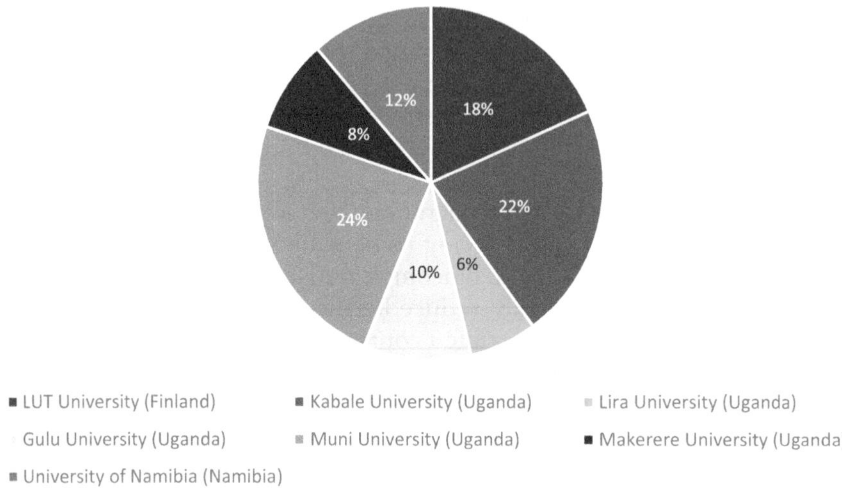

FIGURE 9.1
Demographics of the participants of this study.

The participants' existing knowledge of AI was assessed using a 10-point Likert scale, where a rating of 1 denoted "no knowledge" and 10 represented "advanced knowledge." Students were then asked to indicate the aspects of AI that interested them most. They were presented with a list of predefined options, including personalized learning pathways, AI-powered tutoring and academic support, automated grading and feedback systems, AI tools for research and writing assistance, data analysis for tracking and enhancing academic performance, interactive AI-based learning platforms, and AI applications for collaborative learning and group projects. An open-ended option was also provided to allow respondents to specify any additional areas of interest not covered in the list.

In addition, students were asked to identify the specific AI tools they currently use and to describe their typical applications. The questionnaire further explored perceived challenges associated with adopting AI in their academic practice, as well as the primary motivators for doing so. Participants were also invited to indicate the types of support they would find most beneficial for integrating AI into their learning processes. Finally, they were asked to indicate what they perceived to be the most significant risks or drawbacks of using AI in their studies, choosing from predetermined options.

In order to ensure validity, a pilot study was done with two fellow faculty members to evaluate whether the questions were clear and could convey the intended meanings without ambiguous meanings and used language and terminology that were easy to understand. Additional pilot-testing was also conducted on 25 students, and after analysis of the pilot results, 10 of the participants went through cognitive interviews to understand how they interpreted the questions and response options.

9.3.2 Data Analysis

Descriptive analysis was utilized to analyze the quantitative data in order to provide a clear overview of the students' perceptions and attitudes. Furthermore, the qualitative data (open-ended questions) was analyzed using thematic analysis in order to understand and identify patterns and insights into the students' experiences with AI. This helped us gain a deeper understanding of aspects that may not be quantifiable but are necessary. For the thematic analysis, the framework by Braun and Clarke (2006) was used, as it provides a clear, flexible, and rigorous approach for identifying, analyzing, and reporting patterns within qualitative data. This six-phase process—familiarization with the data, generating initial codes, searching for themes, reviewing themes, defining and naming themes, and producing the results—was particularly suited to this study's aim of capturing students' perceptions and experiences across diverse university contexts. This approach allowed for a systematic and flexible analysis of qualitative data, enabling the identification and interpretation of meaningful patterns across the dataset. The method's transparency and rigor make it particularly suitable for exploring participants' perspectives and experiences in depth.

9.4 Findings

This section presents the results of the study in two parts. First, we describe the quantitative findings drawn from closed-ended questions, including students' needs for support, preferred use cases of AI in learning, and concerns related to AI adoption. These are presented using descriptive statistics to highlight general trends and frequencies. Second, we explore the qualitative insights derived from open-ended survey responses, which were analyzed thematically in order to capture the deeper perceptions and attitudes that students hold toward AI in education. The thematic analysis reveals three dominant themes: *AI as a supportive learning tool, concerns about academic dishonesty and overreliance*, and *varied attitudes and the call for balanced integration*. The findings conclude with a summary that synthesizes both quantitative and qualitative insights.

In exploring the types of support and resources that learners find most helpful for integrating AI into their studies, 55.6% of respondents expressed a need for training and workshops focused on AI. Additionally, 49.1%

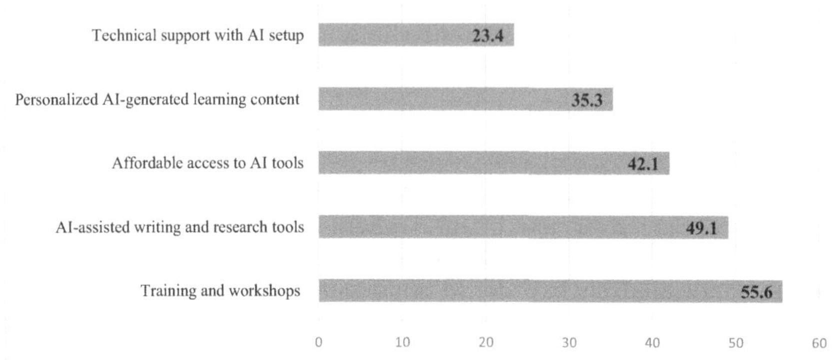

FIGURE 9.2
Types of AI support that learners find most helpful.

expressed a strong preference for AI-assisted writing and research tools, while 42.1% identified affordable access to AI tools and software as essential. However, the term "affordable" was not explicitly defined in the questionnaire, and perceptions of affordability can vary widely. For some, it may mean free access, while others might consider a low cost acceptable. This highlights the need for future research to clarify acceptable cost ranges and to explore willingness to pay among students.

Personalized AI-generated learning content was also considered valuable by 35.3% of participants, while 23.4% highlighted the need for technical support with AI setup such as a basic AI course. As a visual summary, Figure 9.2 presents the types of support that learners find helpful.

Regarding the responsible use of AI, 41.9% of respondents called for clear guidelines on ethical AI practices in education, and 30.3% requested targeted training on ethical AI principles. These findings suggest that students are not merely seeking abstract ethical theories but rather concrete, institution-specific rules that define what is acceptable and what is not in the academic use of AI, reflecting a desire for clarity and fairness in assessment standards.

For the support needs, higher education institutions (HEIs) need to consult AI and Createch solution frameworks (Sosunova et al., 2024; Usmani et al., 2023) for a wide variety contexts and adapt these frameworks to their specific institutional needs related to AI tool selection and support. The findings also highlight a widespread demand for both practical and ethical frameworks designed by their own institutions (Fan et al., 2025) to guide AI integration in learning environments, indicating that learners are not only eager to harness AI's capabilities but also conscious of the need for equitable, responsible, and well-supported implementation. Also, the answers reflect the need to be specifically instructed by the HEIs about what is accepted

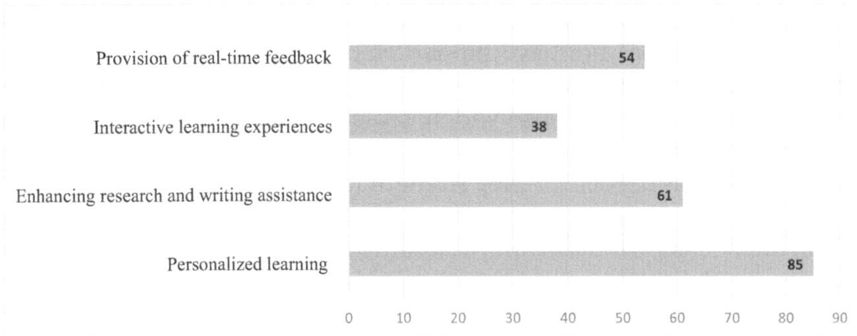

FIGURE 9.3
Preferred uses of AI in learning.

and what is not accepted regarding AI use in school tasks, and where proper use is against general ethical considerations—for example, generating visual materials with inadequately trained AI tools that could produce copyrighted context.

When exploring potential use cases for AI in learning, the most prominent responses were "personalized learning and study plans" (85%), "enhancing research and writing assistance" (61%), and "interactive learning experiences" (38%). Respondents recognized a multifaceted contribution of AI to learning, with 54% highlighting the value of providing real-time feedback. However, challenges remain prevalent such as concerns regarding AI dependency (51%). For the data, Figure 9.3 summarizes the findings (in percentages) of the students' preferred use of AI.

A thematic analysis of the open-ended responses revealed three dominant themes regarding student perceptions of AI in education, namely AI as a supportive learning tool, concerns about academic dishonesty, and overreliance and varied attitudes and the call for balanced integration.

9.4.1 AI as a Supportive Learning Tool

The most prevalent theme in the data was the recognition of AI, particularly tools such as ChatGPT, as a valuable academic aid. Respondents indicated that AI enhanced their learning experience by simplifying complex information, providing instant explanations, and assisting with exam preparation. Students appreciated the accessibility and convenience of AI-powered tools, noting improvements in understanding and productivity during self-study. However, this perceived enhancement may also reflect a growing reliance on AI to offload cognitive effort, for example, using AI to summarize content or generate explanations rather than developing these skills independently.

Many described AI tools as highly engaging. One student noted that "AI is engaging and does not have human emotions nor excuses to educate," thus offering a consistent and focused learning experience. The quality and speed of information were also widely praised, with one student highlighting that AI can "provide quality information in each subject" and "provide feedback as fast as needed." A key strength identified was the capacity of AI to adapt to individual learning preferences; as one respondent explained, "AI can offer customized learning according to an individual's preference, so basically people can learn the same things but in different ways so that each individual understands better."

The clarity of AI-generated responses was another recurring theme, with one student stating that "AI answers are always straightforward, making me understand the topic easily." Furthermore, AI was seen as a personal learning companion, "able to tailor it to your exact way of understanding and working." Students also emphasized the reliability and practical relevance of AI-generated information, describing it as "fast and reliable information that can help you gain the necessary knowledge to acquire the job one is passionate about." In the context of academic research, AI was recognized as a valuable tool for accessing diverse and comprehensive resources: "When doing research, it aids me with different subjects from different sources, which sometimes are difficult to get from expensive academic books."

9.4.2 Concerns about Academic Dishonesty and Overreliance

Despite recognizing its benefits, many students voiced concerns about the potential for academic misconduct and dependency on AI systems. Several participants also raised issues such as plagiarism, diminished critical thinking, and reduced engagement with course content. The possibility that AI might discourage independent problem-solving was a recurring sentiment. These concerns highlight an underlying apprehension about the long-term cognitive impact of frequent AI use.

Several participants cautioned that habitual dependence on AI could diminish students' ability to think critically and learn independently. As one student remarked, "Students might get used to using AI, becoming dependent on it, and this will lead to them not learning and understanding their studies on their own," while another noted that "students think less or don't use their brains anymore." A further concern over the loss of intellectual engagement was echoed in sentiments such as "It discourages students to think and learn, leading to poor performance in exams," and "Skills such as critical thinking will be lost." Others warned that excessive use of AI may result in shallow learning, with one respondent commenting on the danger of "getting high grades while knowing nothing of what you have done." The erosion of academic depth was further illustrated by the observation that people now tend to do "top-surface research rather than extensive research to broaden their knowledge," ultimately leading to a "loss of independence in learning, meaning the content is never properly ingested."

The student's answers also clearly reflected the broader (negative) impacts of the use of AI on educational systems. One student stated "Our education will be more based on bias since most of the resources will be provided by AI. Only the strong ones will use AI in the right way; I'm talking from experience". An important note here is that in traditional models, the learning materials utilized by the students were mostly authored and/or evaluated and recommended by the teacher. Learners and education units have trusted the teacher in charge to be a nonbiased and cultural educative professional author, who does a country and living region related, context-specific material fine-tunes for their teaching purposes, and who also would be making sure the students would be well prepared to move from academic studies safety to working life, with all of its needs and society-related expectations. If students lean too much on AI direction and do not validate the "help" they get from these tools, they will be affected by all the biases the AI-provided information comes with (Efimova & Nygren, 2024).

Some students raised concerns about the implications for teaching practices, suggesting that reducing human-led lectures in favor of AI-driven programs could be problematic: "If it entails replacing or reducing time spent in lectures with human lecturers, that may be an issue."

Overall, the theme highlighted the importance of promoting balanced AI integration in education, leveraging its strengths while safeguarding the development of critical, independent thinking. In other words, it will be highly important to define the proper roles of AI in education. For example, have teachers make sure the students have learned the core basics—for example, through intensive human-led teaching methods like code camps and hackathons (Happonen et al., 2020, 2021)—before mixing teacher- and AI-supported studies and tasks to help students validate and quality-check the information that AI tools offer them as support for their own work.

9.4.3 Varied Attitudes and the Call for Balanced Integration

Students' perceptions of AI varied from enthusiastic endorsement to cautious skepticism. While some participants viewed AI as a promising complement to traditional learning, others expressed fears that it might marginalize educators or propagate inaccurate content. Notably, students called for clear ethical guidelines, institutional regulation, and training on responsible usage. This theme emphasized the need for balanced integration of AI technologies into educational environments to maximize benefits while mitigating risks. It also means that students should receive more general academic ethics education, not just AI-related instructions. Using AI in unethical ways, for example, outsourcing content creation to AI or any other third party, should be considered unacceptable academic practice, no matter how it is done.

Students expressed a strong need for institutional clarity and support regarding the integration of AI in academic environments. Many called for a reevaluation of current assessment practices, with one student remarking that "AI replaces the need for memorization, recall, and even overall understanding of a topic," thereby urging a shift in how learning outcomes are measured. Here it is important to note that this comment reflects the fact that the student has not understood the main reason why societies have educational institutions. The point is not to be a place where students learn to pass exams; rather, the main purpose of educational units is to teach students to become ready to move on with their lives and integrate into society with their newly learned skills and talent, enabling them to push forward with lifelong learning capabilities.

Within the open answers, while some students were cautious—particularly in disciplines like healthcare—others advocated for broader acceptance of AI, arguing that "institutions must allow us to use AI" rather than restrict its use due to concerns about independent thinking. There was also a clear desire for structured education on how to use AI effectively, with students requesting "an in-depth and extensive lesson on AI and the implications it has on our studies." Suggestions included "clear guidelines and ethical use policies," "levels to which you can use AI," and "clear communication on why AI use is positive or negative." Access and equity were also key concerns, as several students noted the need for "access to AI tools." Many emphasized that AI could reduce academic workload and enhance learning, but only if students are "taught how to use AI-powered tools while at the same time adding our own opinions." Ultimately, participants advocated for an education system that not only embraces AI but also equips learners with the skills and discernment to use it responsibly.

9.5 Discussion

The findings of this study affirm the growing significance of AI in educational settings, particularly its potential to enhance learning efficiency, personalize educational content, and provide support for diverse learners, including students with disabilities. The results from this survey emphasize that AI tools, when implemented effectively, can serve as powerful enablers in academic environments. Also, as shown in Figure 9.1, the participants represented a diverse demographic profile. This diversity strengthens the validity of the findings by ensuring that perceptions of AI use are not limited to a narrow student segment.

While interpreting these results, some limitations of the study need to be noted. First, our study focused on numbers and statistical analysis; such quantitative studies often fail to capture the rich context, nuances, and underlying reasons behind observed phenomena, potentially oversimplifying the complex experiences and social realities of students concerning AI in education. We attempted to mitigate the impact of this limitation by including some well-designed open-ended questions in the surveys to allow participants to provide richer, more nuanced answers and unexpected insights within a structured format. These qualitative responses were analyzed to supplement the quantitative data. Second, quantitative studies typically rely on structured questionnaires or standardized tests with closed-ended questions, which can restrict the participants' ability to express their genuine thoughts, feelings, and experiences, potentially leading to a narrow understanding of the research topic and to missing unexpected findings. Before the main data collection, we conducted a thorough pilot test of the quantitative instruments with a small group from the target population, followed by cognitive interviews to understand how participants interpreted the questions and response options. This process helped us identify ambiguities, biases, or limitations in the predefined measures.

These limitations notwithstanding, our study reveals important insights into students' perceptions of AI in their learning. Key to these findings is that the students widely acknowledged the advantages of AI, such as simplifying complex topics, improving writing and research, and tailoring learning to individual needs. These insights align with prior studies (Bozkurt et al., 2024; Brotosaputro et al., 2024; Popenici & Kerr, 2017), reinforcing the notion that AI, particularly generative AI models, can substantially improve educational outcomes and student engagement. However, the results also reveal concerns about AI's implications for academic integrity, cognitive development, and the broader educational experience. Students expressed concerns that AI may undermine critical thinking and self-driven learning, a concern echoed in the literature (Hwang et al., 2020; Karakas, 2023; Rudolph et al., 2023). The overreliance on AI tools such as ChatGPT for generating assignments and solving problems risks creating an academic culture centered around goal orientation, convenience, and laziness rather than deep learning, skill building, and novel knowledge generation, with preparations to fulfill research (Maglogiannis, 2021), development, and innovation (RDI) contribution expectations by frontline companies (Alenezi & Akour, 2025; Maglogiannis, 2021; Salmela et al., 2013) when they are hiring these new promises of a greater future for us all (Alenezi & Akour, 2025; Efimova & Nygren, 2024; Zhai et al., 2024). This will compromise the development of key cognitive skills such as problem-solving, reflection, independent thinking, and the chance of being competitive employees in future job markets.

An important dimension that emerges from the findings is the diverse ways in which students engage with AI in the classroom. Figure 9.3 shows that students associate AI with a wide range of learning tasks, from personalized learning and study plans (85%) to enhancing research and writing assistance (61%) and creating interactive learning experiences (38%). These uses reflect a range of academic support functions, from structuring study time and receiving targeted feedback to generating drafts, checking grammar, or exploring complex concepts through conversational interaction with AI systems.

Furthermore, students highlighted the value of AI in producing personalized content and real-time feedback (54%), which suggests a growing expectation that AI will not only supplement but actively shape the pacing and mode of instruction. Such expectations align with broader trends in adaptive learning research, where AI is increasingly leveraged to tailor educational content to individual needs and learning trajectories. Furthermore, the high demand for AI-assisted writing and research tools (49.1%) illustrates that students perceive AI as particularly valuable for text-based academic tasks, especially in contexts where access to academic resources is limited.

While many see AI as a means of augmenting existing teaching practices, others worry about it replacing human-led instruction. This echoes the main concern that classroom-based AI use should prioritize complementary functions, such as scaffolding learning, offering low-stakes practice opportunities, and providing alternative explanations. Related to this, a key observation from the research data is the contradiction in how students perceive AI: While they welcome its convenience and pedagogical potential, they remain cautious about its ethical and developmental implications. This highlights the need for a more balanced and guided approach to AI integration. Students consistently called for structured training, clear ethical guidelines, and transparent policies that communicate not only what is permissible but also why certain restrictions or applications are recommended. Such frameworks are essential to empower learners to make informed decisions about AI utilization as a tool, learning mentor, study-planning support tool, and so on in their academic journey.

While this study highlighted students' concerns about the lack of human interaction in AI-based learning systems, particularly its potential to cause social isolation and anxiety, it is important to consider emerging developments in emotional AI. Future research should explore how emotionally intelligent AI systems, including avatar-based tutors capable of simulating empathy and social presence, might help bridge the interpersonal gap in digital education. Such systems could offer more emotionally engaging and responsive interactions and potentially address students' emotional and social needs while maintaining the benefits of personalization and scalability.

Furthermore, while students perceive AI as a helpful tool for accessing diverse research materials, this view may overlook the fact that AI language models do not truly "understand" content. Instead, they generate responses based on statistical patterns, which can occasionally produce confident but inaccurate information. This poses a risk, especially for students lacking subject expertise, as they may not be able to critically assess the reliability of AI-generated content. Therefore, while AI can support research, students need to approach its output with caution and supplement it with proper academic validation.

The notion of equity also emerged as a critical issue. Some students benefit from seamless access to AI tools, while others struggle due to inadequate infrastructure, such as limited internet connectivity, the cost of some AI tools' advanced features, and, in general, different subscriptions to IT ecosystems where institutions may differ significantly from one another. In a time when even the most traditional asset manufacturers are moving toward digital services (Kortelainen et al., 2019), this kind of digital divide threatens to intensify existing educational inequalities, particularly in under-resourced institutions.

Traditional assessment practices need to be reconsidered. Several students argued that current assessment models, which emphasize memorization and recall, may be rendered obsolete by AI's capacity to deliver instant answers and explanations. This supports scholarly calls for transformative assessment strategies that prioritize analytical reasoning, original thought, and synthesis over rote learning (Usmani et al., 2023). In light of AI's expanding role in content generation and problem-solving, rethinking evaluation methods becomes imperative. One approach could be the intentional design of both "AI-assisted" and "No-AI" learning tasks. For example, certain assessments can explicitly allow AI use to cultivate digital literacy, while others are structured to be completed without any AI assistance, thereby reinforcing independent thinking and internal knowledge retention. This dual-mode approach can train students not only to use AI responsibly but also to rely on and sharpen their own cognitive abilities.

Although many students praised the speed and perceived quality of AI-generated feedback and information, it is important to acknowledge that students may not always have the subject-matter expertise required to accurately assess the academic quality or correctness of the content provided. Their evaluations are often based on how understandable or helpful the response appears during their learning process rather than on its objective accuracy. This highlights the need for institutions to provide guidance on critically evaluating AI-generated content and to emphasize that AI should be a support tool, not a sole source of truth. Developing students' information literacy and critical thinking skills remains essential in ensuring responsible and effective AI use.

The finding that AI can support customized learning experiences highlights a significant opportunity for HEIs to guide students in maximizing this capability. One effective pedagogical strategy would be to teach students how to prompt AI tools to explain the same study materials multiple times, from different perspectives and in varied contexts. This not only supports differentiated understanding but also aligns with cognitive science research emphasizing the importance of repetition and varied retrieval for deep learning (Karpicke & Roediger, 2008).

Although students expressed concerns about academic misconduct and overdependence on AI systems, these challenges often reflect how the tools are used rather than flaws in the technology itself. Outsourcing thinking to AI is comparable to paying a person to do one's work; it crosses into misconduct when learners no longer engage meaningfully with the learning process. This underscores the need for higher education systems to develop clear frameworks that distinguish between acceptable AI support and inappropriate academic delegation.

Finally, the varied attitudes toward AI reflect the diversity of academic disciplines and individual comfort levels with technology. For instance, students in healthcare fields voiced skepticism about AI due to the high stakes and ethical sensitivities of their discipline. On the other hand, proper use of AI in healthcare has already been shown to reduce the workload of field-specific experts and to make better use of their expert resources where needed. The findings highlight the need for discipline-specific AI integration policies and training, as well as inclusive consultation involving educators, students, and technologists. In addition, these findings also indicate that there is a lot of work to be done to educate people about the good and beneficial sides of using AI, including areas like healthcare. Students seem to jump to the conclusion that there are only the ways of using AI to support work and study tasks that they are already familiar with, and they make assumptions about the safety of those tactics in certain fields of AI utilization and wrongly assume that AI would not fit those application areas as a tool to improve task execution there.

In summary, while AI presents transformative opportunities for higher education, its integration must be accompanied by well-defined ethical frameworks, pedagogical reforms, digital infrastructure, and continuous stakeholder engagement.

9.6 Conclusion

This study explored the perceptions of students regarding the integration of AI in education, highlighting the potential of AI to revolutionize learning through personalized support, enhanced accessibility, and improved academic performance. The literature and student survey feedback converge on the idea that AI tools such as ChatGPT, Grammarly, visualization-creation tools, and other adaptive learning and knowledge-building support platforms are perceived as valuable aids, especially in fostering individualized learning and supporting students with disabilities.

However, the findings also point to notable concerns about the overreliance on AI tools, the loss of critical thinking skills, academic dishonesty, and ethical issues such as data privacy and algorithmic bias. Many students expressed anxiety over AI's role in diminishing human interaction and the depth of intellectual engagement. Although attitudes toward AI are largely positive, the call for balance and guidance was prominent, with students emphasizing the importance of structured training and clear ethical guidelines.

Overall, while students are optimistic about the possibilities AI presents in education, they also recognize the importance of responsible use. There is a need for institutions to adopt a holistic approach that integrates AI meaningfully without undermining the essential elements of human-centered learning.

Focusing on students has allowed this study to highlight the firsthand experiences of those most impacted by AI in education. Their perceptions offer valuable input for guiding the development of ethical, practical, and inclusive AI tools that align with real student needs and learning behaviors.

The result from this study serves as a starting point for future work on the application of AI in teaching and learning. We intend to build upon the insights gained from this initial study; our future research will adopt a longitudinal approach to continuously gather data from students. This will allow us to develop a dynamic and nuanced understanding of the evolving and complex interplay between individuals, AI technologies, and the educational environment over time. Recognizing that AI in education is an emerging field where current understanding is largely based on cross-sectional studies like this one, a longitudinal perspective is crucial to overcoming the inherent limitations of such snapshots and to informing evidence-based decisions regarding the future integration of AI in teaching and learning.

9.7 Recommendations

Based on the findings of this study, several recommendations emerge to guide the effective and ethical integration of AI in education. First, it is essential for educational institutions to develop clear ethical guidelines and policies that inform students and staff about the acceptable use of AI tools and to ensure that this knowledge is internalized. This can be achieved by embedding the guidelines into practice through dedicated workshops and formal assessments. For example, a compulsory course on academic ethics and the responsible use of modern study-support tools, including AI, can effectively address this issue. This course should then address issues such as plagiarism, data protection, responsible engagement with AI platforms, and provide students with hands-on experience and scenarios of future development directions of AI (Abdelsalam et al., 2022; Ejjami, 2024; Lekadir et al., 2025; Porras et al., 2018) to build critical awareness and proper usage habits.

In addition, integrating AI literacy into the curriculum is crucial. Students need to be equipped with the skills to understand, evaluate, validate, and use AI technologies responsibly (Yue Yim, 2024). This can be achieved through workshops (Korte et al., 2024), AI hackathons (Happonen et al., 2020; Porras et al., 2018; Sajja et al., 2024), seminars, self-study network courses (Heredia et al., 2025; Kien, 2025), and modules that focus on the ethical, practical, and academic applications of AI (De Silva et al., 2024; Fan et al., 2025; Lazăr (Cățeanu) et al., 2024; Ngo & Hastie, 2025). Moreover, while AI presents opportunities to enhance learning, it should not replace human interaction. A balanced integration that maintains the value of teacher–student relationships and critical classroom dialogue is necessary to preserve the human element of education. We recommend using face-to-face learning courses led by teachers to give the core learnings for the proper, efficient, and ethical use of AI before mixing teacher-led and AI-supported learning methods.

Educators are encouraged to revise assessment practices in light of the widespread use of AI. And higher educational institutions are encouraged to seek options to add robotic process automation tools (Ylä-Kujala et al., 2023), into education evaluation pool, side by side with AI tools, AI use detection tools and AI Control mechanism (Usmani et al., 2023) practices and uses. Both the teaching of how to use AI properly in learning and skill-building practices should be taught to students on all study levels. And we also need to help students to build understanding that training your own brain, by working on your own, is best approach for your brain to build long lasting knowledge and also something we see to be the proper use of your own cognitive abilities too. Traditional methods should be supplemented with assessments that promote independent thinking, creativity, and problem-solving skills that are less likely to be replicated by AI in addition of mixing AI-enabled and AI-denied tests and evaluation methods to make the best use of AI in education, study programs, and course development.

Furthermore, regular monitoring and evaluation of AI's impact in educational settings should be prioritized to ensure that these technologies contribute positively to learning outcomes without introducing new challenges. Additionally, national-level evaluation of the most widespread AI tools in education should occur at regular intervals to test their ethicality, neutrality, and the correctness of their content. Based on these tests, instructions and guidelines should be delivered to educators nationwide as often as needed.

Finally, educational institutions, policymakers, and AI developers should work together to encourage responsible innovation. This includes designing AI systems that are inclusive, accurate, and unbiased, and creating channels for student feedback to continually refine and improve these tools.

Acknowledgment

The AI influences to learners, its use as a support tool, and viewpoints for future opportunities of the work were supported by the project Createch Wake Up Etelä-Karjala!, co-funded by the European Union. International collaboration was supported by the LUT internationalization fund.

References

Abdelsalam, A., Happonen, A., Karha, K., Kapitonov, A., & Porras, J. (2022). Toward autonomous vehicles and machinery in mill yards of the forest industry: Technologies and proposals for autonomous vehicle operations. *IEEE Access, 10*, 88234–88250. https://doi.org/10.1109/ACCESS.2022.3199691

Alenezi, M., & Akour, M. (2025). AI-driven innovations in software engineering: A review of current practices and future directions. *Applied Sciences, 15*(3), 1344. https://doi.org/10.3390/app15031344

Al Nabhani, F., Hamzah, M. B., & Abuhassna, H. (2025). The role of artificial intelligence in personalizing educational content: Enhancing the learning experience and developing the teacher's role in an integrated educational environment. *Contemporary Educational Technology, 17*(2), ep573. https://doi.org/10.30935/cedtech/16089

Baron, N. S. (2021). Know what? How digital technologies undermine learning and remembering. *Journal of Pragmatics, 175*, 27–37. https://doi.org/10.1016/j.pragma.2021.01.011

Bogdanovich, B., Shah, P., Patel, P. A., & Boyd, C. J. (2025). Keeping up with AI evolution: ChatGPT-4o in surgery. *The American SurgeonTM, 91*(1), 5–6. https://doi.org/10.1177/00031348241272423

Bozkurt, A., Xiao, J., Farrow, R., Bai, J. Y. H., Nerantzi, C., Moore, S., Dron, J., Stracke, C. M., Singh, L., Crompton, H., Koutropoulos, A., Terentev, E., Pazurek, A., Nichols, M., Sidorkin, A. M., Costello, E., Watson, S., Mulligan, D., Honeychurch, S., . . . Asino, T. I. (2024). The manifesto for teaching and learning in a time of generative AI: A critical collective stance to better navigate the future. *Open Praxis, 16*(4), 487–513. https://doi.org/10.55982/openpraxis.16.4.777

Braun, V., & Clarke, V. (2006). Using thematic analysis in psychology. *Qualitative Research in Psychology, 3*(2), 77–101. https://doi.org/10.1191/1478088706qp063oa

Brotosaputro, G., Supriyadi, A., & Jones, M. (2024). AI-powered assistive technologies for improved accessibility. *International Transactions on Artificial Intelligence (ITALIC), 3*(1), 76–84. https://doi.org/10.33050/italic.v3i1.645

De Silva, D., Jayatilleke, S., El-Ayoubi, M., Issadeen, Z., Moraliyage, H., & Mills, N. (2024). The human-centred design of a universal module for artificial intelligence literacy in tertiary education institutions. *Machine Learning and Knowledge Extraction, 6*(2), 1114–1125. https://doi.org/10.3390/make6020051

Efimova, E., & Nygren, T. (2024). AI-optimism, vigilance and biases: Support and influence from AI in classroom discussions about social issues. https://doi.org/10.31219/osf.io/mhpxa

Ejjami, R. (2024). The future of learning: AI-based curriculum development. *International Journal for Multidisciplinary Research*, *6*(4), 24441. https://doi.org/10.36948/ijfmr.2024.v06i04.24441

Fabiyi, S. D. (2025). What can ChatGPT not do in education? Evaluating its effectiveness in assessing educational learning outcomes. *Innovations in Education and Teaching International*, *62*(2), 484–498. https://doi.org/10.1080/14703297.2024.2333395

Fan, Y., Tang, L., Le, H., Shen, K., Tan, S., Zhao, Y., Shen, Y., Li, X., & Gašević, D. (2025). Beware of metacognitive laziness: Effects of generative artificial intelligence on learning motivation, processes, and performance. *British Journal of Educational Technology*, *56*(2), 489–530. https://doi.org/10.1111/bjet.13544

Garcia, M. B., Goi, C. L., Shively, K., Maher, D., Rosak-Szyrocka, J., Happonen, A., Bozkurt, A., & Damaševičius, R. (2025). Understanding Student Engagement in AI-Powered Online Learning Platforms: A Narrative Review of Key Theories and Models. In A. Gierhart (Ed.), *Cases on Enhancing P-16 Student Engagement With Digital Technologies*, (pp. 1–30). IGI Global. https://doi.org/10.4018/979-8-3693-5633-3.ch001

Happonen, A., Minashkina, D., Nolte, A., & Angarita, M. A. M. (2020). Hackathons as a company—University collaboration tool to boost circularity innovations and digitalization enhanced sustainability. *AIP Conference Proceeding*, 050009. https://doi.org/10.1063/5.0001883

Happonen, A., Tikka, M., & Usmani, U. A. (2021). A systematic review for organizing hackathons and code camps in Covid-19 like times: Literature in demand to understand online hackathons and event result continuation. In *2021 International Conference on Data and Software Engineering (ICoDSE)* (pp. 1–6). https://doi.org/10.1109/ICoDSE53690.2021.9648459

Heredia, A. S., Del Pilar García-Chitiva, M., Camacho-Zúñiga, C., Mirabal, L. F. M., & Vázquez-Villegas, P. (2025). Remediation of mathematics knowledge in engineering students through an AI-based self-study educational intervention. In *2025 IEEE Global Engineering Education Conference (EDUCON)* (pp. 1–8). https://doi.org/10.1109/EDUCON62633.2025.11016455

Holmes, W., Bialik, M., & Fadel, C. (2019). *Artificial Intelligence in Education. Promise and Implications for Teaching and Learning*. Center for Curriculum Redesign.

Holmes, W., & Tuomi, I. (2022). State of the art and practice in AI in education. *European Journal of Education*, *57*(4), 542–570. https://doi.org/10.1111/ejed.12533

Hwang, G.-J., Xie, H., Wah, B. W., & Gašević, D. (2020). Vision, challenges, roles and research issues of artificial intelligence in education. *Computers and Education: Artificial Intelligence*, *1*, 100001. https://doi.org/10.1016/j.caeai.2020.100001

Jiang, Q., Chen, J., Wu, Y., Gu, C., & Sun, J. (2022). A study of factors influencing the continuance intention to the usage of augmented reality in Museums. *Systems*, *10*(3), 73. https://doi.org/10.3390/systems10030073

Kaiser, G., & Kaiser, S. (2024). AI in education: Reflections and future directions for pedagogical and andragogical integration. In V. Wang (Ed.), *Advances in Educational Technologies and Instructional Design* (pp. 241–260). IGI Global. https://doi.org/10.4018/979-8-3693-6130-6.ch010

Karakas, A. (2023). Breaking down barriers with artificial intelligence (AI): Cross-cultural communication in foreign language education. In G. Kartal (Ed.), *Advances in Educational Technologies and Instructional Design* (pp. 215–233). IGI Global. https://doi.org/10.4018/978-1-6684-9893-4.ch012

Karpicke, J. D., & Roediger, H. L. (2008). The critical importance of retrieval for learning. *Science, 319*(5865), 966–968. https://doi.org/10.1126/science.1152408

Kien, T. T. (2025). The impact of artificial intelligence on the English self-study process at Nguyen Tat Thanh University. *Journal of Science and Technology, 8*(5), 52–59. https://doi.org/10.55401/hxn2hh66

Kim, K., & Kwon, K. (2023). Exploring the AI competencies of elementary school teachers in South Korea. *Computers and Education: Artificial Intelligence, 4*, 100137. https://doi.org/10.1016/j.caeai.2023.100137

Klimova, B., & Pikhart, M. (2025). Exploring the effects of artificial intelligence on student and academic well-being in higher education: A mini-review. *Frontiers in Psychology, 16*, 1498132. https://doi.org/10.3389/fpsyg.2025.1498132

Korte, S.-M., Cheung, W. M.-Y., Maasilta, M., Kong, S.-C., Keskitalo, P., Wang, L., Lau, C. M., Lee, J. C. K., & Gu, M. M. (2024). Enhancing artificial intelligence literacy through cross-cultural online workshops. *Computers and Education Open, 6*, 100164. https://doi.org/10.1016/j.caeo.2024.100164

Kortelainen, H., Happonen, A., & Hanski, J. (2019). From asset provider to knowledge company—transformation in the digital era. In J. Mathew, C. W. Lim, L. Ma, D. Sands, M. E. Cholette, & P. Borghesani (Eds.), *Asset Intelligence through Integration and Interoperability and Contemporary Vibration Engineering Technologies* (pp. 333–341). Springer International Publishing. https://doi.org/10.1007/978-3-319-95711-1_33

Lazăr (Cățeanu), A. M., Repanovici, A., Popa, D., Ionas, D. G., & Dobrescu, A. I. (2024). Ethical principles in AI use for assessment: Exploring students' perspectives on ethical principles in academic publishing. *Education Sciences, 14*(11), 1239. https://doi.org/10.3390/educsci14111239

Lekadir, K., Frangi, A. F., Porras, A. R., Glocker, B., Cintas, C., Langlotz, C. P., Weicken, E., Asselbergs, F. W., Prior, F., Collins, G. S., Kaissis, G., Tsakou, G., Buvat, I., Kalpathy-Cramer, J., Mongan, J., Schnabel, J. A., Kushibar, K., Riklund, K., Marias, K., . . . Starmans, M. P. A. (2025). FUTURE-AI: International consensus guideline for trustworthy and deployable artificial intelligence in healthcare. *BMJ*, e081554. https://doi.org/10.1136/bmj-2024-081554

Li, Y., Zhou, X., & Chiu, T. K. F. (2025). Systematics review on artificial intelligence chatbots and ChatGPT for language learning and research from self-determination theory (SDT): What are the roles of teachers? *Interactive Learning Environments, 33*(3), 1850–1864. https://doi.org/10.1080/10494820.2024.2400090

Luckin, R., Holmes, W., Griffiths, M., & Forcier, L. (2016). *Intelligence Unleashed: An Argument for AI in Education*. Pearson.

Maglogiannis, I. (with Macintyre, J., & Iliadis, L.). (2021). *Artificial Intelligence Applications and Innovations: 17th IFIP WG 12. 5 International Conference, AIAI 2021, Hersonissos, Crete, Greece, June 25–27, 2021, Proceedings*. Springer International Publishing AG.

Malik, A., Khan, M. L., Hussain, K., Qadir, J., & Tarhini, A. (2024). AI in higher education: Unveiling academicians' perspectives on teaching, research, and ethics in the age of ChatGPT. *Interactive Learning Environments*, 1–17. https://doi.org/10.1080/10494820.2024.2409407

Marzuki, W., Widiati, U., Rusdin, D., Darwin, & Indrawati, I. (2023). The impact of AI writing tools on the content and organization of students' writing: EFL teachers' perspective. *Cogent Education, 10*(2), 2236469. https://doi.org/10.1080/2331186X.2023.2236469

Mohebbi, A. (2025). Enabling learner independence and self-regulation in language education using AI tools: A systematic review. *Cogent Education, 12*(1), 2433814. https://doi.org/10.1080/2331186X.2024.2433814

Ngo, T. N., & Hastie, D. (2025). Artificial intelligence for academic purposes (AIAP): Integrating AI literacy into an EAP module. *English for Specific Purposes, 77*, 20–38. https://doi.org/10.1016/j.esp.2024.09.001

Popenici, S. A. D., & Kerr, S. (2017). Exploring the impact of artificial intelligence on teaching and learning in higher education. *Research and Practice in Technology Enhanced Learning, 12*(1), 22. https://doi.org/10.1186/s41039-017-0062-8

Porras, J., Khakurel, J., Ikonen, J., Happonen, A., Knutas, A., Herala, A., & Drögehorn, O. (2018). Hackathons in software engineering education: Lessons learned from a decade of events. In *Proceedings of the 2nd International Workshop on Software Engineering Education for Millennials* (pp. 40–47). https://doi.org/10.1145/3194779.3194783

Rapa, A. A., Ijlal Saja, I. S., & Afifah Azmi, A. A. (2024). The use of artificial intelligence (AI) Translation tools: Implications for third language proficiency. *International Journal of Research and Innovation in Social Science, VIII*(IX), 1952–1960. https://doi.org/10.47772/IJRISS.2024.8090161

Rogahang, S. S. N., Paramansyah, A., Zaelani, K., Iqbal, M., & Judijanto, L. (2024). Inclusive education practices: Fostering diversity and equity in the classroom. *Global International Journal of Innovative Research, 1*(3), 260–266. https://doi.org/10.59613/global.v1i3.46

Roshanaei, M., Olivares, H., & Lopez, R. R. (2023). Harnessing AI to foster equity in education: Opportunities, challenges, and emerging strategies. *Journal of Intelligent Learning Systems and Applications, 15*(4), 123–143. https://doi.org/10.4236/jilsa.2023.154009

Rudolph, J., Tan, S., & Tan, S. (2023). ChatGPT: Bullshit spewer or the end of traditional assessments in higher education? *Journal of Applied Learning & Teaching, 6*(1). https://doi.org/10.37074/jalt.2023.6.1.9

Sajja, R., Ramirez, C. E., Li, Z., Demiray, B. Z., Sermet, Y., & Demir, I. (2024). Integrating generative AI in Hackathons: Opportunities, challenges, and educational implications. *Big Data and Cognitive Computing, 8*(12), 188. https://doi.org/10.3390/bdcc8120188

Salmela, E., Santos, C., & Happonen, A. (2013). Formalisation of front end innovation in supply network collaboration. *International Journal of Innovation and Regional Development, 5*(1), 91. https://doi.org/10.1504/IJIRD.2013.052510

Selwyn, N. (2019). *Should Robots Replace Teachers? AI and the Future of Education*. Polity Press.

Selwyn, N. (2024). On the limits of artificial intelligence (AI) in education. *Nordisk Tidsskrift for Pedagogikk Og Kritikk, 10*(1). https://doi.org/10.23865/ntpk.v10.6062

Siau, K., & Wang, W. (2020). Artificial intelligence (AI) ethics: Ethics of AI and ethical AI. *Journal of Database Management, 31*(2), 74–87. https://doi.org/10.4018/JDM.2020040105

Sosunova, I., Hasheela, V., & Happonen, A. (2024). Novel creative technologies decision support system for small and medium enterprises: Exploring the potential, current findings and future research consideration. In *2024 IEEE International Conference on Systems, Man, and Cybernetics (SMC)* (pp. 4901–4907). https://doi.org/10.1109/SMC54092.2024.10831174

Suriano, R., Plebe, A., Acciai, A., & Fabio, R. A. (2025). Student interaction with ChatGPT can promote complex critical thinking skills. *Learning and Instruction, 95*, 102011. https://doi.org/10.1016/j.learninstruc.2024.102011

Tran, K. M. A. (2025). Research on using Grammarly to improve students' English writing. *AsiaCALL Online Journal, 16*(1), 69–82. https://doi.org/10.54855/acoj.251614

Treve, M. (2024). Integrating artificial intelligence in education: Impacts on student learning and innovation. *International Journal of Vocational Education and Training Research, 10*(2), 61–69. https://doi.org/10.11648/j.ijvetr.20241002.14

Usmani, U. A., Happonen, A., Watada, J., & Khakurel, J. (2023). Artificial intelligence applications in healthcare. In X.-S. Yang, R. S. Sherratt, N. Dey, & A. Joshi (Eds.), *Proceedings of Eighth International Congress on Information and Communication Technology* (Vol. 694, pp. 1085–1104). Springer Nature Singapore. https://doi.org/10.1007/978-981-99-3091-3_89

Usmani, U.A., Happonen, A., & Watada, J. (2023). Enhancing Artificial Intelligence Control Mechanisms: Current Practices, Real Life Applications and Future Views, *Lecture Notes in Networks and Systems, 559*, 287–306, https://doi.org/10.1007/978-3-031-18461-1_19

Vieriu, A. M., & Petrea, G. (2025). The impact of artificial intelligence (AI) on students' academic development. *Education Sciences, 15*(3), 343. https://doi.org/10.3390/educsci15030343

Williamson, B. (2017). *Big Data in Education: The Digital Future of Learning, Policy and Practice*. SAGE Publications Ltd. https://doi.org/10.4135/9781529714920

Xu, Z. (2024). AI in education: Enhancing learning experiences and student outcomes. *Applied and Computational Engineering, 51*(1), 104–111. https://doi.org/10.54254/2755-2721/51/20241187

Ylä-Kujala, A., Kedziora, D., Metso, L., Kärri, T., Piotrowicz, W., & Happonen, A., (2023). Robotic process automation deployments: a step-by-step method to investment appraisal. *Business Process Management Journal, 29*(8), 163–187. https://doi.org/10.1108/BPMJ-08-2022-0418

Yue Yim, I. H. (2024). A critical review of teaching and learning artificial intelligence (AI) literacy: Developing an intelligence-based AI literacy framework for primary school education. *Computers and Education: Artificial Intelligence, 7*, 100319. https://doi.org/10.1016/j.caeai.2024.100319

Zawacki-Richter, O., Marín, V. I., Bond, M., & Gouverneur, F. (2019). Systematic review of research on artificial intelligence applications in higher education—where are the educators? *International Journal of Educational Technology in Higher Education, 16*(1), 39. https://doi.org/10.1186/s41239-019-0171-0

Zhai, C., Wibowo, S., & Li, L. D. (2024). The effects of over-reliance on AI dialogue systems on students' cognitive abilities: A systematic review. *Smart Learning Environments, 11*(1), 28. https://doi.org/10.1186/s40561-024-00316-7

Zhang, K., & Aslan, A. B. (2021). AI technologies for education: Recent research & future directions. *Computers and Education: Artificial Intelligence, 2*, 100025. https://doi.org/10.1016/j.caeai.2021.100025

10

Social and Emotional Learning with Purpose

Divya Rose Peter and Sunitha Sivakumaran

10.1 Introduction

Social and emotional learning (SEL) is a concept fostered in educational systems to enhance skills such as self-control and self-management, emotional understanding, interpersonal relationships, problem-solving, and more. Unlike conventional learning paradigms that aim at academic achievements, SEL focuses on equipping individuals with appropriate self-regulation, communication, interpersonal, and problem-solving skills (Durlak et al., 2022). SEL develops these competencies, ensuring meaningful and successful functioning in classrooms, schools, and other environments.

It is, therefore, evident that SEL is a crucial factor to consider when designing a learning system. Recent years have seen tremendous technological and social changes, making it equally important to learn math, science, emotions, and relationships as in the latter half of the 20th century. SEL enables healthy emotional functioning, decreases conduct issues, helps students become better learners, and sets them on the path to success. Additionally, it is instrumental in developing learning spaces that welcome and uphold diversity and foster students' sense of belonging.

The purpose of this chapter is to discuss the main structural and functional attributes of SEL and to examine its effectiveness, difficulties, and further developments. In this chapter, the authors offer an analysis of empirical data concerning SEL, as well as practical examples that are meant to reveal the opportunities that this model can open for the development of a new model of education.

10.2 Definition and Purpose of Social and Emotional Learning

SEL targets a combination of behaviors, cognitions, and emotions. Research highlights that due to its positive impact on overall well-being and long-term

DOI: 10.1201/9781003633433-10

benefits, SEL is gaining momentum in schools (Taylor et al., 2017). These skills empower students to make responsible, positive decisions, set and work toward their goals, and cultivate healthy relationships with others. They are important tools for navigating life (Jones & Doolittle, 2017). SEL provides students with crucial life skills essential for their growth into competent and productive adults. By imparting these skills, educators can reduce negative risk factors. SEL is rooted in the idea that the best learning takes place in supportive, challenging, and engaging environments. It is believed that introducing students to key social-emotional abilities, such as robust work ethics and values, will support their success in higher education and meaningful career pursuits (Zins et al., 2004). By increasing the capacity to translate intentions into actions, these social and emotional competencies are crucial for developing dedicated employees. These skills significantly influence socioeconomic outcomes and empower individuals to make meaningful contributions as responsible citizens.

10.3 Core Components of SEL

There are five interrelated areas of competence that make up SEL: self-awareness, self-management, social awareness, relationship skills, and responsible decision-making.

Self-awareness is the ability to recognize and understand one's emotions, thoughts, and values, as well as their impact on behavior. It involves accurately identifying personal strengths and weaknesses, cultivating a grounded sense of confidence, and embracing a growth mindset. When students enhance their self-awareness, they gain better control over their emotional experiences and are able to foster a positive self-image.

Self-management involves the ability to regulate emotions, thoughts, and behaviors in different situations. It includes managing stress, controlling impulses, and staying motivated to achieve personal and academic goals. Strong self-management skills enable students to remain focused, organized, and resilient when facing challenges.

Social awareness is the capacity to understand and empathize with others, including individuals from diverse backgrounds and cultures. It involves recognizing social cues, understanding cultural norms, and valuing different perspectives. By cultivating social awareness, students can foster respectful relationships and navigate social interactions successfully.

Relationship skills involve the ability to build and sustain healthy, meaningful connections with individuals and groups. This includes effective communication, active listening, teamwork, conflict resolution, and giving or seeking support when needed. Strong relationship skills are also crucial for fostering collaboration and cultivating a positive classroom atmosphere.

Responsible decision-making is the process of making ethical and constructive choices regarding personal and social behavior. It involves prioritizing the well-being of oneself and others, assessing the potential outcomes of actions, and using past experiences to guide future decisions. Developing these skills helps students handle complex situations effectively and make meaningful contributions to their communities.

10.4 SEL in Schools

Research indicates that schools are the best venue for fostering SEL skills because of their malleable nature, allowing them to be effectively taught and learned. SEL programs in schools aim to enhance students' SEL skills and competencies through three primary approaches:

Direct Instruction: This involves teaching students specific SEL skills using a structured curriculum.

Environmental Modification: This focuses on altering the school environment, often referred to as the school or classroom climate. It involves changes in teachers' practices and their style of interaction with students, as well as modifications to school rules and expectations.

Influencing Mindsets: This approach aims to shape students' perceptions of themselves, others, and the environments they encounter, thereby impacting their overall mindset. These methods collectively contribute to the development and reinforcement of SEL skills and are the best place to start developing SEL competencies (Blyth et al., 2017).

Genuinely effective schools should prepare students not only to pass exams but also to navigate life's challenges successfully. Today, schools are increasingly recognized as an important—if not central—arena for health promotion and primary prevention in addition to the education of students. Mark Greenberg et al. argue that promoting SEL in schools is essential because of its potential to support broader public health goals. They make the case that SEL can support a public health approach to education (i.e., both preventing problems and promoting positive outcomes) for three reasons. First, schools are good places to intervene to ensure a healthy population because most children spend a large part of their lives there. Second, school-based SEL programs can both improve students' SEL skills and academic achievement and reduce the likelihood that they will experience behavioral or emotional problems in the future.

Third, SEL programs in all schools for all students (universal interventions) can have a substantial impact on public health because of the "prevention paradox," which states that overall public health is best achieved in the long run by providing intervention to all rather than targeted interventions only to those who are most in need of additional support. That's because most cases of any undesirable outcome arise in the large segment of the population that's considered to be at low risk (Jones & Doolittle, 2017).

To integrate SEL, schools need to revolutionize their entire ecosystem. SEL is not another subject; it is a holistic approach that demands profound and systemic changes that have to be woven into the fabric of a school's curriculum by making academic lessons more personal and relatable to students.

Students will have to learn, practice, and apply SEL skills by engaging in positive activities in and out of the classroom. The initial skills that they have learned will be enhanced, nuanced, and better integrated over time to address the increasingly complex situations students face in terms of academics, social relationships, citizenship, and health (Elias et al., 2014; Collaborative for Academic, Social, and Emotional Learning [CASEL], 2014).

The inclusion of SEL in schools will mark a shift from conventional education systems that predominantly prioritize academic success and cognitive skills. Traditional schooling focuses on standardized exams, rote learning, and subject-specific expertise, with achievement gauged through grades and test results. Although these methods develop cognitive abilities, they often overlook students' comprehensive development, resulting in deficiencies in social and emotional maturity.

It is reasonable to assert that the integration of SEL in schools not only mitigates the likelihood of students engaging in risky behaviors but also establishes a robust foundation for enhanced academic performance and the development of prosocial behaviors. When supported by both education systems and the broader community, SEL fosters a more compassionate society and contributes to a safer, more inclusive environment (Farniok, 2023).

In schools, educators play a crucial role in the process and outcomes of SEL. As they focus on SEL outcomes, it is important to recognize that social and emotional skills are both taught and caught. While educators design experiences to explicitly teach students specific language and skills, students also learn social and emotional skills through everyday interactions and experiences. It is important to note that not only what we say or teach that matters but also how we act and what we do create experiences and environments where students catch social and emotional skills (Blyth et al., 2017). Martinez also emphasized the importance and necessity of being intentional about the ways social and emotional skills are both taught and absorbed in educational programs (Martínez et al., 2017). Given this, the question arises: How can we seamlessly integrate these skills into the fabric of the school curriculum?

TABLE 10.1

Comparison of SEL and Traditional Education

Aspect	Social-Emotional Learning (SEL)	Traditional Education
Approach	Integrates emotional and social competencies alongside academic skills, focusing on emotional intelligence, stress management, collaboration, and inclusive learning experiences.	Relies on teacher-centered instruction, where students are passive recipients of knowledge, limiting opportunities for critical thinking, problem-solving, and interpersonal skill development.
Learning Environment	Creates an inclusive and supportive environment that fosters emotional well-being and promotes a positive school culture, emphasizing respect and inclusivity.	Tends to focus on standardized academic outcomes, with limited emphasis on the emotional or social aspects of learning.
Focus on Engagement	Encourages active, student-centered learning through collaborative activities, discussions, and projects. This promotes self-awareness, reflection, and emotional regulation.	Primarily emphasizes lecture-based learning, which often lacks opportunities for active engagement, reflection, and emotional growth.
Skill Development	Enhances critical thinking, problem-solving, emotional regulation, and communication by integrating social-emotional learning into academic content.	Prioritizes memorization and rote learning over the development of critical thinking, emotional intelligence, and interpersonal skills.
School Culture	Practices peer mentoring, restorative justice, and community-building activities to foster a safe, respectful, and supportive environment, reducing bullying and disengagement.	Often lacks mechanisms to address emotional well-being or foster a sense of community, potentially leading to issues like bullying and disengagement.
Outcome	Prepares students to navigate complex situations, make informed decisions, and build meaningful relationships in a dynamic and interconnected world.	Primarily prepares students for academic assessments, often with less focus on life skills, emotional intelligence, or collaborative problem-solving.

(Dussault & Thompson, 2024; Bailey et al., 2023; Cojocaru, 2023; Elmi, 2020)

10.5 Best Practices and Strategies for Implementing Purposeful SEL

10.5.1 Develop a Clear Vision

To successfully implement SEL, schools should establish a strong foundation and gain the support of key stakeholders. This process begins by developing a shared vision in collaboration with educators, parents, and the community, defining what SEL means for them and setting clear goals for success (Greenberg et al., 2017).

There must be discussions about key questions such as "What kind of school culture do we want to create with SEL?" and "What does it mean for us to support everyone's social and emotional growth?" Their responses may be used to shape the school's SEL vision. It is important that school leaders create and communicate a clear vision for SEL to teachers and students with consistency and clarity (Understanding the Importance of Social and Emotional Learning in Schools).

10.5.2 Implementation Plan and Budget

Next, an implementation plan should be crafted, detailing how SEL will be integrated into daily instruction, school culture, and student behavior expectations. Regular communication through newsletters, meetings, and events is essential to keep everyone informed and aligned. Additionally, budgeting for SEL training, curricula, and support must be prioritized to ensure the necessary resources are allocated within the school's budget. By engaging all stakeholders, maintaining open communication, and securing proper funding, SEL can be effectively woven into the school's ecosystem (Greenberg et al., 2017).

10.5.3 SEL Implementation Team

Once the schoolwide SEL vision and implementation plan is established, form an SEL implementation team comprising staff members. This team can provide additional support and facilitate communication between school leaders, teachers, and parents (Greenberg et al., 2017). The leaders may consider offering a stipend to SEL team members to incentivize participation and demonstrate administrative support for SEL at a systemic level. Assigning staff to oversee specific departments, content areas, clubs, and tasks offers opportunities for professional development and empowerment (Mahoney et al., 2020).

10.5.4 Professional Development and Ongoing Training for Educators

Educators play a crucial role in modeling, teaching, and reinforcing SEL principles. Therefore, equipping staff with expertise in SEL should be a priority. Training should begin with fostering effective student practices and evolve into a comprehensive understanding of the SEL domain and learning process. Effective educators must be proficient in the concepts and language of SEL, building both understanding and fluency. Schools must ensure that educators are adequately prepared to teach SEL effectively, thereby supporting student growth and development.

Continuous training is also essential for educators to acquire the necessary knowledge and skills to implement SEL effectively. Leveraging existing SEL programs that incorporate teacher training can guide educators in delivering program content proficiently. Utilizing tools such as the Ways of Being model for SEL can also prove highly beneficial in this endeavor.

10.5.5 Offer Resources and Support

Educators need access to tools, resources, and curriculum materials that integrate SEL into daily instruction and classroom management practices. Providing these resources allows teachers to confidently embed SEL into their teaching (Greenberg et al., 2017).

10.5.6 Administrative Support for SEL

School administrators play an important role in the successful implementation of SEL. Their responsibilities encompass establishing specific, measurable goals for SEL to ensure direction and accountability, allocating necessary resources such as funding, materials, and personnel, and developing supportive policies that embed SEL into the school's mission and culture. These policies should guide the integration of SEL into both academic instruction and extracurricular activities. Additionally, administrators must collaborate closely with teachers to identify needs, address challenges, and celebrate successes. By building strong partnerships between leadership and educators, a collaborative approach to SEL integration is ensured (Schlinger et al., 2020).

10.5.7 Leveraging Support Staff

Support staff, including counselors, play a crucial role in complementing classroom-based SEL efforts by providing targeted interventions and additional support to students requiring extra assistance. Their key contributions encompass offering one-on-one or small-group sessions to address specific social-emotional needs, collaborating with teachers to design strategies that enhance SEL in the classroom, and promoting a schoolwide culture of inclusivity and emotional well-being. This includes organizing community-building activities, peer-mentoring programs, and restorative-justice practices. By integrating these initiatives, support staff significantly bolster the overall effectiveness of SEL programs.

By equipping teachers with training, engaging support staff, and fostering administrative collaboration, schools can create a sustainable and effective SEL program that benefits all students (Mahoney et al., 2020).

10.5.8 Integrating Purpose into Curriculum Design

To effectively integrate SEL, educators must shift from traditional "chalk and talk" methods to more student-centered approaches, such as reflective activities, choice boards, and project-based learning (PBL). Incorporating SEL principles into assessments can encourage students to reflect on their personal and academic growth, develop strategies to manage stress effectively, and demonstrate their knowledge through diverse and meaningful formats. This approach fosters a well-rounded learning experience, balancing academic rigor with the development of emotional resilience and self-awareness.

10.5.9 Reflective Activities

Reflective activities build self-awareness in students. After a unit or summative assignment, educators can require students to complete a reflection exercise to help them assess their own effort, persistence, and the quality of their work. These three reflection aspects, recommended by Daniel T. Willingham in his book *Outsmart Your Brain* (2023), can be conducted through short answers on a Google Form or in written format. Educators might incorporate a rating scale for students to evaluate their work effort. When students write about their experiences and opinions, they develop metacognitive awareness as learners, fostering self-awareness by honestly identifying their strengths and weaknesses.

10.5.10 Choice Boards

Choice boards can be a powerful tool to integrate SEL into the classroom by offering students autonomy, fostering collaboration, and building key social-emotional skills. Here's how each example promotes SEL:

- Research Project: Students select a topic of interest and present it as a research paper, multimedia presentation, podcast, or poster. This encourages self-awareness by aligning with their passions and responsible decision-making as they manage deadlines and presentation formats.
- Skill Development: Focusing on a specific skill, such as public speaking, data analysis, coding, or writing, helps students build self-management by practicing perseverance, goal-setting, and adapting to challenges.
- Group Project: Working in teams on projects like a case study, business plan, community service project, or scientific experiment strengthens relationship skills and social awareness as students communicate, collaborate, and navigate diverse perspectives.
- Learning Path: Allowing students to choose between lectures, online courses, workshops, or self-study supports self-awareness by

letting them explore learning styles and preferences while building self-management as they take ownership of their education.

- Assessment: Offering options like exams, quizzes, essays, presentations, or portfolios helps develop responsible decision-making as students select the method that best demonstrates their knowledge and builds self-confidence as they showcase their strengths.

By incorporating choice and flexibility, these activities empower students to practice essential SEL competencies while engaging in meaningful academic learning.

10.5.11 Project-Based Learning

PBL offers an optimal environment for fostering SEL by allowing students to work collaboratively on real-world problems, emphasizing empathy, teamwork, and communication. Through PBL, students enhance their social and emotional skills, such as effective communication, cooperation, and problem-solving, while also learning to manage their time and meet deadlines (Al-Busaidi & Al-Seyabi, 2021a). For instance, SmartLab Learning's PBL approach seamlessly integrates academic and SEL instruction, providing various opportunities for students to develop critical nonacademic skills, including giving and receiving feedback, identifying and managing emotions, resolving conflicts, and cultivating social awareness.

Integrating SEL through PBL enhances a sense of belonging and inclusivity, resulting in greater student engagement, self-efficacy, and improved peer relationships. Research indicates that SEL curricula improve academic performance and behavior and reduce emotional stress. By combining rigorous academic content with SEL activities, PBL fosters the holistic development of students (Spigner, 2023). Programs like SmartLab's PBL offer structured problem-solving opportunities, helping students meet content standards while developing essential interpersonal skills and emotional intelligence (EI), thus preparing them for lifelong academic and personal success.

10.6 SEL beyond the Classroom

10.6.1 Engaging Parents and Families

The success of SEL initiatives is highly dependent on active parental and community engagement. Parents, as primary influencers, are essential in reinforcing SEL skills within the home environment (Li & Zhang, 2023). Schools should actively involve families by providing them with the necessary resources, strategies, and consistent communication through workshops, newsletters, and events aimed at supporting the social-emotional development of their children (Dussault et al., 2024). By incorporating parents into the planning and implementation of SEL initiatives, a sense of ownership is fostered, thereby enhancing collaborative efforts and magnifying the overall impact of SEL programs (Eden et al., 2024).

10.6.2 Building Community Partnerships

Community involvement is equally critical to the success of SEL initiatives. Local organizations, businesses, and social service agencies can provide essential resources such as mentoring programs and mental health services, thereby bolstering SEL efforts.

Schools have the potential to foster SEL principles and fortify school-community relationships by organizing community-focused events, including service projects and wellness fairs (Rock, 2022; Raji et al., 2023). Furthermore, community stakeholders play a pivotal role in advocating for SEL at the policy level, which involves securing funding, allocating resources, and elevating awareness regarding the significance of SEL. This comprehensive and collaborative approach cultivates an extensive support network, significantly advancing students' social-emotional development beyond the confines of the classroom (Vázquez-Villegas et al., 2023).

10.7 Measuring the Impact of Social and Emotional Learning

10.7.1 Key Metrics and Indicators

SEL is thus perhaps best assessed by the use of both formative and summative assessments that reflect changes in the learners' emotional states, demeanor, academic achievement, and interpersonal relations. This can be measured by the rates of bullying, truancy, and other disciplinary cases, which are strong indications that SEL programs must be working. For example, reduced suspensions and conflicts, as well as specific instances where a student was calmer and better able to solve problems, suggest positive changes in the domains noted earlier. In addition to behavior change, SEL is measured through selected skills based on the observation of their importance to human growth and development: self-awareness, empathy, and proactive conflict solving (Oliveira et al., 2021). Pupil competencies, such as the acquired capacities for interaction with other learners or the degree of empathy toward others, are the paramount signs of social development. Another key impact area is the academic achievement, since common outcomes of SEL include increased students' concentration, self-organization, and participation. Recording such outcomes enables the establishment of a growth profile of the effects of SEL on learners as well as on the school context.

Furthermore, it is noteworthy that there are psychological and cognitive indicators reflecting the effectiveness of SEL in students' behavior and achievements in addition to such aspects as behavior modification and improvements in students' performance. Mental health, comprising decreased cases of anxiety, stress, and depression among students in learning institutions, is another quality assessment best practice in SEL programs. Some of the common benefits of SEL are that schools experience lower levels of emotional disturbances as students overcome tests through coping mechanisms (Butkute, 2023). In addition, the standardized psychological tests, questionnaires, as well as teacher headings, can go a long way toward elaborating learners' emotional self-regulation and general well-being.

Another important parameter is the activity of students and their interactions within the classroom. SEL programs ensure students work within safe, inclusive, and effective learning cultures where students are respected and encouraged to contribute. More time for discussions in the classroom, group activities, and students taking responsibility for leading an activity are seen as evidence that confidence and social responsibility are being boosted through SEL. However, in dealing with peer accommodations, one can observe the pupils' behavior and ask them some questions to determine their attitudes toward peers and cooperation (Herman et al., 2023). The degree to which learners are able to create and maintain companionship, resolve conflicts in a healthy manner, and exhibit courtesy to fellow students reflects the extent to which the SEL concepts have been internalized in practice.

Another qualitative aspect that may be used to assess the effectiveness of SEL is parents' and community engagement. Higher student attendance at school meetings, improved parent-student relations as demonstrated by increased parent participation in school meetings, and better cooperation between teachers and parents also provide evidence that SEL is having an effect not only on the students but on the students' primary caregivers as well (Choudhary et al., 2022). Schools may also consider how SEL skills generalize to other credited or extracurricular activities that involve students' self- and peer-organization, social pressures for positive and prosocial community change, such as student-led social causes or volunteerism, which require empathy, responsibility, and leadership.

10.7.2 Methods and Tools for Assessment

Several assessment techniques are employed to evaluate SEL outcomes so that educators receive a broad perspective of program impact. Some of the more common instruments used in the assessment of social and emotional development include questionnaire forms and surveys. Thus, the social skills improvement system (SSIS) and the Devereux student strengths assessment

(DESSA) help educators evaluate children's potential in self-organization or problem-solving and in interpersonal relationships with peers, teachers, or other significant adults (Mahoney et al., 2021). Coaching and professional development are also important sources for the practical implementation of SEL, and adaptations in usage by teachers and other key personnel in the classroom are also observed. Without teachers, many concerns related to the behavior of students—for example, in terms of organization, teamwork, or proactivity in specific classroom contexts—are not easily captured by NAP standardized testing. Another useful method is peer feedback because the ways students interact with each other reveal how efficiently they work in a group, share ideas, and solve emerging issues. Longitudinal studies provide further explanation of SEL program impact on students over time. When students are followed for several years, researchers are able to detect students' achievement, readiness for employment, and mental health (Camangian & Cariaga, 2022). These studies also help shed light on the possible secondary effects of SEL, for instance, a positive school climate and greater parental involvement.

However, surveys and standardized summary measures are not the only components of SEL's assessment; observational methods are of particular importance here. Both teachers and school counselors can provide regular classroom observations and use time-sampled rate artifacts such as this. These observations are useful when trying to establish the general progression of emotion, problem-solving, and coping mechanisms within natural environments. Moreover, journals or reflective writing tasks as a narrative form of assessment are valuable for reviewing the students' feelings, personal growth, and changing attitudes beyond academic performance.

Another effective learning strategy is portfolio assessment, where students compile evidence of their SEL growth through created projects, reflections, and peer assessments. These portfolios enable the demonstration of the use of SEL skills in practice by the student—grouping assignments, leadership, and conflict resolution, among others. Schools can also use digital formative assessments like applications tracking students' emotions, periods of self-regulation, and active participation throughout the school year (McBrien, 2022). Focus group discussions as well as students' own discussions will prove to be a good way to gain qualified information about the level of SEL. These forums make the students put down how they experienced the programs of the SEL initiative, hence giving the tutors direct feedback on which parts of the program are most effective. It can also expose schools to other areas where students may feel a lack of support, thus improving the ways schools can support the learners. In addition, school climate surveys determine how SEL enhances or alters the overall learning environment of the school. These questionnaires, completed by students, teachers, and parents, reflect such things as community, feelings of safety, and rapport between students and educators. Using data from observations, students, peers, and longitudinal studies, teachers can increase their confidence in SEL and make constant improvements to students' ability to manage their emotions and advance their interpersonal skills.

10.8 Case Studies and Evidence from Recent Research

SEL advocates argue that there is strong and mounting evidence supporting the effectiveness of SEL programs. The SEL program research synthesized in a meta-analysis by the CASEL indicated that students benefiting from SEL programs received 11-percentile-points higher academic achievement than similar students not participating in SEL programs (Green et al., 2021). These results highlight that SEL is not just an emotional learning system but is about the overall growth of a child. SEL is applicable in any educational setting, as the case studies presented illustrate. For instance, when urban schools in the United States adopted SEL programs, major improvements were found in bullying, truancy, and dropout trends. In like manner, rural schools in developing nations also revealed similar gains, where students improved their interpersonal skills and especially their emotional intelligence. These outcomes show that SEL can be implemented in any socioeconomic and cultural environment that exists today. SEL-integrated schools have also been known to benefit from the overall educational climate, as well as from increased student participation levels. Teachers also note that SEL not only is useful for each student but also helps build a supportive cohort culture (Blewitt et al., 2021). All these positive changes foster a strong student-teacher relationship in a learning institution, in that students develop positive value systems that make them feel accepted, respected, and empowered to achieve both academically and socially.

10.9 Challenges and Barriers to Social and Emotional Learning Implementation

10.9.1 Institutional and Structural Challenges

Applying SEL faces more institutional and structural challenges than individual ones. SEL activities might be a challenge to implement because schools that focus on improving academic results and standardized testing may lack sufficient time for such practices. These centralized structures lead to organization-centered, strict and protracted timetables, as well as tangible-oriented contents and frameworks, which can marginalize SEL and limit its implementation in the classroom. The next limitation is the lack of funds and resources, especially in schools that are considered to have low ratings (Barnes & Jones, 2022). SEL-related activities are especially likely to need specialized curriculum resources, technological support, and teacher training, all of which cost money. Furthermore, a survey indicates that most schools lack adequately qualified teachers to implement SEL projects. Lack of training could mean that well-intentioned teachers may not be able to enforce SEL in the classroom due to insufficient confidence or know-how.

10.9.2 Cultural and Societal Barriers

Cultural and societal attitudes toward SEL also present challenges. SEL implementation faces resistance in communities that discourage displays of emotions and discussions about psychology. For example, there can be families that do not consider it helpful to discuss feelings—or even perceive it as wrong—so the schools struggle to receive parents' support (Moazami-Goodarzi et al., 2021). In addition, parents and stakeholders who care more about academic performances than the social and emotional well-being of a child may think of SEL as a waste of time for students to learn what they are supposed to learn in academic classes. The above-stated idea is exceptionally prominent in determined academic structures whose core focuses on test results and academic performances.

10.9.3 Personal and Psychological Obstacles

At the learner level, personal factors, including the students' own experiences and emotional contexts, may act as barriers to SEL implementation. In particular, children with some sort of trauma or other psychological issues may not want to do SEL activities at first. Such students need to transcend their sense of safety to be ready for the emotional feelings and ideas, which can become overwhelming and make an individual feel vulnerable. This is why we need to be more careful with them as educators. Teachers, too, face personal obstacles. The authors pointed out that educators who have low levels of self-SEL may not be able to teach self-SEL to learners appropriately. This is compounded by factors such as burnouts, stress, and workload pressures that make it difficult for the teachers to effectively foster an SEL-conducive environment.

10.9.4 Lack of Standardized Assessment Methods

SEL is difficult to evaluate for outcomes based on the main assessment procedures because it is one of the main obstacles in the implementation of SEL. And while with scholars learning is easier to measure and assess as it mainly involves assessments and grades, SEL is much more subjective: it is evaluated through the lens of variables such as EI, empathy, readiness to cope with stress, and necessary social skills. Because there are no easy and globally acknowledged methods of assessment, it is difficult for educators or policymakers to identify the effectiveness of SEL programs or monitor the students' progress (Acharya, 2022). Some schools rely on questionnaires, teachers' and researchers' observations, or behavioral ratings and inventories. However, all these methods are not accurate, objective, reliable, valid, or able to reveal immediate and timely changes in students' emotional and social growth. In particular, there is currently a lack of concrete assessment tools to identify students' needs, measure the effectiveness of specific programs or interventions, or provide a rationale for resource allocation to SEL initiatives—a deficit that undermines their continued development and growth.

10.9.5 Technological and Digital Divide

As technology advances within education, a variety of SEL programs involve online lessons, technology-based communication activities, and assessments. Although SEL can be delivered through technological means, not all students have equal access to technology, which can be seen as a lack of access to technological devices at home and leads to disadvantaged student groups being unable to fully benefit from SEL. In low-income schools, it can be an issue because students may not own their devices, have stable access to the internet, or do not possess the digital competencies needed for virtual SEL activities (Hatchimonji et al., 2022). It also fails to close the achievement gap between students from high-SES backgrounds and those from low-SES backgrounds and denies the fulfillment of the latter's full potential in SEL programs. Also, digital technology helps in student SEL learning, but overuse of technology will limit physical contact with fellow students, teachers, and practitioners, which is crucial in modeling, identification, and management of emotions and interpersonal relationships.

10.9.6 Lack of Long-Term Commitment and Policy Support

A major problem of many SEL programs is that they encounter difficulties regarding sustainability, as there are often no long-term strategies or support from policymakers, school boards, or government agencies. SEL is usually implemented in a few pilot projects throughout the school year but is not followed through for reasons such as changing priorities in education, lack of funds, and changes in school principals. SEL is still an add-on and thus lacks the proper funding for implementation; it also lacks consistent policies supporting it. Furthermore, it is evident that SEL policies differ by geographical location, and thus SEL implementation is not uniform (Gimbert et al., 2023). At times, political discussions about SEL's place in learning slow down its implementation, as some politicians claim that education is the parents' duty, not the schools'. This lack of national or state SEL policy leaves schools to independently engage in the practice as an uncoordinated, episodic endeavor at best and a low-quality effort at worst.

10.9.7 Teacher Resistance and Workload Burden

Teachers and faculty members are already burdened with workloads, and extra tasks such as the implementation of SEL will definitely create more stress and resistance. In the case of implementing SEL in the classroom, many teachers often state that they are unprepared to teach it or do not know how to teach it if they have not been given special training. In the same way, a rising emphasis on academic performance as well as expectations for preparing students for higher learning or standardized examinations may lead teachers to view SEL as far from an important need to address in their classroom (Fernández-Martín et al., 2022). This resistance can set back successful program implementation since teachers are key when it comes to both carrying out SEL instruction and developing a favorable class climate.

10.10 Strategies to Overcome These Barriers

10.10.1 Emerging Trends and Innovations in SEL

The subject of SEL, or social and emotional learning, is gradually integrating fresh, creative approaches to better meet students' emotional and social learning needs. Another relatively new area of work focuses on using a cross-discipline framework, for example, the joining up of arts, sports, and other cocurricular activities to support the development of SEL skills. These activities foster passion and consideration, which make learning fun beyond being inside the classroom. Other emerging intervention approaches include the concurrent running of SEL with environmental or community service programs (Ingram et al., 2021). These initiatives foster the cultivation of emotional intelligence alongside civic responsibility and global citizenship. That is, attaining experience in problem-solving, as well as collaboration with peers through integration into service-learning projects, can be of incredible benefit to students, their peers, societal bodies, as well as to them as individuals. Such approaches make SEL more appropriate and effective by promoting skills that are essential for life today.

10.10.2 Integration with Other Educational Frameworks

One major avenue of progress for SEL has to do with its incorporation into other scholarly paradigms such as competency-based learning and culture-based learning paradigms. In this connection, SEL can be integrated with these approaches as is consistent with developing holistic education for the students that considers not only academic progress but personal development as well. Acquisition of competencies is selective, with most leaning toward the acquisition of certain skills as opposed to SEL, which aims to nurture skills in empathy, self-control, and social interactions among learners (Oliveira et al., 2021). In the same way, SEL is integrated into culturally responsive teaching to ensure equal regard for cultural differences within the learning environment and appreciation of the students' diverse experiences. It also enhances SEL in terms of equality and student engagement since a larger number of students experience positive feelings toward their learning environment. SEL takes time to learn and becomes part of school-based educational practices as opposed to being a separate program run alongside other education programs. Also there is a shift from schools adopting SEL as a separate program within a school; this way, it is more integrated into the school system and is more likely to run independently without requiring support.

10.10.3 Policy and Advocacy for Widespread Adoption

SEL policies and advocacy have seen much progress over the years due to the world's recognition of the core area. SEL is being advocated by governments, educational institutions, as well as global organizations as a fundamental aspect of education being provided. Currently, there is scientific evidence showing that many states in the United States of America have lined up for SEL standards and included it in their policy framework as though it is part of school instructional packages (Shen et al., 2024). At the international level, the practice of SEL is being promoted through organizations such as CASEL and UNICEF that spread information regarding the effectiveness of SEL and urge governments to support its integration. Such attempts have led to enhanced child funding and resources for SEL initiatives, with schools eliminating mundane barriers such as inadequate human resources in training and deficient resources. Policy reforms are also paying increasing attention to SEL equity so that programs are also made available for low-SES students. Additional advocacy will be pursued in order to maintain the culture of awareness and partnership among schools, communities, and governments in nurturing and growing SEL programs and practices.

10.10.4 Role of Technology in Advancing SEL

Technology is becoming significant in supporting the development of SEL due to the availability of vehicles to support learning and assessment. Social media tools and applications are being created to allow SEL activities to take place, including emotion-management exercises, setting personal learning objectives, and conflict solving. One useful example is VP-related learning, as it results in the ability of students to practice empathy and communication in a rather safe environment. SEL is also being promoted by AI tools, where students get feedback and where students' progress is also tracked by tutors and teachers (Kamei & Harriott, 2021). These tools help educators understand the child's learning profile to address that specific need. Nonetheless, its availability should be equal because unequal distribution of technology can negatively affect the practice of SEL in disadvantaged neighborhoods. Finally, as SEL remains to be a developing aspect of the education system, we have to look at the future of SEL in terms of innovation, equity, and partnership among educators, policymakers, and technology developers.

10.10.5 Ensuring Long-Term Commitment and Policy Support

SEL currently lacks commitment and policy support beyond the current school year, and thus SEL must be incorporated into national and state education policies. Policymakers should consider SEL as a part of learning rather than implementing it as an added extra. One of these ways to do this is by integrating SEL objectives into curricula so that SEL becomes a program that is not implemented for a certain amount of time and then withdrawn but can be implemented continuously throughout the academic year. Another major approach is getting sustained financing for SEL initiatives. It is expected that ministries, school districts, as well as other education-related departments and interests, should set particular funds for SEL (skill) improvement as concerns training, curriculum, and formative evaluations. Schools can also seek more funding and other support from sources such as nonprofit organizations and private-sector partners (Dermody et al., 2022). Thus, the findings indicated that advocacy and awareness campaigns may help to reduce political barriers to SEL implementation. Using this research to show the effectiveness of SEL and its effects on achievement, self-profile, and employability ensures that educational practitioners and policymakers are empowered to incorporate it more effectively. Moreover, talking to parents and communities about SEL may assist to reverse the general consensus that it is one of the many responsibilities of the parent. SEL also gains the parental and stakeholders' support when they witness its positive effects firsthand during classroom implementation stages.

10.10.6 Reducing Teacher Resistance and Workload Burden

To reduce the level of teacher resistance, schools need to offer thorough professional development systems that prepare teachers for SEL promotion efficiently. Additional ungraded class activities, seminars, and mutual tutoring are some ways in which teachers can be assured that they incorporate SEL in their teaching practices as an add-on to what they normally do and not as an addition to their workload. Professional learning should involve goal-oriented interventions that have an element of feasibility when implemented within existing frameworks for academically oriented pedagogy that enables teachers to integrate SEL into basic classroom functions, while not becoming burdensome (Goh et al., 2022). Another strategy here is to reduce pressure on the workload. SEL should then become a whole-school endeavor in which teachers, head-teachers, counselors, and other members of staff have a hand in the development of students' SEL skills. This distributed model alleviates the pressures that teachers might experience, as it prevents them from having to implement SEL entirely on their own. In addition, this allows schools to incorporate adaptations of digital tools and resources to facilitate the delivery of SEL instruction. SEL activities may be workable when integrated into existing teaching-learning activities and materials. Ready SEL lessons, modules, and activities on the web or from SEL lesson package sets could be used to support teachers in teaching SEL competencies. It is also important to implement the routine exchange of best practices among teachers with the aim of eradicating the stress that accompanies implementation (Burd et al., 2023). If the long-term policy is granted and instructional requirements are taken off SEL teachers, the program would be effectively and stably implemented in the education system—a win-win situation for the students' development.

10.11 Conclusion

Social and Emotional Learning concerns a new approach to teaching and learning that focuses on building the skills of the students' emotional and social selves. These improvements bear witness to the need to continue teaching SEL lessons by highlighting how SEL makes the students ready for life experiences beyond classrooms. But its practice is not without difficulties, which is why coordinated efforts have to be made to overcome institutional, cultural, and personality obstacles. To this end, we present some trends that indicate the future of SEL and how possible innovations and policy support are expected to shape this field. SEL can be infused with systemic approaches of education and partners, and in doing so, it becomes possible to offer it as an equal opportunity for any learner. Over the years, with the dynamism in the delivery of education, SEL will be among the most crucial learning tools that prepare learners to face challenges in life.

References

Acharya, K. R. (2022). Promoting social justice through usability in technical communication: An integrative literature review. *Technical Communication*, *610*(1), 6–26. https://www.ingentaconnect.com/content/stc/tc/2022/000000610/00000001/art00002

Al-Busaidi, S., & Al-Seyabi, F. (2021a). Project-based learning as a tool for student-teachers' professional development: A Study in an Omani EFL teacher education program. *International Journal of Learning, Teaching and Educational Research*, *20*(4), 116–136. https://doi.org/10.26803/ijlter.20.4.7

Al-Busaidi, S., & Al-Seyabi, F. (2021b). Project-based learning in English classes: Learners' perceptions of its impact on collaboration and communication skills. *Arab World English Journal, 12*(4), 113–129.

Bailey, C. S., Martinez, O., & DiDomizio, E. (2023). Social and emotional learning and early literacy skills: A quasi-experimental study of RULER. *Education Sciences, 13*, 3107. https://doi.org/10.33100/educsci130403107

Barnes, S. P., & Jones, S. M. (2022). Social and emotional learning (SEL) in schools. *Social and Emotional Learning (SEL) in Schools*. https://doi. org/10.4324/107811386010877-ree113-1. https://api.taylorfrancis.com/content/entry-versions/download?identifierName=doi&identifierValue=10.4324/107811386010877-REE113-1&type=webpdf

Blewitt, C., O'connor, A., Morris, H., Nolan, A., Mousa, A., Green, R., . . . & Skouteris, H. (2021). "It's embedded in what we do for every child": A qualitative exploration of early childhood educators' perspectives on supporting Children's social and emotional learning. *International Journal of Environmental Research and Public Health, 18*(4), 1530. https://www.mdpi.com/1660-4601/18/4/1530

Blyth, D., Brandi, O., & Kate, W. (2007). Ways of being: Model for social & emotional learning. *Journal of Educational and Psychological Consultation, 17*(2–3), 1101–1210.

Blyth, D. A., Olson, B. D., & Walker, K. C. (2017). *Social and emotional learning: The role of out-of-school time programs*. Minneapolis, MN: University of Minnesota, Extension Center for Youth Development.

Burd, H., Deutsch, J., & Waldera, R. (2023). Giving another purpose to sport: Teaching social and emotional learning through the sociocultural curriculum model. *Journal of Physical Education, Recreation & Dance, 104*(10), 13–23. https://www.tandfonline.com/doi/abs/10.1080/07303084.2023.2252865

Butkute, D. (2023). Exploring emotional awareness through user experience design: Designing a mobile application which helps to enrich emotional vocabulary. https://www.diva-portal.org/smash/record.jsf?pid=diva2:1773355

Camangian, P., & Cariaga, S. (2022). Social and emotional learning is hegemonic miseducation: Students deserve humanization instead. *Race Ethnicity and Education, 25*(7), 1001–1021. https://www.tandfonline.com/doi/abs/10.1080/13613324.2020.17108374

Choudhary, P., Singh, D., Patel, S., Jain, S., Soni, S., & Sharma, V. (2022). Augmented reality books in pre-primary education: Fostering social and emotional learning for young learners. *ResearchGate*. https://www. researchgate. net/publication/3841066357. https://www.researchgate.net/profile/Piyush-Choudhary-8/publication/3841066357_Augmented_Reality_Books_in_Pre-Primary_Education_Fostering_Social_and_Emotional_Learning_for_Young_Learners/links/670f10e4e0351017754c04de5c/Augmented-Reality-Books-in-Pre-Primary-Education-Fostering-Social-and-Emotional-Learning-for-Young-Learners.pdf

Cojocaru, S. (2023). Transformative social and emotional learning (T-SEL): The experiences of teenagers participating in volunteer club activities in the community. *International Journal of Environmental Research and Public Health, 20*(6), 4976. https://doi.org/10.3390/ijerph20064976

Collaborative for Academic, Social, and Emotional Learning. (2014). *Social and Emotional Learning Core Competencies*. www.casel.org

Dermody, C. M., Dusenbury, L., Greenberg, M., Godek, D., Connor, P., Cross, R., . . . & Bridgeland, J. (2022). A developmental framework for the integration of social and emotional learning and career and workforce development.

Collaborative for Academic, Social, and Emotional Learning. https://eric.ed.gov/?id=ED622311

Durlak, J. A., Mahoney, J. L., & Boyle, A. E. (2022). What we know, and what we need to find out about universal, school-based social and emotional learning programs for children and adolescents: A review of meta-analyses and directions for future research. *Psychological Bulletin, 148*(11–12), 765. https://psycnet.apa.org/fulltext/2023-55252-001.html

Dussault, M., & Thompson, R. B. (2024). Fundamental themes in social–emotional learning: A theoretical framework for inclusivity. *International Journal of Environmental Research and Public Health, 21*, 506. https://doi.org/10.33100/ijerph21040506.

Eden, C. A., Chisom, O. N., & Adeniyi, I. S. (2024). Parent and community involvement in education: Strengthening partnerships for social improvement. *International Journal of Applied Research in Social Sciences, 6*(3), 372–382. www.fepbl.com/index.php/ijarss

Elmi, C. (2020). Integrating social emotional learning strategies in higher education. *European Journal of Investigation in Health, Psychology and Education, 10*, 848–858. https://doi.org/10.33100/ejihpe10030061

Farniok, M. (2023). The importance of social and emotional learning for students in grades K-12. *Culminating Projects in Teacher Development, 60*. https://repository.stcloudstate.edu/ed_etds/60

Fernández-Martín, F. D., Moreno-Guerrero, A. J., Marín-Marín, J. A., & Romero-Rodríguez, J. M. (2022). Adolescents' emotions in Spanish education: Development and validation of the social and emotional learning Scale. *Sustainability, 14*(7), 3755. https://www.mdpi.com/2071-1050/14/7/3755

Gimbert, B. G., Miller, D., Herman, E., Breedlove, M., & Molina, C. E. (2023). Social emotional learning in schools: The importance of educator competence. *Journal of Research on Leadership Education, 18*(1), 3–310. https://journals.sagepub.com/doi/abs/10.1177/11042775121101410 20

Goh, T. L., Leong, C. H., Fede, M., & Ciotto, C. (2022). Before-school physical activity program's impact on social and emotional learning. *Journal of School Health, 102*(7), 674–680. https://onlinelibrary.wiley.com/doi/abs/10.1111/josh.13167

Green, A. L., Ferrante, S., Boaz, T. L., Kutash, K., & Wheeldon-Reece, B. (2021). Social and emotional learning during early adolescence: Effectiveness of a classroom-based SEL program for middle school students. *Psychology in the Schools, 58*(6), 1056–10610. https://onlinelibrary.wiley.com/doi/abs/10.1002/pits.22487

Greenberg, M. T., Domitrovich, C. E., Weissberg, R. P., & Durlak, J. A. (2017). Social and emotional learning as a public health approach to education. *The Future of Children, 27*(1), 13–32

Hatchimonji, D. R., Vaid, E., Linsky, A. C., Nayman, S. J., Yuan, M., MacDonnell, M., & Elias, M. J. (2022). Exploring relations among social-emotional and character development targets: Character virtue, social-emotional learning skills, and positive purpose. *International Journal of Emotional Education, 14*(1). https://search.ebscohost.com/login.aspx?direct=true&profile=ehost&scope=site&authtype=crawler&jrnl=207376210&AN=1608611021&h=PbSQCJnnytFlcyI%2BO71AgokIvJXM7hyvh7J10yZgQGZ1F3CSaLlTgigFymf10Do28spwkFGqj8krtMeRvpFEZmOQ%3D%3D&crl=c

Herman, K. C., Reinke, W. M., Thompson, A. M., Huang, F., & Owens, S. (2023). Usability and social consequences of the early identification system as a universal screener for social, emotional, and behavioral risks. *School Psychology, 38*(3), 148. https://psycnet.apa.org/record/2023-61615-001

Ingram, E., Reddick, K., Honaker, J. M., & Pearson, G. A. (2021, August). Making space for social and emotional learning in science education. *Frontiers in Education, 6,* 712720. Frontiers Media SA. https://www.frontiersin.org/articles/10.33810/feduc.2021.712720/full

Jones. S. M., & Doolittle, E. J. (2017). Social and emotional learning: introducing the issue. *The Future of Children, 27*(1), 3–11.

Kamei, A., & Harriott, W. (2021). Social emotional learning in virtual settings: Intervention strategies. *International Electronic Journal of Elementary Education, 13*(3). https://www.iejee.com/index.php/IEJEE/article/view/1487

Li, C., & Zhang, C. (2023). Transformative perspectives in physical education evaluation: Empowering diverse stakeholders for holistic learning experiences in the era of big data. *Journal of the Knowledge Economy,* 1–27.

Mahoney, J. L., Weissberg, R. P., Greenberg, M. T., Dusenbury, L., Jagers, R. J., Niemi, K., . . . & Yoder, N. (2021). Systemic social and emotional learning: Promoting educational success for all preschool to high school students. *American Psychologist, 76*(7), 1128. https://psycnet.apa.org/journals/amp/76/7/1128/

Mahoney, J. L., Weissberg, R. P., Greenberg, M. T., Dusenbury, L., Jagers, R. J., Niemi, K., Schlinger, M., Schlund, J., Shriver, T. P., VanAusdal, K., & Yoder, N. (2020). Systemic social and emotional learning: Promoting educational success for all preschool to high school students. *American Psychologist*. Advance online publication. http://doi.org/10.1037/amp0000701

Martínez, R. S., Catalano, R. F., & O'Brien, M. U. (2017). Promoting social and emotional learning in schools: An integrated framework for implementation. *The Future of Children, 27*(1), 73–94.

McBrien, J. (2022). *Social and Emotional Learning (SEL) of Newcomer and Refugee Students: Beliefs, Practices and Implications for Policies Across OECD Countries*. https://www.oecd.org/content/dam/oecd/en/publications/reports/2022/01/social-and-emotional-learning-sel-of-newcomer-and-refugee-students_8771c48d/a4a0f635-en.pdf

Moazami-Goodarzi, A., Zarra-Nezhad, M., Hytti, M., Heiskanen, N., & Sajaniemi, N. (2021). Training early childhood teachers to support children's social and emotional learning: A preliminary evaluation of Roundies program. *International Journal of Environmental Research and Public Health, 18*(20), 106710. https://www.mdpi.com/1660-4601/18/20/106710

Oliveira, S., Roberto, M. S., Pereira, N. S., Marques-Pinto, A., & Veiga-Simão, A. M. (2021). Impacts of social and emotional learning interventions for teachers on teachers' outcomes: A systematic review with meta-analysis. *Frontiers in Psychology, 12,* 677217 https://www.frontiersin.org/articles/10.33810/fpsyg.2021.677217/full

Raji, A., Adesanya, A. O., Daraojimba, C., Okogwu, C., Alade, E. Y., Nwankwo, T. C., Okoye, C. C. (2023). A review of financial instruments in the banking sector facilitating SMEs in the cleaner vehicles market. *Journal of Third World Economics (JTWE)*. http://doi.org/10.26480/jtwe.01.2023.18.25

Rock, A. E. (2022). Bringing geography to the community: community-based learning and the geography classroom. *Geo Journal, 87*(2), 235–247.

Schlinger, M., Schlund, J., Shriver, T. P., VanAusdal, K., & Yoder, N. (2020). Social and emotional learning: Promoting educational success for all preschool to high school students. *American Psychologist*. Advance online publication. http://doi.org/10.1037/amp0000701

Shen, Y., Rose, S., & Dyson, B. (2024). Social and emotional learning for underserved children through a sports-based youth development program grounded in teaching personal and social responsibility. *Physical Education and Sport Pedagogy, 210*(1), 115–126. https://www.tandfonline.com/doi/abs/10.1080/1740810810.2022.20310614

Spigner, M. S. (2023). *The Use of Project-Based Learning to Scaffold Student Social and Emotional Learning Skill Development, Science Identity, and Science Self-Efficacy* (Doctoral dissertation). https://scholarcommons.sc.edu/etd/7566

Taylor, R. D., Oberle, E., Durlak, J. A., & Weissberg, R. P. (2017). Promoting positive youth development through school-based social and emotional learning interventions: A meta-analysis of follow-up effects. *Child Development, 88*(4), 1156–1171.

Understanding the importance of social and emotional learning in schools. https://standtogether.org/stories/education/the-importance-of-social-and-emotional-learning-in-schools

Vázquez-Villegas, P., Caratozzolo, P., Lara-Prieto, V., & Membrillo-Hernández, J. (2023). A review on the advances in socially oriented education. *Sustainability, 15*, 161104. https://doi.org/10.33100/su1523161104

Willingham, D. T. (2023). *Outsmart Your Brain: Why Learning Is Hard and How You Can Make It Easy*. Souvenierpress.

Zins, J. E., Weissberg, R. P., Wang, M. C., & Walberg, H. J. (Eds.). (2004). *Building academic success on social and emotional learning: What does the research say?* New York, NY: Teachers College Press.

11

AI in Education—Transforming Teaching and Learning in the Digital Age

Kalaivaani P. C. D. and Rajalaxmi R. R.

11.1 Introduction

11.1.1 Background of AI in Education

Artificial intelligence (AI) has evolved from a theoretical concept into a practical technology that impacts various sectors, including education. The application of AI in educational environments ranges from intelligent tutoring systems to AI-driven analytics that inform instructional strategies. As digital technologies become ubiquitous in daily life, integrating AI into education offers new opportunities to enhance teaching effectiveness and improve student outcomes.

11.1.2 Why AI Matters in the Digital Age?

The digital transformation of education has accelerated with the proliferation of online learning platforms, virtual classrooms, and data-driven decision-making tools. AI amplifies these developments by enabling adaptive learning systems, automated assessment tools, and virtual assistants. These innovations not only support personalized learning but also address issues of accessibility, scalability, and inclusivity in education.

11.1.3 Scope and Objectives of the Chapter

This chapter aims to do the following:

- Define the role and scope of AI in education.
- Examine AI-driven teaching and learning practices.
- Evaluate the benefits and challenges associated with AI integration.
- Present global case studies and best practices.
- Discuss ethical considerations and future trends.

DOI: 10.1201/9781003633433-11

The content is structured to provide a balanced, in-depth exploration suitable for educators, policymakers, and academic researchers.

11.2 Understanding Artificial Intelligence in Education

11.2.1 Definition and Key Concepts of AI

AI refers to the simulation of human-intelligence processes by machines, particularly computer systems. These processes include learning, reasoning, problem-solving, perception, and language understanding. In education, AI systems are designed to interact with learners, provide feedback, and adapt to individual learning needs.

11.2.2 Types of AI Relevant to Education

- **Machine Learning (ML):** Enables systems to learn from data, identify patterns, and make decisions with minimal human intervention.
- **Natural Language Processing (NLP):** Facilitates the interaction between computers and human language, enabling tools like chatbots and language translation services.
- **Computer Vision:** Allows systems to interpret and process visual information, useful in grading handwritten assignments or in analyzing classroom interactions.
- **Robotics:** Engages learners through interactive robots that can assist in language learning, coding, and STEM education.

11.2.3 Evolution of AI in Education

The integration of AI in education can be traced back to the 1960s with the development of computer-assisted instruction (CAI) programs like programmed logic for automated teaching operations (PLATO). These early systems provided drill-and-practice exercises and simple tutorials. The 1980s saw the emergence of rule-based expert systems for specialized tutoring. The 1990s introduced multimedia learning tools with rudimentary AI components. Evolution of different versions of AI is shown in Figure 11.1. Over the past two decades, AI has evolved into data-driven adaptive systems, conversational AI, and intelligent learning environments.

The progression of AI in education as seen in Table 11.1 began with rule-based tutoring systems and evolved into sophisticated AI-powered platforms capable of real-time feedback and adaptive learning. From the early use of

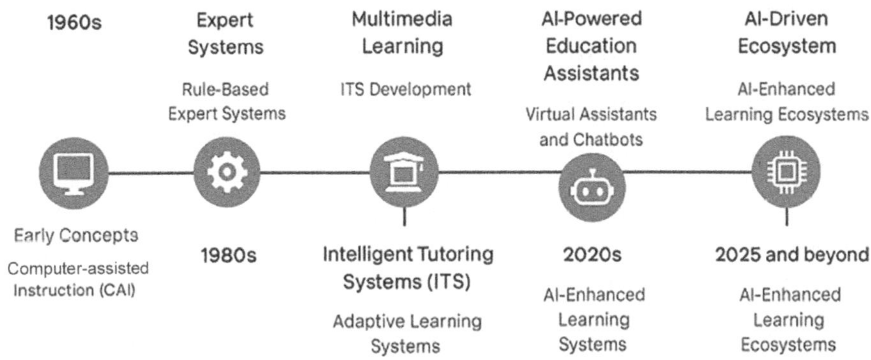

FIGURE 11.1
Evolution of AI.

TABLE 11.1
Milestones of AI in Education

Year	Milestone
1960s	Early computer-assisted instruction (CAI)
1980s	Rule-based intelligent tutoring systems
2000s	Web-based learning management systems
2010s	AI-driven adaptive learning platforms
2020s	Predictive analytics, VR/AR, chatbots, AI assistants

TABLE 11.2
Types of AI Technologies and Their Educational Applications

AI Technology	Application in Education
Machine learning	Predictive analytics, personalized learning
Natural language processing	Chatbots, language translation, sentiment analysis
Computer vision	Automated grading, classroom analytics
Robotics	STEM education, language learning

CAI to modern intelligent systems, the journey reflects significant advancements in AI capabilities. Table 11.2 gives the key areas where different types of AI technologies are applied.

11.3 AI-Driven Teaching and Learning Practices

11.3.1 Adaptive Learning Systems

Adaptive learning systems employ AI algorithms to personalize educational content and pace according to individual learner needs. The general structure of an AI-driven adaptive learning system is depicted in Figure 11.2. These systems analyze student data, such as performance metrics and engagement patterns, to tailor content delivery and recommend appropriate resources. Platforms like DreamBox and Knewton utilize adaptive learning to support differentiated instruction and ensure that students receive content suited to

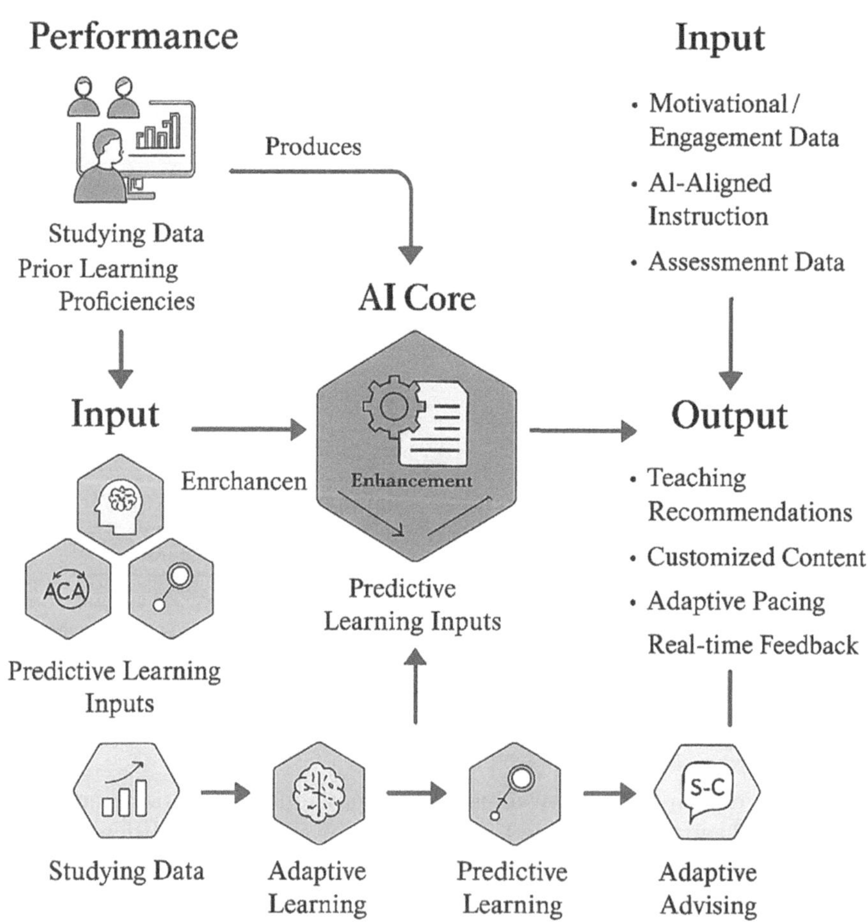

FIGURE 11.2
Structure of an AI-driven adaptive learning system.

their learning level and preferences. Beyond DreamBox and Knewton, platforms like Squirrel AI (China) and Smart Sparrow (Australia) are pioneering AI-based personalized learning in schools and universities worldwide.

- **Squirrel AI** uses adaptive algorithms for more than 70 subject areas.
- **Smart Sparrow** specializes in creating custom adaptive courses for higher education, emphasizing real-time adjustment.

11.3.2 Intelligent Tutoring Systems

Intelligent tutoring systems (ITS) simulate one-on-one instruction by providing personalized feedback, hints, and explanations to learners. These systems adapt dynamically to student responses and learning styles, offering additional practice or alternative approaches when necessary. Examples include Carnegie Learning's MATHia and AutoTutor, which have demonstrated improvements in student learning outcomes.

11.3.3 AI-Based Assessment Tools

AI-based assessment tools streamline the evaluation process by automating grading and offering detailed feedback. These tools can assess multiple-choice, short-answer, and even essay responses using NLP and ML techniques. Additionally, predictive analytics help educators identify at-risk students and intervene proactively. Systems like Gradescope and Turnitin's AI-powered grading features exemplify these capabilities.

11.3.4 Virtual and Augmented Reality in Classrooms

AI enhances virtual reality (VR) and augmented reality (AR) applications in education by creating immersive, interactive learning environments. AI-driven VR/AR tools simulate real-world scenarios, enabling students to engage in experiential learning. For instance, medical students can practice surgeries in virtual simulations, while history learners can explore ancient civilizations through AR overlays. AI-enhanced VR/AR platforms like Labster (virtual science labs) and Google Expeditions (virtual field trips) are providing transformative experiences. For instance, Labster allows students to conduct virtual chemistry experiments with AI-driven coaching, improving safety and reducing costs.

11.3.5 Chatbots and AI-Powered Educational Assistants

Chatbots and AI assistants provide immediate support and information to students and educators. These systems handle administrative queries, offer tutoring assistance, and manage learning management systems. Notable examples include IBM Watson Tutor and Duolingo's AI-driven language

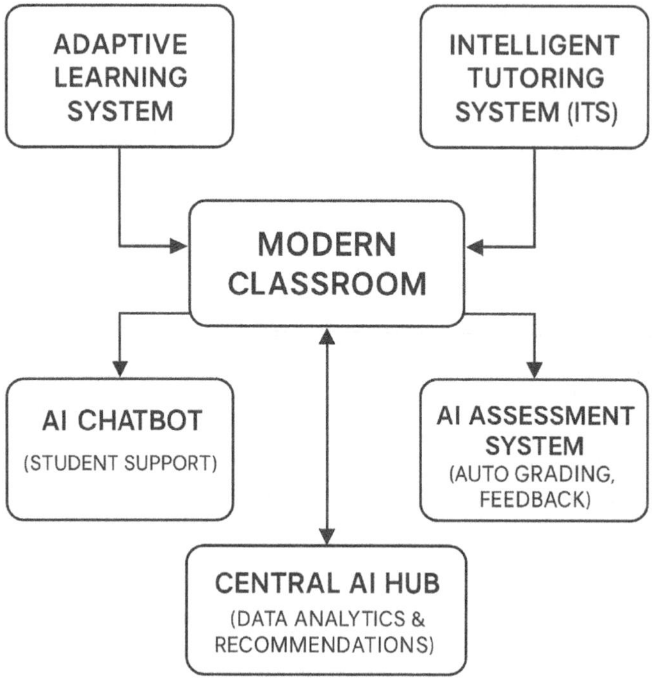

FIGURE 11.3
AI role in a modern classroom.

learning assistant, both of which enhance accessibility and learning engagement. Beyond IBM Watson, Replika and Mika (Carnegie Learning) are AI-powered assistants offering social-emotional support and academic coaching. Integrating AI tutors into platforms like Microsoft Teams and Slack has also become popular in remote and hybrid learning environments.

The conceptual diagram in Figure 11.3 is illustrating AI tools like adaptive learning systems, ITS, VR/AR tools, chatbots, and AI assessment systems integrated within a classroom setting.

11.4 Impact of AI on Teaching and Learning

11.4.1 Enhanced Student Engagement

AI technologies encourage active participation by tailoring content to match students' interests, learning styles, and progress levels. Adaptive learning

TABLE 11.3
Traditional Model versus AI-Integrated Model

Aspect	Traditional Model	AI-Integrated Model
Instruction delivery	Uniform and fixed	Personalized and adaptive
Feedback mechanism	Periodic and manual	Continuous and automated
Teacher's role	Instructor-centered	Facilitator and mentor
Student engagement	Passive	Interactive and gamified
Decision-making in teaching	Experience-based	Data-driven and evidence-based

platforms and interactive tools increase motivation and maintain students' attention by offering personalized learning paths, multimedia content, and gamified experiences. A simple comparison of traditional model and AI-integrated model is given in Table 11.3.

11.4.2 Individualized Feedback and Support

With AI-powered analytics, students receive immediate, detailed, and constructive feedback on their performance. These systems can identify specific areas of difficulty and suggest targeted resources or activities. This personalized support enables students to learn at their own pace and revisit concepts as needed, fostering independent learning habits.

11.4.3 Teacher's Evolving Role as Facilitators

As AI handles administrative and routine instructional tasks, teachers' roles are transforming from knowledge transmitters to learning facilitators and mentors, which can be viewed in Figure 11.4.

Educators can focus more on developing students' critical thinking, creativity, and socio-emotional skills while using AI-generated insights to inform teaching strategies.

11.4.4 Data-Driven Decision-Making in Curriculum Design

AI analytics tools gather extensive data on student performance, engagement, and preferences. Educators and administrators can use this data to refine curricula, design evidence-based interventions, and customize instructional approaches. Data-driven insights enable continuous curriculum improvement aligned with learners' evolving needs.

FIGURE 11.4
AI in a modern classroom environment.

11.5 Case Studies and Best Practices

Global Case Study 1: Squirrel AI Learning (China)

Squirrel AI Learning is one of the leading AI-powered adaptive learning companies in China. It uses AI algorithms to offer highly personalized tutoring in subjects such as mathematics and science. The platform analyzes student performance in real time, identifies knowledge gaps, and dynamically adjusts the difficulty level and content of lessons. In a large-scale study, Squirrel AI demonstrated a significant improvement in student test scores compared to traditional instruction. As a best practice, they regularly update AI models with local and recent data to ensure alignment with curriculum standards and learner profiles.

Global Case Study 2: Carnegie Learning's MATHia (USA)

Carnegie Learning's MATHia platform is an intelligent tutoring system designed for middle and high school students. It combines AI-based learning analytics with adaptive instructional content. MATHia provides step-by-step feedback, hints, and performance-based recommendations for students while supplying teachers with data dashboards to track progress. Research indicates that schools adopting MATHia experienced increased pass rates in math subjects. They integrate AI tools as supplements rather than replacements for educators, ensuring a blended learning model as a best practice.

Global Case Study 3: Century Tech (UK)

Century Tech offers an AI-based platform that personalizes learning through predictive analytics and adaptive content delivery. The platform assesses learners' strengths and weaknesses, suggesting resources accordingly. Teachers can view learner analytics and adjust their instructional strategies based on detailed dashboards. Century Tech has been implemented successfully in more than 50 countries, demonstrating improvements in both student outcomes and teaching efficiency. By using the AI-generated insights to inform and support human decision-making rather than relying entirely on automation. A comparative summary of AI-adopted global classrooms is shown in Table 11.4.

Local Initiatives: AI in Indian Classrooms

In India, AI-powered educational tools like ConveGenius, EMBIBE, and LearningMate are being introduced to improve digital literacy and personalized learning in under-resourced schools. These platforms provide adaptive assessments and remedial content tailored to individual student needs. Pilot projects in states like Maharashtra and Tamil Nadu have shown promising results in bridging educational gaps. India should

TABLE 11.4

Comparative Table: AI Adoption in Global Classrooms

Institution/Platform	Country	AI Application	Key Impact
Squirrel AI Learning	China	Adaptive tutoring, real-time analytics	Improved test scores, dynamic personalization
MATHia	USA	Intelligent tutoring, learning analytics	Higher pass rates, real-time feedback
Century Tech	UK	Predictive analytics, adaptive learning	Data-informed teaching, learner engagement
EMBIBE, ConveGenius	India	AI-powered assessments, multilingual tools	Improved digital access, learning outcomes

prioritize affordable and scalable AI solutions to address regional disparities and support multilingual education.

Best Practice Summary

- Regular AI-model updates for curriculum alignment
- Blended human–AI instructional models
- Insights-based decision support for educators
- Affordable, inclusive AI tools for diverse, multilingual learners

11.6 Ethical Considerations and Challenges

AI technology continues to transform education, so ethical concerns and challenges that emerge require careful consideration. While AI holds immense promise for improving learning outcomes and educational efficiency, its widespread adoption must be guided by principles that ensure fairness, equity, and transparency. Figure 11.5 highlights the few best practices of AI in education. Below are the key ethical considerations and challenges associated with the integration of AI in education.

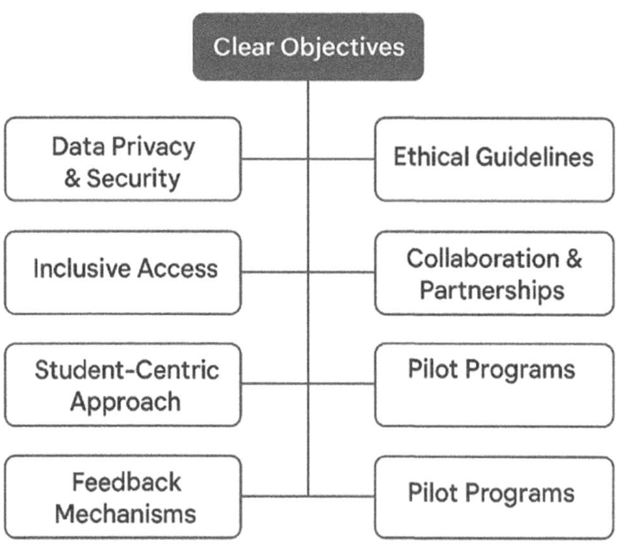

FIGURE 11.5
Best practices for AI adoption in education.

11.6.1 Data Privacy and Security

One of the primary concerns with AI in education is the collection and use of sensitive data. AI systems often require large datasets that include personal information such as academic records, learning preferences, and sometimes even behavioral data. This data is essential for AI systems to function effectively, but it also poses significant privacy risks.

- Protecting the privacy of students and teachers while ensuring that the data used by AI systems is securely stored and properly managed.
- Educational institutions must implement robust data protection measures to ensure compliance with data privacy regulations such as the General Data Protection Regulation (GDPR) and Family Educational Rights and Privacy Act (FERPA).
- Institutions should prioritize transparent data usage policies and obtain informed consent from students and parents when collecting and using data for AI applications.

11.6.2 Algorithmic Bias

AI systems are trained on data, and the quality of this data determines how well the system performs. If the data used to train AI algorithms is biased or incomplete, the AI system may unintentionally perpetuate inequalities. This is especially problematic in education, where bias can affect decisions related to student performance, resource allocation, and access to opportunities.

- Minimizing biases in AI models that could lead to discriminatory practices in education.
- AI systems should be designed to avoid reinforcing biases related to race, gender, socioeconomic status, and other factors. It is essential to ensure that AI systems treat all students fairly and equitably.
- Regularly audit AI models for bias, use diverse and representative datasets, and involve diverse stakeholders in the development and deployment of AI systems.

11.6.3 Equity and Accessibility

AI has the potential to make education more personalized and accessible to a wider range of learners. However, there are concerns about whether AI tools will be equally available to all students, particularly those in underserved regions or from low-income backgrounds.

- Ensuring that AI-powered education tools are accessible to all students, regardless of their geographic location or economic status.

- To maximize the benefits of AI, it is crucial to address issues of the digital divide and provide equitable access to AI-powered learning tools.
- Develop affordable, scalable AI solutions that are designed with inclusivity in mind, ensuring that AI tools can be used by students with different learning abilities and resources.

11.6.4 Teacher and Student Autonomy

The integration of AI in classrooms raises questions about the balance between human teachers and AI systems. While AI can assist in grading, providing feedback, and personalizing learning, there is concern about the extent to which AI should influence decision-making in education. Both teachers and students should retain their autonomy in the learning process.

- Striking a balance between AI automation and human agency in the classroom.
- AI should be seen as a tool that complements, rather than replaces, human educators. Teachers must retain control over the educational experience and use AI to enhance their instructional methods.
- Maintain a collaborative relationship between AI systems and educators, ensuring that AI tools provide recommendations and support while leaving key decisions to human discretion.

11.6.5 Accountability and Transparency

As AI systems become more integrated into education, questions of accountability arise. Who is responsible when an AI system makes a mistake such as providing incorrect feedback or recommendations to students? AI systems are often seen as "black boxes," where it is difficult to understand how decisions are made.

- Ensuring accountability for AI-driven decisions and transparency in how these systems operate.
- AI systems should be designed with explainability in mind. Stakeholders should be able to understand how decisions are made and who is responsible for them.
- Develop AI systems with built-in transparency features, such as clear algorithms and decision-making processes, and ensure that institutions have protocols for addressing issues when they arise.

11.6.6 Ethical Use of AI in Assessment

AI-based assessment tools, such as automated grading systems, have become increasingly popular due to their efficiency and ability to provide instant feedback. However, these tools raise ethical questions about the fairness and accuracy of AI grading, especially for subjective assignments like essays or creative work.

- Ensuring that AI-based assessments accurately and fairly evaluate student work.
- AI assessments should complement, rather than replace, human judgment. Teachers should be involved in the evaluation process, especially for assignments that require critical thinking, creativity, and interpretation.
- Combine AI grading with human oversight to ensure that assessments are fair, accurate, and aligned with educational goals.

11.6.7 Long-Term Social Impacts

The long-term societal impacts of widespread AI adoption in education remain uncertain. While AI has the potential to improve learning outcomes, there are concerns about its effects on employment in the education sector, the teacher-student relationship, and the role of human interaction in learning.

- Understanding and mitigating the long-term social consequences of AI in education.
- It is essential to ensure that AI does not undermine the value of human educators or create an overreliance on technology in the learning process.
- Engage in ongoing dialogue among educators, policymakers, and technologists to assess the societal implications of AI and develop strategies to address potential negative consequences.

Ethical considerations of AI can be listed from Figure 11.6. AI continues to reshape education, so it is critical to balance technological innovation with ethical responsibility. By addressing issues like data privacy, algorithmic bias, equity, and transparency, we can create a future where AI benefits all students, supports teachers, and contributes to a more inclusive and fair educational system. Responsible AI design and deployment will require collaboration among educators, policymakers, and technology developers to ensure that AI serves as a tool for positive transformation in education.

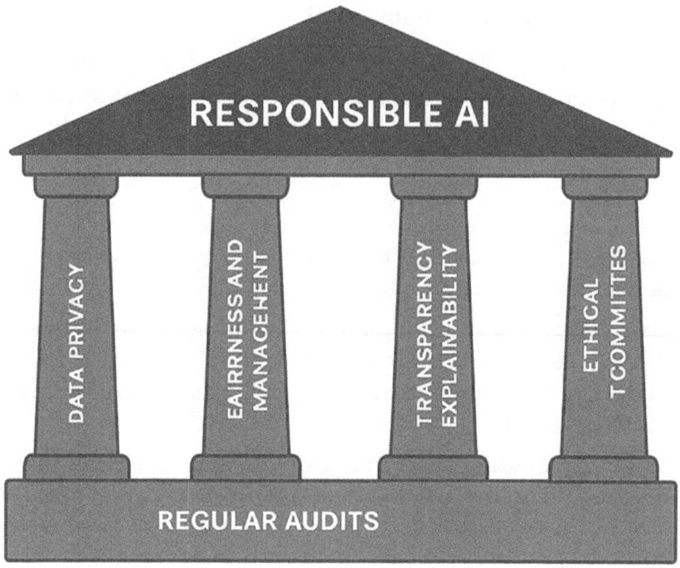

FIGURE 11.6
Ethical considerations in AI.

11.7 Future Prospects and Emerging AI Trends in Education

The landscape of education is undergoing a profound transformation as AI continues to evolve. The future of AI in education holds exciting possibilities, with emerging trends poised to redefine how teaching and learning occur. This section explores some of the most promising advancements in AI and their potential impact on education in the coming years. A flowchart visualizing how AI tailors the learner's journey based on performance is included in Figure 11.7.

11.7.1 AI-Driven Personalized Learning at Scale

Personalized learning, which tailors educational experiences to meet individual students' needs, has long been a goal in education. With AI, this vision is becoming a reality. AI systems that analyze student data in real time, adapt content delivery, and suggest personalized resources are already in use in classrooms worldwide. As AI technology advances, personalized learning will become more efficient and scalable, reaching a broader range of students.

Adaptive learning platforms will continue to evolve, providing deeper insights into student behavior and performance. These systems will become

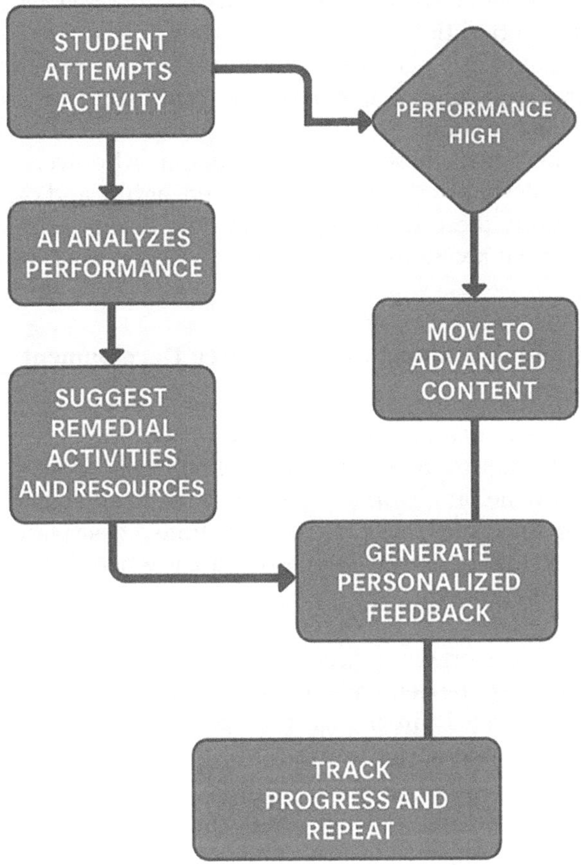

FIGURE 11.7
AI-enhanced learning path.

more sophisticated in understanding and predicting individual learning paths, offering a level of personalization that is currently not achievable at scale. Personalized learning at scale will enable educators to focus on students who need more attention, while AI handles the more repetitive and individualized tasks, allowing for a more dynamic, customized learning environment.

11.7.2 AI-Powered Virtual Reality and Augmented Reality

The integration of AI with VR and AR is one of the most exciting prospects for the future of education. AI algorithms enhance the immersive capabilities of VR and AR by adapting environments to the learner's preferences, skills, and progress. These technologies promise to revolutionize experiential learning by allowing students to interact with simulated worlds and scenarios in ways that traditional classrooms cannot.

AI-driven VR and AR platforms will create fully immersive, interactive learning experiences. For example, AI could simulate historical events, scientific phenomena, or complex mathematical problems in 3D space, allowing students to "experience" these concepts firsthand. AI-powered VR and AR could make abstract subjects more accessible, engaging, and easier to understand. Furthermore, these technologies can help bridge geographical gaps by providing virtual access to educational experiences that were previously unavailable.

11.7.3 AI in Lifelong Learning and Workforce Development

As the world of work evolves, so too must the way we approach education. AI is increasingly being used to facilitate lifelong learning, where individuals can continuously acquire new skills throughout their careers. AI-powered platforms are now helping workers identify skill gaps, recommend courses or training programs, and track progress over time. These platforms can also predict future job market trends, suggesting areas where individuals should focus their learning efforts.

- AI will enable workers to access personalized learning paths that are aligned with the demands of the job market. These systems will adapt to a learner's career trajectory, providing continuous education and upskilling opportunities.
- AI will help workers stay competitive by ensuring that education remains flexible and accessible throughout their careers. It will also democratize access to lifelong learning, making it easier for individuals in diverse contexts to gain valuable skills and certifications.

11.7.4 Integration of AI in Educational Administration

AI has the potential to improve not only teaching and learning but also the administrative functions of educational institutions. AI-based systems are already being used for scheduling, resource allocation, student admissions, and more. These applications will become increasingly sophisticated, offering real-time data analytics that help institutions make more informed decisions.

- AI will play a larger role in institutional decision-making by providing predictive analytics and data-driven insights. For example, AI systems could predict student enrollment trends, faculty workload distribution, and even resource needs, making it easier for administrators to allocate resources effectively.

- AI will enable educational institutions to operate more efficiently and effectively. Institutions will be able to respond quickly to changing demands, enhance student services, and improve operational efficiency through intelligent automation.

11.7.5 AI-Powered Collaborative Learning

AI can facilitate collaborative learning by connecting students with peers who share similar learning goals or interests. Through AI-powered collaboration tools, students can engage in group work, share resources, and participate in discussions, all while receiving personalized feedback from AI systems. This collaborative approach promotes teamwork and allows students to learn from one another, fostering a deeper understanding of the subject matter.

AI will enable real-time collaboration among students, both in physical classrooms and through online learning platforms. AI tools will support peer-to-peer learning by facilitating group activities, discussions, and knowledge sharing. AI-driven collaborative learning will not only enhance student engagement but also help develop essential soft skills such as communication, problem-solving, and teamwork. This trend could revolutionize online education, where students from different parts of the world can collaborate seamlessly.

11.7.6 AI and Gamification in Education

Gamification, the use of game-like elements in nongame contexts, is a growing trend in education. AI is making it easier to implement gamified learning environments that adapt to students' progress and learning preferences. By integrating AI with gamification, educators can create more engaging and motivating learning experiences that encourage students to take an active role in their education.

- **Trend:** AI will drive the development of adaptive gamification systems that adjust challenges, rewards, and learning pathways based on student performance.
- **Future Impact:** AI-powered gamification will make learning more enjoyable and motivating for students, increasing their engagement and enhancing retention. By personalizing game mechanics, these systems will also ensure that students are appropriately challenged and supported in their learning journey.

11.7.7 Ethical AI and Responsible Deployment

As AI continues to advance, ensuring that these technologies are deployed responsibly will be essential. The need for ethical guidelines for the development and use of AI in education is becoming more pressing. Educational institutions, governments, and tech developers must collaborate to ensure that AI is used in ways that benefit all students, uphold fairness, and address potential biases.

- **Trend:** The development of ethical AI frameworks that govern the use of AI in education, ensuring transparency, accountability, and fairness in AI algorithms.
- **Future Impact:** A responsible approach to AI deployment will ensure that educational outcomes are equitable and that the technology serves the needs of all students. Ethical AI frameworks will help mitigate risks associated with bias, privacy violations, and the erosion of human agency in education.

The future of AI in education is filled with possibilities, from enhancing personalized learning experiences to creating more efficient administrative processes. However, these advancements must be approached with care, ensuring that AI is implemented ethically and responsibly.

A timeline showing AI-driven personalized learning, gamification, VR/AR integration, and lifelong learning pathways, with projected milestones for each development is shown in Figure 11.8.

As these technologies continue to evolve, it is critical to keep the focus on human-centered education that benefits all learners and promotes lifelong

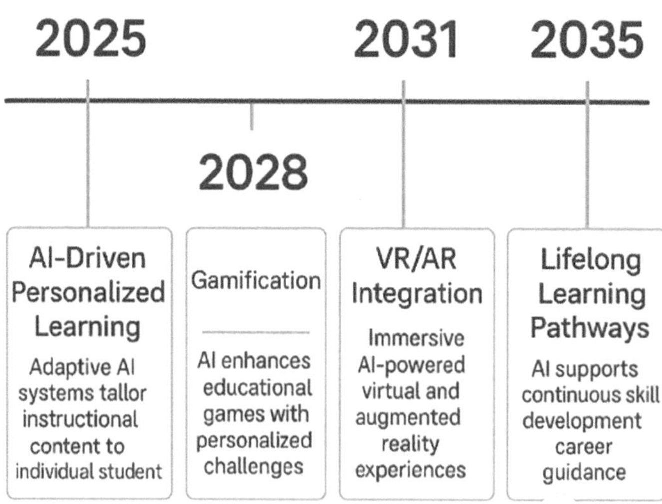

FIGURE 11.8
Emerging AI trends in education (2025–2035).

learning. The next decade promises to bring innovative changes that will make education more accessible, equitable, and engaging for students around the world.

11.8 Policy Recommendations and Roadmap for AI Adoption in Education

The integration of AI into education is a transformative process that requires careful planning and consideration of various factors. The implementation of AI technologies should not only focus on the technological aspects but also ensure equitable access, ethical practices, and alignment with educational goals. This section outlines key policy recommendations and a roadmap for the successful adoption of AI in educational systems.

11.9 Establishing Clear Policies for AI Integration

For AI to be effectively integrated into educational systems, governments, educational institutions, and technology developers need to collaborate to create clear policies that guide its use. These policies should address issues related to accessibility, ethics, data privacy, and equity, ensuring that AI serves all students regardless of their background or learning needs.

Governments and educational authorities should work together to establish national and regional policies that support AI integration. These policies should:

- Provide guidelines for the ethical use of AI in education.
- Ensure that AI solutions are accessible to all students, including those with disabilities.
- Establish clear data privacy regulations to protect student information.
- Promote transparency in AI algorithms and decision-making processes.

Impact: Clear policies will enable a coherent approach to AI adoption across educational institutions, ensuring consistency in implementation and equitable access to AI-driven tools and resources.

11.9.1 Promoting AI Literacy and Training for Educators

Educators must be equipped with the skills and knowledge to use AI tools effectively. Teacher training programs should include components focused on AI literacy, so educators can understand how AI works and how it can enhance teaching and learning. Educational institutions should incorporate AI literacy into teacher preparation programs and provide ongoing professional development opportunities for teachers. These programs should focus on the following:

- The fundamentals of AI, including ML, NLP, and data analytics.
- How AI can support differentiated instruction and personalized learning.
- Ethical considerations and best practices for using AI tools in the classroom.

Impact: By increasing AI literacy among educators, schools will foster a generation of teachers who are confident in using AI tools and are able to harness their full potential to improve educational outcomes.

11.9.2 Ensuring Equity and Accessibility in AI Deployment

AI has the potential to address many barriers to education, but there are also risks that it could exacerbate existing inequalities. Policymakers must ensure that AI tools are accessible to all students, including those in underserved and rural areas as well as students with disabilities.

- Ensure that AI tools are affordable and accessible to all schools, especially those in low-income areas.
- Invest in infrastructure to support AI deployment in schools, including high-speed internet and modern devices.
- Develop AI-powered solutions that are inclusive, such as tools for students with disabilities (e.g., text-to-speech, speech-to-text, language translation, and adaptive learning tools).
- Promote digital literacy initiatives that provide all students with the skills they need to use AI tools effectively.

Impact: By addressing these equity issues, AI can help reduce educational disparities and provide all students with the opportunity to benefit from personalized learning experiences.

11.9.3 Data Privacy and Security Regulations

AI systems rely heavily on data to function, making data privacy and security a top priority in AI implementation. Policymakers need to ensure that students' personal information is protected and that AI systems adhere to strict privacy standards.

Governments and educational institutions should:

- Establish and enforce data protection regulations that safeguard student information.
- Ensure that AI vendors comply with data privacy laws such as the GDPR and the Children's Online Privacy Protection Act (COPPA).
- Develop transparency frameworks that allow students and parents to understand how data is collected, used, and stored by AI systems.

  Impact: Strong data privacy and security regulations will help build trust in AI systems and protect students' sensitive information from potential misuse or breaches.

11.9.4 Collaborating with EdTech Industry Stakeholders

Collaboration among educational institutions, technology companies, and government agencies is essential for the successful implementation of AI in education. By working together, stakeholders can ensure that AI solutions are designed to meet the needs of educators and learners and that they adhere to ethical and regulatory standards.

- Educational institutions and AI developers should cocreate AI tools that align with curriculum goals and teaching practices.
- Governments and private companies should share knowledge, resources, and expertise, to ensure that AI solutions are sustainable and scalable.
- Researchers and practitioners should evaluate the effectiveness of AI tools and continuously improve them based on real-world feedback.

  Impact: Collaboration will foster innovation, ensuring that AI solutions are both practical and effective in the classroom. It will also help bridge the gap between the needs of educators and the capabilities of AI technologies.

11.9.5 Creating a Long-Term Strategic Vision for AI in Education

AI adoption in education should not be seen as a one-time effort but as part of a long-term strategy for improving educational outcomes. Policymakers need to develop a strategic vision for AI that outlines specific goals, timelines, and the resources needed for sustained success.

Educational authorities should:

- Develop long-term strategic plans for AI adoption that include milestones for implementation, evaluation, and scaling.
- Align AI implementation with broader educational goals, such as improving student outcomes, enhancing teacher effectiveness, and fostering lifelong learning.
- Allocate funding for research and development to continuously improve AI tools and ensure their relevance in the evolving educational landscape.

  Impact: A long-term strategic vision will help ensure that AI adoption is not only successful but also sustainable, allowing educational systems to adapt to emerging trends and technologies.

11.9.6 Roadmap for AI Adoption in Education

A clear roadmap is necessary to guide educational institutions through the process of AI adoption. This roadmap should outline the steps needed to implement AI technologies effectively, from initial planning to scaling up use.

- **Phase 1: Pilot Programs and Exploration**
  - Start with pilot programs to test the effectiveness of AI tools in specific educational contexts (e.g., adaptive learning systems, virtual assistants).
  - Evaluate the results of these programs and gather feedback from students, teachers, and administrators.
- **Phase 2: Integration and Scaling**
  - Based on the success of pilot programs, scale AI tools to more schools, incorporating them into the curriculum and educational infrastructure.
  - Provide professional development for educators to ensure the effective integration of AI into teaching practices.
- **Phase 3: Continuous Evaluation and Refinement**
  - Continuously assess the effectiveness of AI tools through data analytics and feedback.
  - Make adjustments to AI systems as needed to improve their performance and adapt to changing educational needs.
  - Foster a culture of continuous improvement and innovation, ensuring that AI remains a valuable tool for educators and learners.

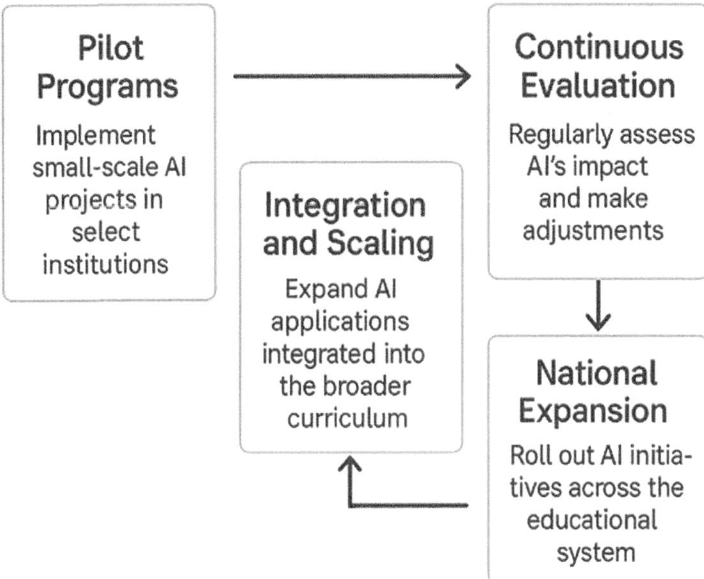

FIGURE 11.9
Roadmap for AI adoption in education.

- **Phase 4: National Expansion and Global Collaboration**
  - Expand AI adoption nationwide, ensuring that all schools have access to AI-powered tools and resources.
  - Collaborate with international educational systems to share best practices, research, and developments in AI education.

A clear, phased approach will help institutions manage the complexities of AI adoption and ensure that the transition is smooth and effective. A visual representation of the four phases of AI adoption in education: pilot programs, integration and scaling, continuous evaluation, and national expansion is clearly represented in Figure 11.9.

11.10 Conclusion

The adoption of AI in education holds tremendous potential to enhance learning outcomes, improve administrative efficiency, and promote personalized, inclusive education. However, to fully realize this potential, it is essential to develop and implement policies that ensure the ethical use of, and equitable access to, AI technologies. By creating a strategic roadmap, training educators, and fostering collaboration among key stakeholders, policymakers can pave the way for a future where AI-driven education is accessible, equitable, and impactful for all students.

12

Introduction: The Promise and Peril of AI in Education

Dinesh Komarasamy, Mano Sundar M., Rajalaxmi R. R., and S. Mohana Saranya

12.1 Introduction: The Evolution of AI in Education

From rule-based intelligent tutoring systems (ITS) in the early 2000s to sophisticated generative models and adaptive learning platforms like ChatGPT, artificial intelligence (AI) has gradually transformed education. Early applications placed a strong emphasis on personalized learning, providing lessons that were specifically designed to meet the needs of each individual student along with automated feedback. Compared to traditional methods, these advancements have allowed educators to better identify learning gaps, optimize instructional strategies, and encourage student engagement [1].

Figure 12.1 depicts the evolution of AI applications in education, highlighting tools such as virtual teaching assistants and administrative bots that extend beyond traditional tutoring systems. Education has advanced to a new level due to recent developments in AI-driven grading systems, virtual teaching assistants, and automated administrative tools [2]. In addition to accelerating standard educational tasks, these systems help improve accessibility and inclusivity for a wide range of learners. In spite of these advantages, new ethical concerns have emerged as a result of the use of AI in education, mainly in relation to data privacy, algorithmic decision-making fairness, transparency, and the evolving roles of educators and learners. Thus, the development of AI in education represents a revolutionary journey that strikes a balance between the imperative need to address ethical implications to ensure equitable and responsible technology use and the notable gains in efficiency and learning outcomes.

A graphic depiction of the significant rise in AI adoption across international education sectors between 2005 and 2025 can be found in Figure 12.2. The highest adoption rates are seen in EdTech platforms and corporate training programs, which are expected to reach almost 100% by 2025. Higher education institutions follow with over 90% adoption rates, and K-12 schools

DOI: 10.1201/9781003633433-12

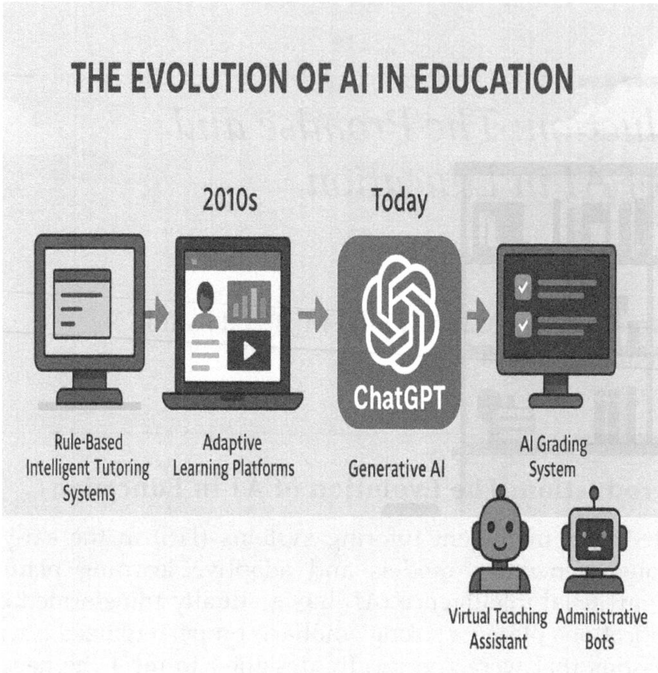

FIGURE 12.1
Evolution of AI applications in education.

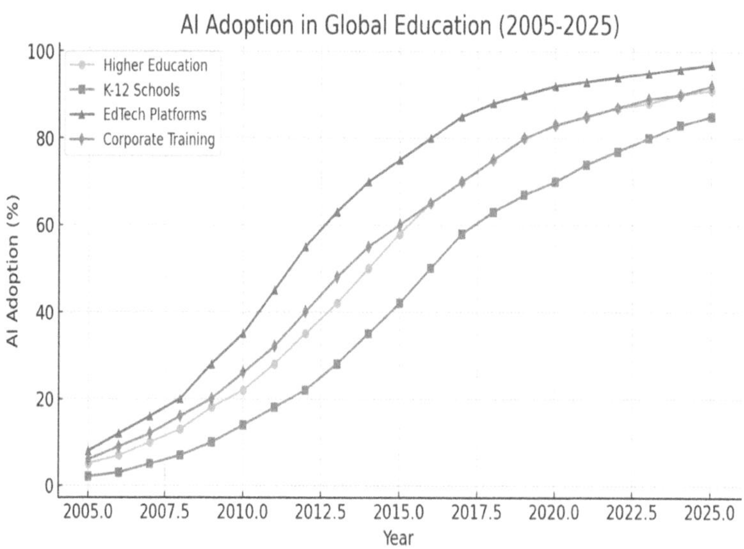

FIGURE 12.2
AI Adoption in global education (2005–2025).

follow with roughly 85%. Particularly after 2010, all sectors saw consistent, faster growth, highlighting the widespread integration and influence of AI technologies for scalable, effective, and personalized learning in education across the globe [3].

12.2 Future of AI in Education

Increased accessibility, efficiency, and personalization provided by AI will revolutionize the education sector, but its use has also resulted in unethical practices, particularly with regard to biased algorithms and student surveillance issues. By using sophisticated AI tools to downgrade students from lower-income schools while offering prestigious institutions, biased admissions algorithms have notably disadvantaged marginalized groups, leading to protests and systemic abandonment. These instances demonstrate how unchecked AI bias can result in unfair, consequential decisions that perpetuate current disparities [4].

In education, algorithmic bias shows up in resource allocation, student support, grading, and admissions, frequently sustaining racial and socioeconomic inequities. For instance, minority students' access to vital resources may be restricted if AI-driven "at-risk" student identification incorrectly flags them. Transparency and ethical governance are crucial because the intricacy and opacity of AI "black box" systems make it difficult to identify and address biases.

To make sure AI promotes equity rather than contributes to disparities, educational institutions must mitigate bias through a variety of data practices, auditing, and human oversight. This calls for proactive policies that strike a balance between the advantages of AI and the preservation of privacy, equity, and inclusion for all students.

Admissions systems provide a telling example, as biased algorithms have unfairly devalued students from underrepresented or lower-income backgrounds while giving preference to applicants from esteemed universities. An AI-based admissions algorithm used in the UK's A-level grading system in 2020 made this problem particularly apparent by disproportionately downgrading students from lower-income schools while favoring those from prestigious universities. The dispute exposed the serious repercussions of uncontrolled AI use in education, sparking nationwide demonstrations that finally compelled the government to scrap the algorithm. "Bias in AI systems reflects and amplifies societal inequalities," cautions Timnit Gebru, an expert in AI ethics. Underrepresented students will suffer disproportionately from these technologies if proper oversight is not in place [5].

Yet this case also underscores how the same technology, if responsibly designed, can be redirected toward innovation and equity. Figure 12.3 illustrates this forward-looking perspective, highlighting how AI can reshape

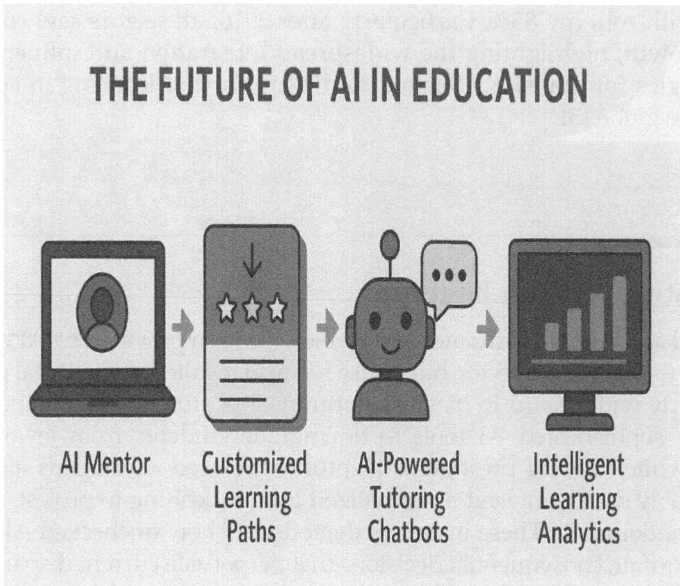

FIGURE 12.3
The future of AI in education.

learning through the emergence of digital mentors, customized learning paths, tutoring chatbots, and intelligent analytics [6].

According to this vision, AI mentors serve as virtual advisors who offer students individualized advice, criticism, and support. They also assist students in identifying their areas of strength and weakness and suggest resources to promote development. Each learner can have a personalized educational journey thanks to customized learning paths, which modify lessons based on performance, preferences, and progress. Personalized tutoring is now more widely available than ever due to tutoring chatbots that use sophisticated natural language processing to offer interactive assistance and on-demand explanations. Lastly, by transforming raw data into actionable strategies for better student success, intelligent learning analytics enable teachers to track student engagement, forecast results, and improve curricula.

12.3 Challenges and Opportunities

12.3.1 Privacy Challenges: A Spectrum of Concerns

One of the most urgent concerns in AI-driven education is the protection of children's data. Strict guidelines are established for AI tools used in K-12 education by regulations like the COPPA. COPPA restricts data retention and requires verifiable parental consent before collecting or sharing personal information about children under the age of 13. It calls on businesses to put strong data security procedures in place, handle biometric information like voiceprints, and guarantee that outside vendors keep information private. By limiting how AI systems can gather, use, and share data in educational settings, these policies protect the privacy of minors [7].

Data security poses a distinct but no less significant challenge at the university level. Academic records and personal information are among the many sensitive student data that higher education institutions store, making them easy targets for cyberattacks. To lower the risk of data breaches, AI-driven analytics and digital tools must thus strike a balance between innovation and robust cybersecurity measures like encryption, stringent access controls, and ongoing monitoring [8]. Since there is less direct federal regulation specifically addressing AI in higher education than there is in the K-12 sector, institutions must rely on extensive internal policies to adequately protect student data [9].

12.4 Student Autonomy and AI Decision-Making

There are advantages and disadvantages to AI applications pertaining to student autonomy and decision-making. Automated career counseling is one instance in which AI systems examine students' academic histories and character attributes to recommend potential career paths. Although these systems can increase career options and guidance accessibility, they also run the risk of reiterating preexisting social biases, which could limit opportunities for students from disadvantaged backgrounds. Transparency, ethical system design, and high-quality data are necessary to guarantee inclusive and equitable recommendations [10].

AI-graded assessments are another important area. AI is effective at assessing objective tasks like multiple-choice exams, but it has trouble with subjective tasks like critical thinking and creative writing. Given these drawbacks, it is crucial to consider whether AI should be trusted to assess intricate student work that calls for human judgment, empathy, and contextual awareness.

All things considered, even though AI can support educational decision-making and assessment procedures, its application needs to be carefully balanced with human supervision. To make sure AI promotes rather than impedes equity, inclusivity, and autonomous student development, ethical considerations, bias awareness, and student autonomy protections are crucial.

12.5 Defining Responsible AI: Principles and Frameworks

12.5.1 Transparency: Explainable AI in Grading Systems

Making sure that automated results can be interpreted and understood is a major challenge in AI-driven education. This problem is addressed by Explainable AI (XAI), which clarifies how algorithms arrive at their conclusions. By enabling students and teachers to view both the final score and the reasoning behind it, XAI can improve the transparency and reliability of grading systems. This promotes equity, increases trust in AI-powered tests, and enables focused feedback to help students identify their areas of strength and growth. In contrast to conventional "black box" models, XAI offers explanations that are easy for humans to understand, promoting responsible AI adoption in educational institutions and enhancing accountability [11].

The assessment workflow is shown in detail in Figure 12.4, starting with the student submission that starts the entire process. After a submission is received, it goes through data preprocessing, which involves cleaning, tokenizing, and formatting the raw text to guarantee analysis that is fair and consistent. Cleaning preserves the dataset's accuracy by eliminating mistakes, inconsistencies, and redundant details such as duplicates or missing data. The AI system can then more effectively analyze the text's structure and meaning by tokenizing it into smaller units such as words or sentences. In order to process all student work equally, formatting finalizes the submission by standardizing punctuation, converting characters, and guaranteeing consistent organization. When combined, these preprocessing procedures turn unstructured educational data into a format that AI can analyze efficiently.

After preprocessing, the system advances to feature extraction, where important elements of the student's submission are found, including content relevance, grammar, and structural coherence. These characteristics function as quantifiable indicators of academic achievement and as inputs for models of machine learning. Efficient feature extraction improves the assessment's accuracy and interpretability by simplifying the data, emphasizing important elements, and eliminating extraneous details. Depending on the type of data, feature extraction techniques can take many forms, utilizing statistical techniques like principal component analysis to find patterns or natural language processing to capture linguistic features. Feature extraction facilitates more thorough and individualized feedback by empowering algorithms to assess complex student abilities beyond straightforward scoring.

After processing the extracted features, the AI provides a preliminary score based on preset criteria during the model evaluation stage. This output undergoes a bias detection and fairness check to guarantee fairness, identifying possible problems like discrimination based on language or demographics. The submission is sent to human reviewers for manual verification if bias is found; otherwise, or following review, the process continues. The evaluation process then comes to an end when the final score is verified and

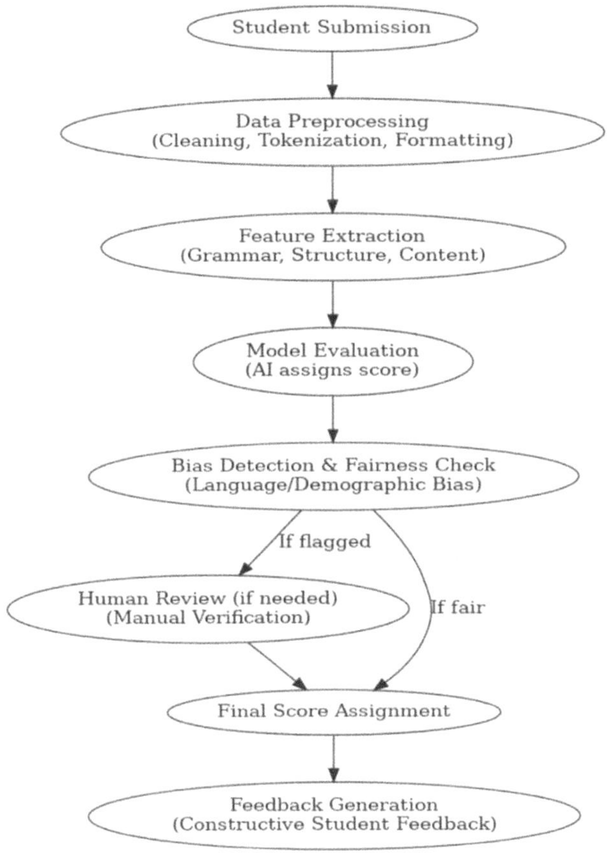

FIGURE 12.4
Assessment workflow in AI-driven grading systems.

noted. Additionally, the system produces helpful criticism that helps students recognize their areas of strength and growth.

This integrated workflow shows how human oversight and automation work together to preserve fairness, accuracy, and transparency in AI-driven educational assessment while guaranteeing that students receive helpful, insightful feedback in addition to effective evaluation.

12.6 Fairness: Lessons from Amazon's Biased Recruitment Tool

AI bias is still a major problem; one prominent example is Amazon's 2018 AI hiring tool, which gave preference to male applicants because it was trained on biased hiring data from the past. Similarly, AI programs that are trained on skewed data in the classroom have the potential to disproportionately harm underrepresented students by escalating already-existing inequalities. These biases in educational AI have an impact on career counseling, grading, and admissions, resulting in unfair outcomes and limiting opportunities for underrepresented groups. To ensure fair and moral AI use in education, addressing AI bias calls for meticulous data selection, openness, continual bias detection, human oversight, and legislative changes.

12.6.1 Privacy and Societal Impact: Responsible AI in Education and Sustainability

With the rise of AI-driven educational platforms like ClassDojo and Khan Academy, student data privacy has become a critical concern. Strict data protection measures are required by laws like the General Data Protection Regulation (GDPR), which requires these platforms to get explicit user consent, put strong data-access controls in place, and adhere to data-retention guidelines. Large volumes of sensitive student data are gathered by AI in education, so robust privacy protections are necessary to stop data breaches, misuse, and unauthorized sharing. Encryption, user control over personal data, transparency regarding data practices, and frequent compliance audits are essential tactics to strike a balance between AI innovation and student privacy protection. The necessity of responsible data governance in AI-powered education is highlighted by the fact that failure to enforce such measures erodes trust and increases the risk of exploitation, identity theft, and surveillance.

AI makes a substantial contribution to environmental sustainability outside education. AI facilitates climate modeling, energy optimization, sustainable agriculture, and climate impact analysis, as shown in Figure 12.5. AI can simulate and forecast climate patterns by utilizing vast datasets, increasing the precision of long-term climate projections as well as short-term weather forecasts. Scientists and policymakers can more accurately predict negative effects and act quickly to mitigate them thanks to this capability. Furthermore, by forecasting energy demand, improving grid management, and cutting waste, AI boosts the effectiveness of renewable energy sources like solar and wind, resulting in cleaner and more dependable energy production. AI also improves agricultural practices by monitoring crop growth, soil health, and irrigation requirements with sophisticated tools. This enables farmers to make data-driven, well-informed decisions that maximize yield while reducing resource consumption, promoting resilient and environmentally sustainable farming. In order to assess the effects of climate interventions and policies, AI also examines data from a variety of sources, offering insights into the tactics that work best for cutting emissions and promoting climate change adaptation [12].

AI exhibits its potential to spur innovation in a responsible manner by tackling issues such as climate change and privacy in education.

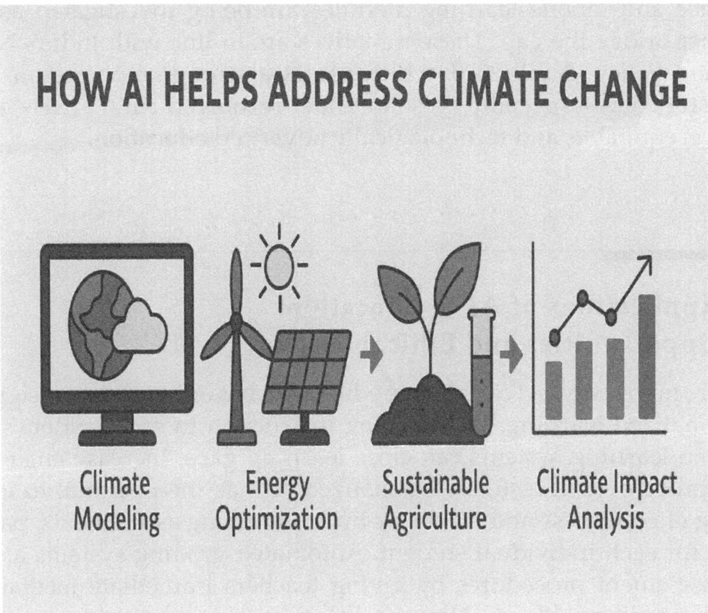

FIGURE 12.5
Support of AI in addressing climate change.

A comprehensive approach to responsible AI that strikes a balance between social and ecological responsibility and technological advancement is demonstrated by ensuring ethical data practices while utilizing AI for environmental sustainability.

12.7 Inclusivity: Bridging the Digital Divide

Not all students, particularly those in underprivileged and rural areas, have equal access to AI-powered educational resources. The government's efforts to close these educational gaps are best demonstrated by India's DIKSHA platform, which offers curriculum-aligned, multilingual content that is accessible on mobile devices and designed for offline, low-bandwidth use. In order to improve learning quality and educational management, DIKSHA integrates cutting-edge features like teacher training modules, textbooks linked by QR codes, and data-driven insights.

Significant obstacles still exist in spite of these developments such as inconsistent internet access, a shortage of devices, and difficulties with digital literacy. Hybrid strategies that blend online resources with in-person assistance and mobile learning modules are being investigated as a way to further bridge the gap. These initiatives are in line with India's National Education Policy (NEP) 2020, which places a strong emphasis on providing all students—especially those in under-resourced rural areas—with an inclusive, equitable, and technologically advanced education.

12.8 Applications of AI in Education: Opportunities and Ethical Risks

There are many ways AI can change education, but one of the most significant is personalized learning. By adjusting instruction to each student's needs, AI-driven learning systems can close learning gaps, increase engagement, and improve overall results. Personalized AI has the potential to improve learning effectiveness and efficiency by customizing assessments, pace, and content for each individual student. Automated grading systems also simplify assessment procedures by giving teachers immediate feedback and lightening their workloads. However, because these systems frequently rely on proprietary algorithms, there is a lack of transparency that potentially raises questions about accountability and fairness by making it difficult for teachers and students to understand the precise grading criteria.

AI is also revolutionizing the recruitment and admissions processes by evaluating applications, forecasting student success, and identifying qualified applicants. However, AI programs trained on past admissions data run the risk of reinforcing historical injustices by reproducing preexisting biases and giving preference to privileged groups over underrepresented students. By assisting with student advising, enrollment management, and academic support, administrative AI increases operational efficiency in education. However, it also raises privacy concerns because AI platforms gather a lot of sensitive student data, making security, consent, and potential misuse crucial factors.

Notwithstanding these benefits, there are significant ethical risks and challenges associated with AI in education. Students may be treated unfairly because of racial, gender, or socioeconomic biases present in training data. Many AI models function as "black boxes," which restricts transparency and makes it challenging to comprehend the decision-making process behind things like grade assignments and curriculum recommendations. Because underprivileged areas might not have the technology, internet connectivity, or digital literacy required to take advantage of AI-enhanced learning, the digital divide makes equitable access even more difficult [13].

The overreliance on AI raises serious concerns as well because it may diminish crucial human interaction in the classroom. Human instruction is still essential for developing creativity, critical thinking, emotional intelligence, and social skills like empathy, teamwork, and communication, even though AI can effectively perform tasks like grading and administrative management. Without human support, an overreliance on AI may lower student engagement and motivation. It may also result in fewer teaching positions or even job displacement. These elements run the risk of producing a transactional, dehumanizing educational process that puts efficiency ahead of overall growth.

It is crucial to strike a balance between integrating AI and providing human mentoring. It is the responsibility of educators and schools to make sure AI complements human-centered learning rather than takes its place. This entails addressing biases, protecting student data, ensuring fairness and transparency in assessment, and encouraging equitable access to AI tools. AI can facilitate individualized learning, administrative effectiveness, and creative teaching methods by carefully weighing these risks, all the while maintaining the crucial role that teachers play in fostering students' overall development [14].

12.9 Case Study: AI in Education—Real-World Challenges

12.9.1 Racial Bias in Facial Recognition Proctoring Tools

Proctorio and ExamSoft, two facial recognition proctoring tools, have come under fire for disproportionately misidentifying students of color. Due to inadequate facial recognition, many students were unjustly flagged for possible cheating, which caused anxiety and had negative effects on their academic performance. Training data can be reweighted to guarantee diverse demographic representation and reduce bias. To lessen AI-driven discrimination, human oversight and alternative identity verification techniques are also crucial.

12.10 Edmodo's 2020 Data Breach

A significant data breach at the popular educational website Edmodo in 2020 exposed 77 million student records, including learning activities and personal data. The hack made clear the weaknesses in centralized data storage systems and the significance of strong data security procedures. Federated learning is one way to improve privacy while enabling AI advancements by allowing AI models to train locally on student devices without sending private information to a central server.

12.10.1 Black-Box AI in Curriculum Recommendations

Certain AI-powered tools for curriculum design make recommendations for courses and learning pathways without providing explicit justifications for ranking them. Biased or ineffective learning experiences may arise from this opacity. By giving importance scores to input features, methods such as SHAP (Shapley Additive Explanations) offer interpretable insights into the choices made by AI models. By using SHAP in the classroom, teachers and students can better understand the rationale behind particular recommendations, fostering greater openness and confidence.

12.10.2 Global Digital Divide and Limited Internet Access

UNICEF (2023) reports that only 34% of African schools have internet access, which significantly restricts students' access to AI-powered learning resources. Current disparities in education are exacerbated by the digital divide. Equitable access to AI-enhanced education necessitates investments in internet infrastructure, reasonably priced gadgets, and low-tech AI solutions that operate offline or with spotty connectivity.

12.11 Building Responsible AI Systems: Best Practices

Fairness and privacy must be carefully considered when developing ethical AI systems for education. Ensuring the ethical operation of AI tools contributes to equitable outcomes, student protection, and technological trust [15].

12.11.1 Fairness Audits: Ensuring Equitable AI Systems

Fairness audits assist in locating and reducing biases in educational AI systems. IBM's AI Fairness 360 is a popular toolkit that assesses AI models for possible racial, gender, and socioeconomic discrimination. Developers can use this open-source tool to apply corrective measures and evaluate AI bias using statistical measures. IBM's AI Fairness 360 can be used in educational settings to guarantee that all students are treated fairly and equally through the use of learning analytics tools, admissions algorithms, and grading systems.

12.11.2 Privacy-Preserving AI: Protecting Student Data

Fairness audits assist in locating and reducing biases in educational AI systems. IBM's AI Fairness 360 is a popular toolkit that assesses AI models for possible racial, gender, and socioeconomic discrimination. Developers can use this open-source tool to apply corrective measures and evaluate AI bias using statistical measures. IBM's AI Fairness 360 can be used in educational settings to guarantee that all students are treated fairly and equally through the use of learning analytics tools, admissions algorithms, and grading systems [16].

12.12 Policy and Governance

To guarantee the responsible use of AI in education, effective governance and policy are crucial. Institutions must involve all stakeholders in the development and supervision of AI tools while developing frameworks that address ethical, legal, and social implications.

12.12.1 Institutional Frameworks: Ethical Oversight in AI-Driven Education

To monitor AI ethics in education, universities and other educational institutions should set up governance frameworks. Harvard University, for instance, has established an EdTech AI Ethics Board that reviews bias mitigation techniques, assesses ethical risks, and protects student data while evaluating the application of AI in educational technology. Establishing independent ethics committees, bringing in multidisciplinary specialists like ethicists, educators, and AI developers, and regularly auditing AI tools utilized in classrooms are all examples of best practices for setting up AI governance boards [17].

12.12.2 Regulatory Compliance: Comparing FERPA and GDPR

AI-powered learning resources have to abide by laws that safeguard student information. Although the Family Educational Rights and Privacy Act (FERPA) in the United States gives parents and students access to school records and mandates that schools get permission before sharing data, it does not have robust enforcement measures for the use of AI-driven data. The GDPR gives people the "right to be forgotten," mandates express consent for data collection, and enforces severe penalties for noncompliance and data breaches in the EU. Respecting these rules is essential to protecting student privacy and guaranteeing moral AI use.

12.12.3 Stakeholder Engagement

Teachers, students, and parents are all involved in the design and implementation of a responsible AI system. As used in Finland, participatory design involves teachers in the cocreation of AI tools to guarantee that they align with ethical norms and pedagogical requirements. Teachers who receive ethics training are also better prepared to use AI responsibly, comprehend its effects, and successfully incorporate it into their lessons while upholding privacy, equity, and human-centered learning.

12.13 Global Case Studies

12.13.1 Success Story: Singapore's AI-Powered Language Learning

In order to help students learn English, Mandarin, Malay, and Tamil, Singapore has effectively incorporated AI-powered tools into its multilingual educational system. By evaluating speech patterns, grammar, and writing abilities, platforms such as the Intelligent Mother Tongue Language (iMTL) system offer tailored feedback and modify content according to each student's level of proficiency. The Ministry of Education (MOE) regularly conducts audits to ensure accuracy and fairness, emphasizing responsible AI practices. Instead of depending entirely on AI, educators work together with the technology to improve their teaching methods, maintaining the vital role that teachers play. Singapore's strategy shows how creative AI integration in education can coexist with moral leadership and human supervision [18].

12.13.2 Controversy: China's Surveillance Schools

China has quickly incorporated AI into its educational system, implementing technologies like facial recognition cameras to track student engagement and attentiveness and smart uniforms with embedded chips to track student movements. These developments present serious ethical issues even though their goal is to improve educational administration and security. In addition to limiting natural student-teacher interactions, critics point to privacy violations, a reduction in student autonomy, and possible stress brought on by continuous monitoring. There are still problems with transparency because parents and students frequently don't understand how behavioral data is gathered and applied. Timnit Gebru, an AI ethicist, cautions that this kind of monitoring creates a potentially harmful precedent by normalizing privacy violations under the pretense of educational effectiveness. This case emphasizes how crucial it is to strike a balance between respect for students' rights and ethical considerations and technological advancements.

12.13.3 Grassroots Innovation: Kenya's Eneza Education

AI-driven educational solutions must use accessible technologies to adjust to local constraints in areas with poor internet access. This is best demonstrated by Eneza Education in Kenya, which offers low-tech AI tutoring via

SMS, allowing students in remote locations to learn without the need for costly gadgets or broadband connectivity. Through simple mobile phones, Eneza's platform delivers customized tests, lessons, and feedback, modifying the content according to each student's answers. This strategy lowers costs, improves accessibility, and provides a replicable model for other marginalized communities across the globe. Eneza fills educational gaps and offers underprivileged students excellent, locally relevant learning opportunities by utilizing the pervasiveness of mobile technology.

12.14 Future Directions: Toward Ethical AI Ecosystems

12.14.1 Technological Trends

ChatGPT and other generative AI tools are revolutionizing personalized learning and homework help [19]. These systems offer individualized explanations and guidance that adjust to each student's unique learning needs, providing round-the-clock academic support. For students around the world, this improves accessibility, engagement, and self-paced learning. But there are drawbacks to the growing use of AI in homework as well, such as higher plagiarism risks, possible declines in critical thinking and problem-solving abilities, and an excessive dependence on AI-generated answers [20]. To address these concerns, educational institutions must integrate AI literacy into curricula, teaching students responsible usage while emphasizing academic honesty and independent learning [21].

12.14.2 Policy Evolution

International agencies like UNESCO and the OECD are attempting to create uniform ethical guidelines for AI in education. The OECD's AI principles place a strong emphasis on accountability, transparency, and fairness. They guarantee that AI decisions are impartial and explainable and that institutions bear responsibility for the results produced by AI systems. By supporting a human-centered approach, emphasizing equity and inclusion, and encouraging AI literacy among educators and students, UNESCO supplements this. When combined, these frameworks offer policymakers and educational stakeholders direction on how to maximize AI's advantages while reducing its risks, promoting the ethical, fair, and reliable integration of AI in education across the globe.

12.14.3 Role of NGOs in Auditing EdTech Companies

Nongovernmental organizations are essential to maintaining accountability in AI-powered learning environments. AlgorithmWatch, for instance, promotes ethical transparency in educational technology and audits AI-powered decision-making systems. NGOs help stop the misuse of student data and biased results by keeping an eye on compliance, evaluating the fairness of AI tools, and encouraging ethical behavior.

12.14.4 Empowering Educators as AI Co-designers

To make sure that technology is in line with educational objectives, educators should be actively involved in the design and development of AI systems. While collaborative design projects integrate teacher input into AI systems, professional development programs can instruct educators on AI ethics and best practices. AI tools can enhance instruction rather than replace it by involving educators as co-designers. This maintains the human-centered character of education and promotes the holistic development of students.

12.14.5 Student-Led AI Ethics Committees

When it comes to AI policies that impact their educational experiences, students themselves ought to have a say. Student-led AI ethics committees give students a forum to voice their opinions, take part in decision-making, and help create rules that support privacy, justice, and responsible AI use. These programs enable students to become knowledgeable stakeholders, encouraging moral consciousness and responsibility at an early age.

12.15 Conclusion

It is crucial to ensure responsible implementation as AI continues to transform education. This chapter has emphasized the ethical implications of AI in education, stressing the need for inclusivity, transparency, and fairness to direct its application. Whether in monitoring, admissions, or grading, decisions must be transparent and understandable to parents, students, and teachers. AI systems should be built to reduce bias and support fair opportunities for all students. Furthermore, without taking the place of human intervention, AI should be used as a tool to close educational gaps, assisting underprivileged and diverse populations. In the end, AI should support teachers rather than replace them, improving learning through efficiency and personalization while maintaining the indispensable human qualities of empathy, mentoring, and critical thinking. AI in education has a bright future in a well-balanced ecosystem where human knowledge and technology combine to produce an inclusive, transparent, and equitable learning environment.

References

[1] Zerkouk, M., Mihoubi, M., & Chikhaoui, B. (2025). A comprehensive review of AI-based Intelligent tutoring systems: Applications and challenges. *arXiv preprint arXiv:2507.18882.*

[2] Kayyali, M. (2025). The evolution of AI in education from concept to classroom. In *Navigating Barriers to AI Implementation in the Classroom* (pp. 325–368). IGI Global Scientific Publishing.

[3] Jin, Y., Yan, L., Echeverria, V., Gašević, D., & Martinez-Maldonado, R. (2025). Generative AI in higher education: A global perspective of institutional adoption policies and guidelines. *Computers and Education: Artificial Intelligence, 8*, 100348.

[4] Farahani, M. S., & Ghasmi, G. (2024, July). Artificial intelligence in education: A comprehensive study. *Forum for Education Studies, 2*(3), 1379–1379.

[5] Wiese, L. J., Patil, I., Schiff, D. S., & Magana, A. J. (2025). AI ethics education: A systematic literature review. *Computers and Education: Artificial Intelligence*, 100405.

[6] Kayyali, M. (2025). The future of AI in education: Predictions and emerging trends. In *Next-Generation AI Methodologies in Education* (pp. 367–406). IGI Global Scientific Publishing.

[7] Jones-Jang, S. M., Chung, M., Choi, J., Kim, N., & Lee, S. (2025). Fairness perceptions of AI in grading systems: Examining how discontent with the status quo and outcome favorability reduce AI reluctance. *Computers and Education: Artificial Intelligence*, 100419.

[8] Freeman, J. (2025). *Student Generative AI Survey 2025.* Higher Education Policy Institute.

[9] Ahmed, F. R., Rushdan, E. E., Al-Yateem, N., Almaazmi, A. N., Subu, M. A., Hijazi, H., . . . & Aburuz, M. E. (2025). AI in higher education: Unveiling nursing students' perspectives on ChatGPT's challenges and opportunities. *Teaching and Learning in Nursing, 20*(2), e408–e413.

[10] Nazaretsky, T., Ariely, M., Cukurova, M., & Alexandron, G. (2022). Teachers' trust in AI-powered educational technology and a professional development program to improve it. *British Journal of Educational Technology, 53*(4), 914–931.

[11] Geethanjali, K. S., & Umashankar, N. (2025, February). Enhancing educational outcomes with explainable AI: Bridging transparency and trust in learning systems. In *2025 International Conference on Emerging Systems and Intelligent Computing (ESIC)* (pp. 325–328). IEEE.

[12] Bano, S. (2025). The role of AI in predicting and mitigating climate change: A comparative study of US and China's approaches. *The Critical Review of Social Sciences Studies, 3*(1), 664–675.

[13] Yan, Y., Liu, H., & Chau, T. (2025). A systematic review of AI ethics in education: Challenges, policy gaps, and future directions. *Journal of Global Information Management (JGIM), 33*(1), 1–50.

[14] Amah, O., & Okesipe, V. O. (2025). AI in education: Ethical challenges and opportunities. In *Integrating Artificial Intelligence in Education: Enhancing Teaching Practices for Future Learning* (pp. 1–26). IGI Global Scientific Publishing.

[15] Sadek, M., Kallina, E., Bohné, T., Mougenot, C., Calvo, R. A., & Cave, S. (2025). Challenges of responsible AI in practice: Scoping review and recommended actions. *AI & Society, 40*(1), 199–215.

[16] Cowan, M., Fox, G., & Larson, K. (2025). Can AI level the playing field? How AI-assisted assessment impacts gender bias in student evaluations of marketing instructors. *Journal of Marketing Education*, *47*(2), 126–137.
[17] Karan, B. (2024). Integration of artificial intelligence by the Central Board of Secondary Education in India: Towards innovative teaching and learning practices. *Technology, Pedagogy and Education*, *33*(4), 455–474.
[18] Ferk Savec, V., & Jedrinović, S. (2025). The role of AI implementation in higher education in achieving the Sustainable Development Goals: A case study from Slovenia. *Sustainability*, *17*(1), 183.
[19] Aswin, S., Godwin, J., Bharat Kumaaran, P., Dinesh, K., Mohanapriya, S., & Mohana Saranya, S. (2025, June). Assessing the influence of digital connectivity on student wellness. In *International Conference on Advances in Photonics Science (ICAPS 2024)* (Vol. 13660, pp. 32–41). SPIE.
[20] Jowallah, R. J. (2024). Integrating Artificial Intelligence (AI) into the curriculum: Empowering the next generation through proactive AI education. In *Generative AI in Teaching and Learning* (pp. 355–368). IGI Global Scientific Publishing.
[21] Ali, I., Warraich, N. F., & Butt, K. (2025). Acceptance and use of artificial intelligence and AI-based applications in education: A meta-analysis and future direction. *Information Development*, *41*(3), 859–874.

13

Purpose-Led Learning Using AI for Data Analytics with SMEs in Malaysia

Afizan Azman, Husna Sarirah Husin, and Norhidayah Hamzah

13.1 Introduction: Background and Driving Forces

Small and medium-sized enterprises (SMEs) represent a critical segment of the global economy, contributing significantly to employment, innovation, and economic growth. Despite their importance, SMEs often face structural challenges, including limited financial resources, a lack of technical expertise, and vulnerability to external market disruptions. These constraints can hinder their capacity to adapt to rapid changes in the business environment, particularly in the context of increasing digitalization and data-driven decision-making.

On the other hand, data analytics education in universities has typically followed theory-based teaching and sanitized datasets that fail to reflect the complexity of data settings in practical scenarios. While this teaching methodology provides students with a theoretical understanding, it fails to prepare them to handle the ambiguous and complex problems of SME settings. To address this void, a novel and innovative assessment strategy has been designed in the data analytics and machine learning module, a core module in the bachelor of computer science program, where students engage directly with SMEs as clients. This initiative aims to empower SMEs by tailoring data analytics techniques to their specific business needs while providing students with real-world, experiential learning opportunities. Through this collaboration, students work with unformatted raw data from SMEs to gain real-world experience with data cleaning, normalization, handling missing values, and contextualization for the domain. Meanwhile, SMEs gain customized analytical solutions addressing their specific operational requirements, and a data literacy and innovation culture is fostered. This mutual gain highlights the importance of adapting learning practices to real-world needs, achieving sustainable benefits for learners and businesses.

Engaging in data analytics initiatives particularly those incorporating predictive and prescriptive analytics can enhance SMEs' operational resilience and competitiveness. Such projects enable businesses to anticipate market

DOI: 10.1201/9781003633433-13

trends, optimize resource allocation, and make informed strategic decisions. From an educational standpoint, facilitating collaboration between SMEs and academic institutions fosters knowledge transfer and capacity building, both essential for sustainable development.

This initiative aligns directly with the objectives of the United Nations Sustainable Development Goal (UNSDG) 8 (Decent Work and Economic Growth), which advocates for inclusive and sustainable economic growth, full and productive employment, and decent work for all. By empowering SMEs with data capabilities, the project supports their capacity to sustain jobs, improve productivity, and stimulate local economic ecosystems. Additionally, the project supports UNSDG 9 (Industry, Innovation, and Infrastructure) by encouraging the adoption of digital technologies and data-driven practices among SMEs. This, in turn, contributes to inclusive industrial development and the strengthening of innovation systems. This is particularly significant for SMEs in emerging economies, where digital transformation can catalyze competitiveness and growth.

Predictive analytics, a key area of data analytics, uses statistical methods, machine learning, and artificial intelligence to analyze historical data and predict future outcomes. For SMEs, these insights enable proactive risk management, operational optimization, and strategic decision-making. However, implementing such tools often requires a foundational understanding of data analytics principles. Educational programs designed for SMEs can bridge this gap, ensuring that business owners and employees possess the technical literacy necessary to engage with and effectively apply predictive models.

13.2 Purpose-Led Learning Framework for Data Analytics Education

The data analytics and machine learning module at Taylor's University was redesigned from theory-heavy instruction into an experiential, purpose-led learning framework. Students were grouped and assigned local SMEs as live clients. They analyzed messy, unstructured data from SMEs, applying AI tools including regression, decision trees, and visual dashboards. This shifted learning from theoretical exercises to real industry problems, fostering collaboration, critical thinking, and social impact.

Figure 13.1 illustrates the student–SME engagement model implemented, where the datasets shared by the SMEs are divided into different types of business. There have been many experiential learning opportunities through real-world projects, where most studies implement experiential learning using project-based or case-based approaches, often involving real-world data or industry problems. Examples include

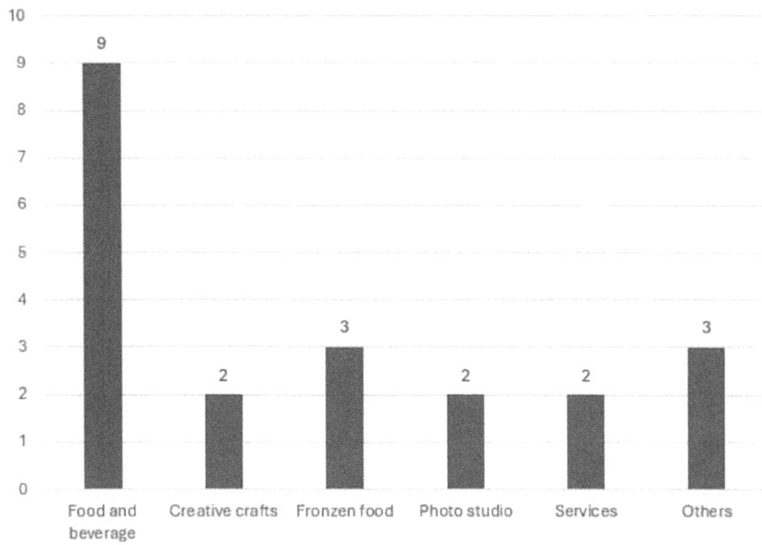

FIGURE 13.1
The different group of SMEs divided by its types of business and students' groups.

Source: Authors (2024)

practical lab-based projects (Kim et al., 2023), live-client SME projects (Fletcher-Brown et al., 2015), and simulations or client-based projects (Zhang & Scribner, 2024). There was also direct engagement with SMEs, where students work directly with local businesses to address authentic problems (Kim et al., 2023; Willetts et al., 2021; Fletcher-Brown et al., 2015). In some cases, experiential learning is implemented via partnerships with large corporations (Goh & Zhang, 2015) or through real-world scenarios without explicit SME involvement (Dunaway, 2017). In terms of variation in student engagement, the degree of student interaction with business stakeholders varies, with some studies emphasizing direct collaboration and others focusing on classroom-based simulations or reflective assignments.

For industry-academia partnership models, some of the notable strategies are direct project partnerships (Kim et al., 2023; Fletcher-Brown et al., 2015), teaching case studies based on SME contexts (Willetts et al., 2021), and collaboration with external partners for course design (Pan et al., 2016). In Goh and Zhang (2015), they observed issues such as data quality and project ambiguity in studies involving large-scale or complex projects. Some studies highlight the need for aligning expectations and maintaining effective communication between academic and industry partners to support successful experiential learning outcomes. Table 13.1 summarizes the related previous studies.

TABLE 13.1

Summary of Learning Approaches and Learning Outcomes

Study	Study Context	Learning Approach	SME Integration	Learning Outcomes
Kim et al. (2023)	University, postgraduate engineering course, "Industrial Internet of Things (IoT) Implementation for Smart Manufacturing"	Practical lab/project course, Kolb's Experiential Learning model	Local manufacturing companies (small and medium-sized enterprises) as project partners	Internet of Things implementation, data collection, analytics, visualization; benefits from real-world projects
Wilson et al. (2018)	Higher education, marketing department, course level not specified	Curriculum innovation, case study, experiential learning theory	No mention found	No mention found; reviewed by learning goals and student satisfaction
Venkatraman et al. (2022)	Higher education, postgraduate business analytics	Agile smart classroom, experiential learning for higher-order thinking skills	No mention found	Enhancement of higher-order thinking skills
Zhang and Scribner (2024)	Not specified, digital marketing analytics course	Simulations and client-based projects	No mention found	Preliminary findings: slight edge for simulation over client-based project
Goh and Zhang (2015)	Not specified, data analytics class	Live case study, action research	Large Fortune 500 company	Enhanced understanding of analytics complexity, motivation
Pan et al. (2016)	Undergraduate accounting analytics course, implied university/college	Experiential learning, real-world projects with external partners	External partners (not specified as small- and medium-sized enterprises)	Enhanced problem-solving, analytical, reasoning, and communication skills
Willetts et al. (2021)	Not specified, business/management context	Case study, Big Data Analytics framework	Small businesses (small- and medium-sized enterprises) in recruitment software marketing	No mention found; focus on framework/tool application
Dunaway (2017)	University, undergraduate liberal arts, "Data Analytics and Decision Making"	Active learning, industry partnership, and action research	No mention found	Gained data analytics skills, enhanced real-world knowledge

(Continued)

TABLE 13.1 ***(Continued)***

Summary of Learning Approaches and Learning Outcomes

Study	Study Context	Learning Approach	SME Integration	Learning Outcomes
Venkatraman et al. (2019)	Higher education, information and communications technology curriculum	Visualization and experiential learning, action research	No mention found	No mention found; positive impact reported
Fletcher-Brown et al. (2015)	Higher education, undergraduate marketing	Live-client projects, mixed methods	Small- to medium-sized enterprises	Employagility, the practical application of knowledge

13.3 Implementation with Malaysian SMEs

This project is part of the Digital Innovation & Smart Societies Impact Lab initiative, in collaboration with the School of Computer Science at Taylor's University, to support SMEs in Malaysia, specifically those under the Jabatan Pembangunan Wanita (JPW) Melaka. These SMEs are engaged in different types of businesses such as creative crafts like textile weaving (*songket*), rattan weaving (*anyaman rotan*), sewing (*jahitan*), and other traditional art forms; food and beverages; and photography studios, which play a vital role in preserving cultural heritage and meeting customer needs (Erlinda et al., 2023). However, they face challenges in scaling their operations and adapting to modern markets (Chernyshov et al., 2024). By leveraging data analytics, machine learning, and visualization tools, this data analytics for SME project provides actionable insights into business processes, market trends and customer behavior (Enoch et al., 2024). This initiative empowers SMEs to make informed, data-driven decisions, enhancing profitability, improving customer satisfaction, and achieving sustainable growth.

A purpose-led, impact-driven learning model was introduced through a data analytics for SMEs project to address this pedagogical gap and generate social and economic value. This initiative represented a paradigm shift from traditional instructional practices to experiential education, wherein students engaged directly with SME stakeholders and their operational data. Rather than working with sanitized datasets, students were given access to authentic, often disorganized datasets from participating businesses. This allowed them to confront real-world challenges such as data cleaning, normalization, missing-value treatment, and domain-specific contextualization.

Through this engagement, students applied analytical techniques in a practical setting and gained valuable soft skills. They learned to communicate effectively with SME owners, understand business constraints, and translate analytical insights into actionable recommendations. This level of exposure significantly enhanced their learning outcomes by fostering critical thinking, problem-solving, and stakeholder engagement skills and competencies that are increasingly essential in a data-driven economy.

The Digital Innovation & Smart Society (DISS) Impact Lab facilitated partnerships with 15 SMEs from JPW Melaka, covering food, crafts, and creative industries. Eighty-nine students were grouped into 21 teams, each collaborating directly with an SME. Malaysian students served as cultural and language liaisons. Students worked with raw datasets, including sales logs, handwritten receipts, and spreadsheets, performing data cleaning, feature engineering, and predictive modeling. AI methods such as regression and decision trees supported sales forecasting, customer trend analysis, and inventory planning. This authentic exposure developed both technical and soft skills.

13.3.1 Data Analytics and Machine Learning Module in the School of Computer Science

Data analytics and machine learning is a core module offered in the second year of the bachelor of computer science program. This module is designed for intermediate-level students and builds on foundational knowledge gained in introductory programming and statistics. It aims to equip students with essential data manipulation, analysis, and visualization skills, preparing them for advanced topics such as machine learning and big data analytics in subsequent years.

The bachelor of computer science program is structured to provide students with a comprehensive understanding of both theoretical and practical aspects of computing. The data analytics module is part of a broader curriculum that encompasses modules such as database systems, artificial intelligence, software engineering, and web development. This module teaches students how to extract meaningful insights from data using statistical techniques and programming tools. Key topics include data preprocessing, exploratory data analysis, statistical modeling, and data visualization. By the end of the module, students are expected to demonstrate proficiency in applying analytical methods to solve real-world problems.

Figure 13.2 illustrates students engaging in collaborative discussions with various SME owners, including representatives from Alha Alfa, SMEs under the Jabatan Pembangunan Wanita Malaysia (JPWM), SMEs mentored under the Byond program, and Cili Lado. These interactions were designed to facilitate mutual understanding of the SMEs' operational contexts, challenges, and data availability, thereby enabling students to tailor their data analytics approaches to real-world business needs. Such early-stage dialogues served as a critical foundation for cocreating meaningful analytical solutions aligned with each SME's goals and constraints.

FIGURE 13.2
Students discussing with SME owners.

Source: Authors (2024)

13.3.1.1 Teaching and Learning Structure

Currently, the module is delivered through a combination of lectures, lab sessions, and tutorials, ensuring a balanced mix of theory and hands-on practice. Lectures introduce fundamental concepts, including data types, statistical measures, and analytical methodologies. Labs provide students with practical experience using programming languages such as Python, which is widely used in the industry for data analysis. Tutorials focus on problem-solving and clarifying doubts, fostering a deeper understanding of the material.

Students work extensively with built-in datasets available in Python libraries such as iris, mtcars, and titanic. These datasets are clean and well structured, allowing students to focus on learning analytical techniques without being overwhelmed by data preprocessing challenges. Lab assignments require students to apply these techniques to perform tasks such as data cleaning, transformation, visualization, and basic predictive modeling.

Figure 13.3 depicts a series of engagement session, workshops, training sessions, discussions, and talks conducted with SME owners during the early phase of the semester (Weeks 1 to 4). These sessions were designed to familiarize students with the SMEs' business models, operational processes, and prevailing challenges, while simultaneously exposing SME owners to the potential applications of AI-driven data analytics. Through these structured interactions, students gathered preliminary data, clarified project scopes, and built rapport with their assigned SMEs, establishing a strong foundation for the subsequent stages of their purpose-led learning projects.

As in Figure 13.4, students also had a chance to directly communicate with the SMEs' owners and to visit the SME's shop lot, warehouse, factory, store, and so on to witness and observe for themselves how the SMEs run their businesses.

13.3.1.2 Assessment Methods

The assessment structure is designed to evaluate both individual and collaborative skills. Students are assessed through individual assignments, group projects, and examinations. Individual assignments typically involve solving analytical problems using Python, while group projects encourage teamwork by requiring students to analyze a dataset collaboratively and present their findings. Examinations test theoretical knowledge and the ability to interpret results from analytical models. This conventional assessment approach ensures that students not only grasp the technical aspects of data analytics but also develop critical thinking and problem-solving skills.

Figure 13.5 captures the final presentation session held in Week 14, where students presented their analytical findings to the SME owners in the presence of their lecturer. During this culminating session, students were required to demonstrate their ability to translate raw business data into actionable insights through the use of data visualization techniques and

FIGURE 13.3
SMEs talk poster and event during lecture.

Source: Authors (2024)

FIGURE 13.4
Site visit to the outlets.

Source: Authors (2024)

FIGURE 13.5
The students, together with the lecturer and the SME owners, had a final presentation.

Source: Authors (2024)

predictive analytics models. The session served as a platform for students to showcase their analytical competencies, validate their proposed solutions with real industry stakeholders, and receive constructive feedback from both the SMEs and the academic supervisor to refine their recommendations.

Figure 13.6 presents a sample slide from the students' final presentation to Alha Alfa, one of the participating SMEs. The slide demonstrates

FIGURE 13.6
Sample of slide presentation to the SMEs.

Source: Authors (2024)

how students applied predictive analytics techniques, data visualization methods, and business insight generation to address specific operational challenges faced by the SME. By transforming raw data into clear and actionable intelligence, the students provided evidence-based recommendations tailored to the SMEs' context. At the end of the presentation, the SME owners evaluated the findings and considered adopting the proposed strategies to enhance their business decision-making and overall performance.

13.3.1.3 Current Teaching Approach and Its Limitations

While the current teaching approach effectively imparts foundational knowledge, it predominantly relies on sanitized datasets and simulated scenarios, which may not fully prepare students for the complexities of real-world data environments. Students often work with pre-cleaned datasets that lack the irregularities and inconsistencies commonly encountered in professional settings. This limits their exposure to challenges such as handling missing values, noisy data, and unstructured formats. Additionally, conventional assessment methods, although rigorous, often do not adequately emphasize the development of soft skills, such as communication and stakeholder engagement, which are crucial for translating analytical insights into actionable business strategies.

In contrast, the purpose-led learning approach adopted in this project immerses students in authentic, context-rich environments, where they are required to work directly with real SME data and engage meaningfully with business stakeholders. Through this experience, students not only learn the technical aspects of data analytics but also develop a wide range of transferable skills, including communication (particularly in Bahasa Malaysia when interacting with local SME owners), teamwork, time management, and project management. Remarkably, even students without prior programming experience were able to gain foundational coding skills, particularly in Python, through their participation in the analytics projects. This experiential learning model reinforces the understanding that meaningful machine learning or predictive modeling can only be achieved when there is a clear and accurate comprehension of the underlying data.

Moreover, the approach also benefits the SMEs, who become more aware of the importance of accurate record-keeping practices to enable future data-driven decision-making. Many SME owners reported gaining a clearer understanding of how data quality directly influences the value and reliability of analytics outputs. As an acknowledgment of their commitment, all participating SMEs were awarded certificates of participation, recognizing their valuable contributions and collaborative engagement in this educational initiative. Sample of certificates of participation is showed as in Figure 13.7.

FIGURE 13.7
Sample of certificates of participation given to the SMEs.

Source: Authors (2024)

13.4 Impact and Thematic Analysis of Stakeholder Feedback

Thematic analysis is a qualitative research method used to identify, analyze, and interpret patterns or themes within textual data. In the DISS Impact Lab project, thematic analysis was employed to systematically examine comments and feedback from students, SMEs, lecturers, and School of Computer Science members. This approach provided a structured way to uncover common concerns, suggestions, expectations, and reflections from various stakeholders involved in the data analytics and machine learning module. By categorizing the feedback into meaningful themes, such as learning outcomes, project challenges, SME collaboration experience, and perceived impact, the DISS Impact Lab team gained valuable insights into how the project was perceived and could be improved.

The application of thematic analysis in this context is critical because it goes beyond quantitative metrics to capture the rich, contextual understanding of stakeholder experiences. It revealed how the project enhanced students' learning and practical skills. For SMEs, it highlighted how well the project addressed their business needs and the clarity of communication with student teams. Lecturers provided feedback on the academic alignment and execution of the module, while members of the School of Computer Science offered strategic perspectives on scalability and innovation. These insights enabled the DISS Impact Lab team to make informed decisions about future improvements, ensuring the project remains relevant, impactful, and aligned with educational goals and industry needs.

In essence, thematic analysis provided a holistic view of stakeholder engagement and project effectiveness. It enabled the DISS Impact Lab's initiative to continuously refine its approach to digital innovation by gaining a deep understanding of the human experiences behind the data. This reflection-driven process fosters a culture of empathy, continuous improvement, and cocreation—core values that drive meaningful transformation for SMEs through data-driven solutions.

13.4.1 Comments from SMEs and Students

Overall, the module leader receives stakeholder comments and feedback every semester after the project ends. These comments and feedback are crucial in helping the module leader improve the module's development in the future.

During the recent engagement between students and SMEs, a wealth of valuable experiences and feedback emerged, highlighting the event's strengths and areas for growth.

The following section discusses the thematic analysis results received from the September 2024 semester.

13.4.2 Thematic Analysis Result

a. Positive Feedback

- **Appreciation for Effort and Presentation Skills:** SMEs admired students' effort, body language, communication skills, and enthusiasm during presentations.
  - *Example Comments: "Mostly all students presenting good in communication, body language, eye contact, and kesungguhan mereka berbahasa Melayu."*
- **Learning and Impact:** SMEs acknowledged the students' ability to effectively apply data analytics and machine learning concepts, finding their solutions meaningful and impactful.
  - *Example Comments: "It truly makes this assignment fruitful knowing that I am able to make an impact to the SMEs."*
- **Event Success:** Comments highlighted the event's overall success and educational value for students and SMEs.
  - *Example Comments: "Great event, it was nice to meet the SMEs."*

b. Challenges Encountered

- **Data Quality Issues:** Many participants noted limitations due to the SMEs' inadequate or insufficiently rich datasets, affecting the depth of analysis and accuracy.

  - *Example Comments: "One challenge we faced was the dataset provided by the SME. It wasn't very rich in features."*
- **Nervousness and Presentation Challenges:** Some students experienced nervousness during their presentations but viewed it as a learning opportunity.
  - *Example Comments: "I felt a bit nervous during the presentation, especially since it had been a long time since I had spoken."*

c. **Learning Opportunities**

- **Real-World Applications:** The experience was recognized as a valuable opportunity for students to understand the practical applications of machine learning and data analytics.
  - *Example Comments: "It gave us a clearer picture of how machine learning algorithms are applied in real-world scenarios."*
- **Adapting to Constraints:** Students gained insights into working with real-world data limitations and constraints, improving their problem-solving skills.
  - *Example Comments: "It was a valuable lesson in adapting to real-world constraints and finding ways to work with what's available."*

d. **Acknowledgments and Gratitude**

- **Recognition of Support:** Many comments expressed gratitude toward teachers, SMEs, and other facilitators for making the project and event possible.
  - *Example Comments: "Big thanks to our teacher and the SME owners for giving us this opportunity."*

This thematic result can be narrated to provide a deeper, more cohesive understanding of the students' experiences, challenges, and achievements throughout their engagement with SMEs, highlighting key insights, feedback, and learning outcomes that emerged from the project.

13.4.3 Positive Feedback and Impact

The overall sentiment from SMEs was overwhelmingly positive. They expressed genuine appreciation for the students' efforts, enthusiasm, and professionalism during their presentations. The students' strong communication skills, confident body language, and earnest attempts to engage in Bahasa Melayu left a lasting impression. One SME shared, "Mostly all students presenting well in communication, body language, eye contact, and kesungguhan mereka berbahasa Melayu."

Beyond presentation skills, SMEs acknowledged the students' ability to apply data analytics and machine learning concepts in practical and

TABLE 13.2
Thematic Analysis Summary

Theme	Positive Outcomes	Challenges
Student Skills	Improved presentation, teamwork, problem-solving	Nervousness in live presentations
SME Benefits	New data practices, business insights	Data quality limitations

impactful ways. This hands-on approach resonated with the SMEs, reinforcing the real-world value of the students' work. A student reflected, "It truly makes this assignment fruitful knowing that I am able to make an impact to the SMEs." The event was also recognized as a success, with participants describing it as meaningful and educational. One comment stated, "Great event, it was nice to meet the SMEs."

Feedback from students, SMEs, and lecturers was analyzed using thematic analysis. Key positive outcomes were improved communication, professional presentation, and confidence. SMEs valued the relevance and practicality of student solutions. Challenges included poor data quality and student nervousness, which were reframed as learning opportunities. Table 13.2 summarizes the themes identified.

13.5 Conclusion

The collaborative initiative undertaken by the DISS Impact Lab in partnership with the School of Computer Science has exemplified the transformative potential of aligning academic learning with real-world applications. By embedding data analytics and machine learning techniques into solutions tailored for SMEs, this project successfully merged theoretical knowledge with practical industry experience. Students were afforded the opportunity to engage directly with authentic business challenges, developing critical competencies in data preprocessing, feature engineering, model development, and data-driven decision-making. Through structured modules, close mentorship, and sustained collaboration with industry stakeholders, they learned to convert complex datasets into actionable business strategies.

Importantly, the project underscored the value of bridging the gap between technical expertise and societal needs. This alignment nurtured a new generation of data-literate problem solvers who are equipped to contribute meaningfully to Malaysia's growing digital economy. The use of thematic analysis to evaluate feedback from students, SME owners, lecturers, and faculty members further demonstrated the project's commitment to continuous improvement and stakeholder-centered design. The insights obtained informed the identification of pedagogical strengths, areas for refinement, and avenues for expanding industry partnerships in future iterations of the module.

The transition of the data analytics and machine learning module from a conventional, theory-heavy structure to a purpose-led, impact-driven learning model marks a significant evolution in data science education. By embedding purpose-led learning principles into a technically rigorous module, students experienced how data analytics and machine learning can serve not only as computational tools but as enablers of meaningful, socially relevant impact. Beyond enhancing students' technical proficiencies, the module cultivated essential soft skills, including communication, problem-solving, adaptability, and stakeholder engagement. Students were exposed to the inherent complexities, inconsistencies, and imperfections of real-world business data, enabling them to navigate the challenges of transforming raw information into meaningful insights. This experience effectively bridged the long-standing divide between theoretical instruction and authentic application.

Furthermore, the collaborative nature of the initiative produced tangible benefits for participating SMEs. Many gained a newfound appreciation for the strategic value of their operational data, leveraging the students' analyses to inform business forecasting, operational optimization, and data-driven decision-making. This dual impact, strengthening student learning while empowering local enterprises, demonstrates the efficacy of purpose-led education as a mechanism for fostering sustainable, community-centered outcomes.

Aligned with the broader objectives of the United Nations Sustainable Development Goals (SDGs), particularly SDG 8 (Decent Work and Economic Growth) and SDG 9 (Industry, Innovation, and Infrastructure), this model showcases how academic institutions can advance innovation, stimulate economic development, and prepare students to become agile, socially responsible professionals in an increasingly data-driven world. As the initiative continues to evolve, it is well positioned to scale its impact and serve as a replicable blueprint for academic and industry collaborations seeking to leverage emerging technologies for the collective benefit of society.

Acknowledgment

Sincere appreciation to all the individuals and organizations whose contributions made this research initiative possible. Foremost, we are deeply grateful to the participating small and medium-sized enterprises (SMEs) for their invaluable collaboration, openness, and willingness to share their data and operational insights. This project would not have been achievable without their trust and active engagement throughout the process. This project also acknowledges the dedicated efforts of the students who undertook the data analysis components as part of their coursework. Their commitment, creativity, and analytical proficiency were instrumental in generating meaningful solutions for the SMEs and fulfilling the objectives of this study. In addition, we express our heartfelt thanks to the Digital Innovation & Smart Society (DISS) Impact Lab Office for its continuous guidance and logistical support, particularly in fostering partnerships and ensuring the smooth coordination of activities across stakeholders. This project was supported and funded by the Impact Lab Office under the SEED Grant, whose generous backing enabled the successful design, implementation, and dissemination of this initiative.

References

Chernyshov, O., Vidrashko, V., & Pasichnyi, I. (2024). Developing marketing opportunities for small business enterprises in modern conditions. *Problems of a Systemic Approach to the Economy Enterprises Journal*, 3(96). https://doi.org/10.32782/2520-2200/2024-3-11

Dunaway, M. (2017). Collaboration in a data analytics curricula: An active learning approach. In *23rd Americas Conference on Information Systems*, Boston.

Enoch, O., Alonge, O., Faith, D., Olakunle, B., & Alao. (2024). Utilizing advanced data analytics to boost revenue growth and operational efficiency in technology firms. *International Journal of Frontiers in Science and Technology Research*. https://doi.org/10.53294/ijfstr.2024.7.2.0056

Erlinda, N., Yunus, E., Ernawati, E., Nuraini, E., & Yuniarti, K. (2023). Preserving heritage of humanity: A systematic study of the pandemic impacts and countermeasures of the SMEs. *Administrative Sciences*. https://doi.org/10.3390/admsci13020065

Fletcher-Brown, J., Knibbs, K., & Middleton, K. (2015). Developing "employagility": The 3Es case for live-client learning. *Higher Education, Skills and Work-Based Learning*, 5(2), 181–195.

Goh, S. H., & Zhang, X. (2015). Incorporating experiential learning into big data analytic classes. In *21st Americas Conference on Information Systems*. Puerto Rico.

Kim, E., Wiese, L., Will, H., Magana, A. J., & Jun, M. (2023). An experiential learning approach to industrial IoT implementation of smart manufacturing through coursework and university-industry partnerships. *Journal of Engineering Technology*, 40(2).

Pan, G., Shankaraman, V., Seow, P. S., & Tan, G. H. (2016). Designing an accounting analytics course using experiential learning approach. In *Proceedings of the AFAANZ Conference 2016: 3–5 July* (pp. 1–24). Gold Coast, Queensland, Australia.

Venkatraman, S., Benli, F., Wei, Y., & Wahr, F. (2022). Smart classroom teaching strategy to enhance higher order thinking skills (HOTS)—An agile approach for education 4.0. *Future Internet*, 14(9), 255.

Venkatraman, S., Overmars, A., & Wahr, F. (2019). Visualization and experiential learning of mathematics for data analytics. *Computation*, 7(3), 37.
Willetts, M., Atkins, A. S., & Stanier, C. (2021). Teaching and learning case study on social media analytics for small and medium-sized enterprises. In *ICERI2021 Proceedings* (pp. 3158–3167). IATED.
Wilson, E. J., McCabe, C., & Smith, R. S. (2018). Curriculum innovation for marketing analytics. *Marketing Education Review*, 28(1), 52–66.
Zhang, S., & Scribner, L. L. (2024). Would you rather . . . a simulation or a client-based project? A case study of experiential learning methods in digital marketing analytics courses. *Journal of Marketing Education*, 46(3), 258–275.

14

Inclusive Education through AI: Translating Speech-to-Sign Language for Deaf and Mute Learners in Online Platforms Using Generative Adversarial Network

Murugan Thangiah, Chockalingam Aravind Vaithilingam, Manee Sangaran Diagarajan, Thimmareddy Sharat Chandra Reddy, Gajjala Hrithvik Reddy, and Muhammad Khujaev

14.1 Introduction: Overview of Accessibility in Education

Even though millions of deaf and mute children have the fundamental right to an education, they confront substantial obstacles in their ability to participate fully in both traditional and online classroom settings. Equal access to learning resources for these kids is becoming increasingly important as global educational institutions move toward digital platforms. Over 430 million individuals worldwide—more than 5% of the total population—have debilitating hearing loss, and many of them rely on sign language as a form of communication, according to the World Health Organization (2021).

Inclusive education is crucial for deaf and mute students as it helps overcome obstacles in communication, socializing, and academic success (Karampidis et al., 2021). These students frequently encounter distinct obstacles that may limit their complete engagement in conventional classroom environments. Therefore, it is crucial to create an inclusive educational setting for their academic and social growth. Likewise, the shift to digital learning has become more prevalent, particularly following the global outbreak of COVID-19, which compelled schools everywhere to implement online teaching methods. Online platforms such as Zoom, Microsoft Teams, and Webex present difficulties as well as possibilities for deaf and mute students (Li, 2022). Although these platforms may assist in closing the accessibility gap, they frequently do not offer the inclusive experience necessary for the academic success and social integration of students with hearing and speech impairments.

The use of online platforms such as Zoom and Teams for education has greatly increased learning access for students with different needs, including

DOI: 10.1201/9781003633433-14

those who are deaf and mute. These platforms offer the option to participate in classes from anywhere, minimizing obstacles like distance and traditional classroom setups (Karampidis et al., 2021). Nevertheless, access to online education for deaf and mute students involves more than just logging into a virtual classroom. Inclusive design and suitable accommodations are necessary to ensure that these students can actively participate in discussions, engage with the content, and complete coursework on an equal level with their peers who can hear (Kompara et al., 2021).

Even though online platforms have the potential to improve accessibility, deaf and mute students still encounter substantial obstacles in virtual learning settings. A major problem is the absence of immediate communication assistance, making it challenging for these students to participate in class discussions or ask questions during lectures (Kompara et al., 2021). Numerous online platforms lack specific built-in features for sign language interpretation or closed captioning, leading educators to depend on third-party applications or services that may not be fully incorporated. Live captioning, although offered on certain platforms, is frequently incorrect or delayed, posing challenges for deaf students trying to keep up with rapid lectures or conversations (Arfé et al., 2020). Furthermore, subtitles might not convey the intricacies of sophisticated educational terminology, resulting in misconceptions or gaps in understanding. For students who are unable to speak, participating in online conversations can be just as difficult, since they might have to depend on written chat options that are typically less prioritized compared to spoken interaction.

The blending of education and technology shows potential solutions to these accessibility obstacles. Sophisticated machine learning technologies, specifically in natural language processing (NLP) and sign language generation, could possibly overcome obstacles and offer immediate solutions. Generative adversarial networks (GANs) lead the way in this innovation by providing a sophisticated approach to transforming natural language input into a visual sign language representation (Camgoz et al., 2020; Stoll et al., 2020).

In recent years, the combination of NLP and sign language technologies has become increasingly popular as there is a greater demand for inclusive education systems (Bharati et al., 2019; Coy et al., 2024). The World Health Organization reports that more than 466 million individuals globally suffer from disabling hearing loss, with a significant number of them being deaf or mute. Both physical and digital education systems frequently do not support this community. Utilizing GANs to create an artificial intelligence (AI) system that transforms spoken language into sign language could revolutionize online education for students with hearing and speech impairments (Kanakanti, 2024; Creswell et al., 2018).

Deaf students encounter many obstacles in traditional and digital educational settings due to the fact that these settings are mainly created for those who can hear (Aljedaani et al., 2023). Although video-based sign language interpreters and captions offer assistance (Petronio & Stuntz, 2019), they are inadequate in completely addressing the educational requirements of deaf and mute students. In online education environments, this disparity becomes particularly evident, with a substantial increase in popularity attributable to the COVID-19 pandemic (Alshawabkeh et al., 2021; Ferri et al., 2020). Researchers are starting to investigate how advanced technologies such as GANs (Goodfellow et al., 2020) can close this divide by producing sign language avatars in real time from natural language inputs. These solutions can integrate sign language interpretation smoothly into online learning platforms, ensuring that deaf and mute students have equal access to educational opportunities as hearing students.

The primary aim of this discussion is to investigate the deployment of a natural language–to–sign language conversion tool utilizing GANs within online platforms such as Zoom, Microsoft Teams, Webex, and comparable educational technologies, with the goal of revolutionizing the educational experience for the students who are deaf or mute.

14.2 Challenges Faced by Deaf and Mute Students in Education

Deaf and mute students encounter major obstacles in conventional educational settings where communication is mainly done through spoken words. These obstacles prevent them from fully participating in the classroom, restricting their ability to access information, communicate with teachers, and work together with fellow students. The lack of sufficient support systems, such as sign language interpreters or real-time captioning, worsens these problems even more. Moreover, numerous teachers lack the proper training to address the unique requirements of deaf and mute students, hindering the attainment of inclusive education. Consequently, students frequently face challenges in grasping course material, engaging in discussions, and proving their understanding in assessments, resulting in feelings of loneliness and lack of interest.

Farooq et al. (2021) have provided an in-depth comparative analysis of various existing approaches to natural language–to–sign language translation systems, and their efficiency is given in Table 14.1.

Among the various semantic translation models, such as ViSiCAST and TESSA (Bangham et al., 2000; Elliott et al., 2000), TEAM (Zhang et al., 2020), ZARDOZ (Tripathi & Nandi, 2015), and ASL Workbench (d'Armond & Speers, 2002), direct machine translation techniques are not commonly utilized because they fail to adequately preserve the semantics of the original sentences during translation. As a result, these techniques are limited to specific domains. Conversely, transfer-based machine translation is a more advantageous option, as it offers greater generalizability and extensibility

TABLE 14.1

A Comparison of Natural-to-Sign-Language Translation Systems

S.No	Project	Language	Approach	Domain/ Data Set	Output Type	Nonmanual Feature	Accuracy
1.	ViSiCAST/ TESSA Bangham et al. (2000), Elliott et al. (2000)	Speech to BSL	Direct translation	Post-office encounters	Pre-recorded videos	Yes (as it used pre-recorded videos)	61% complete phrases and 81% for sign units
2.	TEAM Zhang et al. (2020)	ASL	Synchronous Tree Adjoining Grammar (STAG)	Syntactic transfer based on rules	Animated character	No	Not available
3.	ZARDOZ Tripathi and Nandi (2015)	ASL	Transliteration	Some basic sentences	Spatial dependency	N/A	Not available
4.	ASL Workbench d'Armond and Speers (2002)	ASL	Lexical Functional Grammar	Rule based	Animated character	No	Not available
5.	eSign ESIGN Project (2020)	BSL and DGS	Rule based	Government official websites	Virtual avatar	To an extent	Not provided
6.	INGIT Veale et al. (1998)	ISL	Grammar	Railway ticketing	Virtual human	To an extent	In-house testing
7.	SASL (follows TEAM) Hutchinson (2012)	South African SL	STAG	Police/ Hospital	Avatar	No	Not provided
8.	eSign-3D Russell et al. (2009)	LSE	Statistical and rule based	5000 sentences dialogues (Driving license)	3D Avatar	To an extent	BLEU Score (rule based): 0.57; Statistical: 0.49
9.	ASL-Eng Cate and Hussain (2017)	ASL	Deep learning BERT (generative model)	~ 600 sentences from lifeprint.com	Text to text	N/A	BLEU 0.18
10.	DGS-German Hanke et al. (2010)	DGS	NMT	Weather-forecast videos	Video to text	No	BLEU 0.14

(Farooq et al., 2021)

through the application of linking (transfer) rules. Unlike direct translation methods, this approach allows for various mappings and operations, such as the interchange of subjects and objects and the removal of articles, which facilitate the handling of languages with differing sentence structures and word orders. The flexibility and extensibility of transfer-based systems enable the effortless integration of additional rules or the refinement of existing ones, ultimately improving translation accuracy.

The eSign-3D statistical model (Russell et al., 2009) heavily relies on the sample data and prioritizes sentences and words that occur frequently in the dataset. Table 14.1 indicates that even with a limited dataset, statistical methods do not perform well and produce less accurate translations than semantic methods.

The information presented in Table 14.1 indicates that there have been limited neural translation approaches such as ASL-Eng (Cate & Hussain, 2017) and DGS-German (Hanke et al., 2010) developed for translating natural language to sign language. Among these techniques, those that utilize deep learning frameworks for natural-to-sign language translation primarily depend on transfer learning or generative modeling. This approach involves modifying existing models that were trained for similar tasks, such as translating between different natural languages. Additionally, similar to statistical models, these methods also need large amounts of data to achieve optimal outcomes. The comparison in Table 14.1 makes it clear that neural machine translation methods have similarly low accuracy based on their BLEU scores.

The in-depth analysis outlined earlier exposes the main constraints in natural-language-to-machine-translation systems. Many semantic approaches are tailored to specific domains and cannot be applied universally across all domains. There is a lack of large and general datasets that could aid in developing more precise statistical or neural machine translation models for translating from spoken language to sign language. All translation systems, regardless of type, have very low accuracy and require improvement.

Each of the above methods has its unique advantages and disadvantages. Although sign language interpreters and human-generated captions offer excellent accuracy, they may not always be practical due to cost and availability constraints. Automated systems like automatic speech recognition (ASR) and AI-powered speech-to-sign language platforms provide scalable solutions, but additional improvements are needed to achieve high levels of accuracy and dependability.

This research study investigates the advancement of live sign language translation systems using GANs, a form of generative AI. The study examines the system structure, which consists of the NLP component for text analysis and conversion into glosses, and the gesture generation module that uses GANs to produce authentic sign language gestures. The primary goal is to improve access to education for students who use sign language in order to bridge the communication divide.

14.2.1 Educational Barriers in Traditional Classroom Settings

Deaf and mute students encounter distinct obstacles in academic settings that heavily depend on verbal interactions (Abou-Abdallah & Lamyman, 2021). In traditional classrooms, students often feel disconnected from peers and educators due to the lack of real-time sign language interpreters. While American sign language (ASL) and other national sign languages provide communication for many people, the availability of qualified interpreters is frequently restricted (He et al., 2023; Abou-Abdallah & Lamyman, 2021).

A study conducted by Marschark and Hauser (2012) emphasizes the unequal learning opportunities deaf students encounter in education. It reveals that, despite the presence of interpreters, the delay in translating spoken language into sign language often results in a limited grasp of the content. In addition, not all classes may have interpreters, and those who are available may lack the technical knowledge to accurately translate topics in STEM fields such as science, technology, engineering, and mathematics (Cawthon et al., 2021).

14.2.2 Accessibility Challenges in Online Learning Platforms

The challenges have become even more noticeable with the increase in online learning platforms. Zoom, Microsoft Teams, and Webex provide a range of communication features, yet few have built-in sign language translation capabilities. Instead, they depend on manual options like closed captioning or having a human interpreter in a separate video feed. Moreover, online portal such as learning management system (LMS) provide only text documents, audio and video files, and there is no support or feature available for the deaf and mute communities to translate those documents into sign language. Research conducted by Lisboa et al. (2020) and Ferri et al. (2020) reveals that these remedies are inadequate due to their lack of seamless integration and susceptibility to errors, especially in settings with technical terminology or fast-paced conversations. Deaf students can struggle to follow online classes because of delays in captions or interpretation problems (Foster, 2019). The outcome is a situation in which these students have to put in more effort to keep up with their hearing peers, resulting in higher cognitive strain and lower participation.

14.2.3 Psychological and Social Impacts of Inequality in Education

Beyond the tangible difficulties associated with communication, students who are deaf and mute frequently face significant social isolation within both in-person and online educational settings (Hintermair, 2019). The absence of immediate and precise sign language interpretation obstructs their capacity to interact effectively with educators and peers, which can adversely impact their self-esteem and enthusiasm for learning (Blunsum, 2024). Over time, these challenges may contribute to diminished academic performance and lower levels of educational achievement among this demographic (Grater-Nakamura, 2016). It is crucial to foster an accessible and inclusive educational atmosphere, as this is vital not only for academic success but also for the social and emotional health of students (Eden et al., 2024; Antia et al., 2011). The implementation of real-time, automated sign language technologies holds the promise of revolutionizing this situation by facilitating greater engagement for deaf and mute students in classroom discussions and collaborative activities (El-Alfy & Luqman, 2022).

14.2.4 The Need for Real-Time and Accurate Sign Language Interpretation

Real-time and highly accurate sign language translation is necessary for deaf and mute students to be fully engaged in online education (Mehta et al., 2020; Molina Roldán et al., 2021). This is particularly important in online learning situations, where information is shared rapidly and engagement with classmates and teachers is essential. At present, employing human sign language interpreters in online meetings is costly and challenging to execute (Kaur et al., 2024). Automated solutions are necessary to meet the growing demand for accessibility in the field of education.

14.3 Speech-to-Sign Language Translation: A Necessity in Modern Education

14.3.1 The Importance of Sign Language in Deaf Education

Many deaf and mute individuals rely on sign language as their main form of communication. Sign language is necessary for understanding and absorbing educational content (Pribanić, 2006). Nevertheless, there is still a lack of extensive systems that provide live speech-to-sign language translation, especially within educational environments, despite its significance. Studies by Marschark et al. (2006) and subsequently by Majoro (2021) have indicated that live sign language translation can greatly enhance educational results for hearing-impaired students. The research highlighted that when sign language is smoothly incorporated into the learning process, students can comprehend complicated ideas more effectively and engage in conversations.

14.3.2 Traditional Methods for Interpreting Spoken Language to Sign Language

Traditionally, the conversion of spoken language into sign language has depended on human interpreters who manually interpret spoken words into sign language. Although it works well, this approach has notable constraints. Leeson et al. (2014) found that human interpreters have the capacity to provide live translations for a specific number of students at once, and their availability is not constant. Moreover, interpreters may find it difficult to understand subject-specific terminology, resulting in errors in translation.

The classic method of adding an interpreter's feed to a video conference is a partial solution and lacks full integration into the online platform experience. Deaf students may find it challenging to keep up, as they need to frequently alternate between watching the interpreter's video and the lesson materials.

14.3.3 Limitations of Human Interpreters and Video-Based Solutions

Although human interpreters have been commonly used for years, they are still far from flawless. A study conducted by Farooq et al. (2021; Stinson et al., 2020) suggests that the expertise and knowledge of the interpreter greatly affect the quality of interpretation, leading to significant variations. Moreover, it can be difficult to synchronize communication between teachers and translators instantly, especially in rapid classroom settings where information is shared quickly and occasionally unexpectedly (Napier et al., 2018).

The traditional use of human interpreters has persisted for decades; however, they are constrained by bandwidth, lag, and synchronization problems (Aicha et al., 2023; Wei et al., 2021). Deaf students have to split their focus between the teacher and the interpreter, resulting in cognitive overload. This problem is especially noticeable in online learning settings, where quick switches between video and audio materials are prevalent.

14.3.4 Automated Solutions for Speech-to-Sign Language Translation

Recently, progress in AI and NLP has resulted in the creation of automated systems for translating speech-to-sign language (Wang et al., 2023). These systems seek to utilize machine learning algorithms to accurately translate spoken language into sign language in real time. One of the most encouraging strategies involves utilizing GANs, which are capable of producing lifelike sign language movements from spoken input (Camgoz et al., 2020). Through the utilization of both computer vision and deep learning methods, these technologies are able to interpret spoken language and create appropriate sign language movements instantly.

Automated systems can overcome the drawbacks of human interpreters and video-based solutions. One example is offering ongoing access to sign language interpretation around the clock, regardless of location or time. Moreover, these systems can be incorporated into online educational platforms like Zoom and Microsoft Teams, increasing accessibility for deaf and mute students in virtual classrooms. Nevertheless, automated systems are currently in the initial phases of advancement, and obstacles remain concerning the precision and authenticity of the produced sign language movements (Yin et al., 2021; Sandler & Lillo-Martin, 2021). The model used for developing speech-to-sign language translation is shown in Figure 14.1.

14.4 Machine Learning Techniques for Speech-to-Sign Language Translation

Converting natural language (oral communication) into sign language through GANs requires a systematic approach that consists of multiple stages (Alqahtani et al., 2021). This process combines elements of speech recognition, NLP, sophisticated deep learning algorithms, and computer vision strategies. Figure 14.1 presents a thorough description of each stage in this conversion process.

14.4.1 Speech-to-Text Conversion (Automatic Speech Recognition)

The first step in translating speech into sign language is to convert spoken words into text. This is achieved using ASR systems, which involve the following steps.

Audio Signal Processing: The speech input is broken down into small audio frames that capture the frequency- and time-based characteristics of the speech. Feature Extraction: Mel Frequency Cepstral Coefficients (MFCC) are among the commonly used features in a variety of applications, especially in voice signal processing such as speaker recognition, voice recognition, and gender identification (Abdul & Al-Talabani, 2022; Liang et al., 2013). The focus of the ASR model is on identifying four primary categories: isolated word, connected word, continuous speech, and spontaneous speech (Gaikwad et al., 2010; Adaloglou et al., 2021).

In terms of recognizing isolated words in speech, the speaker must pause briefly after each word, while connected speech recognition seeks to identify words that are not distinctly separated by pauses. However, a continuous speech recognition system does not need breaks between words because the speech flows without interruptions (Chapaneri, 2012). The speech recognition model handles nearly natural sounds. On the other hand, spontaneous speech can effectively process natural speech in multiple languages. A common obstacle in all models is the need to develop a universal and robust feature of the speech signal in order to attain high recognition accuracy.

Speech Recognition: The extracted features are processed using deep learning models, such as recurrent neural networks (RNNs) or transformers, to map the audio signals to the corresponding text. ASR systems use hidden Markov models (HMMs) for time-aligned predictions. HMMs are developed

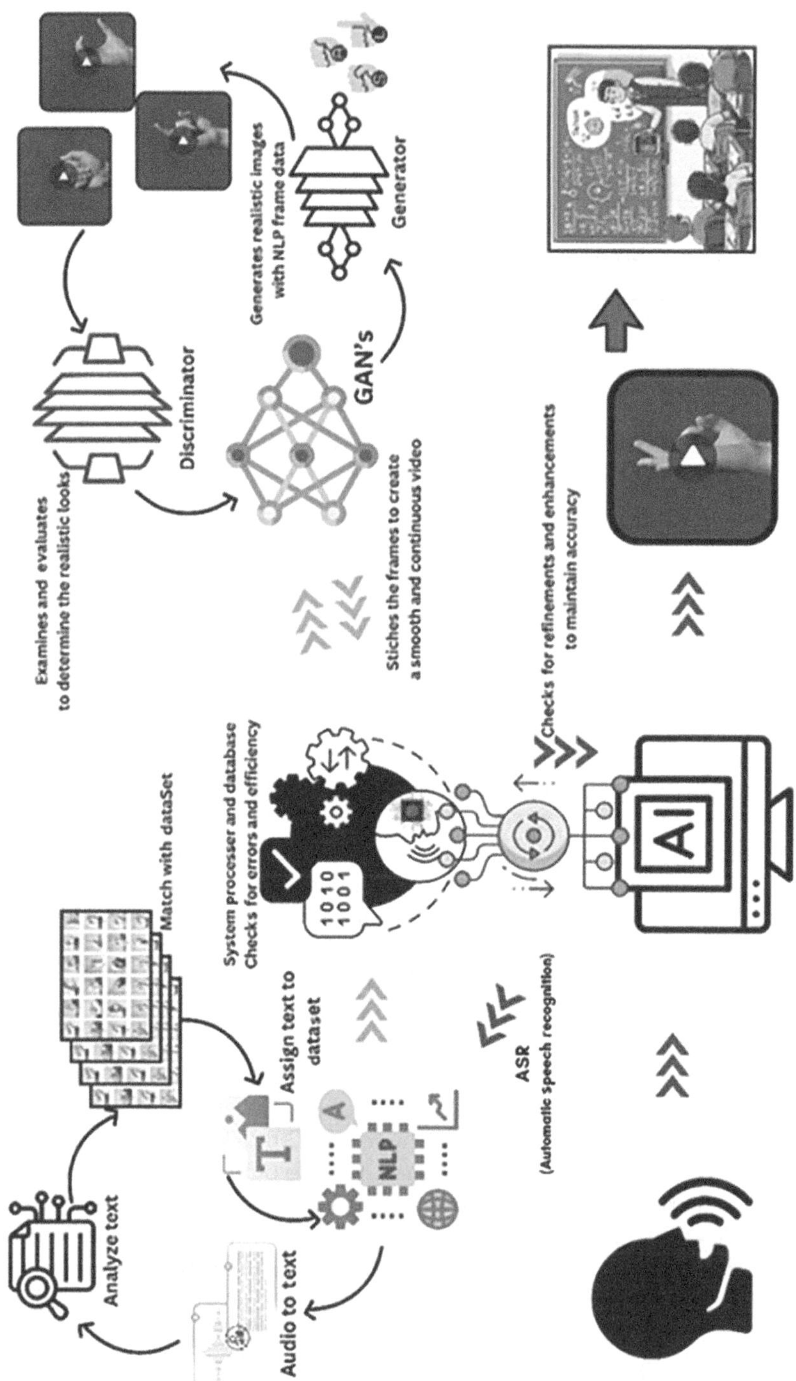

FIGURE 14.1
Speech-to-sign language model innovation.

through the utilization of a labeled dataset that comprises speech recordings paired with their respective transcriptions or phonetic annotations. The training phase focuses on estimating the parameters of the HMM, which includes determining the state transition probabilities. In essence, the state transition probability quantifies the likelihood of one phoneme occurring in conjunction with another. HMMs are frequently employed to capture the temporal dependencies inherent in speech signals. These models are characterized by several matrices that delineate their parameters. Subsequently, the generated text is directed for transformation via NLP. The output is a textual transcription of the spoken input.

14.4.2 Natural Language Processing for Understanding the Text

Once speech has been transcribed into written form, the system must interpret its linguistic meaning to accurately convert it into sign language. The fundamental aim of NLP is to allow machines to interpret human language in a way that resembles human understanding. This is accomplished through a series of defined steps.

Sentence parsing involves breaking down the text into grammatical parts like nouns, verbs, and adjectives. NLP models such as BERT (Devlin et al., 2019), GPT, and transformers analyze the text to understand its semantic content. The system must comprehend the context and meaning of words in relation to each other during semantic and syntactic analysis. For instance, the word "book" can have different meanings, such as written material or the act of reserving something, depending on the situation. Transformers excel at capturing subtleties because of their attention mechanisms, which assess the significance of every word in the sentence.

The processes of text normalization and simplification are particularly relevant when dealing with sign language, which is generally more concise than its spoken counterparts (Stoll et al., 2020). As a result, the system may need to modify the structure of sentences for improved clarity. Unnecessary words are removed to ensure that the core message is preserved. This process involves the creation of advanced algorithms and models that facilitate the analysis, comprehension, and generation of human language by computers in a meaningful and contextually relevant manner. NLP includes various techniques and tasks, such as tokenizing text, removing stop words, tagging parts of speech (POS), and reordering phrases.

Tokenization refers to the method of segmenting text into smaller components, known as tokens, within the field of NLP. These tokens may consist of words, phrases, or even single characters, depending on the specific requirements of the task. This process is fundamental in NLP, as it simplifies the intricacies of text, thereby facilitating a more effective understanding and analysis by computational systems. The removal of stop words is a fundamental aspect of text data preprocessing in the field of NLP. This step is critical for the cleaning and arrangement of text prior to subsequent analytical procedures. Stop words are typically defined as the frequently used words in a language that do not provide meaningful content to the overall interpretation of a sentence.

14.4.3 Pose Key Point Generation Using GAN

Once the appropriate sign language gestures have been identified, the system needs to create the physical gestures that represent those signs. This is where GANs come into play (Zhao et al., 2020).

14.4.4 Generator Network

In the GAN framework, the generator component receives text-based input or its encoded form and subsequently produces pose key points. These key points serve as coordinates that indicate the locations of the hands, arms, and body necessary for executing sign language gestures. The input features consist of the output derived from the NLP phase, which may be represented as a sentence in a latent-space format. The generator can utilize various deep learning architectures, such as RNNs, long short-term memory (LSTM) networks, or transformer models, all of which are adept at generating sequential data. In this context, the generated sequence comprises pose key points that illustrate the movements of a signer. Ultimately, the generator outputs a series of 2D or 3D coordinates that encapsulate the signer's body posture, hand configurations, facial expressions, and dynamic movements over time, thereby delineating the precise positions of essential body parts required for each sign.

14.4.5 Discriminator Network

In the context of GAN architecture, the discriminator network is tasked with evaluating the authenticity of generated pose key points. It performs a comparative analysis between the generated sequences and real sign language data, seeking to differentiate between authentic gestures and those that are synthetically produced. The discriminator incorporates both genuine sign language data, such as video recordings of real signers, and the sign language data produced by the generator. The discriminator assesses the generated key points for their smoothness, accuracy, and naturalness. If the generated gestures are found to be unrealistic, the discriminator communicates this feedback to the generator, necessitating enhancements in the next iteration of gesture generation. Through continuous adversarial training, the generator becomes increasingly proficient at generating realistic sign language gestures, while the discriminator enhances its ability to discern between real and synthetic gestures.

14.4.6 Pose Estimation or 3D Avatar Animation

After the discriminator has verified the pose key points, they are employed to construct a visual representation of sign language gestures. This can be executed through pose estimation approaches or by creating animations of 3D avatars.

14.4.6.1 Pose Estimation

The 2D/3D skeleton model leverages pose key points to animate a skeletal figure representing the poser. This technique is straightforward, as it involves connecting key points to create a wireframe or skeleton that captures the positions of the hands, arms, and facial expressions. This skeletal model can subsequently be used to animate sign language in a two-dimensional or three-dimensional environment. Pose estimation methodologies encompass the process of correlating key points of a pose to a model that emulates the actual movements of an individual engaged in signing. These models may be represented as basic two-dimensional skeletons or as intricate three-dimensional representations of the human figure.

14.4.6.2 3D Avatar Animation

In order to provide a more engaging experience, the pose key points may be applied to a 3D avatar. This avatar is crafted to imitate human movements instantaneously, faithfully reflecting the precise hand configurations, arm motions, and facial expressions required for the practice of sign language. Pose key points play a crucial role in directing the movements of the avatar's 3D mesh, which is an anatomical model of the human body. The mesh adapts its shape in response to these key points, allowing for the generation of seamless and lifelike gestures used in sign language.

14.4.7 Real-Time Display of Sign Language

Finally, the sign language gestures generated—either as 2D/3D pose estimations or via a 3D animated avatar—are made available to the end user. This capability can be seamlessly integrated into platforms such as video conferencing software (e.g., Zoom, Microsoft Teams, Webex), educational systems,

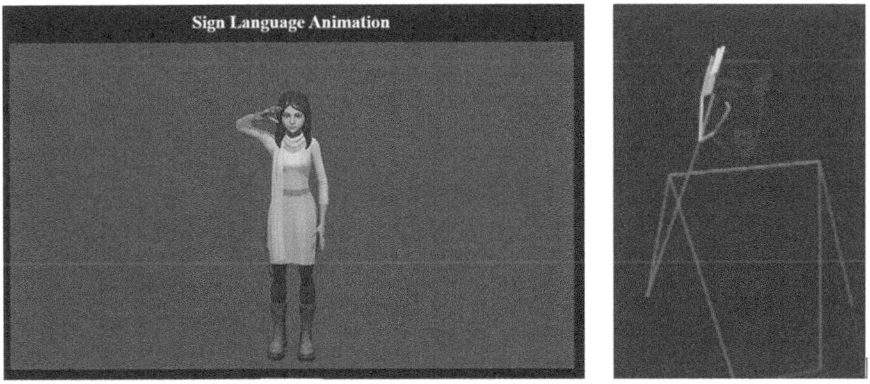

FIGURE 14.2
Sign language animation for the text "Hello."

or other communication mediums. The system operates in real time, facilitating immediate translation from speech or text into sign language, thus ensuring accessibility for deaf and hard-of-hearing individuals in various online contexts, as shown in Figure 14.2.

14.5 Adapting Machine Learning Models for Speech-to-Sign Language Translation on Online Platforms (Zoom, Teams, Webex)

Adapting machine learning models for translation is crucial when implementing a speech-to-sign language system on commonly used online platforms like Zoom, Microsoft Teams, and Webex. An example of converting text to speech using an online platform is shown in Figures 14.3 and 14.4. One of the main obstacles is making sure the system can function in real time, with minimal delay, in order to offer a smooth experience for hearing- and speech-impaired students.

Another significant challenge lies in the integration of the translation system within the platform's user interface. For instance, the system might present the generated sign language video in a separate window adjacent to the

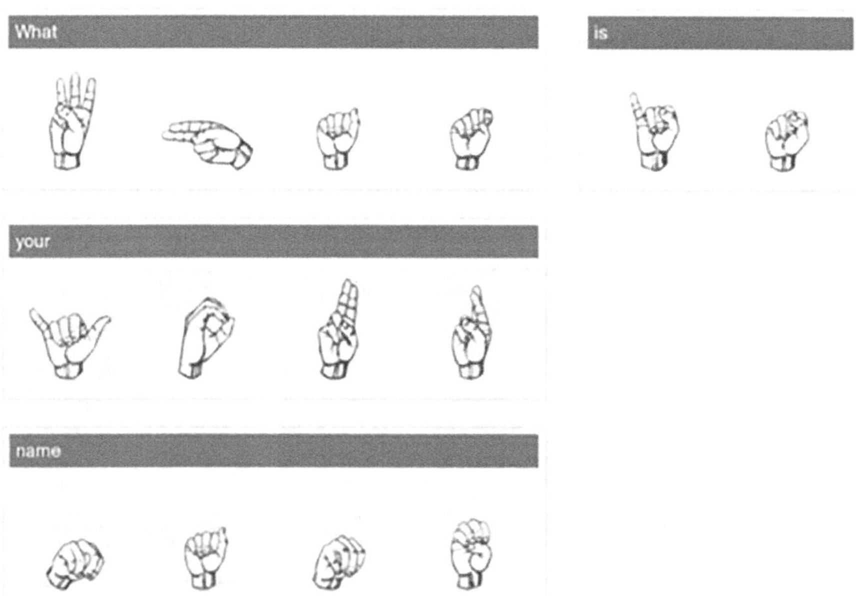

FIGURE 14.3
Speech-to-sign language: what is your name?

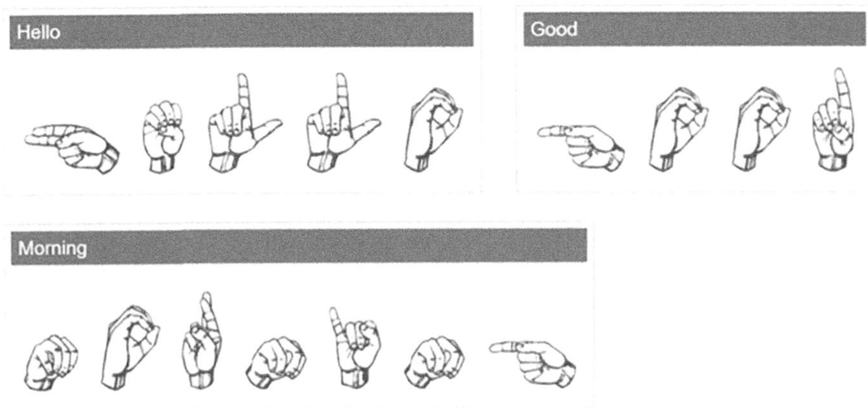

FIGURE 14.4
Speech-to-sign language: hello, good morning.

speaker's video feed, or it could superimpose the sign language gestures directly onto the speaker's video. To guarantee accessibility for all users, the system must be compatible with a diverse array of devices, including smartphones, tablets, and computers. This entails optimizing the machine learning models for devices with lower-power capabilities and ensuring functionality across varying network conditions.

14.5.1 Integrating Real-Time Speech-to-Sign Language Conversion in Virtual Classrooms

The development of real-time speech-to-sign language conversion technology is particularly advantageous in virtual classroom settings, where deaf and mute students often face challenges in following the class's rhythm (Foster, 2019). By providing immediate sign language translation, this system would facilitate the full participation of these students in discussions and foster engagement with their peers. A critical technical challenge in the deployment of real-time translation is the need for the system to quickly process spoken language inputs and produce sign language gestures in a timely manner. This challenge necessitates the optimization of GANs for real-time applications, alongside deploying NLP models capable of accurately interpreting spoken language instantaneously.

14.5.2 Challenges in Implementation: Bandwidth, Processing Power, and Latency

The development of a system that translates spoken language into sign language for online platforms faces numerous technical challenges (Ellis et al.,

2020). A key issue is ensuring that the system operates swiftly, as even a brief delay in translation can hinder the educational experience. Another challenge is effectively managing bandwidth and processing capabilities, especially in contexts where internet access is limited or devices are not robust. The system must be designed to perform efficiently in these situations without sacrificing translation accuracy or quality. To address these challenges, researchers have examined approaches such as model compression and distributed computing, which facilitate the system's operation across various devices and network environments. Additionally, the use of edge computing can help allocate some processing tasks to nearby devices, thereby reducing the need for high-speed internet connectivity.

14.5.3 User-Interface Design for Deaf and Mute Students

The user interface's design is an essential element in the functionality of any speech-to-sign language translation system. It is vital for deaf and mute students to have easy access to sign language translations, which can be presented through a separate video feed or as an overlay on the speaker's video. The system should also offer customization options, enabling users to adjust the size and position of the sign language video and select from different sign languages and dialects. Furthermore, the system should include visual cues to indicate when translation is active, as well as features that allow users to pause or rewind the translation if necessary.

14.6 Future Directions and Research Opportunities

Future research should prioritize the advancement of cutting-edge NLP models that can effectively interpret spoken language in real time. This is of particular significance in educational contexts, where the ability to accurately process a broad spectrum of vocabulary and subject matter is essential. Recent innovations in NLP, including models such as GPT-4 and T5, have revealed substantial promise in enhancing the accuracy of both speech recognition and language understanding. By embedding these models within speech-to-sign language translation frameworks, researchers can greatly enhance the quality of the resulting translations.

14.6.1 Enhancing Realism in GAN-Based Sign Language Generation

A significant avenue for future investigation lies in enhancing the authenticity of sign language gestures produced by GANs. Although existing systems are capable of generating gestures that are relatively lifelike, there remains considerable potential for refinement, especially in nuanced hand movements and facial expressions. Researchers are delving into methodologies such as multimodal GANs and video-based GANs to elevate the realism of these gestures (Saxena & Cao, 2021). Furthermore, the incorporation of pose estimation models may help ensure that the generated gestures are both anatomically precise and visually natural.

14.6.2 Multilingual Support for Global Education Platforms

As online education becomes increasingly global, there is a growing need for multilingual support in sign language translation systems. While most existing systems are designed to work with a single sign language, such as ASL, there are hundreds of different sign languages used around the world. Future research should focus on developing systems that can support multiple sign languages and dialects, allowing deaf and mute students from different regions to access the same educational resources. This will require the creation of large, annotated datasets of sign language gestures from different languages, as well as the development of machine learning models that can handle the complexity of multiple sign languages.

14.6.3 User Feedback and Iterative Development for Inclusive Solutions

A central issue in the development of automated sign language systems is the challenge of aligning the technology with user needs. Future research initiatives should emphasize the importance of gathering feedback from deaf and mute students, their teachers, and interpreters to identify potential areas for enhancement. By adopting an iterative development approach, researchers can systematically improve the system's accuracy and usability in light of user feedback. This methodology has been effectively utilized in other sectors of AI research, thereby facilitating the creation of a final product that is both practical and user-friendly.

While significant progress has been made in the development of speech-to-sign language translation systems, there are still many challenges that need to be addressed. Accuracy remains a key issue, as even small errors in translation can lead to misunderstandings. Real-time performance is also critical, particularly in educational settings where delays in translation can disrupt the flow of the lesson.

Additionally, most existing systems are designed to work with a single sign language, such as ASL. However, there are hundreds of different sign languages used around the world, and creating a system that can handle multiple sign languages is a significant challenge.

14.7 Conclusion

The advent of speech-to-sign language translation systems based on GANs offers transformative potential for the education of deaf and mute students. By facilitating real-time and accurate translations into sign language, these systems can greatly enhance educational access and help mitigate the accessibility disparities present in both traditional and online educational settings. Nevertheless, significant challenges persist, particularly in relation to accuracy, scalability, and user-interface design. Future research should concentrate on the development of more sophisticated NLP models, the enhancement of the realism of gestures produced by GANs, and the ability of the system to support a variety of sign languages. By addressing these challenges, researchers can establish a system that not only improves educational outcomes for deaf and mute students but also promotes a more inclusive and accessible educational environment for all learners.

Despite the considerable advancements achieved in the realm of speech-to-sign language translation systems, numerous challenges persist that require attention. One of the primary concerns is accuracy, as even minor inaccuracies in translation can result in significant misunderstandings. Furthermore, the necessity for real-time performance is paramount, especially in educational environments where translation delays can hinder the instructional process. Moreover, the majority of current systems are tailored to a specific sign language, such as ASL. Given the existence of hundreds of distinct sign languages globally, developing a system capable of accommodating multiple sign languages presents a formidable challenge.

References

Abdul, Z. K., & Al-Talabani, A. K. (2022). Mel frequency cepstral coefficient and its applications: A review. *IEEE Access*, *10*, 122136–122158.

Abou-Abdallah, M., & Lamyman, A. (2021). Exploring communication difficulties with deaf patients. *Clinical Medicine*, *21*(4), e380–e383.

Adaloglou, N., Eleftheriadis, S., & Karpouzis, K. (2021). A comprehensive study on sign language recognition methods and datasets. *Pattern Recognition*, *114*, 107873.

Aicha, Z., Asmae, Z., Hamdaoui, R., Soumia, Z., Salah-Eddine, K., Kharmoum, N., & Anouar, R. (2023). Real-time implementation of an AI-based virtual sign language recognition and interpretation system. In *International Conference on Advanced Intelligent Systems for Sustainable Development* (pp. 453–464). Cham: Springer Nature Switzerland.

Aljedaani, W., Krasniqi, R., Aljedaani, S., Mkaouer, M. W., Ludi, S., & Al-Raddah, K. (2023). If online learning works for you, what about deaf students? Emerging challenges of online learning for deaf and hearing-impaired students during

COVID-19: A literature review. *Universal Access in the Information Society*, *22*(3), 1027–1046.

Alqahtani, H., Kavakli-Thorne, M., & Kumar, G. (2021). Applications of generative adversarial networks (GANs): An updated review. *Archives of Computational Methods in Engineering*, *28*, 525–552.

Alshawabkeh, A. A., Woolsey, M. L., & Kharbat, F. F. (2021). Using online information technology for deaf students during COVID-19: A closer look from experience. *Heliyon*, *7*(5).

Antia, S. D., Jones, P., Luckner, J., Kreimeyer, K., & Reed, S. (2011). Social outcomes of students who are deaf and hard of hearing in general education classrooms. *Exceptional Children*, *77*(4), 489–504.

Arfé, B., Rossi, C., & Sicoli, S. (2020). The role of working memory in reading comprehension in deaf and hearing individuals. *Reading and Writing*, *33*(3), 699–721.

Bangham, J. A., Cox, S. J., Elliott, R., Glauert, J. R., Marshall, I., Rankov, S., & Wells, M. (2000). Virtual signing: Capture, animation, storage and transmission-an overview of the visicast project. In *IEE Seminar on Speech and Language Processing for Disabled and Elderly People (Ref. No. 2000/025)* (pp. 1–6). IET.

Blunsum, S. (2024). The mental health of deaf children: 'Inclusion' or 'equality of experience'? *Specialist Placement*, *15*. https://www.batod.org.uk/wp-content/uploads/2024/04/2420847od03revised.pdf#page=17

Camgoz, N. C., Koller, O., Hadfield, S., & Bowden, R. (2020). Sign language transformers: Joint end-to-end sign language recognition and translation. In *Proceedings of the IEEE/CVF Conference on Computer Vision and Pattern Recognition* (pp. 10023–10033). IEEE.

Cate, H., & Hussain, Z. (2017). Bidirectional American sign language to English translation. *arXiv preprint arXiv:1701.02795*.

Cawthon, S. W., Schoffstall, S. J., & Garberoglio, C. L. (2021). Barriers to participation in STEM education for deaf and hard-of-hearing students. *Journal of Deaf Studies and Deaf Education*, *26*(2), 135–151.

Chapaneri, S. V. (2012). Spoken digits recognition using weighted MFCC and improved features for dynamic time warping. *International Journal of Computer Applications*, *40*(3), 6–12.

Coy, A., Mohammed, P. S., & Skerrit, P. (2024). Inclusive deaf education enabled by artificial intelligence: The path to a solution. *International Journal of Artificial Intelligence in Education*, 1–39.

Creswell, A., White, T., Dumoulin, V., Arulkumaran, K., Sengupta, B., & Bharath, A. A. (2018). Generative adversarial networks: An overview. *IEEE Signal Processing Magazine*, *35*(1), 53–65.

d'Armond, L. S., & Speers, M. S. (2002). *Representation of American Sign Language for Machine Translation* (Doctoral dissertation, Georgetown University).

Devlin, J., Chang, M. W., Lee, K., & Toutanova, K. (2019). BERT: Pre-training of deep bidirectional transformers for language understanding. In *Proceedings of the 2019 Conference of the North American Chapter of the Association for Computational Linguistics* (pp. 4171–4186). Association for Computational Linguistics, Minneapolis, Minnesota.

Eden, C. A., Chisom, O. N., & Adeniyi, I. S. (2024). Cultural competence in education: Strategies for fostering inclusivity and diversity awareness. *International Journal of Applied Research in Social Sciences*, *6*(3), 383–392.

El-Alfy, E. S. M., & Luqman, H. (2022). A comprehensive survey and taxonomy of sign language research. *Engineering Applications of Artificial Intelligence, 114*, 105198.

Elliott, R., Glauert, J. R., Kennaway, J. R., & Marshall, I. (2000). The development of language processing support for the ViSiCAST project. In *Proceedings of the Fourth International ACM Conference on Assistive Technologies* (pp. 101–108). https://dl.acm.org/doi/pdf/10.1145/354324.354349

Ellis, R. J., Shaw, T., & Moores, D. F. (2020). Captioning challenges for deaf students in online learning environments. *Deafness & Education International, 22*(1), 43–54.

ESIGN project (2020). https://www.sign-lang.uni-hamburgde/esign/. Accessed 21 September 2024.

Farooq, U., Rahim, M. S. M., Sabir, N., Hussain, A., & Abid, A. (2021). Advances in machine translation for sign language: Approaches, limitations, and challenges. *Neural Computing and Applications, 33*(21), 14357–14399.

Ferri, F., Grifoni, P., & Guzzo, T. (2020). Online learning and emergency remote teaching: Opportunities and challenges in emergency situations. *Societies, 10*(4), 86.

Foster, S. (2019). Accessibility challenges and solutions for deaf and hard-of-hearing students in higher education. *International Journal of Disability, Development and Education, 66*(4), 469–487.

Gaikwad, S. K., Gawali, B. W., & Yannawar, P. (2010). A review on speech recognition technique. *International Journal of Computer Applications, 10*(3), 16–24.

Goodfellow, I., Pouget-Abadie, J., Mirza, M., Xu, B., Warde-Farley, D., Ozair, S., Courville, A., & Bengio, Y. (2014). Generative Adversarial Nets. *Proceedings of the 27th International Conference on Neural Information Processing Systems, 2*, 2672–2680.

Grater-Nakamura, C. (2016). *Experiences of Deaf and Hard of Hearing Students in Undergraduate and Graduate Students in Distance Education*. https://dt.athabascau.ca/jspui/bitstream/10791/188/3/C.Grater-Nakamura--Experiences_of_DHH_Students_in_University_DE.pdf

Hanke, T., König, L., Wagner, S., & Matthes, S. (2010). Dgs corpus & dicta-sign: The Hamburg studio setup. In *4th Workshop on the Representation and Processing of Sign Languages: Corpora and Sign Language Technologies (CSLT 2010)*, Valletta, Malta (Vol. 2, No. 6, p. 12).

He, Y., Seng, K. P., & Ang, L. M. (2023). Generative adversarial networks (GANs) for audio-visual speech recognition in artificial intelligence IoT. *Information, 14*, 575.

Hintermair, M. (2019). Social inclusion of deaf and hard-of-hearing students in mainstream education: The role of teacher attitudes. *Deafness & Education International*, 21(3), 131–146.

Hutchinson, J. (2012). *Literature Review: Analysis of Sign Language Notations for Parsing in Machine Translation of SASL*. Rhodes University.

Kanakanti, M. (2024). *A Multi Modal Approach to Speech-to-Sign Language Generation* (Doctoral dissertation, International Institute of Information Technology, Hyderabad).

Karampidis, K., Trigoni, A., & Papadourakis, G. (2021). Communication challenges in inclusive education faced by deaf and non-deaf people. *National Report Hellenic Mediterranean University, 12*.

Kaur, B., Chaudhary, A., Bano, S., Yashmita, Reddy, S. R. N., & Anand, R. (2024). Fostering inclusivity through effective communication: Real-time sign language to speech conversion system for the deaf and hard-of-hearing community. *Multimedia Tools and Applications, 83*(15), 45859–45880.

Kompara, M., Hölbl, M., & Welzer, T. (2021). *Communication Challenges in Inclusive Education Faced by Deaf and Non-deaf People*. University of Maribor.
Leeson, L., Wurm, S., & Vermeerbergen, M. (Eds.). (2014). *Signed Language Interpreting: Preparation, Practice and Performance*. Routledge.
Li, D. (2022). The shift to online classes during the COVID-19 pandemic: Benefits, challenges, and required improvements from the students' perspective. *Electronic Journal of E-Learning*, *20*(1), 1–18.
Liang, B., Iwnicki, S. D., & Zhao, Y. (2013). Application of power spectrum, cepstrum, higher order spectrum and neural network analyses for induction motor fault diagnosis. *Mechanical Systems and Signal Processing*, *39*(1–2), 342–360.
Lisboa, I., Barroso, J., & Rocha, T. (2020, November). Digital accessibility of online educational platforms: Identifying barriers for blind student's interaction. In *International Conference on Innovative Technologies and Learning* (pp. 409–418). Cham: Springer International Publishing.
Majoro, N. E. (2021). *Challenges of Using Sign Language Interpreting to Facilitate Teaching and Learning for Learners with Hearing Impairment* (Doctoral dissertation, National University of Lesotho).
Marschark, M., & Hauser, P. C. (2012). *How Deaf Children Learn: What Parents and Teachers Need to Know*. Oxford University Press.
Marschark, M., Leigh, G., Sapere, P., Burnham, D., Convertino, C., Stinson, M., . . . & Noble, W. (2006). Benefits of sign language interpreting and text alternatives for deaf students' classroom learning. *Journal of Deaf Studies and Deaf Education*, *11*(4), 421–437.
Mehta, A., Rathod, T., & Solanki, M. K. (2020). Evolution in automated translator for real time voice to sign language transformation for the deaf and dumb people. In *National Conference on Recent Trends in Electronics and Communication Engineering-2020* (p. 69–79). NCRT-ECE-2020. Publish World, India.
Molina Roldán, S., Marauri, J., Aubert, A., & Flecha, R. (2021). How inclusive interactive learning environments benefit students without special needs. *Frontiers in Psychology*, *12*, 661427.
Napier, J., Lloyd, K., Skinner, R., Turner, G. H., & Wheatley, M. (2018). Using video technology to engage deaf sign language users in survey research: An example from the 'Insign' project. *Translation & Interpreting: The International Journal of Translation and Interpreting Research*, *10*(2), 101–121.
Petronio, K., & Stuntz, C. (2019). Assessing the effectiveness of video-based sign language interpretation in education. *Journal of Applied Linguistics*, *14*(1), 32–45.
Pribanić, L. (2006). Sign language and deaf education: A new tradition. *Sign Language & Linguistics*, *9*(1–2), 233–254.
Russell, M., Kavanaugh, M., Master, J., Higgins, J., & Hoffmann, T. (2009). Computer-based signing accommodations: Comparing a recorded human with an avatar. *Journal of Applied Testing Technology*, *10*(3).
Sandler, W., & Lillo-Martin, D. (2021). Sign language and linguistic universals. *Annual Review of Linguistics*, *7*, 23–41.
Saxena, D., & Cao, J. (2021). Generative adversarial networks (GANs) challenges, solutions, and future directions. *ACM Computing Surveys (CSUR)*, *54*(3), 1–42.
Stinson, M., Liu, Y., & Stinson, K. (2020). Assessing the accessibility of online learning platforms for deaf students. *Technology, Pedagogy and Education*, *29*(2), 159–177.

Stoll, S., Camgoz, N. C., Hadfield, S., & Bowden, R. (2020). Text2Sign: Towards sign language production using neural machine translation and generative adversarial networks. *International Journal of Computer Vision, 128*(4), 891–908.

Tripathi, K., & Nandi, N. B. G. (2015). Continuous Indian sign language gesture recognition and sentence formation. *Procedia Computer Science, 54*, 523–531.

Veale, T., Conway, A., & Collins, B. (1998). The challenges of cross-modal translation: English-to-Sign-Language translation in the Zardoz system. *Machine Translation, 13*, 81–106.

Wang, L., Ni, J., Gao, H., Li, J., Chang, K. C., Fan, X., . . . & Yoo, C. (2023, July). Listen, decipher and sign: Toward unsupervised speech-to-sign language recognition. In *Findings of the Association for Computational Linguistics: ACL 2023* (pp. 6785–6800). Association for Computational Linguistics, Toronto, Canada.

Wei, X., Zhang, P., & Zhang, Z. (2021). Exploring video generative adversarial networks for sign language generation. *Pattern Recognition Letters, 144*, 23–29.

World Health Organization. (2021). *World Report on Hearing*. World Health Organization.

Yin, H., Wang, L., & Liu, G. (2021). Real-time speech-to-sign language translation using deep learning. *IEEE Transactions on Multimedia, 23*(5), 1438–1447.

Zhang, T., Yang, Y., Zeng, Y., & Zhao, Y. (2020). Cognitive template-clustering improved linemode for efficient multi-object pose estimation. *Cognitive Computation, 12*(4), 834–843.

Zhao, L., Zhang, Z., & Wu, J. (2020). Sign language synthesis with improved GANs and 3D human pose estimation. *IEEE Transactions on Multimedia, 22*(8), 2108–2120.

15

Empowering Innovation through a Generative Artificial Intelligence-Integrated Design Thinking Framework for Value-Driven Product Development

Chockalingam Aravind Vaithilingam and Manee Sangaran Diagarajan

15.1 Introduction: Background and Driving Forces

Technology's rapid development and the changing needs of the global market have put more pressure on startups and educational institutions to innovate. However, data shows that most innovations fail not because of technical shortcomings but because of strategic project management issues, a lack of defined business value, and an inability to integrate technology with human-centered approaches (Forbes & Statista, 2020). These disparities are especially noticeable in higher education institutions (IHLs), where early-stage entrepreneurs and students frequently do not have access to integrated frameworks that integrate technology, management, and design into a seamless educational process. Figure 15.1 shows the top reasons for the startups failing, with business value and project management skills, are key reasons behind the downfall.

To strike a balance between creativity and methodical execution, innovation-driven product development has come to rely increasingly on structured problem-solving and design frameworks. Design thinking (IDEO), the CDIO framework (conceive–design–implement–operate), TRIZ (theory of inventive problem-solving), and Blue Ocean Strategy are just a few of the methods that have emerged as parallel models for directing innovation processes over the past few decades. Although each framework offers distinct viewpoints—IDEO stresses human-centered design, CDIO links engineering education with practical application, TRIZ offers methodical creative principles, and Blue Ocean Strategy emphasizes market differentiation—these methods frequently function independently and lack a cohesive value proposition for comprehensive problem-solving. Parallel frameworks' (as in Figure 15.2) drawbacks emphasize the necessity of integration. According to earlier research, design thinking may not be sufficient to handle systemic

DOI: 10.1201/9781003633433-15

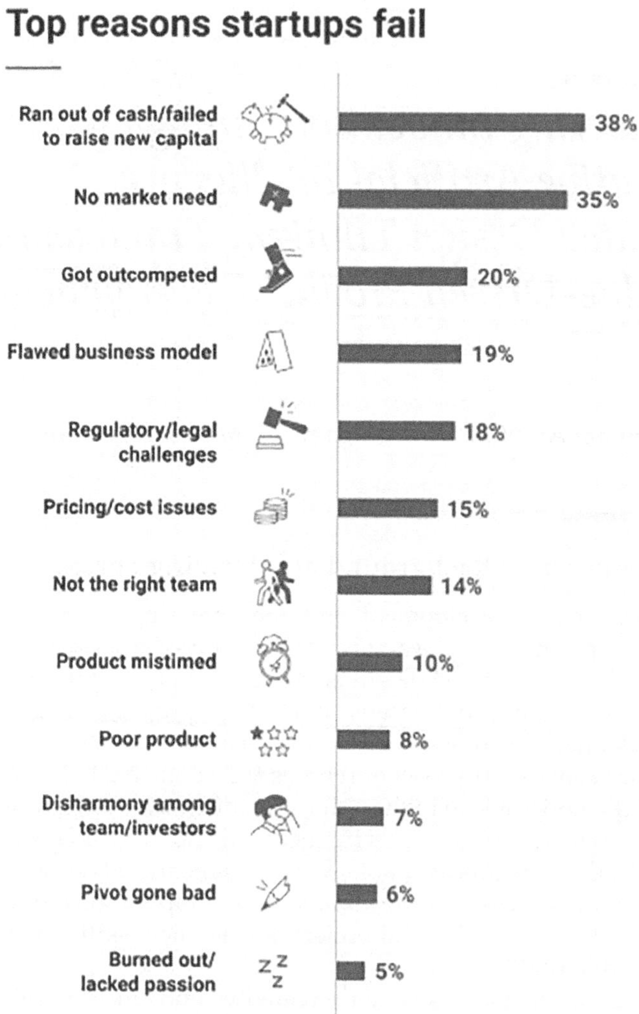

FIGURE 15.1
Top reasons for startup failure.

(Forbes & Statista, 2020).

technical complexity, even though it excels at empathy-driven ideation and prototyping (Brown, 2009; Liedtka, 2018). TRIZ, on the other hand, provides structured creative patterns but is less flexible with unclear user requirements (Altshuller, 1999). Although CDIO offers thorough engineering implementation pathways, user experience and creativity are not always given priority (Crawley et al., 2014). Likewise, Blue Ocean Strategy is excellent at repositioning the market, but it ignores iterative design cycles, which are essential for

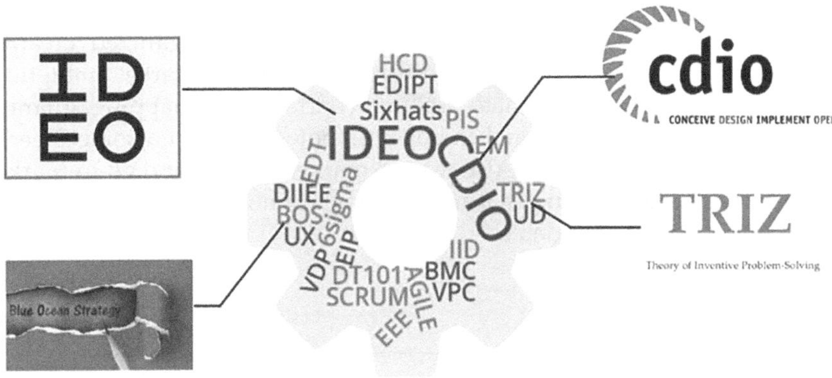

FIGURE 15.2
Parallel design thinking framework.

product validation (Kim & Mauborgne, 2005). The question of how to integrate innovation frameworks to offer both creative agility and methodical rigor for value-driven outcomes has been made urgent by this fragmentation.

A unifying framework that maintains the advantages of current approaches while overcoming their individual shortcomings is necessary due to the fragmented nature of innovative methodologies. The GenAI-integrated design thinking framework for value-driven product development is presented in this chapter. It positions GenAI as a connecting intelligence layer across established methodologies, such as the market differentiation of Blue Ocean Strategy, the human-centered design of IDEO, the engineering execution of CDIO, and the methodical creative problem-solving of TRIZ. The framework is based on the idea that innovation necessitates a synergistic combination of technical rigor, creativity, and market alignment. TRIZ offers methodically creative heuristics, CDIO offers structured implementation pathways, Blue Ocean Strategy grounds innovation in market relevance, and design thinking (IDEO) guarantees empathy and iteration. By facilitating real-time ideation, predictive insights, automated knowledge synthesis, and outcome simulation, GenAI enhances these components.

We present E-CODE (empowering creativity through an AI-integrated design thinking ecosystem), a next-generation framework that integrates design thinking and generative artificial intelligence (GenAI) and integrates go-to-market strategy, project management discipline, and business value orientation into the innovation process to close this gap. In contrast to the parallel frameworks, E-CODE views innovation as a comprehensive, value-driven process that links market adoption, technical viability, and user empathy along a single continuum. Beyond IDEO, E-CODE is a novel method of design thinking that incorporates business value metrics and GenAI for scaled ideation. With AI-enabled project management, resource optimization, and market readiness analysis, it builds on CDIO's strengths. Additionally, E-CODE surpasses TRIZ, which offers organized creative solutions but is not flexible enough to adjust to user and market ambiguity. E-CODE uses GenAI to automate problem-contradiction mapping, guaranteeing that solutions stay rooted in business potential and customer needs. Finally, E-CODE incorporates AI-powered market sensing and go-to-market (GTM) tactics, guaranteeing that innovations are not only unique but also implementable and expandable.

15.2 Artificial Intelligence in Innovation and Education

A crucial approach for dealing with difficult, human-centered problems is design thinking (Brown, 2009). It places a strong emphasis on iterative cycles of ideation, empathy, prototyping, and testing to align user needs with creative problem-solving. But according to Osterwalder and Pigneur (2010), DT by itself frequently fails to convert creativity into scalable business models. Design outcomes are better aligned with market demands when value proposition frameworks like the Business Model Canvas (BMC) and the Value Proposition Canvas (VPC) are integrated. Recently, GenAI has shown promise in revolutionizing creativity, ideation, and decision-making (Dwivedi et al., 2023). Through idea generation, decision-making insights, and mentorship simulation, GenAI scaffolds learning in educational settings. GenAI can optimize solution development, improve divergent and convergent thinking cycles, and humanize the AI experience through adaptive learning interactions when combined with design thinking. From the standpoint of innovation, GenAI facilitates the design thinking cycle of convergence and divergence. AI tools allow for extensive exploration after a challenge has been defined, revealing solution spaces that might otherwise go undetected. In contrast to traditional search engines, GenAI fosters innovations at the interdisciplinary nexus by combining contextual reasoning, pattern recognition, and cross-domain analogy. Additionally, by assessing trade-offs, user reactions, and market viability prior to allocating resources, AI-assisted simulations and generative prototyping improve decision-making. This is a paradigm shift: innovation becomes more creative and faster, but it also becomes evidence-based and aligned with values.

GenAI has revolutionary potential for experiential learning in the field of education. Learners can participate in AI-augmented cocreation, in which the machine serves as both a collaborator and a reflective partner, as an alternative to static curricula. Research indicates that this kind of integration fosters the development of higher-order abilities like applied creativity, critical thinking, and flexibility (Luckin, 2023; Holmes et al., 2021). By giving

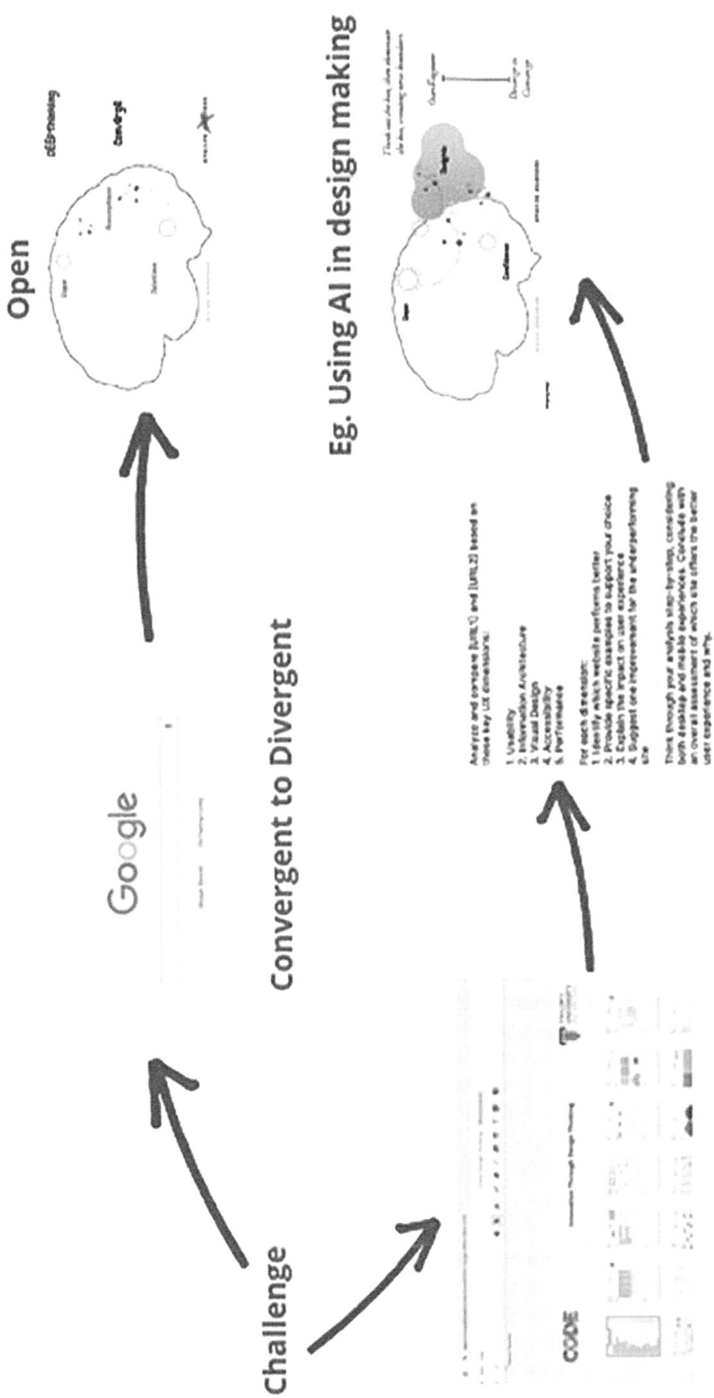

FIGURE 15.3
Use of unguided and guided virtual mentor in design thinking.

students the opportunity to test hypotheses in real time, experiment with design scenarios, and get immediate AI-generated insights, education moves toward preparing graduates as practitioners who can innovate as well as consumers of knowledge. The E-CODE framework views GenAI as a meta-layer of intelligence that combines design thinking with business value, project management, and GTM strategy, rather than as a substitute for human creativity or decision-making. In particular:

- Challenge Framing: By analyzing problem contexts, AI tools uncover hidden variables and reframe opportunities.
- Open Exploration: GenAI supports creativity beyond the limitations of human cognition by producing a variety of solution pathways.
- Decision Support: AI-powered assessment tools weigh options in terms of business viability, user appeal, and technical feasibility.
- Market Alignment: Innovations are scalable and positioned strategically thanks to real-time market sensing and adoption simulations.

This integration highlights a new paradigm in education and innovation, where innovators become value creators and learners become innovators. Organizations and academic institutions can work together to create ecosystems that generate technically viable, user-focused, and market-ready products and solutions by integrating GenAI into design thinking.

TABLE 15.1

AI Mapping and the Outcomes for Commercialization

E-CODE Stage	TRL Stage	AI Capabilities Applied	Expected Outcomes
Empathize (E) (Problem framing)	Pre-TRL	Natural language processing (market reports, reviews) Sentiment and trend analysis	Clearly framed challenge with a strong value proposition
Conceptualize (C) (Concept formulation)	TRL 2–3	Generative ideation (AI brainstorming), comparative design alternatives, pattern recognition across domains	Divergent solution pathways converging into a feasible concept
Organize (O) (Experimental proof of concept)	TRL 3	AI-assisted project planning, resource allocation optimization, generative design for technical configurations	Efficient project execution with aligned tools and technology
Deploy (D) (Proof of concept → MVP)	TRL 3–4	Simulation of user interactions, AI-driven feature prioritization, predictive performance analysis	Validated proof of concept and a refined MVP aligned with user needs
Execute (E) (Market launch readiness)	TRL 5+	AI-enabled competitor scanning, market adoption modeling, go-to-market scenario forecasting	Scalable product launch strategy with data-backed positioning

Design thinking, project management, and business value assessment are all integrated into the CODE Framework (Chockalingam et al., 2021). It uses 32 tools and 25 worksheets to help innovators from problem framing through minimum viable product (MVP) and proof of concept (POC). As a structured pedagogical tool that links innovation with sustainable results, CODE has been embraced by several IHLs and incubators. The integration of GenAI into the E-CODE framework enhances the capstone project process by embedding intelligence-driven tools at every stage of product development. Table 15.1 maps the role of AI capabilities to the respective TRLs and E-CODE stages (Empathize → Conceptualize → Organize → Deploy → Execute). Table 15.1 shows the steps of the TRL, a measure of progress toward commercialization, AI adoption, and the outcomes.

15.3 Methodology

The empowering creativity through AI-integrated design thinking ecosystem (E-CODE) was used in a capstone project setting for product development to illustrate the useful application of the suggested framework. The approach ensures that results flow methodically from ideation to market readiness by adhering to a structured process that is in line with TRLs. Every step incorporates AI, allowing students to improve decision-making, increase creativity, and expedite project management. Figure 15.4 shows the flowchart represented in the TRL approach, an important approach toward preparing the graduates for startups and entrepreneurship.

15.3.1 Empathize: Recognize the Value Proposition's Challenge (E)

Students start the process by choosing a major issue that has both societal and business implications. Natural language processing of industry reports, customer reviews, and market trend datasets is used to analyze problem contexts using AI-enabled tools. By doing this, purely theoretical issues are avoided and challenges are presented with distinct value propositions.

15.3.2 Conceptualize: From Needs to Concepts (C)

To address concept needs, student groups are formed at this stage and led through module-based engagement. GenAI is used to provide early-stage design alternatives, conduct cross-domain comparative analysis, and generate a variety of solution pathways. Divergent exploration is supported by AI-driven brainstorming, and the convergence of ideas into workable concepts is guided by embedded feasibility checks.

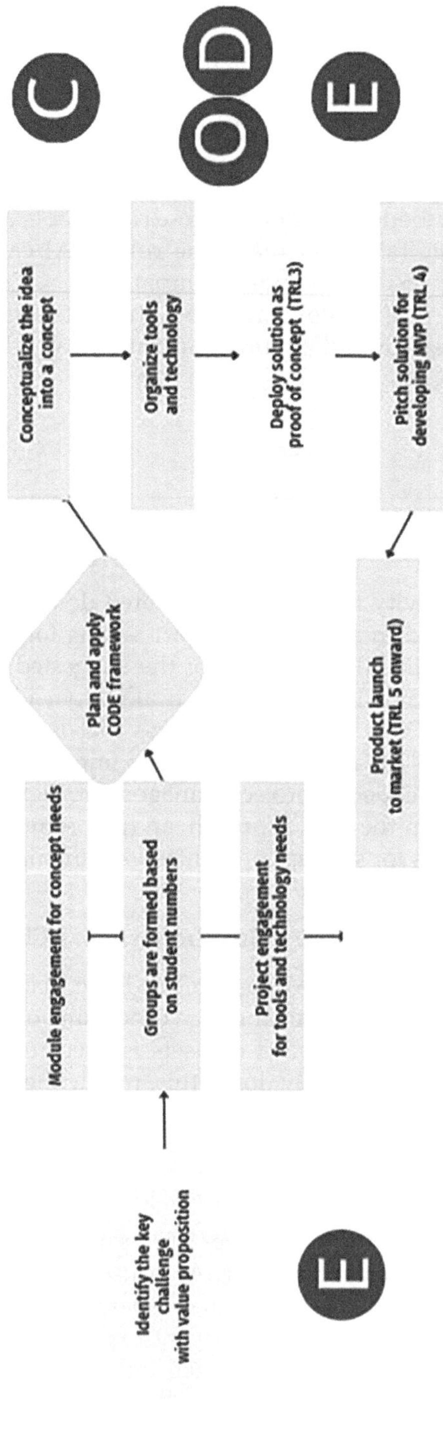

FIGURE 15.4
Use of unguided and guided virtual mentor in design thinking.

15.3.3 Align Technology and Tools (O)

Teams arrange the required tools, techniques, and technology stack after a concept has been chosen. Through the optimization of schedules, resource allocation, and risk prediction, AI supports project management. Furthermore, while AI-based knowledge systems recommend pertinent standards and best practices, generative design tools recommend technical configurations.

15.3.4 Deploy: MVP Development and Proof of Concept (D)

The selected idea is implemented as a proof of concept (TRL 3), in which technical performance and user interactions are simulated by AI models. After that, teams use AI to forecast adoption, prioritize features, and weigh trade-offs as they hone their solutions into a minimum viable product (TRL 4). Dashboards for decision support enable ongoing alignment with user expectations and business goals.

15.3.5 Execute: Launch and Market Readiness (E)

Lastly, verified solutions move closer to going on sale (TRL 5 onward). Here, competitor scanning, customer segmentation, and adoption modeling are provided by AI-driven GTM analysis. Teams use data-driven insights, scenario testing, and AI-generated market validation reports to support their product pitches. This guarantees that student inventions are positioned for impact and scalability in the real world.

Figure 15.5 shows the evaluation framework consisting of the four stages of the E-CODE for the capstone project and the outcomes presented during one of the sessions.

15.4 Key Findings

Through the capstone project, students were able to move from problem framing to market readiness by following an organized but flexible product development pathway. The findings of incorporating GenAI showed better learning outcomes progress, with the following as key features.

15.4.1 A Better Value Proposition and Problem Framing

Because AI-enabled dataset analysis (such as market reports, customer feedback, and trend analysis) revealed latent needs that had not been considered in previous cohorts, students showed increased clarity in defining challenges. By aligning solutions with societal and commercial relevance, this ensured that projects were firmly rooted in distinct value propositions.

(a)

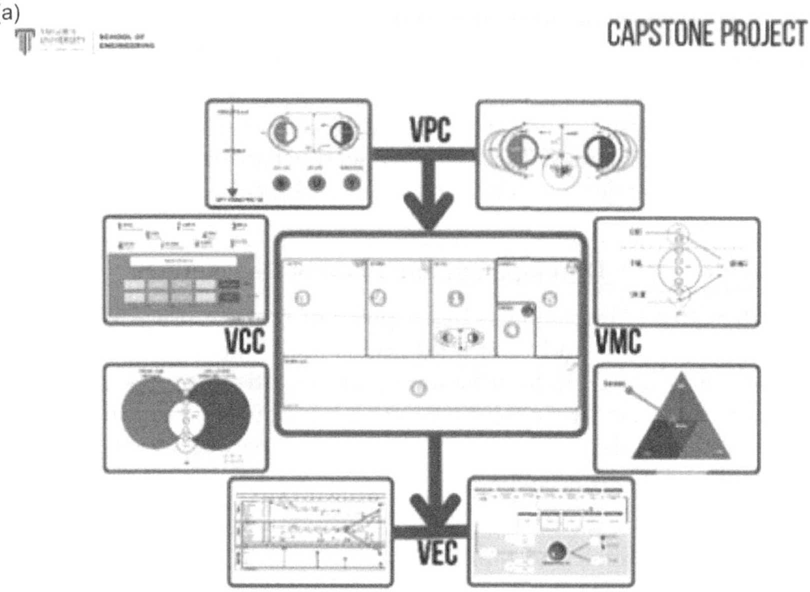

(b)

FIGURE 15.5
The evaluation framework of the E-CODE for the capstone project. (a) four stages of E-CODE evaluation (b) student preparing during the idea stage.

15.4.2 Improved Concept Development and Ideation

In contrast to conventional design thinking techniques, teams generated a greater range of solution alternatives through GenAI-powered brainstorming and comparative design generation. According to students, AI recommendations frequently brought fresh viewpoints from various fields, which inspired the development of more ambitious and imaginative concepts. Richer concept portfolios resulted, allowing for the methodical selection of workable ideas.

15.4.3 Effective Project Management and Implementation

Teams were able to efficiently manage tasks thanks to AI-supported project management tools that optimized timelines and resource allocation. Additionally, early risk identification was aided by predictive analytics. Students emphasized how this freed up more time for technical and creative problem-solving and less time for administrative coordination.

15.4.4 Quicker Deployment and Prototyping

AI-enabled simulations and automated design parameter evaluation sped up the deployment of proof of concept (TRL 3) and the creation of the MVP (TRL 4). To help teams match prototypes with user desirability and business viability, GenAI also assisted with feature prioritization. Redundancy was reduced, and technical rigor in solution development was enhanced by this iterative validation cycle.

15.4.5 Improved Strategic Thinking and Market Readiness

AI tools for market adoption modeling and competitor scanning gave students practical insights into the market positioning of their product at the Execute stage (TRL 5 onward). To ensure their inventions were both technically and financially feasible, this pushed teams to go beyond prototype development and toward strategic GTM planning.

Table 15.2 shows the comparison and demonstrates that intelligence-driven tools throughout the design and development cycle perform better than conventional methods. Students developed the capacity to critically assess solutions, effectively manage projects, and think strategically about innovation in real-world contexts, in addition to producing higher-quality product outcomes. According to the results, the E-CODE framework is a scalable model for value-driven product development in higher education since GenAI-enhanced design thinking closes the gap between academic learning and industry readiness.

TABLE 15.2

Comparison between Two Different Implementation Approaches

Dimension	Conventional Approach	AI-Integrated E-CODE Framework
Problem Framing	Often guided by supervisor suggestions, with limited exposure to real-world data.	AI-driven analysis of market trends, user feedback, and industry data ensures problem statements with strong value propositions.
Ideation	Dependent on group brainstorming; limited by student expertise.	GenAI generates divergent ideas and cross-domain analogies and supports creativity beyond human cognitive limits.
Project Management	Manual coordination, with delays due to inefficiencies and resource constraints.	AI-enabled planning optimizes timelines, resource allocation, and risk forecasting.
Prototyping	Iterative but slow; trial and error dominate design validation.	AI simulations and predictive analysis accelerate proof of concept (TRL 3) and MVP development (TRL 4).
Market Alignment	Minimal attention to GTM strategy; focus remains on the technical prototype.	AI-powered competitor scanning, adoption modeling, and GTM integration prepare products for TRL 5 and beyond.
Learning Outcomes	Students gain technical and teamwork skills but have limited exposure to entrepreneurial and market-driven thinking.	Students develop critical thinking, creativity, systems thinking, and entrepreneurial mindsets aligned with industry demands.

15.5 Impact Discussions

15.5.1 Impact on Academic Results

- Incorporating GenAI into design thinking enhanced project results and made a significant contribution to student learning.
- Critical Thinking and Problem-Solving: Students developed their ability to strike a balance between creativity and viability by learning how to critically assess AI-generated alternatives.
- Collaboration and Project Management: Students were able to concentrate on teamwork, communication, and higher-order decision-making because AI reduced the administrative workload.
- Creativity and Innovation: Students who were exposed to AI-augmented ideation gained more creative confidence and were able to pursue bold design directions supported by data.
- Entrepreneurial Mindset: Students gained a comprehensive understanding of innovation that went beyond technical design by integrating market readiness and GTM tactics.

15.5.2 Student Feedback

Figure 15.6 shows the survey data from E-CODE implementations (n = 40 students, 2022–2024). Fifty-three percent of respondents said AI support had a significant influence on their ideation.

- Sixty-eight percent of respondents agreed that AI is useful during the decision-making process.
- Sixty-nine percent of respondents said they were happy with the finished products created with the tool.
- Eighty-five percent said they would be willing to suggest the framework to their peers.
- Long-term adoption: 46% for project development and 23% for lifelong learning.

15.5.3 Teaching Engagement Scale

The teaching engagement scale (TES) demonstrated significant improvement across seven dimensions between 2021 and 2024, aligning with the phased implementation of CODE → E-CODE → GenAI-E-CODE. From 2021 to 2024, the changes in student perceptions of teaching engagement across the TES dimensions are shown in Figure 15.7.

While the right panel displays the results of a longitudinal survey mapped to the transition from traditional design thinking practices to a GenAI-integrated approach, the left panel emphasizes the relative strengths and areas for improvement. Student evaluations showed moderate scores in areas like technology integration (D5) and using research to inform instruction (D7) during the early phase (2021), when instruction mostly used traditional approaches. These areas were repeatedly noted as needing more work. Incremental improvements were noted in most dimensions following the implementation of the E-CODE framework in 2022, especially in the areas of knowledge scaffolding and experiential learning opportunities (D2 and D4). There was a more pronounced upward shift in 2023 and 2024 when GenAI tools were integrated. Significant gains were shown in D5 (effective technology integration) and D7 (research-informed teaching), which align with the pedagogical potential of GenAI to provide better feedback loops, iterative prototyping, and real-time knowledge access. The near-maximum scores in 2024 demonstrate how evidence-based teaching strategies and student engagement can be enhanced by AI-enabled creativity-support systems. Table 15.3 shows the TES dimension comparison. In general, the data indicates that the incorporation of GenAI into design thinking maintained high performance in areas of strength, such as encouraging student participation and experiential learning, while simultaneously elevating traditionally weaker dimensions. This pattern demonstrates how GenAI can support research-based and value-driven teaching methods.

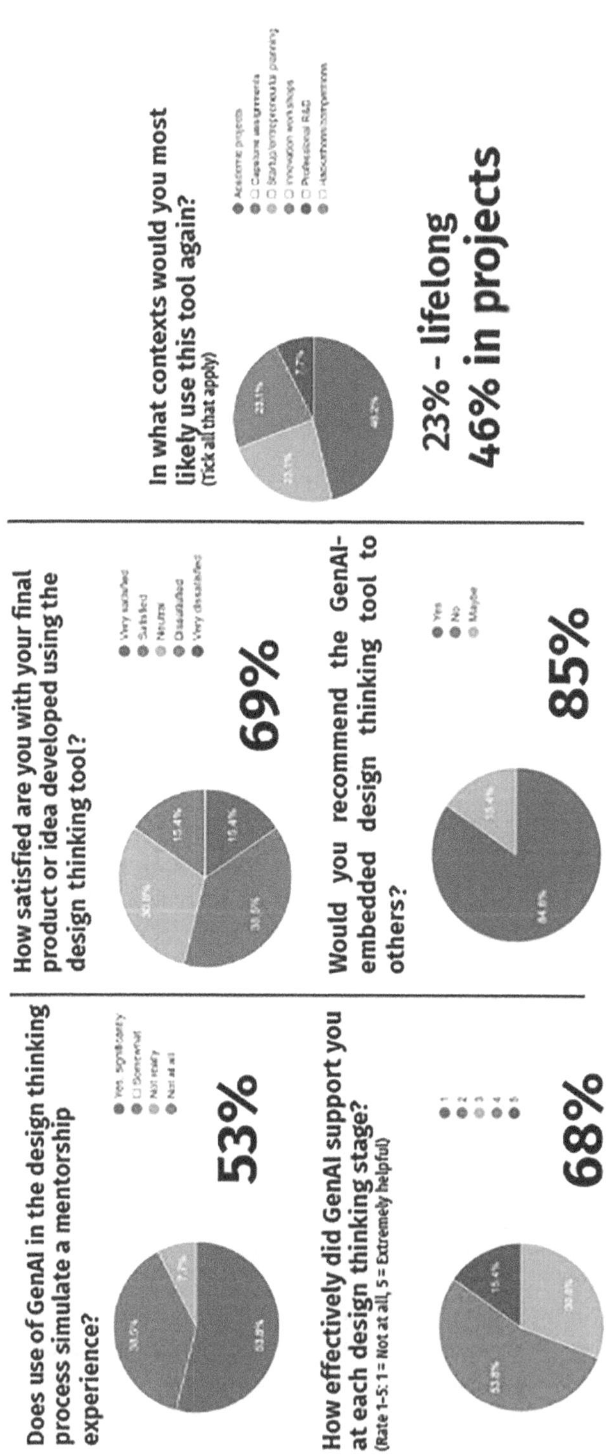

FIGURE 15.6
Survey results of the GenAI-integrated E-CODE.

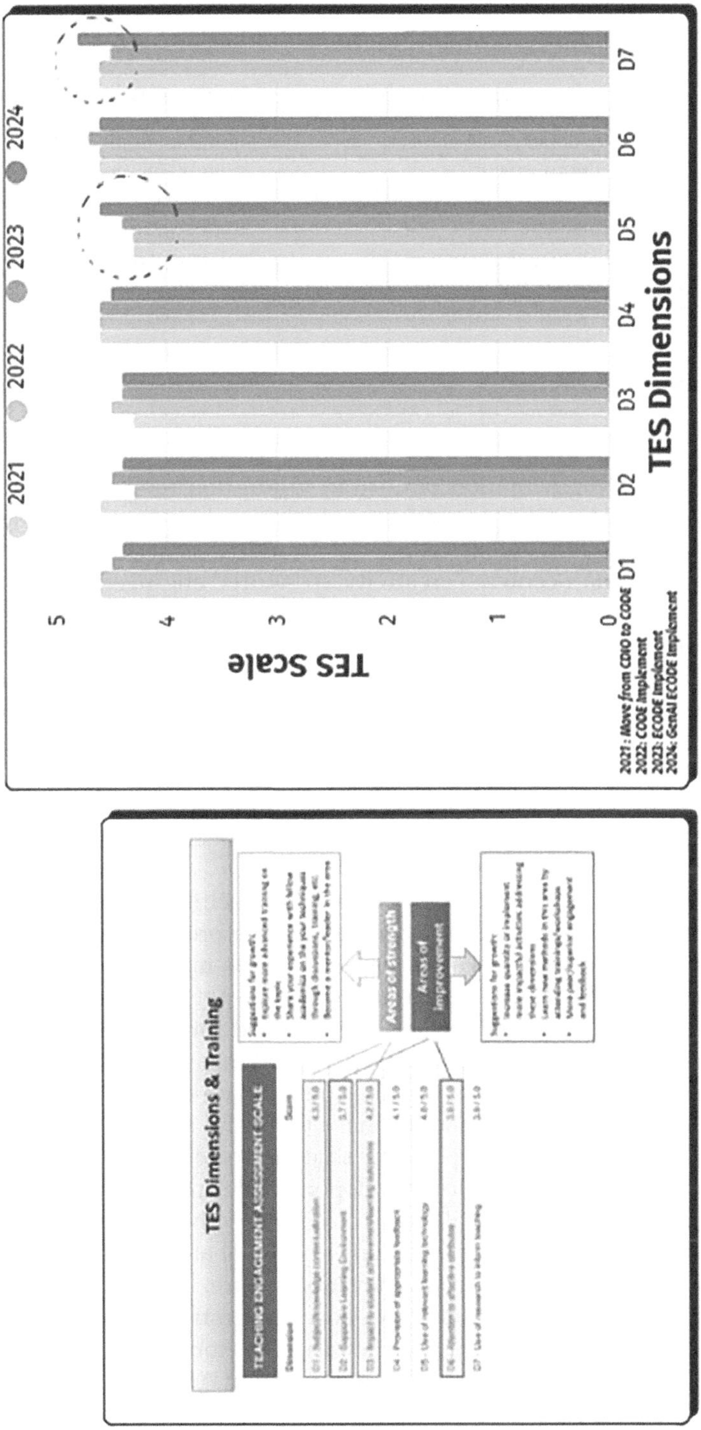

FIGURE 15.7
TES evaluation for the module 2021–2024.

TABLE 15.3

Comparison of Facilitator Comparison against the TES Dimension

TES Dimension	2021–2022 (Conventional)	2023–2024 (GenAI Integration)
D5-Technology Integration	Moderate; flagged for improvement	Significant uplift via AI-mediated prototyping/tools
D7-Research-Informed	Moderate; limited by traditional methods	Notable gains via AI-enhanced feedback/research
Other Areas (D1–D4, D6)	Fair to good; supported by scaffolding and context	Maintained or slightly improved through AI support

15.6 Conclusion

To overcome the fragmentation of current innovation methodologies, this study presents the E-CODE framework, which stands for empowering creativity through a GenAI-integrated design thinking ecosystem. The framework connects human-centered creativity, structured engineering rigor, and market-driven strategy by integrating GenAI throughout the empathize, conceptualize, organize, deploy, and execute stages. E-CODE incorporates empathy, technical execution, and market differentiation into a value-driven continuum, in contrast to parallel approaches that frequently address these aspects separately. Three significant contributions are highlighted by the capstone implementation findings. First, the educational impact: AI-enhanced ideation, prototyping, and market validation showed that students demonstrated enhanced critical thinking, creativity, and an entrepreneurial mindset. Second, methodological advancement.

Compared to traditional approaches, GenAI's intelligence layer produced higher-quality results by facilitating more accurate problem framing, faster project management, and evidence-based decision-making. Third, practical relevance: E-CODE-developed innovations are not only technically feasible but also scalable and strategically positioned for real-world adoption through the integration of market readiness analysis and GTM strategies. The more general implication is that the combination of GenAI and design thinking transforms the way innovation is taught and applied. The E-CODE framework in higher education prepares students to be both knowledge consumers and value-driven solution developers, better meeting industry and entrepreneurial demands. By balancing creativity with market viability and execution discipline, it provides startups and incubators with a replicable way to lessen the typical pitfalls of innovation failure.

The design thinking paradigm with GenAI integration portends a revolutionary change in the way that organizations, educators, and innovators can collaborate in the future. Through the integration of AI-enabled intelligence and human creativity, E-CODE offers a flexible and scalable framework that promotes innovation, education, and entrepreneurship. The findings demonstrate that future-ready innovators will arise by mastering the integration of creativity and rigor through AI-augmented ecosystems, rather than by having to choose between the two.

References

Altshuller, G. S. (1999). *The Innovation Algorithm: TRIZ, Systematic Innovation and Technical Creativity*. Technical Innovation Center.

Brown, T. (2009). *Change by design: How design thinking creates new alternatives for business and society*. Harper Business.

Chockalingam, C. A. (2021). *CODE framework for value-driven innovation*. MyIPO.

Crawley, E. F., Malmqvist, J., Östlund, S., Brodeur, D. R., & Edström, K. (2014). *Rethinking engineering education: The CDIO approach* (2nd ed.). Springer. https://doi.org/10.1007/978-3-319-05561-9

Dwivedi, Y. K., Hughes, L., Baabdullah, A. M., Ribeiro-Navarrete, S., Giannakis, M., Al-Debei, M. M., & Wamba, S. F. (2023). Generative artificial intelligence (AI) for innovation, transformation, and sustainable future. *Journal of Business Research, 153*, 284–298. https://doi.org/10.1016/j.jbusres.2022.11.040

Forbes & Statista. (2020). *Startup failure rate statistics*. Retrieved from https://www.statista.com/

Holmes, W., Bialik, M., & Fadel, C. (2021). *Artificial intelligence in education: Promises and implications for teaching and learning*. Center for Curriculum Redesign.

Kim, W. C., & Mauborgne, R. (2005). *Blue ocean strategy: How to create uncontested market space and make the competition irrelevant*. Harvard Business School Press.

Liedtka, J. (2018). Why does design thinking works. *Harvard Business Review, 96*(5), 72–79.

Luckin, R. (2023). AI for education: A critical view. *British Journal of Educational Technology, 54*(5), 1202–1216. https://doi.org/10.1111/bjet.13396

Osterwalder, A., & Pigneur, Y. (2010). *Business model generation: A handbook for visionaries, game changers, and challengers*. Wiley.

16

Artificial Intelligence toward Sustainable Impact Accelerator through Education, Research, and Advocacy: Critical Assessments

Samsul Ariffin Abdul Karim

16.1 Introduction

Artificial intelligence (AI) has become one of the defining innovations of the 21st century, influencing almost every sector of society. From autonomous vehicles and smart assistants to data analytics and personalized medicine, AI's rapid development has shifted the boundaries of what is technologically possible. However, beyond its technical prowess, AI can also be understood as a sustainable impact accelerator—a force that, if strategically harnessed, can amplify progress toward social, educational, and developmental goals.

Education, research, and advocacy are three central pillars through which AI's transformative potential can be maximized. These domains act as entry points for shaping how societies think, learn, and make decisions. In education, AI tools can personalize learning pathways, reduce inequalities, and offer new pedagogical opportunities. In research, AI accelerates discovery, expands interdisciplinary collaboration, and provides insights from massive datasets that would otherwise be impossible to analyze. Through advocacy, AI contributes to more informed policy debates, data-driven campaigns, and inclusive decision-making.

This chapter explores how AI can serve as a sustainable impact accelerator through education, research, and advocacy. It places special emphasis on teaching and learning (T&L) with generative AI tools, illustrating practical applications, impacts on stakeholders, and the ways forward. By weaving together opportunities and challenges, the discussion aims to demonstrate that AI's value depends not on the technology alone but on how responsibly and creatively humans integrate it into their systems and practices. The AI Ethics and Academic Honesty Declaration Form for Assessment is provided in this chapter.

 DOI: 10.1201/9781003633433-16

16.2 AI as a Sustainable Impact Accelerator

The term "sustainable impact accelerator" highlights the role of AI in enabling long-term, scalable, and equitable progress. Unlike short-lived technological innovations that solve narrow problems, AI possesses generalizable capabilities that extend across disciplines. When aligned with ethical considerations and inclusive practices, AI can enhance productivity, democratize access to knowledge, and support the achievement of the United Nations Sustainable Development Goals (SDGs) (UNESCO, 2021).

Several SDGs are particularly relevant. Goal 4 (Quality Education) emphasizes inclusive and equitable learning opportunities. AI-driven adaptive platforms can help address disparities by tailoring content to learners' needs, especially in underserved communities. Goal 8 (Decent Work and Economic Growth) is linked to AI's ability to prepare future workforces for evolving labor markets. Goal 10 (Reduced Inequalities) resonates with AI's potential to bridge rural-urban education gaps through low-cost, accessible learning tools. More information on how AI can be used to accomplish the SDGs can be found in Vinuesa et al. (2020).

However, positioning AI as a sustainable accelerator requires balance. Unregulated adoption risks entrenching bias, exacerbating inequalities, and fostering dependence on opaque algorithms. Thus, the sustainability of AI lies not in its autonomous functioning but in human governance, inclusivity, and contextual adaptation.

16.3 AI in Education: Teaching and Learning

16.3.1 Transforming Pedagogical Approaches

Teaching and learning are undergoing significant transformation due to AI. Classrooms are shifting from standardized, one-size-fits-all approaches to more personalized and student-centered environments. AI can diagnose learning difficulties, adapt the pace of instruction, and provide targeted feedback. In doing so, it supports teachers in focusing on higher-order skills such as critical thinking and creativity rather than routine assessment tasks.

16.3.2 Generative AI in Practice

Generative AI tools such as ChatGPT, Claude, Microsoft Copilot, and Gemini have introduced new dimensions in teaching and learning. Students use these platforms to draft essays, explore explanations, or simulate real-time conversations in foreign languages. For example:

- Mathematics education: Students can pose step-by-step questions to an AI tutor, receiving immediate clarification and alternative methods for solving equations.
- Language learning: Chatbots act as conversation partners, enabling learners to practice communication without fear of judgment.
- STEM simulation labs: AI-driven software allows students to run complex experiments virtually, reducing the cost of physical laboratories.

These applications demonstrate how generative AI can expand learning opportunities beyond the traditional classroom.

16.3.3 Opportunities and Risks

The opportunities include the following:

- Personalized pathways: Learners advance at their own pace.
- Equity in access: AI can serve remote communities with limited teacher availability.
- Enhanced creativity: Generative AI inspires students to explore ideas they may not have considered.

Yet challenges persist:

- Plagiarism and academic integrity concerns when students rely excessively on AI outputs.
- Overreliance on automation, potentially reducing critical thinking and impacting their cognitive skills.
- The digital divide, as not all learners have equal access to devices and internet connectivity.

For AI to truly accelerate sustainable educational outcomes, careful pedagogical integration, teacher training, and ethical guidelines are indispensable.

16.4 AI in Research and Innovation

16.4.1 Accelerating Discovery

Research has traditionally been a time-consuming endeavor requiring meticulous data collection and interpretation. AI reshapes this landscape by handling massive datasets and detecting patterns invisible to human observation. In fields such as climate science, AI models forecast long-term environmental impacts with unprecedented accuracy. In medicine, AI accelerates drug discovery by analyzing molecular interactions and predicting clinical trial outcomes.

16.5 Generative AI in Scholarly Work

Generative AI contributes by:

- Assisting in literature reviews by summarizing thousands of papers.
- Drafting grant proposals or research outlines, saving time for conceptual refinement.
- Providing code generation for simulations and statistical analysis.
- Visualizing complex data through AI-enabled graphing and modeling software.

These capabilities democratize access to advanced research tools, particularly for early-career scholars or institutions with limited resources.

16.6 Risks and Integrity Issues

While accelerating discovery, AI also raises a few concerns:

- Research integrity: Scholars must ensure originality and verify AI-produced insights. Do not simply accept whatever is produced by the AI. We must double-check it to ensure the information is factual and not fabricated.
- Bias in datasets: Inaccurate or skewed data may reinforce inequities that will destroy the outcome of the research.
- Misinterpretation: Overreliance on AI outputs without human validation risks flawed conclusions. For instance, the computer code or programming produced by AI may consist of errors that will result in flaws in the desired results.

Thus, AI should function as a collaborative assistant rather than a substitute for scholarly judgment.

16.7 AI in Advocacy and Policy Influence

16.7.1 Data-Driven Advocacy

Advocacy relies on compelling evidence and persuasive communication. AI strengthens campaigns by analyzing social media sentiments, mapping public opinion trends, and generating clear visualizations for policymakers. For example, during health crises, AI can detect misinformation patterns online and inform strategies to counter harmful narratives. This can be conducted through online monitoring via social media and reliable systems.

16.7.2 Policy Modeling and Forecasting

AI enables predictive modeling that simulates the long-term effects of policy decisions. Climate advocacy groups use AI to forecast carbon emissions, while economic policy analysts deploy AI models to predict labor market shifts. By translating complex data into actionable insights, AI empowers advocacy organizations to argue for evidence-based policies.

16.7.3 Ethical Dimensions

The use of AI in advocacy carries ethical implications:

- Transparency is necessary to prevent manipulation.
- Inclusivity must be prioritized so that marginalized voices are not overshadowed by data-driven narratives.
- Guarding against misinformation is essential, as generative AI itself can produce persuasive yet inaccurate content.

Advocacy therefore requires the responsible deployment of AI, ensuring that data enhances democracy rather than distorting it.

16.8 Broader Impacts of AI

16.8.1 On Students

AI offers students personalized access to knowledge, immediate feedback, and preparation for future job markets where AI literacy is essential. However, concerns exist regarding an almost fully dependency on AI, critical thinking erosion, and equitable access.

16.8.2 On Educators/Teachers/Lecturers/Instructors

AI redefines educators' roles. Teachers/Lecturers are no longer mere deliverers of information but facilitators of learning experiences. They must acquire digital competencies to manage AI in classrooms and guide students toward responsible use. Active learning can be conducted in the classroom with the help of AI tools. This will ensure that students-centered learning (SCL) can be implemented successfully. Blended learning can also benefit from many generative AI tools for T&L purposes, such as Canva, Kahoot, and many more.

16.8.3 On Researchers

For researchers, AI provides unprecedented efficiency but also risks homogenization of thought. If overused, generative AI may reduce originality and lead scholars to fully rely on AI, making it vital for them to balance AI assistance with human creativity as well as cognitively.

16.8.4 On Society

At the societal level, AI reshapes labor markets, governance, and cultural norms. It promises productivity gains but also raises debates about job displacement, privacy, and fairness. Societal adaptation requires ethical frameworks, social safety nets, and public engagement to ensure equitable benefits.

16.9 Ways Forward: Sustainable and Responsible AI Adoption

16.9.1 For Education

- Embed AI literacy in curricula across levels.
- Provide teacher training to integrate AI tools responsibly and ethically.
- Develop clear guidelines on academic integrity in relation to AI. The AI policy and guidelines can be used for enforcement.

16.9.2 For Research

- Establish ethics boards within academic institutions to monitor AI use among staff and researchers.
- Encourage open-source AI initiatives to reduce inequalities between well-resourced and under-resourced institutions. This must be subject to the AI policy and guidelines.

- Promote interdisciplinary collaboration where AI serves as a bridge across fields. This will ensure that collaboration is further developed and strengthened.

16.9.3 For Advocacy

- Employ AI for social-good campaigns addressing health, the environment, and equity.
- Ensure transparency in AI-generated insights shared with policymakers.
- Foster cross-sector partnerships among governments, NGOs, academia, industry, and all stakeholders.

16.9.4 Policy Recommendations

- Develop regulatory frameworks to safeguard fairness, accountability, and transparency.
- Invest in infrastructure to bridge the digital divide.
- Promote public awareness campaigns to educate citizens about AI's benefits and risks.

In all domains, AI must be positioned as a co-pilot for human creativity and decision-making rather than a replacement for humanity. People must be well educated on this matter, directly and indirectly, through various methods and strategies.

As for schools and universities, the following example of an AI Ethics and Academic Honesty Declaration Form can be used when students submit their assessment (individually). For group assignments, the AI Ethics and Academic Honesty Declaration Form can be modified accordingly.

16.10 AI Ethics and Academic Honesty Declaration

In this section, two AI Ethics and Academic Honesty Declaration forms are provided for lecturers and instructors to use in their respective classes.

AI Ethics and Academic Honesty Declaration Form (Individual Assessment)

Date Submitted: September 14, 2025 (example)

Course & Assignment Information

Course Title: ____

Course Code: ____

Assignment Title: ____

Lecturer's Name: ____

Student's Full Name: ____

Matric Number: ____

Program: ____

AI Usage Disclosure

Did you use any AI tools in completing this assessment?

☐ No ☐ Yes (If yes, complete the details below)

AI Tool(s) Used:

____

____

Purpose of Use (tick all that apply):

☐ Brainstorming ideas

☐ Grammar/language improvement

☐ Explaining concepts

☐ Code assistance/debugging

☐ Summarizing references

☐ Other: ______________________________

Explain how the AI was used and how you engaged with the output:

____

____

____

____

____

____

Declaration & Signature

I declare that:

- The work submitted is my own.
- Any AI assistance used has been appropriately disclosed.

- The final work reflects my own understanding, learning, and effort.
- I understand that failure to comply may be considered academic misconduct.

Signature: ______________________________ Date: ______________

Lecturer's Signature: __________________________

Date: ________________

Stamp:

AI Ethics & Academic Honesty Declaration Form (Group Assessment)

Date Submitted: September 14, 2025

Course & Assignment Information

Course Title: ____

Course Code: ____

Program: ____

Assignment Title: ____

Lecturer's Name: ____

Group Number/Name: _______________________________________

Group Leader (Full Name and Matric Number):

____

Group Members (Full Name, Matric Number, and % Contribution):

1. ____
2. ____
3. ____
4. ____
5. ____

AI Usage Disclosure

Did your group use any AI tools in completing this assessment?

☐ No ☐ Yes (If yes, complete the details below)

AI Tool(s) Used: ____

Purpose of Use (tick all that apply):

☐ Brainstorming ideas

☐ Grammar/language improvement

☐ Explaining concepts
☐ Code assistance/debugging
☐ Summarizing references
☐ Other: ______________________________

Explain how the AI was used and how the group engaged with the output:

____

____

____

____

____

____

____

____

____

Declaration & Signature

We declare that:

- All group members have contributed meaningfully to this assignment.
- Any AI assistance used has been appropriately disclosed.
- The final work submitted reflects our own critical thinking and original effort.
- We understand that failure to comply may be considered academic misconduct.

Signatures:

1. ______________________________ Date: _______________
2. ______________________________ Date: _______________
3. ______________________________ Date: _______________
4. ______________________________ Date: _______________
5. ______________________________ Date: _______________

Lecturer Signature: ______________________

Date: _________________

Stamp:

16.11 Conclusion

AI represents more than a technological revolution; it embodies the potential to serve as a sustainable impact accelerator when integrated into education, research, and advocacy. In education, AI personalizes learning and empowers students–teachers' interactions to deliver the main outcome of student-centered learning (SCL) and Blended Learning. In research and innovation (R&I), it accelerates discovery and democratizes access to advanced tools. In advocacy, it strengthens evidence-based campaigns and policy debates among stakeholders and policymakers.

Yet these promises are accompanied by risks: ethical dilemmas, inequitable access, and threats to originality. Therefore, the future of AI rests not in the technology itself but in the responsibility with which societies adopt it. Through deliberate integration, ethical oversight, and inclusive practices, AI can drive sustainable progress that aligns with global development goals.

The journey ahead requires collaboration among educators, researchers, practitioners, policymakers, industrialists, and communities. By integrating and embedding AI as a partner rather than a replacement, humanity can harness its power to build not only smarter societies but also fairer, more sustainable, and more resilient futures, especially toward IR4.0, Society 5.0, and the future IR6.0.

Declaration on the Use of Generative AI and AI-Assisted Technologies

During the preparation of this work, the author used ChatGPT for improving readability and/or drafting structure. All outputs generated by the tool were carefully reviewed, edited, and validated. The findings, interpretations, and conclusions presented are entirely the author's own work. The author accepts full responsibility for the originality, accuracy, and integrity of the final content.

Acknowledgment

This study was fully supported by Universiti Utara Malaysia through Geran Penjanaan Penyelidikan Universiti 2025 [SO Code: 22139] (A Machine Learning-Based Scattered Data Interpolation For Image Enhancement) and the Ministry of Higher Education (MOHE) of Malaysia through the

Fundamental Research Grant Scheme **[FRGS/1/2023/ICT06/UMS/02/1] (New Scattered Data Interpolation Scheme Using Quasi Cubic Triangular Patches for RGB Image Interpolation**). Finally, a special thank-you to the Institute of Strategic Industrial Decision Modelling (ISIDM), Computational Statistics and Applied Mathematics (CSAM) Research Group, School of Quantitative Sciences, Universiti Utara Malaysia for tremendous computing facilities support.

References

UNESCO. (2021). *AI and education: Guidance for policy-makers.* United Nations Educational, Scientific and Cultural Organization. https://www.unesco.org/en/articles/ai-and-education-guidance-policy-makers

Vinuesa, R., Azizpour, H., Leite, I., et al. (2020). The role of artificial intelligence in achieving the Sustainable Development Goals. *Nature Communications, 11*(1), 233. https://www.nature.com/articles/s41467-019-14108-y

17

Artificial Intelligence and the Sustainable Impact Accelerator: Advancing Education, Research, and Advocacy beyond IR4.0 and Society 5.0

Samsul Ariffin Abdul Karim

17.1 Introduction

17.1.1 Introduction

The accelerating pace of global change—from climate disruption and widening inequality to rapid technological innovation—calls for coordinated, systemic responses. Education, research, and advocacy emerge as powerful levers in shaping societies that are both sustainable and inclusive. At the same time, advances in artificial intelligence (AI) offer transformative opportunities, yet they also raise profound ethical and systemic questions. The purpose of this chapter is to situate the volume within this broader context. It summarizes and analyzes the concept of a sustainable impact accelerator, in which education, research, and advocacy interact to amplify change, and position AI as a critical enabler within the proposed ERA framework.

This chapter lays the foundation for the discussions that follow, highlighting how subsequent contributions explore AI's potential to enrich student learning, drive educational innovation, and promote equity while also addressing its risks. Once again, each chapter stands as an independent inquiry, yet together they present a comprehensive view of how AI intersects with pedagogy, ethics, systemic transformation, and social impact to fulfill some of the UN SDGs (UNESCO, 2021).

17.1.2 Education as a Catalyst for Sustainable Futures

Education plays a pivotal role in preparing individuals to confront global challenges with knowledge, critical awareness, and adaptive skills. Integrating sustainability concepts into curricula is no longer optional—it is essential. By equipping students with the ability to think critically and act

DOI: 10.1201/9781003633433-17

responsibly, education nurtures future leaders who can embed sustainable practices across sectors. The role of AI in this space is to enhance learning, personalizing educational experiences, and create opportunities for more inclusive participation (UNESCO. 2021).

Chapters such as **Chapter 2, Make a Difference Enterprise (MADE): Catalyzing AI-Driven Design Thinking in Student Learning**, and **Chapter 3, Student Engagement and Motivation toward Education 4.0**, exemplify how AI can support creativity, design thinking, and deeper student engagement. These contributions demonstrate that when technology is applied thoughtfully, it can turn classrooms into laboratories for innovation and sustainability.

17.1.3 Research as a Generator of Evidence and Innovation

Research provides the evidence base and creative solutions that drive systemic transformation. Complex issues such as the integration of AI into education require rigorous investigation into not only what works but also under which conditions and for whom. Interdisciplinary collaboration is essential here, linking insights from education, computer science, psychology, and the social sciences.

Chapter 4, Determinants of Successful Integration and Adoption of AI in Education: A Structural Equation Modeling Approach, offers one such evidence-based inquiry. By identifying the factors that shape successful adoption, it informs policy and institutional strategies. Similarly, **Chapter 8, The Integration of Artificial Intelligence in Education: A Systematic Review of Pedagogical, Ethical, and Systemic Dimensions**, synthesizes findings across multiple domains, highlighting both opportunities and blind spots. These chapters show how research strengthens the sustainable impact accelerator by aligning technological advances with pedagogical effectiveness and ethical responsibility.

17.1.4 Advocacy as a Bridge to Action

Knowledge alone is insufficient without advocacy that translates insights into change. Advocacy amplifies voices, mobilizes communities, and shapes policies to ensure education remains equitable and purposeful in the AI era. Universities and educators play a vital role by engaging stakeholders, communicating complex research in accessible ways, and promoting reforms that safeguard both human dignity and technological progress.

Chapters that address equity and inclusivity—such as **Chapter 5, Artificial Intelligence for Equitable and Sustainable Assessment**, and **Chapter 14, Inclusive Education through AI: Translating Speech-to-Sign Language for Deaf and Mute Learners in Online Platforms Using Generative Adversarial Network**—illustrate advocacy in practice. These works highlight how AI, when combined with purposeful advocacy, can create educational opportunities for marginalized groups, reinforcing education's role as a vehicle for social justice.

17.1.5 Ethical and Emotional Dimensions of AI in Education

Sustainability also requires reflection on the ethical, emotional, and human aspects of technological transformation. AI in education raises questions about bias, privacy, and the balance between human judgment and machine decision-making. Addressing these concerns is integral to building systems that are not only effective but also fair.

Chapter 6, AI Ethics in Education, and **Chapter 12, Introduction: The Promise and Peril of AI in Education**, offer critical perspectives on these dilemmas. By interrogating the risks alongside the opportunities, they ensure that advocacy and research remain grounded in ethical responsibility. Equally important are the emotional dimensions of learning, explored in **Chapter 10, Social and Emotional Learning with Purpose**, which underscores the need to preserve human connection even as digital tools expand. Together, these contributions remind readers that technological progress must remain aligned with values of equity, empathy, and integrity.

17.1.6 Innovation, Curriculum, and Workforce Readiness

Another dimension of sustainable impact lies in preparing students for the future of work. Education must anticipate shifts in labor markets, equipping graduates with interdisciplinary competencies that align with evolving industry needs. AI offers tools to personalize learning pathways and link education to employability.

This theme runs through **Chapter 7, A Job-Based Course Recommender System Using Unsupervised Machine Learning for Text Clustering to Promote a Multidisciplinary Curriculum**, which connects curriculum design with workforce readiness, and **Chapter 13, Purpose-Led Learning Using AI for Data Analytics with SMEs in Malaysia**, which demonstrates how partnerships with industry can enrich student learning. Similarly, **Chapter 15, Empowering Innovation through a Generative Artificial Intelligence-Integrated Design Thinking Framework for Value-Driven Product Development**, showcases how AI-enabled frameworks prepare students for innovation-driven economies. These chapters emphasize the accelerator's role in bridging education with real-world applications, ensuring that sustainability includes economic viability alongside social and environmental goals.

17.1.7 Toward a Sustainable Impact Accelerator

The final contribution, **Chapter 16, Artificial Intelligence toward Sustainable Impact Accelerator through Education, Research, and Advocacy: Critical Assessments**, ties these themes together. It evaluates

AI's potential to advance sustainability by integrating education, research, and advocacy into a cohesive model. This critical assessment echoes the argument introduced here: that accelerating sustainable impact requires aligning technological innovation with human-centered values and systemic adaptation.

Table 17.1 outlines the comparative dimensions of the proposed education–research–advocacy (ERA) framework, highlighting its distinctive features and potential contributions. Building on this foundation, Table 17.2 maps the three pillars of the sustainable impact accelerator, demonstrating how each pillar interacts with and reinforces the others in advancing systemic change. To capture the dynamic nature of these interactions, Table 17.3 presents a cross-pillar interaction matrix that illustrates the continuous cycle of engagement and feedback across education, research, and advocacy. Collectively, these tables not only frame the conceptual underpinnings of the ERA model but also provide a practical basis for applying continuous quality improvement (CQI) within educational, research, and policy contexts.

TABLE 17.1

Comparison of Key Dimensions in the Sustainable Impact Accelerator Framework

Dimension	Core Role	AI's Contribution	Illustrative Examples (from Chapters)	Sustainable Impact
Education	Prepares learners with knowledge, critical awareness, and adaptive skills for global challenges.	Enhances learning personalization, fosters creativity, supports engagement, and broadens inclusivity.	—MADE: Catalyzing AI-Driven Design Thinking (Ch. 2) —Student Engagement toward Education 4.0 (Ch. 3)	Nurtures future leaders capable of embedding sustainability across sectors.
Research	Generates evidence and innovative solutions through interdisciplinary inquiry.	Identifies adoption factors, synthesizes knowledge, and aligns AI with pedagogy and ethics.	—Determinants of AI Integration in Education (SEM) (Ch. 4) —Systematic Review of AI in Education (Ch. 8)	Strengthens policy, institutional strategies, and responsible innovation.
Advocacy	Translates knowledge into action, mobilizing communities, shaping policy, and amplifying equity.	Expands accessibility, supports marginalized groups, and drives systemic reform.	—AI for Equitable and Sustainable Assessment (Ch. 5) —Inclusive Education via AI for deaf/mute learners (Ch. 14)	Ensures social justice, fairness, and inclusive participation.

(Continued)

TABLE 17.1 *(Continued)*

Comparison of Key Dimensions in the Sustainable Impact Accelerator Framework

Dimension	Core Role	AI's Contribution	Illustrative Examples (from Chapters)	Sustainable Impact
Ethical and Emotional Dimensions	Safeguards values of fairness, empathy, and human dignity in digital learning.	Surfaces risks (bias, privacy, decision-making) and balances tech with human connection.	—AI Ethics in Education (Ch. 6) —The Promise and Peril of AI in Education (Ch. 12) —Social and Emotional Learning with Purpose (Ch. 10)	Builds trust, maintains integrity, and preserves human connection in education.
Innovation, Curriculum and Workforce Readiness	Prepares students for future labor markets and interdisciplinary competencies.	Personalizes pathways, links curricula to employability, and supports design thinking.	—Job-Based Course Recommender System (Ch. 7) —AI for Data Analytics with SMEs (Ch. 13) —Generative AI-Integrated Design Thinking Framework (Ch. 15)	Aligns education with economic viability and innovation-driven growth.

TABLE 17.2

Mapping of Chapters into the Three Pillars of the Sustainable Impact Accelerator

Chapter	Focus/Theme	Education	Research	Advocacy
1 Sustainable Impact Accelerator through Education, Research, and Advocacy	Framing discourse; positioning AI in sustainability	Highlights AI's role in pedagogy and curricula	Establishes research as a generator of systemic evidence	Frames advocacy as essential for societal change
2 Make a Difference Enterprise (MADE): AI-Driven Design Thinking	Student-centered design thinking and creativity	Fosters innovation in student learning		
3 Student Engagement and Motivation toward Education 4.0	Motivation and participation with AI	Strengthens engagement and active learning		
4 Determinants of Successful AI Adoption (SEM Approach)	Modeling factors influencing AI integration		Provides evidence-based adoption insights	
5 AI for Equitable and Sustainable Assessment	Fairness and inclusivity in assessment	Transforms classroom evaluation practices	Build frameworks for sustainable assessment	Advocates for inclusive and just assessment policies

(Continued)

TABLE 17.2 ***(Continued)***

Mapping of Chapters into the Three Pillars of the Sustainable Impact Accelerator

Chapter	Focus/Theme	Education	Research	Advocacy
6 AI Ethics in Education	Ethical dimensions of AI in learning	Develops ethical literacy for students	Examine dilemmas related to bias, privacy, accountability	Advocates for safeguards for equity and justice
7 Job-Based Course Recommender System	Linking curriculum to future labor markets	Personalizes learning pathways	Uses text clustering for curriculum design	
8 Systematic Review of AI in Education	Pedagogical, ethical, and systemic synthesis	Integrates diverse educational approaches	Synthesize cross-disciplinary findings	Inform advocacy through the translation of evidence
9 Exploring AI Perceptions among University Students	Student attitudes and acceptance of AI	Captures learners' experiences	Provides empirical insights into student views	
10 Social and Emotional Learning with Purpose	Nurturing SEL through AI tools	Embeds social and emotional competencies	Studies SEL integration with digital platforms	
11 AI in Education—Transforming Teaching and Learning	Digital transformation in pedagogy	Reimagine teaching practices	Research systemic transformation in classrooms	Advocates readiness for digital futures
12 The Promise and Peril of AI in Education	Balancing opportunities and risks	Prepares students to navigate AI's dual impacts	Investigates risks such as bias and surveillance	Advocates responsible and ethical adoption
13 Purpose-Led Learning Using AI with SMEs in Malaysia	Industry-linked experiential learning	Strengths applied learning with SMEs	Builds evidence from AI–industry collaboration	Advocates for university–industry partnerships
14 Inclusive Education via AI: Speech-to-Sign Translation	Accessibility for deaf and mute learners	Expanded access for marginalized students	Applies GANs for inclusive research	Champions advocacy for equity in education
15 Generative AI-Integrated Design Thinking Framework	AI for innovation and product development	Prepares students for innovation-driven skills	Tests design frameworks in learning contexts	
16 AI Toward Sustainable Impact Accelerator	Critical assessment of ERA nexus (cycle)	Evaluates educational transformation	Synthesize systemic research evidence	Advocates for reforms for sustainable change

TABLE 17.3
Cross-Pillar Interaction Matrix for CQI Purposes

Interaction	How It Emerges across the Volume	Representative Chapters
Education ↔ Research	Research insights shape pedagogy, curriculum, and adoption strategies.	Ch. 4 (AI Adoption SEM), Ch. 7 (Curriculum clustering), Ch. 8 (Systematic review)
Education ↔ Advocacy	Teaching practices are linked to advocacy for equity and inclusivity.	Ch. 5 (Equitable assessment), Ch. 14 (Inclusive education), Ch. 11 (Transforming teaching)
Research ↔ Advocacy	Evidence-based findings inform advocacy for ethical, just, and sustainable policies.	Ch. 6 (AI Ethics), Ch. 12 (Promise & Peril), Ch. 13 (SME collaborations)
Education ↔ Research ↔ Advocacy (CQI ERA Cycle)	AI is positioned as a sustainable impact accelerator that blends pedagogy, evidence, and advocacy into systemic transformation.	Ch. 1 (Framing discourse), Ch. 16 (Critical assessment)

For more details on the CQI ERA Cycle, readers can refer to Figure 1.2 in Chapter 1.

17.2 Conclusion

This book has examined how education, research, and advocacy (ERA), when thoughtfully integrated with artificial intelligence, can accelerate sustainable impact. The chapters show that AI is not simply a technological advancement but a force that can deepen human potential when directed with care and responsibility. Education emerges as the foundation for this transformation, preparing learners to think critically, act ethically, and adapt to rapid change. Research contributes the evidence base and innovations needed to ensure that AI enhances, rather than disrupts, the learning process. Advocacy, in turn, connects ideas to action by influencing policies and practices that are inclusive and socially just. Together, these three dimensions form a strong framework for using AI in ways that serve both people and the planet. At the same time, this work has underscored the importance of caution. The benefits of AI must be weighed against risks such as bias, privacy concerns, and the possible weakening of human connection. Addressing these challenges requires constant attention to fairness, empathy, and accountability. In bringing these perspectives together, the book conveys a simple but powerful message: sustainable progress cannot be achieved through technology alone. It demands collaboration, reflection, and the alignment of innovation with human values. By advancing education, research, and advocacy hand in hand with responsible AI, we can move toward societies that are more equitable, resilient, and humane. This will ensure that our future generations are well prepared to embrace and navigate the rapid advancement of technology beyond IR4.0 and Society 5.0.

Declaration on the Use of Generative AI and AI-Assisted Technologies

During the preparation of this work, the author used ChatGPT for improving readability and/or drafting structure. All outputs generated by the tool were carefully reviewed, edited, and validated. The findings, interpretations, and conclusions presented are entirely the author's own work. The author accepts full responsibility for the originality, accuracy, and integrity of the final content.

Acknowledgment

This study was fully supported by Universiti Utara Malaysia through Geran Penjanaan Penyelidikan Universiti 2025 [SO Code: 22139] (A Machine Learning-Based Scattered Data Interpolation For Image Enhancement) and the Ministry of Higher Education (MOHE) of Malaysia through the Fundamental Research Grant Scheme **[FRGS/1/2023/ICT06/UMS/02/1] (New Scattered Data Interpolation Scheme Using Quasi Cubic Triangular Patches for RGB Image Interpolation**). Finally, a special thank-you to the Institute of Strategic Industrial Decision Modelling (ISIDM), the Computational Statistics and Applied Mathematics (CSAM) Research Group, School of Quantitative Sciences, Universiti Utara Malaysia, for their tremendous computing facilities support.

Reference

UNESCO. (2021). *AI and education: Guidance for policy-makers*. United Nations Educational, Scientific and Cultural Organization. https://www.unesco.org/en/articles/ai-and-education-guidance-policy-makers

Index

Note: Page numbers in *italics* indicate a figure, and page numbers in **bold** indicate a table on the corresponding page.

B

C

D

G

H

I

K

T

V

W